149

WAR
WITHOUT
END

Michael T. Klare

WAR WITHOUT END

American Planning for the Next Vietnams

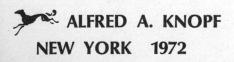 ALFRED A. KNOPF

NEW YORK   1972

Library of Congress Cataloging in Publication Data

Klare, Michael T., 1942-   War without end.

Bibliography: p.
1. U. S.—Military policy. 2. U. S.—Foreign relations—1945- I. Title.
UA23.K63   1972   355.03'35'73   79-154932   ISBN 0-394-46214-9

Manufactured in the United States of America

FIRST EDITION

This book is dedicated to the people of Vietnam and the United States who have participated in the struggle against the American intervention in Southeast Asia.

Acknowledgments

Work on *War Without End* began in February 1968, and occupied most of my time in the succeeding three and a half years. During this period numerous individuals gave their time and energy to help bring this project to fruition. While it is not possible to mention all of the people who provided assistance along the way, I would like to identify some of those whose help has been most valuable and beneficial.

My first expression of gratitude must be reserved for my brother, Karl E. Klare, of the Political Studies Department at Adelphi University, who prepared several drafts for the Introduction and who provided extremely valuable criticism of the manuscript as a whole. *War Without End* has been enriched enormously as a result of his cooperation and concern.

Since October 1967 I have been a staff member of the North American Congress on Latin America (NACLA), an independent, nonprofit research organization that is dedicated to the collection, analysis, and dissemination of information about United States imperial operations in Latin America and other Third World areas. As a member of NACLA, I have had many occasions to visit and work with members of other organizations in the radical research movement, including the National Action/Research on the Military-Industrial Complex (NARMIC) of the American Friends Service Committee, the Africa Research Group (ARG), and the Pacific Studies Center (PSC). Without the support, encouragement, and cooperation of my colleagues in NACLA and these other groups, I never could have completed a project on the scale of this book.

An investigation of American counterinsurgency planning for the next Vietnams unavoidably required study of a great many unrelated fields, and I was fortunate, in this effort, to have the assistance of several colleagues in the preparation of certain specialized passages. A special debt of gratitude is owed to Carol Brightman, for her guidance in developing the analysis in Chapter 4 (Social Systems Engineering), and to Chris Robinson, for help in preparing the draft of Chapter 7 ("The Electronic Battlefield").

At each stage in the development of this book, I have profited from the advice of friends and colleagues who took time from their own work to read parts of the manuscript and make recommendations for its improvement. Among those who have helped in this way are: Fred Goff and Mike Locker of NACLA, Eqbal Ahmad of the Adlai Stevenson Institute, Gabriel Kolko of York University (Ontario), Derek Shearer of Dispatch News Service, Wilfred Burchett, and Adam Schesch. Without their valuable suggestions and criticisms, *War Without End* would undoubtedly have been much less convincing.

Among the many individuals who provided support and encouragement when the obstacles ahead seemed most formidable are: Karen and Banning Garrett of PSC, Jack A. Smith of *The Guardian*, Carey McWilliams of *The Nation*, Giles Kotcher, Amy Kesselman, Jim Fishman, Eric Prokosch, Patty Berens, and my parents, Mr. and Mrs. Charles Klare.

This book is partially based on research conducted under a grant furnished by the Louis M. Rabinowitz Foundation. I am deeply indebted to the Trustees of the Foundation for their support and encouragement.

I am grateful to the editors of *Commonweal* for permission to include excerpts from two of my articles, "The Sun Never Sets on the American Empire" and "Policing the Empire," and to the editors of *The Nation* for reassignment to me of the copyright on two articles, "The Great South Asian War" and "Thailand: Counterinsurgency's Proving Ground."

Finally, I owe a special debt of gratitude to my editors at Alfred A. Knopf—Angus Cameron, who encouraged me to proceed with a serious analytical study of this subject, and Dan Okrent, who provided valuable criticism and supervised the final work of revision and editing.

Michael T. Klare
September 25, 1971

Contents

Foreword

If the Pentagon Papers have accomplished nothing else,
they document conclusively that the men who operate at
the highest levels of American diplomacy and military
power have a toughness and clarity of mind and inclination
that is their true hallmark. Contrived sentimentality, seem-
ing naiveté, concern for public moods—they have feigned
these characteristics to deliberately manipulate mass opinion in order to avoid an intellectual confrontation with
their domestic victims that could, were mystifications
stripped aside, have profound political consequences and
lead to the emergence of an American opposition that
would have a political as well as moral basis of resistance
to the direction of this society.

The question that will someday preoccupy a growing
number of Americans whose intellectual armor and tranquillity have been torn asunder by the Vietnam war is
why, in light of the irrefutable evidence, they did not far
earlier comprehend the purpose and quality of their soci-

ety, not just after 1965 but during preceding decades as well. With insight and knowledge comes immunity to conscious deception and deliberate falsehood. To possess that understanding, to know far more precisely the nature of the society and its structure, is also to anticipate its consequences and to know infinitely better how, and where, to oppose the performance of social and human evil by those who wield power. The attainment of that insight, after the shocking apathy and confusion of the postwar decades, may very well become a national passion for those who desire both a new society and personal integrity. For even if they cannot transform power merely by understanding it, at least in its larger contours, more and more Americans will never again wish to become gulled and silent—if unwitting—accomplices elsewhere to the infliction of such evil as their leaders have levied upon the peoples of Indochina.

Obfuscation of reality by conventional wisdom is not merely the result of official press releases, however, but one of the necessary by-products of the condition of American social science and scholarship. Academic social science, in the name of empiricism, cultivates a narrow specialization that has encouraged the avoidance of reality by dealing with the most minute, discrete aspects. More general theories or overviews of the entire society have simply not been produced as a normal outcome of research in depth. Grand theory, such as it is, has been left to obscurantists or, much more often, to witty literary stylists who, despite marginal criticisms, make all of the society's problems appear relatively easily soluble within the existing social structure—John Kenneth Galbraith, A. A. Berle, and Peter Drucker are but the best known among them.

On the part of the critics of American society on the Left, all too often the "correct" phrase and posture has become a substitute for true insight and knowledge, and not since C. Wright Mills has there been a credible radical assault on some major aspect of the status quo. The sterility necessarily concomitant with a purely deductive line explains only part of this void. Lack of adequate research in depth into the institutional workings and mechanics of the social structure is far more consequential, for only by investigating a system closely can one understand it. Facile, incorrect generalizations about the nature of reality—from the Left as well as from purveyors of conventional wisdom— are possible only where their analytic premises and contentions are not convincingly challenged. Insofar as effective opposition requires clarity in order to forestall the dangerous consequences of constituted power, as well as the wisdom with which to seek to replace it, it also must possess a great deal of information. For individuals who seek to attain and preserve their intelligence and sensibility amidst a colossus that inflicts evil at home and abroad, such insight is no less precious. Indeed, it is inconceivable, either out of desire for social change or intellectual reformation, that Americans can avoid a far more profound knowledge of the operational aspects of their own nation. Obtaining it is a prerequisite for any future that is superior to the present, and essential for a rejection of the debilitating, impressionistic apologies of middle- and highbrow American social science, which reinforces the cultivated illusions of the status quo with cant and irrelevance masked as pseudo-objectivity.

Michael T. Klare's *War Without End* succeeds brilliantly and convincingly in staking out a vast area of American foreign policy where average citizens and erstwhile experts alike have virtually no serious comprehension. In managing to avoid all the pitfalls of sterile academism as well as lightheaded radical phraseology, and by mastering and genuinely distilling and comprehending a vast literature on U.S. military and foreign policy, he has qualitatively advanced our social knowledge in a manner that finally makes discussion of future American interventions based on ignorance inexcusable. No one who reads closely in his sources would be able to arrive at conclusions different from his. A consideration of the merits and contents of his book is superfluous here and is no substitute for the texture and value of the work itself. Suffice it to say, it is a major building block in radical scholarship that one hopes will be followed by books of similar scope and accomplishment in other fields. For a comprehension of the planning —past and future—of American globalism, *War Without End* has no rival.

Yet Michael Klare has not simply digested an unprecedented mass of data prerequisite for understanding; he has accepted a historical truth that makes his wealth of information explicable. Basically, the traditional interpretation of the Cold War postulates a kind of uneasy peace between the United States and Russia after World War II, but it minimizes and even ignores the sustained postwar violence and intervention that has characterized U.S. foreign policy outside of Europe. In brief, it is a theory of international relations between advanced industrial nations with nuclear power, and until now no one has offered a convincing and documented alternative explanation of the relationship of the United States to Third World nations in the process of revolution and the assertion of true national independence.

This interaction between the United States and the Third World has both a socioeconomic dimension, with geopolitical aspects, and a technological phase that impinges not only on the causes of U.S. interventionism but also on the economics of defense procurement.

The relationship of the successive administrations in Washington to the national revolutionary movements in the Third World is not simply a question of Indochina— which is but the highest expression of the postwar struggle of the United States to impose its hegemony in the former colonial regions and Latin America. It is, above all, determined by a strategy for international economic and political integration that anticipates new interventions, one that the U.S. has scarcely abandoned. Indeed, *War Without End* irrefutably shows how America's leaders have sought to learn the epic lessons of Vietnam in their planning for future wars, calculating the manner in which it can utilize mercenaries, local *compradors*, and regional allies as both a complement to and substitute for American military forces. The United States is preparing men who have the same social goals, or whom it simply can buy, for the future crucifixions of nations in places whose names are hardly familiar to serious and concerned Americans unaware of the plans and dreams of generals who have already shown their mettle in Indochina. The Nixon Doctrine of Asians fighting Asians on behalf of America's (and perhaps also of Japan's) goals is the loftiest if least candid, expression of this new outline for future local wars.

The problem, of course, is that the United States' local allies are neither motivated nor effective, and in the end often mobilize a greater local resistance and patriotic opposition to foreign domination, or even so profoundly dislocate the domestic economy as to escalate the scale of revolutionary upheaval and struggle. That, indeed, was the lesson of China immediately after World War II, and later of Vietnam. Partially to compensate for this, as well as to overcome the natural disadvantages of controlling only six percent of the population of a vast globe, the leaders of the United States have also planned to fight a technologically intensive war against decentralized opponents in fields and jungles, hoping thereby to accomplish with "hardware" what has eluded their ideological appeals.

There is a fascinating exoticism to this planning for warfare essentially between machines and men—as there are warnings. Vietnam, after all, was a technological and fiscal extravaganza that makes pale the David and Goliath analogy. In the end, while the Indochinese people have suffered immeasurably, they have also defeated U.S. military power in what is surely one of the epic contests of human history. For there is a kind of futile and pathetic as well as dangerous aspect to America's technological fetishism that Mr. Klare fully comprehends and discusses. And its failure transcends the fact that the necessarily crucial socioeconomic allies and objectives of the United States in its interventionist efforts are no less irrelevant and impossible.

⎸The pseudosophistication of "think tank" planners and kept university brains cannot acknowledge the limits of American power, or the irreversible, uncontrollable condition of contemporary civilization, so long as they are paid to work within the carefully defined assumptions and goals of various military agencies.⎸This failure, however, and the desperate efforts to improvise new means by which to transcend it, are precisely dissected in the brilliant exposition that follows. It is the story of chimerical planning and research to make certain that the next major intervention after Vietnam avoids the same pitfalls.

But what is failure to some is gain to others, because to the defense procurement establishment the name of the game is not necessarily success but the continuous effort to attain it. Indeed, never-ending search itself can be more profitable than the acquisition of the ultimate successful weapons, which might perhaps inflict greater harm on military contractors than would total American hegemony and tranquillity in the world. And in view of the arbitrary personal loyalties of Pentagon leaders and the theory of maintaining a company as part of a mobilized technological capacity, it is not at all surprising to see weapons concepts and contractors selected for reasons that frequently have little to do with efficiency and economy. The choice of weapons that, stated candidly and accurately, are pure boondoggles is a legacy of the immediate postwar expansion of the military and the initial selection of the hardly functional B-36 bomber in 1948. While the TFX and the C-5A aircraft are more recent examples of the same principle, in effect, purely political and economic criteria have had an enormous influence on the choice of weaponry since 1946. Because of the propensity to develop strategic theories to rationalize the weapons that some service interest desires, or because some influential company knows how to build or win support for its arms, the image of the United States as the giant with feet of clay is the appropriate one that emerges from Mr. Klare's splendid study. But even clumsy titans can inflict immense human and social misery on others and on themselves. This too we can see as the consequence of the global strategy and weaponry that have been mapped and procured in Washington, for the future as well as the past.

Incapacity to adjust to failure is a function of the need of a social system with vested interests to attain ends absolutely essential to it, and what seems irrational in Vietnam today does not by any means suggest the lesson of defeat. Rather, it will alter only the methods by which it will continue to hope to attain the same objectives. From the viewpoint of learning from past failures and abandoning the effort, the Korean War should have been sufficiently instructive to the men in Washington. Vietnam was not the first unsuccessful massive war against an agrarian, decentralized nation, nor will it be the last until there is a basic transformation of the American economy and its instinctive but also quite necessary expansionist impulses. Therefore it is possible for Michael Klare to outline accurately the plans for future Vietnams in the following pages. It is a vision of the torment of other lands—and of our own.

Still, the pathetic quality of the geopolitical and military planning of successive administrations in Washington has never been more apparent than today. They virtually ignored entirely the problem of the morale and fighting capacity of their own armed forces, a shoal that may cause disaster totally regardless of success or failure with plans in other areas. Officials underrated the venality and cost of their kept allies, who could pilfer and black-market U.S. military and economic aid far more quickly than the Treasury might ever sustain the flow. And Washington remained oblivious of what the profound economic consequences of its extravagant military spending might be for the general health of a national economy that could not always be doctored with arms expenditures. Nor did it comprehend that the literal application of fixed objectives for an area might so distort the priorities of the United States as to tie it down in one region, Southeast Asia, while others, such as Latin America, thereby enjoyed a relative immunity that removed to a historically unprecedented extent that dread inhibition to change—fear of Yankee intervention.

If a decade ago we had had the insight into the plans, objectives, and assumptions of U.S. strategy in Indochina that the Pentagon Papers have revealed, resistance to the war there would have been far greater and more effective, and the government could not have deluded and outflanked it so often. In this sense, the culpability of a large part of the American people for the war crimes their leaders have committed must also be linked to the total failure of purveyors of conventional wisdom—in universities and the press—to examine and publicize the kinds of documents and sources that Michael Klare has now mastered in regard to possible future Vietnams. The man in the street did not know, but a fashionable cynicism and naiveté among the respectable and sanctioned authorities made clarity and public consciousness extremely difficult if not impossible. When the treason of the intellectuals becomes the subject of a period of national remorse, this failure to enquire and assert their critical insights will rightfully be noted. No such defense of ignorance, and justification for apathy and inaction, will be possible during the 1970's. For *War Without End* links our past to our future, thereby helping us to struggle to redefine and change it for the welfare of the American people as well as all humanity.

Gabriel Kolko

WAR
WITHOUT
END

Introduction

In every important respect, *War Without End* is a product of the struggle in the United States against America's intervention in Southeast Asia. The book's genesis can be traced to the earliest teach-ins and forums on the war, when dissident scholars first began to challenge the government's position on Vietnam. As the American military effort escalated, public opposition to the war multiplied and a strong need developed for "hard" information on the origins of the war, its place in U.S. global strategy, and its significance for the future of American relations with Asia and the other less-developed areas of the world. In response to this need, many scholars and researchers initiated a broad and penetrating analysis of the whole thrust of America's postwar foreign policy, calling into question every assumption of Cold War scholarship and journalism. A number of important critical studies were ultimately published, and became required reading for the many "underground" courses on Vietnam that sprang up at campuses all over the country. Over the course of time this educational offensive deepened the commitment of the antiwar forces while isolating the purveyors of government doctrine. *War Without End* was written in this spirit of confrontation and debate; it represents an attempt to examine in detail one aspect of the Vietnam conflict—the development of new strategies and techniques for counterinsurgency—while contributing to the broader assault on the assumptions of American foreign policy.

Most of the information presented here has been obtained from U.S. government documents or from the publications of military associations, military contractors, or military information services (see the Research Guide for a survey of these sources). While every effort has been made to present an accurate and complete picture of current military programs, I make no pretense of neutrality in discussion of the broader issues of policy—but rather seek to strengthen the arguments of those who would limit the government's power to intervene in future conflicts like Vietnam. By presenting detailed information on the Pentagon's counterinsurgency apparatus, *War Without End* will hopefully demonstrate that it is not enough to call for withdrawal from Vietnam when the government still has the capacity to begin new Vietnams elsewhere, and that *only the complete dismantling of the Pentagon's intervention capability* (and related military and police assistance programs) *will guarantee that we will not be dragged into more Vietnams.*

America's continued maintenance of an intervention capability is not, in itself, sufficient cause for us to fear the outbreak of further Vietnam-type hostilities. It is the general thrust of American foreign policy itself that gives rise to this fear. An examination of available information suggests that the underlying considerations which propelled the United States into a disastrous war in Indochina are still in effect and have the capacity to lead us into similar conflicts elsewhere. While a detailed evaluation of U.S. policy is beyond the scope of this book, *War Without End* will attempt to show that certain consequences of that policy—like the intervention in Southeast Asia—are not the fortuitous products of bureaucratic parlaying but rather the predictable outcome of an American drive to secure control over the economic resources of the non-Communist world.[1]

This conclusion is inevitable if one goes beyond the current obsession with the *minutiae* of intervention (as, for example, is found in commentaries on the Pentagon Papers) to ask the *fundamental* questions raised by the war:

First, why has the United States intervened with such intensity and intractability in Southeast Asia? What is really at stake in Vietnam? Our expeditionary forces are systematically destroying the rural society of South Vietnam. One cannot help asking again and again: Why has the most powerful nation on earth found it necessary to pursue such a brutal and seemingly unproductive course in a small, agricultural nation thousands of miles away?

Second, what motivates the peasants of Vietnam to fight so long and so hard against such seemingly hopeless odds? What could possibly impel poor men and women, armed with relatively primitive weapons, to go into battle year after year against napalm, antipersonnel bombs, and supersonic jets—and against an enemy with ten soldiers for each of theirs? Opposed by a military apparatus that boasts every technological innovation of the atomic age as well as virtually unlimited funds and manpower, why haven't the Vietnamese peasants buckled under and given up their struggle?

A good part of the answers to these questions emerges from an understanding of the crisis of "underdevelopment" in the impoverished nations of the Third World.* Any student of this subject would have to conclude that a crucial determinant of international relations and conflict in the coming decades will be the refusal of the once-colonial nations of Africa, Asia, and Latin America to any longer accept the poverty and stagnation to which they are condemned by the workings of the capitalist system. This is not to say, of course, that every potential crisis can be analyzed solely in terms of the issue of underdevelopment —a full range of other factors will continue to play a major role in international affairs. Such factors include rivalries among the advanced capitalist powers, as well as between them and the Communist world; disputes within the Communist bloc; internal disorders in the advanced capitalist nations; and essentially nationalist considerations. But the backdrop, the setting of future events, will be the long-run attempt of the advanced capitalist nations to maintain their position of preeminence in industrial production and world trade on the one hand, and the struggle of the peoples of the Third World to achieve self-determination and control over their own economic development on the other.[2]

In popular mythology the United States is a nation whose founding ideals enshrine the concept of self-determination for all peoples—the right of every nation to seek its own future unhampered by outside interference. (Such, indeed, is the official explanation given for our intervention in

* The "Third World" is a rough designation for the generally poor and underdeveloped nations of Africa, Asia, Oceania, and Latin America. The term was coined to distinguish these nations from the advanced capitalist countries (the United States, Great Britain, West Germany, France, Japan) on the one hand, and from the Soviet bloc on the other. While used here for the sake of convenience, the term "Third World" is actually a misnomer since the underdeveloped countries are in fact dependencies of the advanced capitalist countries, and do not constitute an independent bloc.

South Vietnam.) That the United States upholds this ideal is, and always has been, largely unquestioned—so unchallenged, in fact, that the assumption has found its way into the writings of generations of historians and political commentators. The reality behind the ideal, however, is quite another matter: American political, business, and financial leaders have always taken for granted the right— if not the *mission*—of the United States to expand its industry, trade, and way of life beyond its borders.

Throughout our history, prominent statesmen have consistently viewed territorial and commercial expansion as the solution to one or another of the key domestic problems plaguing the country at the time. Thus early American leaders saw Florida, the Mississippi Basin, Cuba, Mexico, and parts of Canada as open territory for expansion (a process that some hoped would maintain the precarious balance between slave and nonslave states and thus prevent a clash between North and South). Similarly, westward expansion, entailing a ruthless war of extermination against the Indians, was seen as a "safety valve" that could alleviate the violent class antagonisms and successive economic crises engendered by industrialization in the East. When the West had been settled, the "frontier thesis" was elaborated into the notion that the United States could continue to avoid violent class warfare and economic downturns by expanding the "frontier" overseas—that is, by aggressive expansion of the American share of world trade.

The importance of foreign markets to the stability and prosperity of the United States was made abundantly clear during the last quarter of the nineteenth century when the nation was rocked by a series of severe depressions followed by the outbreak of violent labor struggles. These crises, and the need for foreign markets to compensate for the lack of sufficient domestic demand for the products of American industry, led most businessmen to conclude that overseas expansion was essential if further depressions and labor conflicts were to be avoided. While there was considerable debate regarding the *mechanisms* of expansion—particularly about the benefits of imitating the European powers by acquiring colonies—few questioned the general goal. To quote from a State Department circular of April 1898:

It seems to be conceded that every year we shall be confronted with an increasing surplus of manufactured goods for sale in foreign markets if American operatives and artisans are to be kept employed the year around. The enlargement of foreign consumption of the products of our mills and workshops has, therefore, become a serious problem of statesmanship as well as of commerce.[3]

Even Woodrow Wilson—who is considered in the popular imagination to have been a great champion of democratic ideals and national self-determination—argued that: "If we are not going to stifle economically, we have got to find our way into the great international exchanges of the world. . . . *The nation's irresistible energy has got to be released for the commercial conquest of the world.*"[4] (Emphasis added.)

The release of America's "irresistible energy" in the world economy has determined much of our history over the past seventy-five years; from the late nineteenth century on, a major objective of American foreign policy has been the acquisition of new outlets for American trade and investment. The imperial role of the United States has been obscured, however, by our failure to acquire the formal trappings of an empire. With the crucial exceptions of Puerto Rico, Hawaii, the Philippines, and a number of other Pacific and Caribbean islands, American expansion has been achieved without the acquisition of colonial territories. As symbolized by the great documents of American imperialism, the Monroe Doctrine and the Open Door Notes, the United States has always attempted to establish its hegemony through aggressive investment and trade, and by maneuvering the less developed nations into dependent economic, political, and military relationships.∫ While the European powers sought to maintain direct political control over the destinies of their foreign territories, the United States has forged an "invisible empire" secured by financial arrangements, business operations, military and economic aid agreements, and the creation of client regimes.

The immediate motives behind expansion of America's invisible empire and the actual mechanisms of control have changed through the years. Nevertheless, the relationships forged between the United States and its overseas dependents have followed a consistent pattern: each linkage is designed to meet some current need of the American economy while further securing the dependent status of the colonial economy. Although the specific content of these relationships is constantly undergoing modification, it is possible to identify three major goals of American business operations in the Third World today. The United States needs unhampered access to and control of overseas trade to serve as a market for the products of American industry (and of American-owned plants located abroad), as an outlet for the surplus of U.S. investment funds, and as a source of key raw materials and cheap labor.

In the decade prior to 1968, domestic sales of manufactured products rose 50 percent while sales of American-owned plants abroad increased over 110 percent.[5] The growing sales of U.S.-affiliates is not limited to affluent Europe: between 1957 and 1962, sales of U.S. manufacturing affiliates in Latin America rose from $2.4 billion to $4.2 billion, an increase of over 70 percent.[6] (For a regional breakdown of U.S. investments and earnings abroad, showing the pronounced growth in both during the 1960's, see Table 1 below.) The importance of these figures is underscored by the contribution to domestic economic growth made by the operations of U.S. corporations abroad. By 1964, earnings from overseas sources accounted for nearly one-fourth of domestic nonbank corporate profits.[7] In the

Table 1

U.S. DIRECT INVESTMENTS ABROAD, 1960 & 1969

(Dollars in millions)

Country or region	Book value at year end		Earnings	
	1960	1969	1960	1969
All areas	31,865	70,763	3,566	7,955
Canada	11,179	21,075	718	1,542
Europe	6,691	21,554	769	1,855
Japan	254	1,218	32	181
Australia, New Zealand, and South Africa	1,195	3,854	162	393
Latin American Republics and other Western Hemisphere	8,365	13,810	970	1,634
Other areas	4,181	9,250	915	2,349

Source: David T. Devlin and George R. Kruer, "The International Investment Position of the United States: Developments in 1969," *Survey of Current Business* (October 1969), pp. 21–37. (Prepared with data supplied by the U.S. Department of Commerce.)

postwar period, when sales in domestic markets have often lagged, foreign investment has been one of the relatively few consistent sources of profit growth and capital accumulation.

Overseas expansion is not just *important* to the American economy, it is *vital*. This can be seen by considering the case of raw materials. The Pentagon maintains a list of strategic and critical raw materials (as a guideline for its stockpiling program) that are vitally necessary for the production of war materiel. (These raw materials are also essential to the production of many items used in everyday life.) Eighty to 100 percent of the supply needed by this country of more than half of these strategic materials must be obtained abroad; for 52 of the 62 materials on the Pentagon list, at least 40 percent has to be secured abroad.[8] The strategic significance of this data is clear: a Senate committee concluded in 1954 that should the United States be denied access to the mineral-rich nations, "to a very dangerous extent, the vital security of this Nation [would be] in serious jeopardy."[9]

The Senate's concern is easily justified by considering the materials required for production of a jet engine—an item important to both the national defense and the domestic economy. Among other materials, each jet engine requires certain quantities of columbium, chromium, and cobalt. The actual quantities needed are relatively small, but without them it would be impossible to produce a single jet engine at the present level of technology. The United States must obtain *100 percent* of its supply of these three minerals from abroad. Table 2 lists the major, non-Communist bloc suppliers of these minerals, with their percentages of total "Free World" production. No more graphic presentation of the strategic significance

Table 2

**SOURCES OF SELECTED MINERALS
USED IN PRODUCTION OF A JET ENGINE**

Mineral	Country	Percentage of Free World Production in 1966
columbium	Brazil	54
	Canada	21
	Mozambique	18
chromium	South Africa	31
	Turkey	19
	Southern Rhodesia	19
	Philippines	18
	Iran	5
cobalt	Congo (Kinshasa)	60
	Morocco	13
	Canada	12
	Zambia	11

Source: U.S. Department of the Interior, *Minerals Yearbook 1966*; Percy Bidwell, *Raw Materials* (New York, 1958); and Harry Magdoff, *The Age of Imperialism* (New York, 1969), p. 53.

of the Third World to the American economy and way of life can be made: with the exception of Canada's columbium and cobalt, these minerals can be obtained only in countries experiencing the seething turmoil born of nationalism and the struggle against economic stagnation. Revolution, guerrilla warfare, and urban unrest have been the common experience of at least eight of these countries in the postwar era, and revolutionary movements are still active in half of them. As noted by Gabriel Kolko, "American and European industry can find most of their future sources [of critical minerals], so vital to their economic growth, *only in the continents of upheaval and revolution.*"[10] (Emphasis added.)

As one studies recent world history, it becomes clear that to ask, "Is expansionism really necessary for the United States?" is quite beside the point since expansionism *has* been the outcome of our foreign operations. The relevant question concerns the motive forces of history itself: *Why* has the United States recurrently acted in an expansionist fashion for at least three-quarters of a century? In seeking an answer, one finds that common-sense realism drives businessmen to maintain and protect favored trading and investment positions, to seek a stable sociopolitical climate for their long-term investments abroad, and to frustrate the parallel efforts of foreign competitors. This outlook has led entrepreneurs to secure as much control over foreign economies as they can manage (and the U.S. government is prepared to protect). As noted by economist Harry Magdoff,

The concentration of economic power in a limited number of giant firms became possible in many industries precisely because of the control by these firms over raw material sources. The ability to maintain this concentrated power, to ward off native and foreign competitors, to weaken newcomers, and to conduct affairs in accordance with monopolistic price and production policies depended on the alertness and aggressiveness of the giant firms to obtain and maintain control over major segments of the supplies of raw materials—*on a world scale.* . . .[11]

Thus to talk of the United States without its invisible empire is to conjure up an abstraction that bears little resemblance to our history or to this country as it is now: the richest and most powerful nation on earth, with a distinctive set of institutions, class relations, and cultural norms—all of which have been shaped by our imperial past.* To paraphrase Harry Magdoff, maintenance of a commercial empire is not a *policy* of any given administration or political party, nor does it result from the machinations of a few unscrupulous corporations. Expansionism is not a matter of choice for capitalist America: *it is the way of life of this society.*[12]

When one turns to a discussion of the problem of "underdevelopment" in the Third World, it is normal to encounter another set of myths about capitalist operations abroad. Most Western economists tend to represent underdevelop-

---

* The economic system that is characterized by the subordination of foreign economies to the needs of the domestic economy is technically known as imperialism. This term has, in recent years, been robbed of content through repeated misuse and overuse, and accordingly has not been used here. For the record, however, it is worth including this definition of imperialism, proposed by Fred Block in the *Berkeley Journal of Sociology* (Vol. XV, 1970):

> By imperialism, I mean the control by nationals of one country over economic resources in another country, whether these resources are labor, capital, commodities, land, or mineral resources, such that the resources are used largely for the benefit of the foreign nationals. The key concept is control, whether it is exerted directly, as in the classical colonial situation, or indirectly, as, e.g., in the manipulation of international commodity prices.

ment as a condition to which some nations are condemned by fate—by the *natural* poverty of their resources—or by ethnic or racial deficiencies. Actually, underdevelopment is the complex of *social* relationships that result from a situation in which production in the "underdeveloped" country is geared to the fulfillment of the needs of the "developed" country (also called the "metropolitan" country), rather than to the achievement of autonomous, self-generating growth serving local needs. The capacity of some nations to become and remain "developed" thus requires the conscious planning of "underdevelopment" (that is, dependency) into the economies of others. Given this analysis, it is clear why the term "Third World" is indeed a misnomer: underdevelopment in the poor countries is the result of capitalist development in the advanced countries. This point is eloquently expounded by economist Paul Sweezy in the following passage:

Capitalism as a world system had its origins in the late fifteenth and early sixteenth centuries when Europeans, mastering the art of long-distance navigation, broke out of their little corner of the globe and roamed the seven seas, conquering, plundering, and trading. Ever since then capitalism has consisted of two sharply contrasting parts: on the one hand a handful of dominant exploiting countries and on the other hand a much larger number of dominated and exploited countries. *The two are indissolubly linked together, and nothing that happens in either part can be understood if it is considered in abstraction from the system as a whole.* It is important to stress that this is as true of "modern capitalism," meaning the global capitalist system of the last half of the twentieth century, as it was of the predominantly mercantile capitalism of the period before the Industrial Revolution. . . . We thus do not subscribe to the usage which equates "modern" with "developed." The underdeveloped part of the system is as modern as the developed part.[13]

In order to further understand the crisis of underdevelopment in the contemporary world, it is necessary to outline some of the forces that have structured underdevelopment into Third World economies, and to identify the operations of the American economy as they reinforce or alter those forces.

By far the most common traditional system for exploitation has been the creation of what is known as "monoculture" in Third World countries. This has entailed the organization of entire economies around the sale of one or two export crops (or minerals), thereby gearing those nations to the vicissitudes of the world market. The status of such economies is extremely dependent and precarious, since even minuscule fluctuations in world prices will have a tremendous impact on the income of the producing nation. The Brazilian economy, for example, loses about $25 million per year if the price of coffee drops one cent on the world market.[14] Kenya's fate is bound to sales of coffee in the same way, Ghana's to cocoa, Ceylon's to tea, Chile's to copper, and Venezuela's to oil, to choose but a few examples.

Gearing an economy to export crops has necessarily been accompanied by the breakup of age-old agrarian patterns. Giant, cash-crop plantations or *haciendas* are substituted for the smaller subsistence farms that produced foodstuffs for local consumption, thus driving people off the land and creating what economists call "surplus population." By the same token, monoculture causes starvation in even the richest agricultural regions since all arable land is used for speculation in export crops. Native farmers dispossessed by the monoculture system are reduced to permanently underemployed or unemployable paupers; the vast, impoverished shantytowns that surround most Third World capitals are the living monument to this form of underdevelopment.

Structuring an economy around one or two basic export items enriches the foreign interests which control the plantations and mines and the small native elite which manages them. Since raw materials are normally brought to the advanced countries for processing into finished products, the dependent status of the original country is assured. The underdevelopment of the Third World is further exacerbated by the fact that while the prices of manufactured goods on the world market are holding steady or rising, the prices of most foodstuffs and raw materials supplied by the Third World have shown a long-run tendency toward relative decline.[15] The poorer nations are becoming poorer; they have less and less to offer on the world market with which to purchase the capital goods they need to begin the journey out of backwardness.

The obvious way out of monoculture is diversification, but the developing nations are trapped in a vicious circle: the only way (within the structures of free enterprise) that they can obtain the wherewithal to diversify—heavy machinery, technical expertise, and the like—is to buy it on the world market in return for the primary products they already produce. That is, in order to diversify they must produce even greater quantities of their major export items (which, as noted above, are declining in value over time). This process only serves to make the underdeveloped countries even more dependent on the world market, where prices are normally set by the advanced nations.

Any discussion of American investment in the Third World must be qualified by taking into account a recent shift in attitude on the part of U.S. businessmen, particularly the most established and secure among them. In the past decade there has been a trend toward increased investment in manufacturing enterprises and consumer industries. This trend has been accompanied by calls for enlightened social and economic progress in the Third World: agrarian reform, diversification, tariff reform, the creation of regional common markets, and the development of a prosperous middle class. (These are the themes, for instance, that emerge from John F. Kennedy's plan for the Alliance for Progress and Nelson Rockefeller's 1969 report to President Nixon, *Quality of Life in the Americas.*) The impetus behind these progressive prescriptions is not so much a humanitarian concern for the peoples of the poorer nations as an acknowledgment of the changing needs of the American economy. The Third World is no longer exclusively seen as a source of raw materials but as a potentially vast market for the changing products of American industry, including heavy machinery, high-technology goods, and expensive consumer items.[16]

Major reforms will be necessary for the Third World to absorb new products and investments. The old mechanisms which caused ever-increasing impoverishment must be modified and replaced with new structures that permit the retention of some local wealth and encourage the development of a consumption-oriented middle class. Hence the "progressive" attitudes of some U.S. businessmen that have surfaced—the willingness to invest in local industrial enterprises, to employ more foreign managers and technicians, and so forth. These trends, and the new ideologies of "modernization" with which they are celebrated, should not be allowed to obscure the fact that current U.S. economic practices—no less than those of the past—are designed to service the metropolitan economy by controlling the inputs and outputs of Third World economies.* Expan-

---

* The overall effect of American investment policies in the Third World can be measured by considering data on net capital flows—that is, the question of whether or not overseas investment causes money to flow into Third World economies. Despite the heavy outflow of capital from the United States for investment abroad, the fact is that *more capital is coming in than is going out.* U.S. Department of Commerce figures indicate that between 1950 and 1965, the total flow of investment funds from the United States to the rest of the world totalled $23.9 billion, while the corresponding capital inflow from profits was $37 billion. Of these amounts, $14.9 billion flowed from the United States to Europe and Canada and only $11.4 billion flowed in the opposite direction, for a net *outflow* of $3.5 billion. Between the United States and all the other countries—that is, mainly the poor and underdeveloped ones—the situation was reversed: $9 billion in investments flowed out to these countries while

sion of U.S. manufacturing subsidiaries in underdeveloped
nations may constitute some impetus to diversification and
provide employment for native workers, but in the long
run it will skew the local economy in ways that are beneficial to American interests while perpetuating dependency.
Thus, development of an automobile industry will enrich
a small local elite (and nurture the market for such luxury
items) while bringing huge profits to the American purveyors of technical expertise, financial credit, specialized
components, and assembly equipment. However, without
the development of crucial basic industries (steel, machine
tools, petrochemicals) and the institution of a planned
economy, no nation can begin the journey toward self-
sustaining growth—the only course that will enable it to
relieve the poverty and misery of the great mass of its
citizens.

We have seen that economic operations in the underdeveloped countries are vital to the continued prosperity of
American business. Likewise, we have seen that domination of Third World economies by American business
interests leads to dependence, an irrational allocation of
resources, and outright stagnation in the underdeveloped
countries. Increasingly, the people of the Third World can
calculate the outcome of these relationships with absolute
precision; they can see that no future awaits the mass of
their compatriots but unmitigated poverty, that their aspirations for a better life will be forever compromised by
the tiny oligarchies that are allied to foreign interests, and

$25.6 billion in profits flowed in from them, for a net *inflow* of $16.6
billion. (Andre Gunder Frank, *Capitalism and Underdevelopment in
Latin America*, New York, 1967, pp. 305–6.) Contrary to public mythology, the direction of capital flow is not altered by the foreign aid
program. Current legislation requires that most foreign aid revenues
be spent in the United States, that goods purchased under the program be shipped in American vessels, and that repayments on loans
be paid in dollars or other "hard" currencies.

that the situation is growing worse, not better. (Some Third World economists have gone so far as to call their countries the "underdeveloping" nations to emphasize the growing deterioration of their economies.[17])

At a certain point men and women are compelled to make a choice: either abandon their visions of a better way of life, or take direct action to make them possible. Since World War II, the peoples of the Third World have increasingly turned to the one solution—revolution—that offers any hope of escape from the bonds of underdevelopment. They have embarked upon political revolution to overthrow the repressive and corrupt regimes tied to foreign business interests; social revolution to obliterate the wasteful and oppressive divisions between the elite and the masses; and economic revolution to mobilize native resources for the long journey toward true, self-sustained development.

On the sixth anniversary of the abortive Bay of Pigs invasion, Cuban Premier Fidel Castro delivered a major address in Havana on the role of armed struggle in the Latin American movement for justice and equality. Beginning with an analysis of the crisis facing capitalism, he noted that American business was driven "to increase its exploitation . . . to deplete Latin American resources more and more." Since the population of Latin America was growing faster than its economy, "What," he asked, "will be the inevitable outcome of a situation in which misery and hunger lead year by year to more misery and hunger?" There can be no answer, he maintained, but revolution. *"This revolution is the outcome of a historical need,"* Castro said, *"not the result of caprice or personal will. No one will be able to impose that revolution, as no one will be able to prevent it; for that revolution is the outcome of a vital necessity. It is the only path open to the peoples of Latin America."*[18] (Emphasis in the original.) On the issue of whether armed struggle was necessary to achieve this revolution, he declared:

Thus far history has shown us a *single* road—our own history of today and yesterday and always, the history of the peoples who have made their revolutions. . . . The peoples have found themselves forced to struggle; they have had to struggle. They have had to fight not because they like to spill blood, not because they like war, but because they are faced with the alternative of slavery or sacrifice; they are forced to pay for their freedom and justice with their blood and sacrifice.[19]

In the coming conflagration, Castro warned in another speech, the imperialists will discover that their modern armies and superior armaments will not intimidate the heretofore silent masses of Latin America:

This epic before us is going to be written by the hungry Indian masses, the peasants without land, the exploited workers. . . . An epic which will be carried forward by our people, despised and maltreated by imperialism, our people, unreckoned with till today, who are now beginning to shake off their slumber. . . .

Already they can be seen armed with stones, sticks, machetes, in one direction and another, each day, occupying lands, sinking hooks into the land which belongs to them and defending it with their lives. They can be seen carrying signs, slogans, flags: letting them flap in the mountain or prairie winds. And the wave of anger, of demands for justice, of claims for rights, which is beginning to sweep the lands of Latin America will not stop. . . .

For this great mass of humanity has said, "enough!" and has begun to march. And their giant march will not be halted until they conquer true independence. . . .[20]

Although many Americans may not accept Castro's prognosis, it is abundantly clear that great numbers of people in the Third World *do* accept it, and are prepared to act on their convictions. And while the architects of American foreign policy may question the validity of this prognosis, their response to it—as manifest in the long, brutal intervention in Southeast Asia and the preparations for future interventions elsewhere—suggests that they consider it a major threat to the stability of the invisible empire.

Central to Fidel Castro's vision of the revolutionary

struggle in the Third World is the conviction that the global military and police apparatus of the imperial powers can be cast off by the great masses of the population acting in concert. The same principle has been adopted by other revolutionary leaders as the cornerstone of an evolving body of doctrine for rebellion against Western-backed client regimes. Drawing upon the experience of the Red Army in China, the Viet Minh in Vietnam, the FLN in Algeria, and the guerrilla forces in Cuba, Third World revolutionaries posit that insurgent forces can triumph over imperial armies or Western-trained client troops if there is sufficient popular backing for the revolution. In their view, the superior firepower, training, and mobility of professional armies can be offset by guerrilla tactics if masses are willing to supply the insurgents with food, recruits, and intelligence, and if they are prepared to participate in demonstrations, strikes, acts of civil disobedience, and other forms of harassment. Once the masses side with the revolution, they argue, no combination of purely military measures can guarantee the survival of an unpopular regime. This approach by necessity stresses the primary importance of *political* work in the revolutionary struggle; only when the general population is convinced of the *legitimacy* of the revolution can the insurgents safely engage in armed combat against the incumbent regime.

American management of the Vietnam war has not taken this reasoning into account. Confronted by the persistent failure of the Saigon regime to win a measure of support from the South Vietnamese peasantry, many American apologists have attempted to attribute the National Liberation Front's organizational strength to the use of terrorism or to its capacity to undermine development projects. In the words of Walt W. Rostow, the Front's "task is merely to destroy, while the government must build and protect what it is building." This conclusion is contradicted, according to Eqbal Ahmad of the Adlai Stevenson Institute, by every serious study of revolutionary movements:

Given the inevitable, and generally vast, disparity of military strength between the guerrillas and the government, the success of a revolutionary movement depends on covert and sustained support from a substantial part of the population. Revolutionary warfare . . . demands patience under prolonged suffering, and a resolute conspiracy of silence and militancy. A people can summon up such strength only if it feels morally alienated from its formal rulers, when the latter's title to authority is actively rejected by the masses.

Once a revolutionary movement enters the guerrilla phase, its central objective is to confirm and perpetuate the moral isolation of the discredited regime by creating "parallel hierarchies." The major task of the movement, then, is not to outfight but to out-legitimize and out-administer the government. It must establish a measure of land reform, reduce taxes, provide some education and social welfare, and maintain a modicum of economic activity. A revolutionary guerrilla movement which did not have these constructive concerns and structures to fulfill its obligations to the populace would degenerate into banditry.[21]

These strands of revolutionary doctrine, when reduced to general principles, constitute the essential components of strategy for what have come to be called "wars of national liberation"—wars, that is, that combine the struggles for national independence and socialist revolution.[22] In the past decade, national liberation movements have been formed in scores of countries to organize resistance to the incumbent regime and to win popular support for a revolutionary program. Some of these movements have become quiescent in time, while others—the National Liberation Front of South Vietnam among them—have had a major impact on world history.

This book is concerned with the changes in American military doctrine that have been instituted in response to the challenge of armed revolutionary struggles in the Third World, and with the plans now being made for U.S. military activity in the world environment of the 1970's and 1980's. As we shall see, the established military policy of the early Cold War era—the strategy of "Massive Retaliation"—was considered inadequate for defense against revolutionary movements by the national security advisers who joined the White House staff under John F. Kennedy. Through the efforts of these men, and with the backing of the President and the Secretary of Defense, the focus of American military planning shifted from the dynamics of thermonuclear combat among the advanced industrial nations to the threat of guerrilla uprisings in the remote areas of the Third World.

Military doctrine is not formulated on the basis of abstract principles or unchanging laws; the armed forces of a nation are nothing more nor less than an instrument of national policy—an instrument, that is, of those with the power to make that policy. In the United States, the making of foreign policy has been, for all practical purposes, the exclusive prerogative of the business elite that has dominated the Executive departments since the late nineteenth century.[23] Of course, one cannot say that this elite constitutes a monolithic bloc with a unified policy orientation. Differences of outlook, competing short- and long-term interests, and conflicting power foci have always existed. But in the most general sense, the business community that dominates the American foreign policy apparatus has shared a common interest in the continued growth of capitalism, the Open Door in world trade, and the expansion of our "invisible empire." In the words of Harry Magdoff:

What matters to the business community, and to the business system as a whole, is that the option of foreign investment (and foreign trade) should remain available. For this to be meaningful, the business system requires, as a minimum, that the political and economic principles of capitalism should prevail and that the door be fully open for foreign capital at all times. . . . How much or how little an open door may be exploited at any given time is not the issue. The *principle* must be maintained, especially for a capitalist super-power like the United States, and especially when it is being challenged widely and openly.[24]

Given the intertwined relationship of American business and government, it is not surprising that the ultimate arm of national policy—the military—has been used consistently to defend, expand, and maintain our informal empire. For over a century, the employment of U.S. forces abroad has been governed by the principle of business expansionism; again and again, American troops have been sent to the Third World to guarantee our access to key markets and sources of raw materials, and to protect American properties from expropriation. This pattern of military intervention is graphically documented in a chronology of the "Instances of Use of U.S. Armed Forces Abroad, 1798–1945," prepared at the request of the late Senator Everett Dirksen and published in the *Congressional Record*. Of the nearly 160 occasions on which American forces were employed abroad between 1798 and 1945, an overwhelming majority involved occupation of a Third World country. Between 1900 and 1925, for instance, U.S. troops were dispatched overseas "to protect American interests" or "to restore order" during "periods of revolutionary activity" in China (seven times), Colombia (three times), Cuba (three times), the Dominican Republic (four times), Guatemala (twice), Haiti (twice), Honduras (seven times), Korea (twice), Mexico (three times), Morocco, Nicaragua (twice), Panama (six times), the Philippines, Syria, and Turkey (twice). Of the longer interventions, American soldiers occupied Haiti from 1915 to 1934 "to maintain order during a period of chronic and threatened insurrection," and Cuba from 1917 to 1933 "to protect American interests during an insurrection and subsequent unsettled conditions."[25]

Following World War II, American military strategy was reshaped by the nation's Cold War leadership to accord with the principal foreign policy goals of the era: the stabilization of Western European capitalism and the prevention of further Soviet advances in Europe and Asia. The officers who assumed leadership of the military apparatus at this time had all risen to prominence during the World War, and they naturally turned to their wartime experience for guidance in the formulation of combat doctrine. The strategies they adopted, and the weapons they acquired, were appropriate to what they perceived as the greatest threat to American national interests—a Third World War in Europe precipitated by an invasion by the Soviet Red Army.

By the late 1950's, it had become apparent to some American strategists that the maintenance of nuclear supremacy —secured at the expense of other military programs—had left us vulnerable to attack by armed revolutionaries. The stability of our "invisible empire" in the Third World was shaken by unexpected rebel successes at Dien Bien Phu in 1954, in Cuba in 1959, and in Algeria in 1962. These events, coming at a time when trade and investment in the Third World were becoming increasingly critical to the metropolitan economy, forced a complete reevaluation of American military strategy. If our invisible empire were to be preserved, and American expansion in the Third World facilitated, it would be necessary to develop new strategies and techniques for defeat of guerrilla armies in underdeveloped areas. U.S. troops would once again be sent abroad to "protect American interests" and "to restore order" during "periods of chronic and threatened insurrection."*

---

* This prognosis was confirmed by the Douglas Aircraft Company in an extraordinary report prepared for the Army Research Office in 1965. The report was originally titled "Pax Americana," and subsequently retitled "Strategic Alignments and Military Objectives" when the Senate Foreign Relations Committee became interested in the document. Although classified secret, Senator Karl E. Mundt man-

John F. Kennedy, who entered the White House during a period of mounting revolutionary activity in Southeast Asia, recognized that the next World War would not be a major confrontation in Europe but rather an unending series of "limited" conflicts in the Third World.* Under his leadership, the American military establishment was enlarged and restructured to assure our success in conflicts of this kind. Simultaneously, Pentagon thinking was remolded to account for the changes in our defense posture: *underdevelopment,* not the expansion of the Soviet

---

aged to see a copy and later provided the Senate Foreign Relations Committee with these extracts from the report's "General Conclusions":

> While the United States is not an imperialistic nation she exhibits many of the characteristics of past imperiums and in fact has acquired imperial responsibilities.
>
> The Army will be the major military instrument in the continuation of U.S. leadership whether at home or abroad.
>
> Probably the most important future role of the Army will be in the role of nationbuilding [that is, pacification and civic action] and in keeping secure the frontiers of the U.S. imperium. Relevant here is the Army's past and present role in the Philippines, Taiwan, Europe, South Korea, Thailand and now South Vietnam.

* This outlook was confirmed statistically in 1966 by the Policy Planning Staff of the Office of the Assistant Secretary of Defense for International Security Affairs (OASD/ISA) in a memorandum prepared for Defense Secretary McNamara. In an analysis of the 164 "internationally significant conflicts" during the period 1958–66, Colonel David R. Hughes of the OASD/ISA staff provided the following breakdown of conflict situations:

Overt military conflicts between states	15
Prolonged irregular or guerrilla-type insurgencies	76
Brief revolts, coups, uprisings	73
Total	164

Poor countries, according to Hughes's analysis, figured in an overwhelming majority of these conflicts. (*Adelphi Papers,* No. 46, March 1968, p. 15.)

Red Army, was now seen as the gravest threat to the American empire. As former Secretary of Defense Robert S. McNamara explained in 1966:

Security is development, and without development there can be no security. A developing nation that does not, in fact, develop simply cannot remain secure for the simple reason that its own citizenry cannot shed its human nature.

If security implies anything, it implies a minimal measure of order and stability. Without internal development of at least a minimal degree, order and stability are impossible. They are impossible because human nature cannot be frustrated indefinitely.[26]

Herein lies the great dilemma of current American foreign policy. While the military understands that unalleviated poverty leads to revolution, the business interests that play a key role in determining policy cannot allow the Third World to undergo genuine, self-sustained economic growth. For them to do so would be to undermine the very system that guarantees their profits and power. The only solution that has been found to this dilemma has been to turn McNamara's formula around, and to argue that without stability there can be no development. If the revolutionary movements of the Third World can be extinguished, the argument goes, the resulting climate of stability will give capitalism the chance to bring some measure of prosperity to the Third World and thereby reduce the likelihood of revolt. (Circular reasoning, perhaps, but at least it avoids the embarrassment of examining why people revolt in the first place.) Since masses of peasants are often stripped of their livelihood in the process of "modernization" and thus become an unstable element in Third World societies, the militarization of such societies is seen as a necessary evil on the tough journey to development. Furthermore, when such societies are threatened by "subversive forces" seeking "to mislead and excite" the unruly peasants, a client government is justified in using brutal force to crush the "conspirators" (usually viewed as agents of a foreign government), and, if necessary, the "misguided" peasants along with them. Finally, if such a government is threatened by collapse as a result of uncontrollable public unrest, it is appropriate for the United States to lend its hand in restoring order so that the entrenched regime "can get back to the job of development." Such reasoning, advanced by policymakers like Walt W. Rostow, is usually given as the explanation for our intervention in South Vietnam and for similar "police actions" in Lebanon, Laos, and the Dominican Republic.[27]

It is now possible to essay an answer to the two questions that framed this discussion. The poor people of the world will fight so persistently against great odds because the generations of unrelieved suffering they have endured, and the stagnation they see around them, inform them that their only hope for a decent and just future is a revolution against underdevelopment and the political system that perpetuates it. The American corporate elite will have us fight so persistently to suppress revolutions because they view this struggle as the only way to maintain their power and privilege—that is, as the only way to preserve their way of life. There can be no reconciliation in this conflict. The rewards at stake are far too great. Only through revolution can the people of the Third World begin the process of development and acquire some measure of self-dignity; only through counterrevolution can the American business elite preserve its wealth and power. For the United States, the only possible outcome of this global conflict is participation in a long series of "limited" conflicts, police actions and "stability operations"—the *War Without End*.

Part One

THE COUNTER-INSURGENCY ESTABLISHMENT

Chapter 1

FROM DETERRENCE TO COUNTER- INSURGENCY

—The Kennedy Response to Wars of National Liberation

When the Kennedy Administration took office in January 1961, the United States possessed a military capability powerful enough to ensure that any attack on this country would be followed automatically by the complete destruction of the aggressor's own cities and bases. America's strategic capability, consisting of a multitude of nuclear-armed intercontinental ballistic missiles and Strategic Air Command bombers, had been created at tremendous cost by the Eisenhower Administration. Underlying this buildup was the strategy of "Massive Retaliation," which held that the very threat of nuclear reprisal was enough to deter an attack on this country or any of our NATO allies. As embodied in Eisenhower's "New Look" military policy, Massive Retaliation obliged the defense establishment to concentrate American armed strength at one end of the military spectrum—all-out nuclear war. President Kennedy was soon to discover, however, that the expansion of our nuclear arsenal had been achieved at the expense of the nation's conventional military forces (particularly the infantry), and thus of our ability to engage in conflicts at the other end of the spectrum. In fact, the further we moved away from nuclear war in the military spectrum, the less capable we were of succeeding in combat. The United States was weakest, it appeared, in the area of "low-intensity conflict"—limited warfare, guerrilla warfare, and small-scale police actions.

During the 1950's, when the Soviet Union was regarded as the greatest threat to U.S. national security, this imbalance in our military capabilities did not seem dangerous. Although each postwar crisis had been settled without recourse to nuclear attack, it was felt that these local episodes (including the Korean war) were secondary in importance to the impending war with Russia. As Pentagon correspondent John Tompkins has written: "From the end of World War II through the fifties, each crisis, each coup, each revolt was seen as a possible scheme to divert our attention from World War III—the great East-West confrontation that we were sure was coming. The bomb might be unsuitable for such local troubles, but we were going to win World War III with it."[1]

The problem with this outlook was that World War III —an endless succession of many small wars—had already begun. The major challenge to U.S.-NATO supremacy has not come from the Soviet Army but from rebellious peasants in the underdeveloped countries of Africa, Asia, and Latin America. Armed with primitive weapons but undeterred by America's nuclear capabilities, amateur soldiers have engaged Western armies in Vietnam, Cambodia, Laos, Thailand, Malaya, Algeria, Angola, Mozambique, Cuba, and the Dominican Republic. It is the struggle between these Third World revolutionaries and the guardians of Western economic domination—arising from the irreconcilable conflict between the aspirations of the developing nations and the exigencies of Western capitalism—that constitutes the impetus to the war without end.

By the late 1950's, a handful of academic military strategists and dissident Army generals had come to realize that American hegemony in the Third World was highly vulnerable to armed liberation movements. Arguing that nuclear stockpiles had failed to deter the outbreak of guerrilla movements (because the United States had shown itself unwilling to risk a nuclear war over what appeared to be noncritical objectives), these critics called for a military buildup in the neglected areas of the military spectrum in order to assure an American military victory in *any* armed encounter.

The critics of Massive Retaliation, while questioning many tenets of current military policy, did not deviate from the orthodox Cold War position on the need to contain Communist expansion on a global front. Robert E. Osgood of the Washington Center of Foreign Policy Research notes that under the prevailing consensus, "a local Communist aggression even in an intrinsically unimportant place could jeopardize American security by encouraging further aggressions in more important places, leading to a chain of aggressions that might eventually cause World War III." This view, vigorously propounded by Secretary of State John Foster Dulles, did not—as its critics contended—"depend on the assumption that international Communism was under the monolithic control of the Soviet Union . . . but it did depend on an assumption that amounted to the same thing in practice: that a successful aggression by one Communist state would enhance the power of the Soviet Union, China, and other Communist states *vis-à-vis* the United States and the free world."[2] By acquiring a limited war capability, the argument ran, the United States would be able to contain Communist influences at its periphery, making a nuclear showdown between the superpowers unnecessary while preventing the gradual erosion of Free World hegemony.

Since there is some confusion concerning the meaning of limited war, conventional war, and unconventional warfare, it is worth providing a definition of each. A *limited* war, according to Robert Osgood, "is generally conceived to be a war fought for ends far short of the complete subordination of one state's will to another's and by means involving far less than the total military resources of the belligerents, leaving the civilian life and the armed forces of the belligerents largely intact and leading to a bargained termination." Of course, a war that is limited for one side might be total for the other side, as when a superpower uses less than its total resources to subjugate a backward nation.

A *conventional* war is fought with non-nuclear weapons by the regular armed forces of a nation; such a war may be limited or, as in the case of World War II, entail the total mobilization of the belligerents' warmaking capabilities. *Unconventional warfare* usually connotes operations conducted by irregular military units (guerrillas, commandos, intelligence operatives, etc.) with light arms or, occasionally, with outlawed weapons such as chemical or biological agents, and involves a degree of violence which falls below the level of full-scale hostilities. Typical unconventional operations include sabotage, assassination, ambushes, hit-and-run attacks on isolated outposts, and clandestine propaganda campaigns. When performed by a nation technically at peace, such operations are usually covert and are conducted by secret or semisecret organizations. In the United States, unconventional warfare activities are usually called special operations, and various "special" units have been formed to conduct them.

U.S. interest in limited war strategy first emerged in response to the Korean war, which was largely fought with World War II weapons despite an overwhelming American superiority in nuclear armaments. It flourished in a handful of university-based foreign-policy research institutes and in the Army, which suffered gradual reductions in strength throughout the Eisenhower period. (The standing Army was cut from twenty divisions to fourteen, entailing a reduction of from 1,500,000 to 870,000 men.) The opponents of Massive Retaliation have been described by Osgood as "strategic revisionists" who "rejected the thesis of the Eisenhower-Dulles Administration that the United States would spend itself into bankruptcy if it prepared to fight local aggression locally at places and with weapons of the enemy's choosing." The revisionists, according to Osgood, sought "to save American military policies from the thralldom of misguided budgetary restrictions imposed at the expense of security needs."[3]

One of the leading members of the revisionist caucus was General Maxwell D. Taylor, a former Army Chief of Staff, who wrote *The Uncertain Trumpet* in 1959 to publicize his belief that "Massive Retaliation as a guiding strategic concept has reached a dead end." Taylor, who served on the Joint Chiefs of Staff under President Eisenhower, recalled that "in its heyday, Massive Retaliation could offer our leaders only two choices, the initiation of general nuclear war, or compromise and retreat." From its earliest days, he suggested:

Many world events have occurred which cast doubt on its validity and exposed its fallacious character. Korea, a limited conventional war, fought by the United States when we had an atomic monopoly, was clear disproof of its universal efficacy. The many other limited wars which have occurred since 1945— the Chinese civil war, the guerrilla warfare in Greece and Malaya, Vietnam, Taiwan, Hungary, the Middle East, Laos, to mention only a few—are clear evidence that, while our massive retaliatory strategy may have prevented the Great War—a World War III—it has not maintained the Little Peace: that is, peace from disturbances which are little only in comparison with the disaster of general war.[4]

As a replacement for Massive Retaliation, Taylor proposed the strategy of Flexible Response. This name, he wrote:

suggests the need for a capability to react across the entire spectrum of possible challenge, for coping with anything from general atomic war to infiltrations and aggressions such as [now] threaten Laos and Berlin. . . . The new strategy would recognize that it is just as necessary to deter or win quickly a limited war as to deter general war. Otherwise, the limited war which we cannot win quickly may result in our piecemeal attrition or involvement in an expanding conflict which may grow into the general war we all want to avoid.[5]

The development of a Flexible Response capability— entailing a buildup of America's "General Purpose" (i.e., non-nuclear) forces—would enable the United States to respond to each crisis with precisely that degree of force required to assure our success. With such a capability, Taylor argued, we would no longer have to choose between "nuclear war, or compromise and retreat."

In developing his arguments for a new strategic doctrine, Taylor had the backing and advice of a small but influential group of academic strategists, most of whom were associated with the Council for Foreign Relations in New York, the Center for International Affairs of Harvard University, or the Center for International Studies of the Massachusetts Institute of Technology. These civilians had their first major opportunity to influence policy in 1957, when the Senate Foreign Relations Committee established a Special Committee to Study the Foreign Aid Program. The chairman of this committee, Max Millikan of MIT's Center for International Studies, chose many prominent advocates of the revisionist position to prepare the required background papers. In its final report to the Senate, the study group headed by Millikan criticized the reliance on a deterrence strategy, concluding that "its exclusive focus on Soviet-initiated action ignores the real possibility that the two-thirds of the world's population outside the Iron Curtain just emerging into political and economic awareness may become an *independent source of turbulence and change*, and that interaction among the 'uncommitted' countries could overnight threaten the precarious East-West balance."[6] (Emphasis added.)

These views were given further elaboration in the following year when Panel II of the Special Studies Project of the Rockefeller Brothers Fund delivered its report on "International Security: The Military Aspect." Prepared under the direction of Henry A. Kissinger (ten years before he was to become President Nixon's key foreign-policy adviser), this report concluded: "Even if we succeed in deterring all-out war by the threat of total annihilation, our country and the rest of the free world remains in peril. For we cannot expect to counter limited military challenges by the response appropriate to all-out surprise attack." Since the Communists could well benefit from this apparent impasse, the report insisted that "it is therefore imperative that in addition to our retaliatory force we develop units that can intervene rapidly and that are able to make their power felt with discrimination and versatility. . . . Our mobile forces must be tailored to the gamut of possible limited wars, which may range from conflicts involving several countries to minor police actions."[7]

This prophetic statement—written at a time when widespread resistance to the Ngo Dinh Diem government in South Vietnam was just beginning to cause concern in Washington—had no significant impact on the military policies of the Eisenhower era. President Kennedy, on the other hand, was deeply impressed by these arguments, and in 1961 the advocates of Flexible Response were invited to participate in the new Administration. Maxwell Taylor became the President's principal military adviser and was later promoted to Chairman of the Joint Chiefs of Staff. Walt W. Rostow of MIT and McGeorge Bundy of Harvard, both early proponents of the Flexible Response strategy, became the President's key foreign-policy advisers.[8] Roger Hilsman, another outspoken critic of prevailing military doctrine, was made director of the State Department's Bureau of Intelligence and Research.[9]

Thus under Kennedy the policy of Flexible Response became established Pentagon doctrine. With almost evangelical zeal, the new policymakers set out to rebuild the Defense establishment to ensure that it would be capable of responding to threats arising at *any* level of the military spectrum. They were determined, Osgood recalls, to fill every military gap in the strategy of containment:

To safeguard American security and restore American prestige it would be necessary, among other measures . . . to build up the United States' capacity to fight limited wars without resorting to nuclear weapons. If the Communists could be contained at the level of strategic war and overt local aggression, the new administration reasoned, the Third World would be the most active arena of the cold war and guerrilla war would be the greatest military threat.[10]

THE KENNEDY DOCTRINE

No member of the new Administration was more concerned with the problem of revolutionary warfare than the President himself. Maxwell Taylor recalled in 1965 that Kennedy "first became aware of the problem during an early visit to South Vietnam, when the French were still in the throes of the guerrilla war against the Viet Minh. When he became President, he soon found that among his principal international problems were the situations in Laos and South Vietnam; and gradually developed a growing awareness of the extent of these problems." The President's personal interest in developing a response to these problems, according to Taylor, "inevitably had vast repercussions throughout all the executive branches."[11] Roger Hilsman remembers that from the beginning of his Administration, the President "hammered on the point that guerrilla warfare was different from any other kind and that it required new tactics and doctrines."[12] Hilsman cites a 1962 speech at West Point in which Kennedy declared:

Subversive insurgency is another type of war, new in its intensity, ancient in its origins—war by guerrillas, subversives, insurgents, assassins; war by ambush instead of by combat; by infiltration, instead of aggression, seeking victory by eroding and exhausting the enemy instead of engaging him. . . . It requires in those situations where we must counter it . . . a whole new kind of strategy, a wholly different kind of force, and therefore a new and wholly different kind of training.[13]

Finding scant strategic guidance in the Army field manuals, Kennedy "read the classic texts on guerrilla warfare by Red China's Mao Tse-tung and Cuba's Che Guevara, and requested the appropriate military men to do the same."[14] Soon thousands of State Department and Pentagon officers were studying Mao and Che in the special courses on counterinsurgency that the President had ordered set up for U.S. personnel attached to embassies and missions in the Third World.[15]

When he discovered that the military establishment was not disposed to move quickly in the area of guerrilla warfare, Kennedy used his authority as Commander-in-Chief to get new programs started. The American counterguerrilla effort was sadly lacking in ingenuity and leadership, former White House aide Theodore Sorensen recalled in 1965, and the President, "far more than any of his generals or even McNamara, supplied that leadership."[16] As a start, he created a high-level interdepartmental committee—the "Special Group for Counterinsurgency"—to coordinate all United States activities in this area. Edward Lansdale, an Air Force colonel with close ties to the CIA, was invited to develop new counterinsurgency manuals for the Army and to test his ideas in South Vietnam. After attending a mock guerrilla battle at Fort Bragg, North Carolina,* Ken-

* The Special Forces exercise, conducted on October 12, 1961, was described by one of the journalists present as follows:

As the President watched, seated at the edge of a small pond, troops stormed a beachhead, machine guns rattled, rockets and

nedy ordered a fivefold increase in Special Forces strength and directed that they wear the green beret—theretofore outlawed by the Joint Chiefs of Staff as a symbol of elitism.[17] In response to the Special Forces buildup, the Navy and Air Force each created its own counterguerrilla unit—the Sea/Air/Land teams (SEAL's) and Special Operations Forces (SOF), respectively.[18] The President's pride, however, was still the Army Special Forces. According to Sorensen, Kennedy wanted the Green Berets to be "a dedicated, high-quality elite corps of specialists, trained to train local partisans in guerrilla warfare, prepared to perform a wide range of civilian as well as military tasks, able to live off the bush, in a village or behind enemy lines."[19] Kennedy personally supervised the selection of new jungle equipment, and ordered more helicopters, lightweight field radios, and high-powered rifles for the Special Forces.[20] In an assessment of American counterinsurgency programs, General Taylor told the 1965 graduating class of the International Police Academy (itself a Kennedy innovation): "I think we should look to President Kennedy as the architect in large measure of the programs and policies of my government and eventually of many other govern-

---

flares exploded and helicopters showered the area with propaganda leaflets. It looked like the Fourth of July in a snowstorm. As part of the demonstration, a soldier wearing a rocket-assisted flying belt took off from an amphibious cargo carrier and literally flew three hundred feet over the water directly toward the Chief Executive. (David Wise, "Guerrillas Growl for Kennedy," New York *Herald Tribune*, October 13, 1961.)

Former Green Beret Master Sergeant Donald Duncan, who participated in the exercise while a student at Fort Bragg, later described this event as an elaborate farce: "So few qualified men were around that the judo and [other stunt] teams were imported from the Ranger School at Fort Benning. . . . Much of the equipment shown, including the rocket, had never been seen before and probably would never be seen again. . . ." (*The New Legions*, New York, Random House, 1967, p. 146.)

ments directed at facing the challenge of what was originally called subversive insurgency."[21]

Sharing the President's concern with the threat of revolutionary warfare was the new Secretary of Defense, Robert S. McNamara. In his annual posture statement to Congress, McNamara stated in 1962 that "there has come into prominence, in the last year or two, a kind of war which Mr. Khrushchev [in a speech delivered January 6, 1961] calls 'wars of national liberation' or 'popular revolts,' but which we know as insurrection, subversion, and covert armed aggression. . . . We have a long way to go in devising and implementing effective countermeasures against these Communist techniques. But this is a challenge we must meet if we are to defeat the Communists in this kind of war. It is quite possible that *in the decade of the 1960's the decisive struggle will take place in this area.*"[22] (Emphasis added.)

While Kennedy and McNamara were in agreement on the need for a crash program to upgrade America's limited war capability, they discovered that budgetary restraints and Pentagon inertia could hold up their plans indefinitely. When, however, the Soviet Union announced its intention to sign a separate peace treaty with East Germany (thus jeopardizing Western access to Berlin), they evidently saw an opportunity to rally popular support for a major buildup of non-nuclear forces. Although Soviet diplomats maintained that Western access to Berlin would be assured under the treaty arrangement, the White House allowed a crisis atmosphere to develop in this country until, in a dramatic eleventh-hour address, Kennedy asked the American people to back his plans for an expansion of the armed forces and the acquisition of new weapons.[23] The Berlin crisis speech, made to a nationwide radio and television audience on July 25, 1961, was followed the next day by the introduction of special legislation in Congress.[24] Specifically, Kennedy asked for $3.4 billion to raise Army strength from 870,000 to 1,000,000 men, to add 29,000 men to the Navy and 63,000 to the Air Force, and to create a special $1.8-billion fund for purchase of non-nuclear munitions and equipment.[25] The President emphasized that these additional forces and arms were not required for Berlin alone: "That isolated outpost is not an isolated problem," he told the nation. "The threat is world-wide. Our effort must be equally wide and strong, and not be obsessed by a single manufactured crisis."[26]

Not surprisingly, many analysts concluded that the July 25 speech represented the death knell of Massive Retaliation as a guiding military strategy, and its replacement by Maxwell Taylor's strategy of Flexible Response. Thus Joseph Alsop wrote three days later:

The idea of a conventional infantry engagement on the approaches to Berlin is hard to grasp, simply because Western military thinking fell into such grave decay in the period of American nuclear monopoly. It became an accepted notion that Western armies, and especially American armies, ought never again to submit to the danger and discomfort of non-nuclear combat. This notion was sanctified and made official doctrine, when the "New Look" strategy was imposed upon the Pentagon, for strictly budgetary reasons, in the autumn of 1953.

But the "New Look," always bitterly opposed by the President's military adviser, Gen. Maxwell Taylor, has now been roundly rejected by President Kennedy himself.

Alsop added that the turning point occurred when the Pentagon presented a plan at the White House "for sending a few trucks down the autobahn toward Berlin, and then blithely pushing the button for a thermonuclear war if the trucks were halted."[27]

Certainly the President's speech bore the strong imprint of the Flexible Response strategy position. Against the threat posed by Communist aggression, he declared, "we need the capability of placing in any critical area at the appropriate time" forces large enough "to meet all levels of aggressor pressure with whatever levels of force are required." Although Kennedy stressed the defensive nature of these measures, he hinted that the United States was prepared to deploy its forces abroad to counter subversion and other threats arising below the threshold of nuclear war. "We intend," he declared, "to have a wider choice than humiliation or all-out nuclear action." This aggressive, interventionist response to the challenge of revolutionary war can quite properly be called the Kennedy Doctrine. Adherence to this doctrine prompted the President to send U.S. combat advisers and Special Forces commandos to South Vietnam, and led inevitably to the commitment of American ground troops.

A BLUEPRINT FOR COUNTERREVOLUTION

The Berlin crisis of July 1961 produced the necessary Congressional climate for approval of the President's plans for expansion of the nation's non-nuclear forces. The armed forces quickly grew in strength from 2,500,000 to 2,750,000 men, and the Defense budget was raised to $47 billion—as much as was spent during the height of the Korean war. These actions gave Kennedy and McNamara the necessary authority and resources to build a counter-guerrilla capability into the American military establishment. Still lacking, however, was a long-range program to govern the design and utilization of this capability. In order to obtain expert advice on the development of such a program, Kennedy in 1962 established an ad hoc inter-departmental committee—the Special Group for Counter-insurgency—to pool the views of his principal military and civilian advisers.[28] Under the chairmanship of Maxwell Taylor, the Special Group met weekly to review all government activities in the area of counterinsurgency and unconventional warfare, and to make recommendations for the initiation of new programs and/or the modification of existing ones.* Besides General Taylor, the Special Group's membership included Deputy Undersecretary of State U. Alexis Johnson, Director of Central Intelligence John A. McCone, Chairman of the Joint Chiefs of Staff General Lyman L. Lemnitzer, Deputy Secretary of Defense Roswell L. Gilpatric, Foreign Aid Administrator Fowler Hamilton, Director of the U.S. Information Agency Edward R. Murrow, and Special Assistant to the President for National Security Affairs McGeorge Bundy. The President himself was represented by the Attorney General, Robert F. Kennedy.

Through a continuous process of interaction between the Special Group, the President, and the Secretary of Defense, a program for the development of an American counterinsurgency apparatus began to emerge. (Rather than acknowledge the counterrevolutionary nature of its operations in the Third World, the Pentagon has chosen the clinical term "counterinsurgency" to describe its response to movements for national liberation.†) Although never

---

* Something like the Special Group has been revived by the Nixon Administration. During the Cambodian crisis of May 1970, the President met daily with an ad hoc body called the Washington Special Action Group (commonly referred to as WASAG). This group is headed by Henry Kissinger, the President's national security adviser, and includes representatives of the CIA, the State Department, the Office of the Secretary of Defense, and the Joint Chiefs of Staff.

† The official Pentagon definition of counterinsurgency, as provided in the *Dictionary of United States Military Terms for Joint Usage,* is: "Those military, paramilitary, political, economic, psychological, and civic actions taken by a government to defeat subversive insurgency." *Insurgency* is defined as "a condition resulting from a revolt or insurrection against a constituted government which falls short of civil war. In the current context, subversive insurgency is primarily communist inspired, supported, or exploited."

reduced to a rigid set of principles, this counterinsurgency schema has governed U.S. defense planning since the early 1960's. The major components of this program are:

Rapid Deployment

From their close reading of Mao and Che, President Kennedy and Secretary McNamara knew that time was a crucial ingredient in revolutionary war strategy, and that in order to be successful a counterinsurgency effort must destroy the guerrilla organization before it gains widespread popular support. They determined, therefore, to provide the American military establishment with a "rapid response" capability allowing for deployment of American troops on the guerrilla battlefield at the first sign of an insurgent uprising. Development of this capability—consisting of giant transport aircraft, fast supply ships, and portable air-base equipment—has come to be called the Rapid Deployment strategy.

The Electronic Battlefield

Kennedy and his advisers recognized that guerrilla struggles are ultimately won or lost on the ground, and that large numbers of infantrymen are normally required to protect "loyal" villages, pacification teams, and government installations in the guerrilla zone from surprise attack. (In Malaya, the British counterinsurgency effort, often cited as a model for American efforts of this kind, required a force of 260,000 government troops to overcome 8,000 guerrillas—a ratio of 33 to 1.) Knowing that American military strength had been concentrated in the air and on the sea, the Kennedy team moved to upgrade the infantry and to enhance its capabilities in the areas of mobility, firepower, communications, and intelligence. By applying American technological knowhow to the problem of detecting guerrilla sanctuaries and warning against guerrilla attacks, they hoped to reduce the ratio of infantrymen to guerrillas. This determination led to the development of new surveillance devices, infiltration alarms, and battlefield computers that together constitute the "Electronic Battlefield."

The Mercenary Apparatus

Since a major aim of revolutionary war is to isolate the incumbent regime from the masses of people, the use of American troops to defend such a regime would inevitably legitimate the arguments of the insurgent movement. Furthermore, no matter how many technological innovations were incorporated into the American military apparatus, participation in a series of drawn-out counterguerrilla campaigns would cause a severe manpower drain on the United States and arouse strong opposition at home. In order to reduce direct American involvement in such conflicts, therefore, Kennedy determined to mobilize local armies for counterinsurgency operations in their own or neighboring countries. By employing native troops, he hoped to limit the manpower drain on the United States while giving the impression that our participation was restricted to support for the self-defense forces of a legitimate government. In Southeast Asia, where this strategy has been carried to its furthest limits, the American mercenary apparatus includes the Central Intelligence Agency's "Secret Army" of Meo tribesmen, the regular armies and police forces of our client states, and "elite" mercenaries from other industrialized nations.

Social Systems Engineering

It is not through military means, ultimately, that a revolutionary movement wins a guerrilla war, but rather through

the superiority of its political positions and its proven
ability to provide needed services to the common people.
Kennedy and his civilian aides were well aware that in
order to counter the genuine appeal of national liberation
movements, they would have to develop a program of
psychological warfare, rural development, and economic
assistance in order to alleviate outstanding social ills and
provide some measure of legitimacy for the incumbent
regime. At the same time, they concluded that it would be
necessary to institute a system of "resources control" (i.e.,
restraints on the movement of people and goods in and out
of the guerrilla zone) in order to undermine the insurgents'
administrative infrastructure. These nonmilitary activities,
collectively known as "the other war" in Vietnam, are
products of the new "science" of "social systems engineering."

This blueprint for the American counterinsurgency apparatus, developed by the Kennedy Administration in 1961
and 1962, was retained by the two succeeding Administrations and remains in force today. That is not to say, however, that the program has not undergone modification or
change of emphasis; even during the Kennedy Presidency,
in fact, certain elements of the scheme received more
emphasis than others. Thus while Kennedy himself was
convinced of the primary importance of political measures
in counterinsurgency, this view was not wholly shared by
his military advisers, who stressed the primacy of military
activities. President Johnson, who was more comfortable
with the regular military than with either professional
counterinsurgents like the Green Berets or with civilian
pacification workers, sent a large expeditionary army to
Vietnam and turned over direction of "other war" activities
to the Pentagon.[29] President Nixon, on the other hand, is
withdrawing American ground forces in Asia and placing

greater emphasis on mercenary operations and the development of an indigenous counterinsurgency establishment.[30] Some elements of Kennedy's scheme—the creation of a rapid deployment capability, for instance—have received unqualified support from both of his successors. Thus Kennedy's promise to develop the means to place American forces "in any critical area at the appropriate time" will reach fulfillment if the C-5A supertransport can be made airworthy. Other programs begun during his Administration, such as the development of new battlefield surveillance systems, are not expected to reach fruition until the late 1970's or even the 1980's.

KENNEDY AND VIETNAM

The guerrilla war in South Vietnam, gradually emerging from modest beginnings in the final years of the Eisenhower Administration, expanded rapidly after Kennedy took office in 1961. (According to Roger Hilsman, U.S. intelligence reports indicated that guerrilla strength rose from 5,000 men in January 1961 to 16,000 a year later.[31]) It was only natural, therefore, that Kennedy chose to use Vietnam as a proving ground for the new counterinsurgency programs and weapons that were coming off the drawing boards in the Pentagon and the military think tanks. Kennedy sent his key foreign-policy advisers—Maxwell Taylor, Walt Rostow, Hilsman, and others—to South Vietnam on inspection trips, and asked them to develop battle plans for the American-directed campaign against the National Liberation Front.[32] Experienced counterinsurgency planners, including the CIA's Edward Lansdale and Great Britain's Sir Robert Thompson, were invited to contribute to the design of these battle plans and to participate in their implementation.[33] The Pentagon sent weapons researchers and training officers to Asia with the mission of developing new arms and combat doctrine for a jungle war. Taylor, who witnessed all this activity from his command post in the Pentagon, told a Congressional committee in 1963:

Here we have a going laboratory where we see subversive insurgency, the Ho Chi Minh doctrine, being applied in all its forms. This has been a challenge not just for the armed services, but for several of the agencies of Government, as many of them are involved in one way or another in South Vietnam. On the military side, however, we have recognized the importance of the area as a laboratory. We have had teams out there looking at the equipment requirements of this kind of guerrilla warfare. We have rotated senior officers through there, spending several weeks just to talk to people and get the feel of the operation, so even though not regularly assigned to Vietnam, they are carrying their experience back to their own organizations.[34]

The decision to convert South Vietnam into a proving ground for American counterinsurgency programs can be traced to two mutually reinforcing factors.

First, Vietnam had all the necessary features for an ideal laboratory: it had a proven guerrilla army with genuine revolutionary credentials, a "nationalist" anti-Communist regime with some claim to popular backing, and a non-white population whose suffering at the hands of American counterinsurgency technicians would cause no undue concern in the United States. As noted in the secret Pentagon history of the war, "Vietnam was the only place in the world where the Administration faced a well-developed Communist effort to topple a pro-Western government with an externally aided pro-Communist insurgency. It was a challenge that could hardly be ignored."[35]

Second, South Vietnam was a new revolutionary front in what Kennedy and his advisers considered "Free World" territory—that is, the American sphere of influence—and thus could not be allowed to fall into the Communists' hands. As we have seen, the strategic revisionists believed implicitly in the Cold War formula that considered any gain in Communist strength, even in a remote and backward corner of the globe, as constituting an unfavorable shift in the balance of power between the United States and the Soviet bloc. Just such a shift of power had occurred under the previous Administration, when Fidel Castro overthrew the client regime of Fulgencio Batista and installed a leftist government in Havana; Kennedy was determined that no such erosion of American power would occur during his incumbency. In a secret memorandum delivered to the President on November 11, 1961, and later incorporated into the Pentagon's history of the war, Secretary of Defense McNamara and Secretary of State Dean Rusk wrote:

The loss of South Vietnam to Communism would involve the transfer of a nation of 20 million people from the free world to the Communist bloc. The loss of South Vietnam would make pointless any further discussion about the importance of Southeast Asia to the free world; we would have to face the near certainty that the remainder of Southeast Asia and Indonesia would move to a complete accommodation with Communism, if not formal incorporation with the Communist bloc.[36]

The Pentagon Papers note that on the basis of this memo, President Kennedy approved the deployment of several thousand advisers and combat support troops to South Vietnam, thus raising to a certainty the likelihood of our becoming involved in a shooting war with the Vietnamese guerrillas.[37]

The Pentagon's study of the war indicates that Kennedy and his advisers did not doubt that, once the United States became fully committed to the struggle in Vietnam, it would be able to overcome any insurgent challenge to the Diem regime. Top Administration officials, according to the study, were convinced that every problem of the Saigon government—including its army's lack of fighting spirit—"could be cured if enough dedicated Americans . . . became involved in South Vietnam to show the South

Vietnamese, at all levels, how to get on and win the war."[38] Defeat, or even stalemate, was considered impossible. There was great implicit faith, the study notes, that the mere introduction of American troops would provide the South Vietnamese "with the élan and style needed to win."[39] Robert Osgood recalls that during Kennedy's incumbency, after the Cuban missile crisis of 1962 and before large numbers of U.S. troops got bogged down in Vietnam, the United States appeared so powerful that many Americans "began to think of the world as virtually monopolar and of America's position in the world as comparable to that of a great imperial power. *The only remaining gap in military containment might be closed if the United States could demonstrate in Vietnam that wars of national liberation must fail.*"[40] (Emphasis added.)

The original Kennedy contribution to the Vietnam conflict was relatively modest—although, as seen in the light of subsequent events, fateful. In National Security Action Memorandum 52, dated May 11, 1961, the President authorized an increase of one hundred men in the U.S. advisory mission in Saigon and the deployment to South Vietnam of four hundred Green Berets to provide training in counterguerrilla operations.[41] Although the numbers involved appear small, even this first expansion of the U.S. military apparatus signaled a willingness to go beyond the 685-man limit that had been imposed on the advisory mission by the 1954 Geneva Agreements. Moreover, the memo called upon the CIA to organize South Vietnamese commando teams for covert raids on North Vietnam and rebel-held portions of Laos.

According to the Pentagon's secret history of the war, President Kennedy's specific orders for the initiation of covert actions called for these steps:

—"Dispatch of . . . agents to North Vietnam" for intelligence-gathering operations.
—"Infiltrate teams under light civilian cover to south-

east Laos to locate and attack Vietnamese Communist bases and lines of communication.

—"In North Vietnam, using the foundation established by intelligence operations, form networks of resistance, covert bases and teams for sabotage and light harassment.

—"Conduct overflights for dropping of leaflets to harass the Communists and to maintain morale of North Vietnamese population, and increase [propaganda] broadcasts to North Vietnam for the same purposes."

—Train "the South Vietnamese Army to conduct ranger raids and similar military actions in North Vietnam as might prove necessary or appropriate."[42]

These decisions transformed the American commitment to Diem from a passive, defensive posture to an activist, combative one: the credibility of the American counterinsurgency apparatus was now at stake.*

Despite this initial infusion of U.S. personnel and resources, the political and military situation in Vietnam continued to deteriorate. Maxwell Taylor, who was sent to Southeast Asia in October 1961 at the President's request, reported on November 1 that only the deployment of U.S. ground troops would save South Vietnam

---

* In a retrospective essay on U.S. policy in Southeast Asia, former Presidential Adviser Walt W. Rostow wrote in 1970: "In making his decisions on Southeast Asia in 1961, President Kennedy did not believe his option was war, if he stood firm on the treaty commitments, versus peace, if he let Laos and Vietnam slide away. He believed the United States, in the end, would not acquiesce [in] the region from Saigon and Vientiane to Singapore and Djakarta falling under the hegemony of a potential enemy. He was conscious, too, . . . that the American performance in Southeast Asia would affect profoundly the stability of other regions of the world. He believed his realistic option was to stand on the treaty commitments—whatever the costs—or see the United States engaged in a wider war fairly soon." ("Domestic Determinants of U.S. Foreign Policy," *Armed Forces Journal,* June 27, 1970, p. 16B.)

from a Communist take-over.* In the November 11 McNamara-Rusk memo cited above, Kennedy was cautioned against the commitment of regular combat troops but was urged to provide Diem with substantial logistical, communications, and intelligence support, including the dispatch of naval patrol vessels and U.S. helicopter airlift companies.

These recommendations were incorporated by the President in National Security Action Memorandum 111, dated November 22, 1961, which approved the buildup of U.S. advisory and support forces in South Vietnam and authorized them to engage in combat operations if fired upon in the pursuit of their mission.[43] Although, as noted in the Pentagon history of the war, Kennedy never approved the use of regular U.S. combat forces to save Diem, he responded to each downward spiral of the crisis by dispatching more advisers and support units and thus, "almost by default," established an American combat apparatus in South Vietnam.† (During the thirty-four

---

* In a cablegram to the President from Baguio, the Philippines, Taylor warned that "the introduction of a U.S. military force into SVN [South Vietnam] . . . is an essential action if we are to reverse the present downward trend of events." In this message, later incorporated into the Pentagon history of the war, he further argued: "The size of the U.S. force introduced need not be great to provide the military presence necessary to produce the desired effect on national morale in SVN. . . . A bare token, however, will not suffice; it must have a significant value." Taylor acknowledged that introduction of the proposed U.S. task force might cause the insurgents to step up their attacks on the Saigon regime, but he concluded, "I do not believe that our program to save SVN will succeed without it." (From the November 1, 1961, cablegram as published in *The New York Times* on July 1, 1971.)

†By January 9, 1962, according to the Pentagon history of the war, the following American forces were active in Vietnam:
—Two Army helicopter companies were flying combat support missions and an air commando unit code-named Jungle Jim was "instructing the Vietnamese Air Force in combat air support tactics and techniques."

months of the Kennedy Presidency, American troop
strength in Vietnam grew from 685 to roughly 16,000.[44])
The Pentagon Papers conclude that John F. Kennedy
transformed the "limited-risk" policy of the Eisenhower
Administration into a "broad commitment" to prevent a
Communist victory in South Vietnam.[45]

In retrospect, it is apparent that once the decision was
made to use South Vietnam as a proving ground for our
burgeoning counterinsurgency apparatus, the Kennedy
Administration had created a new rationale for the continued American presence there. Since our effort in Vietnam was intended to be a model counterinsurgency—the
struggle in which we would demonstrate that wars of
national liberation must fail—we had no choice but to
win the war: a failure to do so would lend credibility to
the proponents of revolutionary warfare and inspire
oppressed peoples everywhere to revolt against the Pax
Americana. As time went on and the earliest American
efforts proved incapable of stopping the insurgents'
advance, this rationale caused President Kennedy to send
more and more advisers and support elements to Vietnam
in order to prevent further setbacks. In the process, a
vicious cycle took command of American policymaking:
the greater our direct involvement in the Vietnam counterinsurgency, the more urgent became our need to avoid
defeat. This urgency is clearly manifested in a January

—United States Navy Mine Division 73, with a tender and five
minesweepers, was sailing from Danang along the coastline to
intercept enemy supply junks.

—American aircraft from Thailand and from the Seventh Fleet
aircraft carriers off Vietnam were flying surveillance and reconnaissance missions over Vietnam.

—Six C-123 spray-equipped aircraft "for support of defoliant
operations" had "received diplomatic clearance" to enter South
Vietnam.

1964 memorandum from Maxwell Taylor, then Chairman of the Joint Chiefs of Staff, to Secretary McNamara recommending an expansion of the American war effort in South Vietnam. In the memo, later incorporated into the Pentagon's history of the war, Taylor commented that the loss of South Vietnam to the insurgents would almost certainly be followed by the collapse of anti-Communist regimes in the rest of Southeast Asia. Then he added:

In a broader sense, the failure of our programs in South Vietnam would have heavy influence on the judgments of Burma, India, Indonesia, Malaysia, Japan, Taiwan, the Republic of Korea, and the Republic of the Philippines with respect to U.S. durability, resolution, and trustworthiness. *Finally, this being the first real test of our determination to defeat the communist wars of national liberation formula, it is not unreasonable to conclude that there would be a corresponding unfavorable effect upon our image in Africa and Latin America.*[46] (Emphasis added.)

The rest is history. In order to protect the credibility of our counterinsurgency capability, President Johnson sent first 100,000, then 200,000, and finally more than 500,000 American troops to Vietnam, turning the conflict there into a limited conventional struggle in which the counter-guerrilla effort became lost. It is only in the present, under the Nixon Administration's Vietnamization program, that an effort is being made to revive the original Kennedy-inspired counterinsurgency campaign against South Vietnam's indigenous rebels.

Chapter 2

RESTRUCTURING THE PENTAGON

—"The McNamara Revolution"

The policy of Massive Retaliation, which dominated American military thinking in the 1950's, led most senior Pentagon strategists to believe that conventional army forces no longer constituted a significant instrument of warfare. In the elaborate war games that occupied the time of most defense analysts, infantry forces were usually given the humble task of serving as a "tripwire" for the more potent nuclear forces. Thus, to cite a typical contingency, if Western Europe should be attacked in force by Soviet infantry, it was assumed that the NATO ground troops on the scene would seek only to hold back the invaders for the few hours that would be necessary to bring nuclear weapons into play. Aside from serving as a tripwire for nuclear forces, the infantry did not figure into any of the standard "scenarios," or strategic timetables, for major East-West confrontations.

The strategic weakness implied by the neglect of our conventional-war forces became increasingly apparent during the Truman and Eisenhower Administrations.\The decade began with a frustrating and inconclusive war in Korea in which 400,000 G.I.'s were held in check by poorly armed "satellite" troops despite overwhelming U.S. superiority in the air and on the sea⏐On the eve of the first engagements, U.S. forces in Korea consisted of only one Army division—the "understrength, ill-equipped, poorly-trained" 24th Infantry.[1] Reinforcements, when they arrived, were equipped for the most part with obsolete World War II weapons. As noted by many historians of the war, the Korean experience left a deep scar on the old-line military establishment. "To many of the higher-ranking American military," Roger Hilsman notes, "the Korean War was a frustrating humiliation. The American Army had been fought to a standstill by Asians, and by Asians whose arms and equipment were somewhat primitive by American standards."[2] With 140,000 casualties and little to show for it, the American public applauded the end of the war and President Eisenhower's pledge to avoid future non-nuclear engagements on the periphery of Asia. Under the fiscal year 1955 budget, the Army's and Navy's armed strength was reduced by one-third, and their budgets cut proportionally. Only the nuclear-oriented Air Force enjoyed an increase in manpower and funding—receiving a 1955 allocation of $16.4 billion, nearly twice that of the Army.[3]

The war in Korea was barely concluded when the United States faced another challenge on the mainland of Asia. In May 1954, Viet Minh troops under the command of General Vo Nguyen Giap began their final assault on the beleagured French garrison at Dien Bien Phu. As the French position grew increasingly desperate, a number of high-ranking Pentagon officials proposed a nuclear attack on Viet Minh positions in the surrounding hills. According to Maxwell Taylor, this plan was overruled because Eisenhower's advisers doubted that "any air attack could be mounted on a sufficient scale to offer success without,

at the same time, endangering the French defenders."
Other emergency schemes, calling for the introduction of
U.S. troops, had to be abandoned because the United
States lacked adequate airlift forces to bring in enough
men in the time available. Taylor concluded from this
experience that "the need was apparent for ready military
forces with conventional weapons to cope with this kind
of limited war situation."[4]

America's ability to come to the aid of an ally under
attack was again tested during the 1958 crisis in Lebanon.
In an analysis of our intervention there, Hanson W.
Baldwin of *The New York Times* observed that "the numbers of men and the amount of equipment transported to
Beirut in the initial increment were far too small and the
time required [to get them there] was too long. . . . If the
United States had faced fairly determined opposition the
small units sent might have been defeated in detail." The
Lebanon episode convinced Baldwin that "today, the air
transport available is not sufficient to move any sizeable
numbers of airborne troops and still carry out the other
emergency tasks required."[5]

On January 1, 1959, and in April 1962, two events
occurred that had a shattering effect on the U.S. military
establishment. The first was the successful guerrilla
campaign waged by Fidel Castro against superior numbers
of U.S.-armed and -trained Cuban government soldiers.
The second was the French decision to abandon Algeria
at a time when the National Liberation Front appeared to
have been defeated on the battlefield. In both of these
struggles, the political and moral dimensions of revolutionary warfare proved stronger than the combined might
of modern and well-equipped armies. These events, which
defied conventional military logic, had a profound impact
upon those few strategists in the United States who had
not become blinded by apocalyptic visions of thermonuclear warfare.

Shortly before the Kennedy Administration was to take office, Henry Kissinger warned that "with fourteen divisions, some of them understrength and most of them less well equipped than their Soviet counterparts, *we are in no position to fight a limited war against a first-class opponent.*" (Emphasis added.) Kissinger argued that America's thermonuclear capability would not deter "minor aggressions" and guerrilla attacks on the United States and its allies, nor would it ensure our success in any such engagements. It was necessary, therefore, to expand and modernize our conventional forces in order to provide the United States with a reliable defense against revolution. "No more urgent task confronts the free world," Kissinger proclaimed, "than to separate itself from the nostalgia for the period of its invulnerability and to face the stark realities of a revolutionary period."[6]

ENTER McNAMARA

As we have seen, the Kennedy Administration was fully committed to the task of upgrading America's non-nuclear forces. No man was better prepared to act on Kissinger's warning than the new Secretary of Defense, Robert Strange McNamara. "When I entered the Defense Department in 1961," he later wrote, "several basic considerations were becoming clear: One of the first things we had to do was to separate the problem of strategic nuclear war from all other kinds of war. Careful analysis revealed two important facts on this point: One was that strategic nuclear forces in themselves no longer constituted a credible deterrent to the broad range of aggression. . . . The other was that we could not substitute tactical nuclear weapons for conventional forces in the types of conflicts that were most likely to involve us in the period of the 1960s."[7] These considerations, according to McNamara, "had an immediate corollary in the obvious need for improvement in our non-nuclear capability. Consequently, we gave our conventional forces early and high priority in 1961."[8] The Berlin crisis of July 1961 provided McNamara with a suitable pretext for increasing Army strength from 870,000 to 1,000,000 men, and for adding $6 billion to the defense budget—much of it spent on conventional-war ammunition and supplies. In addition, the Secretary created a new multi-Service task force for rapid intervention operations, the Strike Command (STRICOM), by combining elements of the Army's Strategic Army Corps and the Air Force's Tactical Air Command.

Noting that while "we must continue to provide for the forces required to deter all-out nuclear war," McNamara insisted that it was imperative that we "see to it that this nation . . . has the kind of forces needed to discourage more limited adventures by the enemies of freedom." As events in Vietnam and Laos demonstrate, he told Congress in 1961, "these adventures may range from guerrilla and subversive activities involving small scattered bands of men to organized aggression involving sizeable regular military units." For this reason, "our limited war forces should be properly deployed, properly trained, and properly equipped to deal with the entire spectrum of such actions; and they should have the means to move quickly to wherever they may be needed on very short notice." The new Secretary of Defense began immediately to carry out the improvements he considered necessary:

As a start we increased the purchase of conventional weapons, ammunition and equipment, expanded the Navy's ship maintenance program, ordered construction of more amphibious transports, and modified Air Force tactical fighters to improve their non-nuclear delivery capability. In addition, we stepped up the pace of training; began revamping the Army reserves; added personnel to the Army and its Special Forces, as well as the Marine Corps and its Reserve; increased airlift capability; and intensified non-nuclear military research and development.[9]

One cannot overemphasize the decisive role played by McNamara in the strengthening and expansion of America's intervention forces.* By mid-1964, he could boast of the following achievements:

A 45 per cent increase in the number of combat-ready Army divisions; a 44 per cent increase in the number of tactical fighter squadrons; a 75 per cent increase in airlift capability (with a 300–400 per cent increase to come); a 100 per cent increase in general ship construction and conversion to modernize the fleet; an 800 per cent increase in the Special Forces trained to deal with counterinsurgency threats.[10]

These achievements, and other McNamara-inspired developments described in subsequent chapters, have so irrevocably altered the composition of the U.S. military establishment that even today it is nearly impossible to conceive of a major Pentagon program that does not bear his imprint. The United States Army of the 1970's, no less than that of the 1960's, is McNamara's Army.

The sweeping changes that McNamara wrought at the Pentagon were possible because legislative action and

* By the same measure, one must note the decisive role played by McNamara in the management of the Vietnam war. Even though, as revealed in published versions of the Pentagon's history of the war, McNamara counseled against the more adventuristic escalations proposed by the Joint Chiefs of Staff and General William C. Westmoreland's headquarters in Saigon, he nevertheless presided over the establishment of the American military apparatus in South Vietnam and saw to it that the apparatus worked smoothly. Alain C. Enthoven and C. Wayne Smith, who worked under McNamara in the Systems Analysis branch of the Office of the Secretary of Defense (OSD), later declared:

> Unlike the determination of peacetime force structures and the defense budget, in which the OSD staff was heavily involved, or even the determination of force deployments to Europe, which also involved OSD, decisions on force deployments to Vietnam were made largely by the President and the Secretary of Defense dealing directly with the U.S. military commander in Vietnam and the Joint Chiefs of Staff. (Quoted in *Armed Forces Journal*, February 1, 1971, p. 40.)

Presidential backing gave him more power than any of his predecessors, and because he possessed the will and the ability to wield this power effectively.

Prior to World War II, the different military services had functioned as more or less autonomous institutions, with their own traditions, weapons, and philosophies of warfare; even after the creation of a unified military command in 1947, each of the services sought to retain its old prerogatives. Critics of the old ways often complained that the Army was armed and trained to fight one kind of war, while the Navy and the Air Force were prepared for totally different kinds of wars. McNamara later wrote that soon after taking office, he discovered that "the three military departments had been establishing their requirements independently of each other." The result, he continued,

could be described fairly as chaotic: Army planning, for example, was based primarily on a long war of attrition; Air Force planning was based, largely, on a short war of nuclear bombardment. Consequently the Army was stating a requirement for stocking months, if not years, of combat supplies against the event of a sizeable conventional conflict. The Air Force stock requirements for such a war had to be measured in days, and not very many days at that. Either approach, consistently followed, might make some sense. The two combined could not possibly make sense.[11]

As noted by *Ramparts* editor Sol Stern, "Each service had its own propaganda machine and its own lobby in Congress. Representatives in both houses became known as 'Army men' (or Navy or Air Force men). Each service fought for its own funds, stressing the value of its own weapons and approaches to war, so that strategic questions were actually fought out on the floor as inter-service rivalries."[12] Although Congress passed a number of measures in the 1950's to strengthen the authority of the Secretary of Defense, the residual privileges enjoyed by the senior career officers in each service prevented the first Secretaries from presiding over a unified and sub-servient constituency. Kennedy and his advisers rec-ognized, therefore, that in order to implement their new military policies it would first be necessary to centralize the decision-making machinery in the Office of the Sec-retary of Defense.

McNamara, an executive at the Ford Motor Company with no previous military experience except a wartime stint as statistical control officer, was relatively unknown outside the business community when he was appointed to the Pentagon's top post. When a student at the Harvard Business School, he had become a disciple of the then new methodology of applying the principles of statistical analysis to business management. Having thoroughly mastered the new techniques, McNamara and some war-time associates offered their managerial talents to the highest bidder in industry, which turned out to be Ford. While some members of this group ultimately moved on to other companies, McNamara had a spectacular career at Ford, rising in fourteen years from manager of the plan-ning and financial office to comptroller, to vice-president and general manager of the Ford Division, and finally—on the day after John F. Kennedy was elected President of the United States—to the coveted position of president of the Ford Motor Company. McNamara's managerial skills made a strong impression on the President-elect's "talent scouts," who suggested him for the post of Secretary of the Treasury; the need for strong leadership in the Pent-agon, however, prompted Kennedy to offer him the top Defense position.[13]

"The challenge of the Department of Defense is com-pelling," McNamara once wrote. "It is the greatest single management complex in history; it supervises the greatest aggregation of raw power ever assembled by man."[14] The new Secretary of Defense approached this challenge in the same manner in which he had faced the complex tasks of administering a gigantic industrial enterprise:

In many respects the role of a public manager is similar to that of a private manager. In each case he may follow one of two alternative courses. He can act either as a judge or as a leader. As the former he waits until subordinates bring him problems for solution, or alternatives for choice. In the latter case, he immerses himself in his operation, leads and stimulates an examination of the objectives, the problems and the alternatives.[15]

For McNamara, the course to be followed was obvious; in *The Essence of Security* he wrote that throughout his tenure as Defense Secretary he was guided by the principle that "the direction of the Department of Defense demands not only a strong, responsible civilian control, but a Secretary's role that consists of active, imaginative and decisive leadership of the establishment at large, and not the passive practice of simply refereeing the disputes of traditional and partisan factions."[16] This principle, wedded to the policy of Flexible Response, was, according to McNamara, the "foundation" upon which he "refashioned and rebuilt the Defense Establishment."[17]

In order to strengthen his control over the decision-making machinery of the Pentagon, McNamara first sought to centralize the command apparatus of Defense intelligence, logistics, communications, and research in the Office of the Secretary of Defense while simultaneously downgrading the importance of the separate service agencies in each of these areas.* Although the legislative authority for such consolidation was provided in 1958

* Some high-ranking officers, including Admiral Hyman G. Rickover, have charged that McNamara attempted to supplant the operational authority of the Joint Chiefs of Staff by establishing a "civilian General Staff" in the Office of the Secretary of Defense. In testimony before a Senate committee in 1968, Admiral Rickover charged that "at the policymaking level the Department now looks like an inverted pyramid, a huge civilian bureaucracy bearing down on the armed forces command over which it exercises almost total control." (U.S. Senate, Committee on Foreign Relations, *Defense Department Sponsored Foreign Affairs Research*, Hearings, May 28, 1968, p. 3.)

by the Department of Defense Reorganization Act, McNamara's immediate predecessors (Neil H. McElroy and Thomas S. Gates, Jr.) had not made any substantial changes in the Pentagon structure.[18] Using powers granted him under the 1958 act, McNamara put into operation the Defense Intelligence Agency (DIA) to replace the separate service intelligence organizations, the Defense Supply Agency (DSA) to oversee procurement of all equipment used by more than one service, and the Defense Communications Agency (DCA) to operate the Pentagon's central communications facilities.[19] The Office of the Director of Defense Research and Engineering (ODDRE), which had a minor coordinating role in the previous administration, was given the task of planning and supervising all Pentagon-sponsored research programs. In addition, specialized agencies were created or modified to manage Pentagon programs in the area of counterinsurgency and limited warfare (see Chapter 5).

Although the Secretary of Defense had sufficient "management authority" to establish hegemony over the Defense establishment, there was, McNamara observed, an "absence of the essential management tools needed to make sound decisions on the really crucial issues of national security."[20] Often comparing the problems of governing the Defense Department to those of governing a large corporation, McNamara set out to endow the Office of the Secretary of Defense (OSD) with the same kind of modern management aids that were available to him as president of Ford. As a start, the staff of the OSD was augmented by bright young scientists and economists from the universities and think tanks, and new Pentagon agencies were set up to oversee the management process. The offices of the various assistant secretaries (Administration, Installations and Logistics, International Security Affairs, Manpower, Public Affairs, and Comptroller) were given considerably increased responsibilities for both day-to-day and long-range supervision of Defense Department operations. Ultimately, a new office, Assistant Secretary of Defense, Systems Analysis (OASD/SA), was created to enhance the authority of the team of civilian analysts (originally stationed in the Comptroller's office) that studied the effectiveness and cost efficiency of proposed weapons systems.*

Most of these managerial measures were designed to give the Secretary of Defense more effective control over the distribution and utilization of defense funds—and thus over the functioning of the military establishment at large.[21] Indeed, on the eve of McNamara's departure from the Pentagon, Frederick Taylor wrote in the *Wall Street Journal* (November 29, 1967): "When Mr. McNamara leaves the Pentagon after having served as Defense chief longer than any other man, he will leave behind a military establishment more firmly under civilian control than at any time in American history. Whether that establishment remains under strong civilian control will be in part up to his successor; a weak Secretary certainly would invite an attempt by the military to move into the vacuum. But the machinery is there for continued civilian dominance."

---

* No McNamara innovation has aroused as much resentment from the professional military as the establishment of OASD/SA. Under the direction of Assistant Secretary of Defense Alain Enthoven, the Systems Analysis staff questioned the utility and comparative value of every weapons system proposed by the three services. Incensed at the growing power of Enthoven and his civilian assistants, the generals turned to their friends in the Congress for relief. Late in 1968, House Armed Services Committee Chairman L. Mendel Rivers tried to abolish the Systems Analysis office. His proposal won the backing of the full House of Representatives, but failed to pass in the Senate. Rivers' campaign against OASD/SA did succeed in swaying Richard Nixon, who promised during the 1968 presidential race to "root out the whiz kids approach" at the Pentagon. While the Systems Analysis staff still functions under Defense Secretary Laird, "its charter has been emasculated—by virtue of a 'treaty' with the Joint Chiefs of Staff—to a much less influential and more passive role of 'evaluation and review.'" (*Armed Forces Journal*, February 1, 1971, p. 37.)

In the preface to *The Essence of Security*, written during his last year in the Pentagon, McNamara acknowledged his debt to the "superb group of colleagues" who helped him reorganize the Defense Department. Since most of these men shared his views on key military and administrative issues, it is worth mentioning by name at least some of the people whom McNamara singled out for special recognition. The list includes: Deputy Secretaries of Defense Roswell Gilpatric, Cyrus Vance, and Paul Nitze; Directors of Defense Research and Engineering Herbert York, Harold Brown, and John Foster; Service Secretaries Stanley Resor, Paul Ignatius, and Eugene Zuckert; Assistant Secretaries of Defense Charles Hitch, Alain Enthoven, John McNaughton, and Arthur Sylvester; and special assistant Adam Yarmolinsky.[22] Although it is not possible in the context of this study to include biographies of all these men, some of whom played key roles in the fashioning of America's counterinsurgency apparatus, it is possible to make a few generalizations about their backgrounds. Most were younger than McNamara (himself younger by far than any previous Secretary), and most were educated at New England prep schools and Ivy League universities. Even a short list of the institutions they attended includes many of the top establishment schools; thus Gilpatric went to Hotchkiss and Yale, Vance to Kent School and Yale; Zuckert to Salisbury Prep and Yale, and Nitze to Hotchkiss and Princeton. Not a few of these men were brought from important posts in the university and think tank communities: all three Defense Research Directors—York, Brown, and Foster—held administrative posts at the University of California's nuclear research laboratories, while economists Hitch and Enthoven were recruited from the RAND Corporation.

McNamara's civilian assistants—or the "Whiz Kids," as they came to be called—were viewed with considerable anxiety by the professional military. Representing the most enlightened thinking of establishment circles, the new Pentagon elite possessed a much broader world view than did their service counterparts. Whereas the generals still considered nuclear war with the Soviet Union to be the most likely conflict we would have to face, the Whiz Kids believed that revolutionary struggles in the Third World constituted the gravest threat to American interests. Loyal only to the Secretary of Defense and each other, these men were immune to the appeals of old service traditions; while occasionally differing with the Secretary on secondary matters, they were uncompromising in their support of his efforts to rationalize Defense spending and to revitalize the nation's conventional-warfare capability.

The reorganization of the Pentagon—described as the "McNamara Revolution" in the press—naturally precipitated many conflicts between the old combat generals and the Secretary's civilian staff; in the ensuing struggle, the newcomers were aided by an unexpected turn of events shortly after Kennedy was inaugurated. As a result of the Bay of Pigs fiasco, the military incumbents of the Pentagon high command lost whatever prestige they still enjoyed. McNamara aides told newsmen that the service chiefs were responsible for certain aspects of the debacle, such as the poor choice made for the landing site. The Joint Chiefs at that time were General Lyman L. Lemnitzer, Chairman; General Thomas D. White of the Air Force; General George H. Decker of the Army; Admiral Arleigh A. Burke, Chief of Naval Operations; and General David M. Shoup, Commandant of the Marine Corps. Within a year, all but Shoup had retired or moved to other posts.[23] To replace Lemnitzer as Chairman, the President chose Maxwell D. Taylor, a man whose views coincided with those of the Secretary of Defense and whose appointment to the Joint Chiefs assured the triumph of McNamara's plans for restructuring the Pentagon.

Chapter 3

THE
SCIENTIFIC
MERCENARIES
—America's Fourth
Armed Service

Considering the academic background of many top Kennedy and McNamara aides, it is not surprising that the university community (in its broadest dimensions) was mobilized at an early point for the Administration's effort to develop new counterinsurgency tactics and techniques. Distrusting the meager limited war theories of the uniformed Pentagon strategists, McNamara's Whiz Kids poured millions of dollars into campus research institutes and nonprofit think tanks for studies of revolutionary warfare and various government countermeasures. The experiences of other colonial powers, particularly France and Great Britain, in fighting national liberation movements were carefully analyzed for possible application to the emerging American counterinsurgency apparatus. Ambitious university researchers were awarded lucrative Defense Department contracts for such purposes as the collection of anthropological data on selected tribes inhabiting strategic areas of South Vietnam, the study of jungle communications equipment in Thailand, and measuring peasant attitudes on government programs in Colombia. Some university organizations became so deeply involved in the Pentagon's counterinsurgency program that they agreed to supply scientists and other technical personnel for the paramilitary agencies of embattled client regimes. Scientists from the University of Michigan, for instance, helped Thai officers locate hidden guerrilla camp sites with the aid of a sensor-equipped C-47 transport aircraft (see Chapter 7). To cite a more famous example, the Michigan State University Group provided police experts to organize Ngo Dinh Diem's secret police and train his palace guard (see Chapter 9). It was only with the later upsurge of antiwar activism on campus—spurred by such events as the May 1970 invasion of Cambodia—that university contractors have elected to abandon such activities.

University scientific resources were first harnessed for military work during the Second World War, when large numbers of technical personnel were required for critical development projects, notably the atomic bomb. Since technological advancement is often considered equivalent to military superiority in the nuclear era, the Pentagon has sought to develop an informal research service that can produce, on demand, the technological innovations required for advanced weapons systems. During the 1950's and early 1960's, Federal expenditures on research and development (R&D) activities grew at the rate of 20 percent a year, reaching $16 billion in 1965. The impact of this largesse on the manpower utilization of America's scientific work force has naturally been tremendous: in 1965, the House Government Operations Committee estimated that two-thirds of all scientists and engineers engaged in R&D work were employed on Federally funded projects.[1] Since roughly 80 percent of all Federal R&D

funds are supplied by the Department of Defense ($7.8 billion in fiscal year 1970], the National Aeronautics and Space Administration ($3.8 billion) and the Atomic Energy Commission ($1.4 billion), it is safe to assume that a majority of these scientists and engineers are committed to defense-related work.*\ This nonuniformed corps of technical personnel constitutes the nation's Fourth Armed Service.[2] (

As one would expect, under Presidents Truman and Eisenhower the civilian research service was employed primarily in the development of nuclear weapons and strategies. When President Kennedy took office in 1961, this service was quickly told to devote a significant portion of its efforts to counterinsurgency studies. The Administration was particularly anxious to secure the cooperation of social scientists and foreign-area specialists in acquiring knowledge about the diverse and unfamiliar peoples who occupy the outlying areas of Africa, Asia, and Latin America, and for the development of strategies for social control (see Chapter 4 for a discussion of such programs). For the most part, the Pentagon has been successful in its efforts to utilize the expertise and skills of the civilian research community; the growth of antiwar sentiment on the campus, however, has caused many academic researchers to be wary of any direct identification with the Defense establishment. Thus American officials at the Agency for International Development mission in Bangkok reported in 1971 that their efforts to evaluate the success of the pacification program in rural Thailand were being hampered by the reluctance of American scholars to work for the government. One official told a reporter from *The New York Times:* "Many of the best American academic specialists on Thailand seem so beset by criticisms and attacks within the United States that significant assistance cannot be ex-

---

* See Appendix B for a detailed table of Federal spending for R&D, 1953–70.

pected from them." |Because of this growing reluctance, the Defense Department has been obliged to establish or support intermediary institutions—like the nonprofit think tanks—that can obtain the services of university personnel without implicating them in military work.|In this chapter, we will look at the various mechanisms employed by the Pentagon to assure the continued productivity of the Fourth Armed Service, and identify the research institutions that are responsible for the development of strategies and hardware for the government's campaign against national liberation movements.

THE INSTITUTIONALIZATION OF RESEARCH

Until well into the twentieth century, new weapons were developed by hit-or-miss experimentation, or through continuous refinement of existing devices. It is only in the past three decades that instrumentalities of warfare have emerged from organized scientific investigations, in which the talents of many researchers are pooled in the quest for novel military systems. The Manhattan Project of World War II is the prototype of all such efforts—at its peak thousands of scientists were engaged in various subtasks of the project, many without being aware of the final objective of their work. In order to mount other large-scale research projects, the War Department found it necessary at the onset of the Second World War to establish a network of mammoth laboratories devoted to intensive research on advanced weapons systems. Since the only reservoir of trained scientific manpower available for such work was the university community, it was inevitable that the nation's institutions of higher education be mobilized for the establishment of a military research service. Products of this wartime mobilization include radar and counterradar instruments, the proximity fuse, and the atomic bomb.

During the course of the war, a number of university laboratories developed into sizable institutions, employing thousands of scientists and technicians. This wartime mobilization of university resources was organized on the basis of expedience and had not been intended to outlast the war. As victory approached, however, the military services and some of the universities sought to prevent the dissolution of these installations. With the dawn of the Cold War, the Pentagon found itself enjoined to "contain Communism" on a front that stretched from Berlin to Seoul, and the civilian research apparatus became a permanent fixture of the academic community.

The outstanding characteristic of university warfare laboratories—the concentration of scientific personnel under conditions of relative autonomy—makes them particularly attractive to the Pentagon as performers of military research work. University research centers have grown in importance in direct proportion to the increasing value placed on this country's "technical intellectual resources," the scientists and engineers whose intellectual efforts lie at the root of all technological advancement. The increased value placed upon these human resources can be detected, according to the Stanford Research Institute (SRI), in the concern expressed by many countries over the loss of their engineers and scientists through the "brain drain," and in the efforts of aerospace companies to sell their technical intellectual capability rather than their technology.[3]

Since there is a limited supply of this important commodity, the motivations, incentives, and working conditions that determine the employment pattern of the scientific work force are matters of great concern to Pentagon research administrators, who naturally seek to employ the best minds available on any given project. Studies of the attitudes of professional research personnel indicate that organizational incentives (such as opportunity for advancement into management) and material incentives (higher salaries) are not closely related to technological productivity. In contrast, professional incentives (e.g., allowing the individual a high degree of freedom and flexibility in choosing his own work assignments in terms of what he feels will be professionally challenging) are "likely to be associated with higher levels of both professional and organizational productivity among scientists and engineers."[4] It is not hard to deduce from these findings that universities provide the environment most likely to assure high technological productivity. In confirmation of this view, Dr. Frederick Seitz, past president of the National Academy of Sciences, told a Senate committee in 1963:

A certain fraction of the best minds find the type of freedom and flexibility peculiar to the university best suited for their work. In addition, the presence of many inquiring young minds in the formative period, particularly the reseach students, adds a particular freshness and vitality to research. I do not mean to say that excellent work is not done elsewhere. . . . What is important is that any program which does not take maximum advantage of the capability of the university will not advance in the most effective way possible.[5]

This analysis has prompted the Defense Department to establish military research centers at selected universities, to enlist the help of university administrators in the creation of independent rescarch organizations (such as the Institute for Defense Analyses), and to offer financial incentives to universities that agree to adopt an existing facility. Where direct university participation has not proved feasible, the Pentagon has found it expedient to create a network of para-universities—independent research organizations (think tanks) that boast a "campus-like environment" and adhere to many rituals of academic life. (The most famous example of this kind of institution is the RAND Corporation.) The nonprofit research organizations identified later in this chapter should be viewed, then, as extensions of the university world and not as unique institutions.

With ample government backing assured, scores of semi-autonomous military research organizations were established by American universities in the postwar period. Some of these installations have come to enjoy a special relationship with the government as Federal Contract Research Centers (FCRC's), also known as Federally Funded Research and Development Centers (FFRDC's). These institutions receive at least 70 percent of their income from Federal agencies, and work "under the direct monitorship of the Government." According to National Science Foundation nomenclature, FFRDC's are "organizational units associated with universities and colleges whose creation and operation are not primarily related to the main function of the administering universities and colleges."[6] FFRDC's receive a substantial portion of Federal research funds available to the university community: in fiscal 1971, university-administered FFRDC's received $730 million from the government, compared with the $1,650 million awarded directly to the universities for R&D activities.[7]

Even when not recognized as FFRDC's, campus research centers can be found at most universities. Most of these institutions engage in research on military and space "hardware"—the mechanical equipment needed to outfit an army or launch a space vehicle. Increasingly, however, such organizations are devoting their energies to the development of "software" systems—the mathematical and analytical models used in systems analysis, operations research, and related methodologies. University research centers have played an important role in the development of military software systems, and many of the nonprofit organizations like RAND and the Institute for Defense Analyses have become noted for this kind of work. University social scientists, foreign-area specialists, and educational researchers have followed the lead of physicists and chemists in setting

up autonomous research centers to benefit from the explosion in Federal research spending.[8] Gerard Piel of *Scientific
American* discussed the proliferation of university-based
software research institutes in a 1965 talk to the American
Philosophical Society as follows:

The new science of "human engineering" at the "man-machine
interface" has brought psychology into the circle of disciplines
favored by the project contract/grant. Regional research institutes, organized at the primary initiative of the Department of
State and the great private foundations to illuminate hitherto
dark regions on the world map, have brought sociology and
anthropology into the ambience of the Department of Defense.
. . . With funds abounding for projects in every field of learning,
the university campus has come to harbor a new kind of
condottieri, mercenaries of science and scholarship hooded with
doctorates and ready for hire on studies done to contract spec-
ification.[9]

THE COUNTERINSURGENCY THINK TANKS

In recent years, approximately 60 percent of all Defense
research funds have been awarded to industrial firms,
while another 20 percent has been spent on the Pentagon's in-house laboratories—leaving 20 percent to be
divided among the universities (10 percent), the university-administered Federal Contract Research Centers (5
percent), and nonprofit research institutions (5 percent).
The distribution of software R&D funds, however, has not
followed this pattern: in fiscal 1966, 39 percent of social
science research funds were awarded to universities, 23
percent each to nonprofit institutes and the in-house labs,
and only 14 percent to industrial firms.[10]

Counterinsurgency software research has been even
more concentrated in the universities and nonprofit institutes; the Institute for Defense Analyses reported in 1965

that except for the 6 percent of such research performed by industrial organizations, all this work was performed by universities and nonprofit research organizations. Four organizations alone—RAND, the Special Operations Research Office, the Research Analysis Corporation, and the Human Resources Research Office—performed 57 percent of social, behavioral, and operations research on counterinsurgency.[11] If we were to add IDA and the Stanford Research Institute to this list, we would be able to account for the great bulk of such work. Because references to these organizations occur throughout this book, brief descriptions of each are provided here.

The Center for Research in Social Systems (CRESS) was founded in 1956 as the Special Operations Research Office (SORO) of the American University in Washington, D.C. CRESS is the Federal Contract Research Center responsible for social science research in the areas of counterinsurgency, psychological warfare, and military civic action. Most of its income ($1.5 million in fiscal 1970) comes from Army contracts. In the 1950's SORO concentrated its efforts on the development of psychological-warfare materials aimed at the Soviet-bloc nations. During the Kennedy Administration, however, SORO was given increased responsibility for counterinsurgency research aimed at the Third World, and was ultimately chosen to coordinate work on Project Camelot (see Chapter 4). In 1966, as a result of the Camelot fiasco, SORO was reorganized as CRESS. The reconstituted organization retained its affiliation with the American University until December 5, 1969, when, as a result of student demonstrations, CRESS was separated from the university. CRESS subsequently announced its affiliation with the American Institutes for Research, a nonprofit organization with substantial counterinsurgency contracts of its own.

CRESS is composed of two divisions: the Cultural Information Analysis Center (CINFAC), and the Social

Science Research Institute (SSRI). CINFAC, originally
known as the Counterinsurgency Information Analysis
Center, was established to "provide a rapid-response
capability system which can effectively store and retrieve
raw data as well as completed studies in counterinsurgency, emphasizing the social, psychological, and economic
sciences." SSRI performs in-depth studies "of unconventional warfare, psychological operations, military assistance programs, and other studies and evaluations of
foreign cultures."[12]

The Human Resources Research Organization (HumRRO)
was founded by the Army in 1951 to institutionalize the
practice of employing university scientists to design training programs and psychological tests for military personnel. Originally a unit of George Washington University
(GW), HumRRO is the Federal Contract Research Center
responsible for the development of methods to improve
the training of the U.S. soldier, and for behavioral-science
research on motivation, leadership, and "man/machine
systems." In October 1969, following a series of student
demonstrations, HumRRO was severed from GW and reconstituted as an independent, nonprofit research organization. HumRRO still receives most of its income ($4.3
million in fiscal 1970) from the Army.

Most of HumRRO's research is concerned with the performance of soldiers under varying conditions of stress
(psychological and physiological), and the development of
new training methods for the Army. HumRRO Division No.
7, Language and Area Training, is responsible for the development of training programs for U.S. personnel assigned
to military missions, advisory groups, Special Forces units,
and other agencies that will bring them into contact with
foreign military personnel. As part of this function, Hum-
RRO tries to develop programs that will help inspire
American servicemen to overcome their unfamiliarity with,

and antipathy toward, militarily significant nonwhite populations such as the Koreans, Laotians, and Vietnamese.[13]

The Institute for Defense Analyses (IDA) was founded in 1956 as a nonprofit research organization by MIT, Stanford University, Tulane, Case Institute, and the California Institute of Technology. The original members of the corporation were later joined by the Universities of Chicago, California, Illinois, and Michigan, and by Columbia, Princeton, and Penn State. This consortium was finally dissolved in the summer of 1968, when, following demonstrations at Chicago and Princeton and the student uprising at Columbia University, IDA became an independent corporation with its own board of trustees. (Many of the university presidents and vice-presidents who represented their schools on IDA's board of trustees before the 1968 reorganization continue to sit on the board as "private citizens.")

IDA's original function was to provide scientific and technical support to the Weapons Systems Evaluation Group of the Joint Chiefs of Staff and to the Advanced Research Projects Agency. Because of its connections with the university community, IDA has been able to recruit many academic scientists to study the effectiveness of proposed weapons systems, ranging from thermonuclear weapons to chemical and biological munitions. As a Federal Contract Research Center, IDA received $10.1 million from the Defense Department in fiscal 1970. IDA also studies cryptography for the National Security Agency, and police command-and-control systems for the Justice Department.[14]

The RAND Corporation was organized by the Air Force in 1946 in order to perpetuate the partnership of university scientists and military men that had been formed during World War II. America's oldest and most famous think tank, RAND maintains campus-like facilities in Santa Monica, California, where security procedures are reported to be tougher than in the Pentagon itself. RAND's major responsibility as a Federal Contract Research Center is the performance of feasibility studies of advanced aerospace vehicles and thermonuclear devices. Much of this work incorporates the systems-analysis and cost-effectiveness methodologies developed by RAND scientists in the 1950's. Project RAND, the organization's basic Air Force contract, accounts for about two-thirds of RAND's $22-million annual budget.

In the early 1960's, RAND was commissioned by the Advanced Research Projects Agency to apply its systems-analysis skills to the study of counterinsurgency and limited warfare. As a result, RAND scientists were dispatched to South Vietnam to learn about underground organizations and guerrilla tactics from prisoners of war and defectors from the National Liberation Front.[15] Recently RAND has sought contracts from various civilian agencies for work on nonmilitary projects; under a substantial contract (more than $1 million) from the City of New York, RAND has investigated the reorganization of one of America's hardest-to-govern cities.

The Research Analysis Corporation (RAC) was founded in 1961 to take over the work of the Operations Research Office (ORO) of Johns Hopkins University, one of the oldest university-based military research organizations. When Johns Hopkins became uncomfortable with ORO's strict security requirements, RAC was established as an independent nonprofit research organization with headquarters in McLean, Virginia. Often described as the Army's equivalent of the RAND Corporation, RAC is the Federal Contract Research Center responsible for systems analysis and operations research for the Department of the Army. RAC's current income from Pentagon contracts is about $ 9 million annually.

RAC's primary mission is to upgrade the combat effectiveness of U.S. troops by conducting operations research on the design, performance, and utilization of Army weapons systems. This work also includes long-range strategic analyses on future threats to U.S. security and possible countermeasures, as well as on-the-spot reviews of weapons effectiveness under battlefield conditions. Recent projects have included studies of the utilization of chemical and biological warfare in counterinsurgency, and the mobilization of minority groups in counterguerrilla operations. RAC is particularly proud of its role in the creation of the Army's 1st Cavalry Division (Airmobile).[16]

The Stanford Research Institute (SRI) was founded in 1946 by Stanford University and a group of West Coast businessmen. In the past two decades, SRI has become one of the nation's largest private research organizations, with a staff of 2,200 and an annual budget of $60 million (of which some $25 million represents Defense contracts). The Institute's headquarters are located in Menlo Park, California, adjacent to the Stanford Industrial Park (occupied by "spin-off" companies that market the products developed in SRI's laboratories). Until January 1970, SRI was a wholly owned subsidiary of Stanford University; in response to student protests, the university at that time sold the Institute to its own board of directors for $25 million.

Pentagon-financed research at SRI has encompassed a wide array of subjects, including chemical and biological warfare and antimissile missile systems. SRI involvement in Vietnam includes a secret study of naval mobility in the Mekong Delta and research on tropical communications. SRI has been particularly conspicuous in Thailand, where some fifty-five Institute researchers are attached to the Thai-U.S. Military Research and Development Center in Bangkok to develop methods for counterguerrilla surveillance and counterinfiltration.[17] (See Chapter 7.)

THE COORDINATION
OF RESEARCH

Under normal operating procedure, each of the research organizations just described is supervised by one of the service R&D agencies and ultimately by the Office of the Director of Defense Research and Engineering (ODDRE) in the Pentagon. This "vertical" command structure is supplemented, however, by a horizontal system of advisory panels and scientific committees that bring together representatives of the Defense Department, the think tanks, universities, and the aerospace industry. To a large extent these panels, most of which have been created during the past twenty-five years, determine the allocation of tasks and resources between the various research organizations.

According to the Department of Defense (DoD) Directive 5030:13 of April 20, 1962, "Regulations for the Formulation and Use of Advisory Committees," such panels are formed "to provide a means of obtaining advice, views, and recommendations of benefit to the operation of the Government from industrialists, businessmen, scientists, engineers, educators, and other public and private citizens whose experience and talents would not otherwise be available to DoD."[18] University scientists, the Stanford Research Institute reports, constitute a majority of the members of these committees, while many panelists have multiple associations with university, industrial, and non-profit R&D organizations.[19] These panels perform essential services for the Pentagon by informing the Defense Department of new scientific discoveries applicable to weapons development; finding the scientists and research organizations best able to accomplish a specified research task; lobbying in the academic community for support of Pentagon research policies; and providing a reservoir of highly skilled scientific manpower available for work on crash military projects.

A 1970 survey by *Armed Forces Journal* determined that there were then 105 military R&D advisory committees, of which the senior panel was the Defense Science Board (DSB).[20] The DSB was established in 1956 in response to a recommendation of the Commission on Organization of the Executive Branch of the Government (Hoover Commission) that a committee be appointed to "canvass periodically the needs and opportunities presented by new scientific knowledge for radically new weapons systems." The Board consists of twenty-eight civilian scientists who "advise the Secretary of Defense, through the Director of Defense Research and Engineering, on scientific and technical matters of interest to the Department of Defense." In effect, the DSB provides the Secretary of Defense and the head of ODDRE with direct access to the nation's R&D industry: "Through its membership of distinguished men representing industry, government and the academic world, the Defense Science Board serves as the connecting link between the Office of the Director of Defense Research and Engineering and the scientific and technical community of the United States."[21] (Because of the pivotal role played by the DSB within the military research apparatus, a list of Board members during 1965–70 is provided in Appendix A.)

The oldest and largest of the service panels, the Air Force Scientific Advisory Board (AFSAB), was established in 1944 to assist the Army Air Force, and was reorganized in 1946 to "advise the Chief of Staff, U.S. Air Force, on all scientific/technical matters relevant to the mission of the Air Force." The AFSAB is composed of some seventy-five members, who serve on one of the nine subpanels on such subjects as Nuclear Warfare, Aerospace Vehicles, and Missile Guidance and Control. The Naval Research Advisory Committee (NRAC) and Army Scientific Advisory Panel (ASAP) were founded in 1946 and 1951, respectively, and perform the same duties for the research chiefs of their respective departments.[22]

One nongovernmental advisory group has come to occupy a particularly influential position in the military
research apparatus: the Jason Division of the Institute for
Defense Analyses. Jason was established in 1958 with the
encouragement of the Pentagon's Advanced Research Projects Agency, which continues to provide financial support.
The group consists of forty-five "outstanding university
scientists who devote as much of their available time as
possible to studies in the vanguard of the scientific aspects
of defense problems."[23] In the first years of Jason's existence, its members reportedly concentrated on "theoretical
analyses of ballistic missile defense and exoatmospheric
detonations." In 1964, however, "a new excursion was
made. Increased government attention to such problems as
counterinsurgency, insurrection, and infiltration led to the
suggestion that Jason members might be able to provide
fresh insights into problems that are not entirely in the
realm of physical science."[24] As a result of this "excursion," Jason in 1966 proposed the cessation of the air war
against North Vietnam and the creation of an "anti-infiltration barrier" across the Demilitarized Zone and southern
Laos (see Chapter 7).

Research on counterinsurgency software is coordinated
by an informal network of ad hoc committees, interagency
government panels, and subcommittees of the advisory
boards identified above. In 1964, for instance, the Defense
Science Board established a subcommittee on behavioral
sciences to review Pentagon research on social conflict and
counterinsurgency. And from June 19 to July 6, 1967, IDA's
Jason Division assembled a "Thailand Study Group" at the
Falmouth Intermediate School in Falmouth, Massachusetts,
to conduct a secret review of counterinsurgency research
in Thailand.[25] In general, the reports of these panels are
kept secret or circulated to members only; in the spring
of 1970, however, it became possible to examine the activities of one of these committees when an antiwar organization, the Student Mobilization Committee, obtained the

minutes of the Academic Advisory Committee on Thailand (AACT).[26]

AACT was founded in 1966 after two University of Michigan professors, Gayl D. Ness and L. A. Peter Gosling, made a trip to Bangkok on behalf of the Agency for International Development (AID) to determine the research needs of the U.S. Operations Mission in Thailand (USOM). In their report, "Suggestions on the Elaboration of a University Role in USOM," Ness and Gosling note that "USOM wants what has been aptly termed a continuing conversation with the universities, or more accurately, with Thai specialists in the universities." Since no single American university had the range of resources required by USOM, they proposed the creation of a "secretariat" of Thai specialists in the universities to "provide liaison among the Mission, the Southeast Asian Development Advisory Group of AID/Washington, the university community, foundations, learned societies, and other groups specializing on Southeast Asia or working on development problems."[27]

The secretariat envisioned by Ness and Gosling was formally constituted on September 6, 1966, when the University of California at Los Angeles received a contract from AID to serve as the administrative "home base" for AACT. The contract specified that UCLA was to "identify research that is being, has been, or will be conducted by universities, foundations and other institutions that may relate to developmental and counterinsurgency activities in Thailand; [and to] evaluate, index and make such research available to AID."[28] An amendment to the UCLA contract, dated September 6, 1968, indicates the range of seemingly harmless functions performed by university scientists to enhance U.S. paramilitary operations in a country that is nominally our ally:

The Contractor will . . . identify, prepare and maintain a current inventory of American scholars with specialized knowledge of or background in Thailand, which can be drawn upon by AID for its specialized needs . . . [and will] organize, coordinate and conduct meetings, seminars or conferences, under AACT auspices, dealing with development and counterinsurgency problems, issues and activities, including research relating to AID operations in Thailand.[29]

With this mandate, AACT members, led by David A. Wilson of UCLA, infiltrated the ranks of Asian scholars to assure the continued flow of knowledge from the academic community at home to the U.S. command in Bangkok. Often the producers of this knowledge are not even aware that they are serving the military establishment: the documents published by the Student Mobilization Committee indicate that AACT members arranged conferences and panels on subjects of interest to USOM without informing participants that they were helping to perfect the U.S. counterinsurgency program in Thailand. (Thus in 1970 AACT persuaded the Association of Asian Studies—AAS —to include a panel on the problems of northern Thailand during its April 1970 meeting, when AACT was unable to convene a conference on this topic under its own name.)

The Academic Advisory Committee on Thailand is only one of many informal groupings that coordinate research on subjects of interest to the Pentagon. Members of these committees—most of whom can boast flawless university accreditation—can be found at every academic meeting and symposium, collecting intelligence on the scholarly output of their colleagues.* During Congressional hearings held in

---

* The documents released by the Student Mobilization Committee (SMC) and other disclosures of university complicity in counterinsurgency research have sent a shock wave through the academic community, compelling many professional organizations to reexamine the codes of ethics that govern the activities of research personnel. After publication of the SMC data, the Ethics Committee of the American Anthropological Association (AAA) determined that "anthropologists are being used in large programs of counterinsurgency. . . . These programs comprise efforts at the manipulation of

1965 to investigate the Project Camelot fiasco, the Director of the Special Operations Research Office, Dr. Theodore Vallance, was asked by one Representative to explain how the work of government-sponsored organizations like SORO was correlated with that of the universities. In reply, Vallance disclosed that several governmental and quasi-governmental agencies maintained inventories of the current research activities of university personnel. The clearinghouses that perform this function, according to Vallance, include the National Science Foundation, the External Research Staff of the Department of State, and the Roper Institute of Williamstown, Massachusetts. In preparing a study on foreign culture, he explained, "We systematically brainpick these various sources to make sure we have the up-to-date information that bears on the development of one of our books." He added, in all innocence, that most of the work of coordination was conducted "through the normal intercourse among people in the scientific world—by attending meetings, corresponding with one another, through publications, and so on."[30]

---

people on a giant scale and intertwine straightforward anthropological research with overt and covert counterinsurgency." This judgment was too strong for AAA president Professor George M. Foster of the University of California, who appointed a new committee, headed by Margaret Mead, to investigate the whole matter. When this ad hoc committee later exonerated AACT members from participation in counterinsurgency activities, Dr. Mead herself came under attack from the AAA membership, which voted—at its 1971 annual meeting—to reject the committee's report. (*The New York Times*, November 21, 1971.)

Chapter 4

SOCIAL
SYSTEMS
ENGINEERING
—Project Camelot
and Its Successors

Throughout the Cold War era, American defense analysts believed implicitly in the proposition that military superiority was defined in terms of firepower, mobility, and other technological factors. In the annual budget message of the Secretary of Defense, it was common to hear America's strategic capabilities measured in the quantity of our ballistic missiles, the megatonnage of our nuclear warheads, and the aerodynamic properties of our latest jet bomber. Not surprisingly, many Pentagon strategists directed the same approach to counterinsurgency planning: if we could marshal a sufficient number of tanks, helicopters, and other equipment on the guerrilla battlefield, presumably any insurgent force would ultimately be destroyed. (This attitude, as shown in the next chapter, has governed most Pentagon research programs of the past decade.) Among the civilian analysts recruited by President Kennedy and Secretary McNamara, however, there developed a countertendency to this attitude which held that political, not technological, answers must be found to the challenge posed by national liberation movements. "The essential core of insurgent warfare is political," Army researcher Michael C. Conley wrote in 1966, "and the counterinsurgent can achieve victory only if he operates skillfully in the political arena." Conley, a Ph.D. on the staff of the Center for Research in Social Systems, warned: "Technology is no substitute for politics; the more the attention of the security forces is absorbed by technology, the closer that force is to political bankruptcy and possible military defeat."[1]

Conley's remarks, contained in a paper on "The Military Value of Social Sciences in an Insurgent Environment," are worth quoting at length because they go a long way to explain why the United States has indeed been reduced to "political bankruptcy" in Vietnam:

An analysis of past Communist-dominated insurgencies and of the current experience in South Vietnam reveals consistent patterns of insurgent behavior. The insurgents' pathway to national power has not been the dramatic seizure of the governmental apparatus, but rather the slow forging of alternative institutions and norms which gradually receive the loyalty of increasing numbers of people. . . .

Only as counterinsurgent forces work with the people are they responding meaningfully to the challenge that the insurgents generate through their mass organization work. . . .

To the extent that the counterinsurgent circumvents the civil population and grasps at technology as an alternative to or subsitute for work among the people, he is, in fact, retreating from the real battlefield.[2]

America's technological orientation, according to Conley, has prevented us from understanding the political characteristics of insurgent struggle, and therefore from developing suitable strategies for success on the "real" battlefield. This strategic vacuum would persist, he argued, until the Pentagon established an extensive program of studies "which could help to fill in portions of the uncharted regions of human behavior in insurgency situations."[3]

The need for systematic social science research in the area of social unrest and insurgency was first expressed by academicians and other civilians engaged in Defense research and development work. One of the earliest presentations of this argument was contained in a series of papers issued by the Smithsonian Institution in 1962 on the potential contribution of social science research to the study of insurgent behavior. In these reports, published collectively as *Social Science Research and National Security*, civilian researchers like Ithiel de Sola Pool and Lucian Pye proposed a multidisciplinary research effort leading to the formulation of analytical models of social change and social control in underdeveloped countries. This recommendation was not taken seriously by the Pentagon, however, until the first phase of U.S. intervention in Vietnam (limited to the involvement of military advisers) neared disaster in 1964. With the collapse of the Strategic Hamlet Program and the growing militancy of antigovernment Buddhists, it was painfully obvious that we could not undertake new social, economic, and political programs in Vietnam without a vastly improved understanding of social processes. The Pentagon was obliged, therefore, to embrace the position of the academicians who had argued for a new research initiative in the social and behavioral sciences. The military establishment's new policy on social research was presented to Congress by Seymour J. Deitchman of the Office of Defense Research and Engineering as follows:

[Counterinsurgency] war itself revolves around the allegiance and support of the local population. The Defense Department has therefore recognized that part of its research and development efforts to support counterinsurgency operations must be oriented toward the people, United States and foreign, involved in this type of war; and the Department of Defense has called on the types of scientists—anthropologists, psychologists, sociologists, political scientists, economists—whose professional orientation to human behavior would enable them to make useful contributions in this area.[4]

To ensure that the efforts of these scientists would be mobilized in the most effective fashion possible, the Defense Department began with an overall review of existing resources for counterinsurgency software research. On April 20, 1964, the Office of the Director of Defense Research and Engineering requested the Defense Science Board to establish a subcommittee to "conduct a study of research and development programs and findings related to ethnic and other motivational factors involved in the causation and conduct of small wars." A similar review was begun at the same time by the Department of the Army, and, on September 2, 1964, ODDRE instructed the other services and the Advanced Research Projects Agency to undertake parallel studies. Under contract to ARPA, the Institute for Defense Analyses prepared a statistical and content analysis of all Pentagon-sponsored social science research on counterinsurgency.

The conclusions of these studies were predictable: the U.S. military's research service had only the most superficial understanding of social dynamics in an insurgent environment. The DSB subcommittee said it succinctly:

The subcommittee's review of the [Defense Department's] research program in the behavioral sciences disclosed serious deficiencies that are not offset by an adequate research effort on the part of the universities and other civilian organizations. Primarily, there is very incomplete knowledge and understanding in depth of the internal cultural, economic, and political conditions that generate conflict between national groups.[5]

To overcome these deficiencies, the subcommittee proposed an expanded program of field research abroad, and the application of systems-analysis modeling to the problems of social conflict.

In its survey of existing research programs, the Institute for Defense Analyses discovered that of the $10.8 million spent on counterinsurgency software research in fiscal 1965, 21 percent was concerned with South Vietnam and Thailand, only 7 percent with Latin America, and none with Africa. The implications were obvious:

There is insufficient evidence that the present program on counterinsurgency will meet the long term needs of the DoD. This is shown most strikingly in the emphasis upon problems of South Vietnam and Southeast Asia and the virtual neglect of the other areas of the world, primarily Africa, but also Latin America. Already, these areas show important signs of social discontent; and delay in developing a better understanding of their problems may lead us to face elsewhere problems similar to those of South Vietnam.

It was therefore imperative, IDA argued, "that we attempt to understand the nature of the social changes that are going on in these countries and the underlying processes which govern them." The basic task, in other words, was to employ conventional social science methodologies in the study of social change in underdeveloped countries; the end product of this effort was not, however, to be a compilation of scholarly reports, but rather the development of strategies for politico-military intervention in areas threatened by revolution. As IDA put it, "In the long run, the development of appropriate theories will most enhance our ability to understand, predict and influence the social changes which confront us around the world."[6]

CAMELOT

The first Pentagon agency to act on these recommendations was the Office of the Chief of Research and Development (OCRD) of the Department of the Army.* Although the DSB and IDA reports were not officially released until 1965, their findings were being circulated in the military R&D community by mid-1964, when the OCRD gave the go-ahead for a multimillion-dollar study of insurgent behavior in underdeveloped countries. This effort, subsequently code-named Project Camelot, was developed by the Special Operations Research Office (SORO) of the American University in consultation with OCRD. When asked by a curious Congressman about the choice of Camelot for the code name of this project, the Director of SORO, Dr. Theodore Vallance, replied: "The label 'Camelot' simply emerged from the basic intent of the story which is relayed in the play [of that name] and in [T. H.] White's book, that is, the development of a stable society with domestic tranquillity and peace and justice for all. This is an objective that seemed to, if we were going to have a code label, connote the right sorts of things."[7] Preliminary work on the project occupied the second half of 1964; by December 4, when Camelot surfaced in the academic community, a staff had already been recruited and Dr. Rex Hopper, chairman

---

* Presumably the Army moved ahead on social science research because of a secret Department of Defense directive assigning it primary responsibility for support of counterinsurgency operations undertaken by friendly governments. Although the directive itself is classified, the Army's former Chief of Research and Development, General W. W. Dick, Jr., told a Congressional committee: "By direction of a higher authority the Army is performing a wide variety of missions in counterinsurgency, military assistance, civic action, and psychological warfare, with regular units, MAAG's [Military Assistance Advisory Groups], missions, mobile training teams, and Special Action Forces in various countries which have requested our assistance." Dick added: "For the Army to be effective in these missions, its commanders and troops must understand the social, political, and economic conditions of the environment confronting them." (U.S. House of Representatives, Committee on Foreign Affairs, *Behavioral Sciences and the National Security, Hearings,* 89th Congress, 2d session, 1966, p. 35.)

of the Department of Sociology and Anthropology at Brooklyn College, had been named director of the project. Camelot received official Pentagon endorsement in March 1965, when, in response to the recommendations of the Defense Science Board, the Director of Defense Research and Engineering "directed that the Army develop a plan for a coordinated program of applied behavioral and social science research in support of counterinsurgency and special warfare on behalf of the entire Department of Defense."[8]

Project Camelot represented, in essence, an attempt to satisfy *all* of the research needs indicated in the studies cited above. As proposed by DSB, Camelot was to include both data-collection and policy formulation phases. In its first public mention of the project, SORO explained:

Project CAMELOT is a study whose objective is to determine the feasibility of developing a general social systems model which would make it possible to predict and influence politically significant aspects of social change in the developing nations of the world. Specifically, its objectives are:

First, to devise procedures for assessing the potential for internal war within national societies;

Second, to identify with increased degrees of confidence those actions which a government might take to relieve conditions which are assessed as giving rise to a potential for internal war.[9]

Camelot was designed, in other words, to develop those *political* strategies for counterrevolution which had been found so sadly lacking in Vietnam.

In introducing Camelot to the social science community, SORO repeated many of the arguments with which we have become familiar. A "working paper" dated December 5, 1964, commented: "In the past, an insurgency has been perceived primarily, if not entirely, as a matter of internal security . . . to be countered when it became overt by military and police actions." It would be much more efficient,

SORO argued, to contain popular disaffection at a pre-insurgency level by initiating programs for "political, economic, social, and psychological development," which would "create an environment of security and popular trust." Although U.S. counterinsurgency doctrine now encompassed noncombative programs of this sort, "there has been no large-scale attempt to analyze the interrelated processes of social conflict and social control." Camelot would now overcome this deficiency: "This project will differ from other efforts to study the symptoms and causes of insurgency, and methods of dealing with it and its preconditions, not only in size and scope but in insisting from the start upon a careful analysis of all components of the problem, and in bringing to bear in a coordinated effort the research talents of the relevant disciplines."[10]

Project Camelot was originally planned as a three- to four-year effort, and was to have cost an estimated $4.5 million—the most ambitious social science research project on record. The early phases of the project were to have included extensive field work overseas culminating in intensive studies of several Latin American countries to identify "critical social parameters that might be indications of social unrest." Most of this work was to have been performed by the SORO staff, although professors from other universities were invited to participate in various aspects of the project, and particularly in the field work abroad. It was this arrangement that ultimately led to the downfall of the whole project.[11]

In the early spring of 1965, an anthropology professor at the University of Pittsburgh, Hugo G. Nuttini, volunteered to assist Camelot by recruiting Chilean social scientists for the field studies to be performed in Latin America. After obtaining SORO's approval for this effort, Nuttini traveled to Chile and began canvassing the university community there for likely participants. Although Nuttini later reported that he had aroused considerable interest in Camelot, not everyone with whom he spoke was equally enthusiastic about the project's objectives or the identity of its sponsor. In April 1965, stories began to appear in Chile's left-wing press that described Camelot as a Pentagon scheme for espionage and intervention in Chile's internal affairs. The controversy spread to the Chilean Senate, and compelled the U.S. ambassador, Ralph A. Dungan, to request unconditional cancellation of the project's Chilean activities. Chile, ironically, was not among the countries that were being considered for intensive field work. (According to the December 5, 1964, "Working Paper" on Project Camelot, the countries being considered for field studies were Bolivia, Colombia, Ecuador, Paraguay, Peru, Venezuela, Iran, and Thailand.) Nevertheless, ⎰the furor that resulted from the outcry in Chile forced the United States government to terminate the project in its entirety.⎱

The cancellation of Camelot had many repercussions, some of them still being felt. On August 2, 1965, President Johnson instructed the Secretary of State to establish procedures to ensure that the government would not again undertake to sponsor research that could adversely affect U.S. foreign relations. These instructions were contained in a letter from the President to Secretary of State Dean Rusk, which read:

Many agencies of the Government are sponsoring social science research which focuses on foreign areas and peoples and thus relates to the foreign policy of the United States. Some of it involves residence and travel in foreign countries and communication with foreign nationals. As we have recently learned, it can raise problems affecting the conduct of our foreign policy.

For that reason I am determined that no Government sponsorship of foreign area research should be undertaken which in the judgment of the Secretary of State would adversely affect United States foreign relations. Therefore I am asking you to establish effective procedures which will enable you to assure the propriety of Government-sponsored social science research in the area of foreign policy. I suggest that you consult with the director of the Bureau of the Budget to determine the proper procedures for clearance of foreign affairs research projects on a Government-wide basis.

The State Department subsequently created the Foreign Affairs Research Council to screen all government-sponsored research on foreign affairs; this body, chaired by the Director of the Department's Bureau of Intelligence and Research, has the power to veto any project considered inimical to the interests of the United States. Even these measures did not satisfy some Pentagon critics in the Senate, who sought to place a ban on all social science research sponsored by the Department of Defense.

The reaction to Camelot in the academic community was particularly severe.[12] Many American scholars complained that their study of foreign cultures was dangerously compromised by the suspicion voiced by foreign academicians that the American university community as a whole was in the service of the military and the CIA.* To support their contention, these scholars pointed to the decision of a Brazilian research organization to cancel a cooperative project with Cornell University as a result of the Camelot publicity; in its letter to Cornell, the organization explained that most Brazilian students could not distinguish one segment of the American academic community from any other, and therefore it was impossible to "maintain and justify a relationship with an institution—the university in the United States—which permits itself to be transformed

* This position was reinforced by a report prepared for the American Anthropological Association by one of its former presidents, Professor Ralph L. Beals of UCLA, who revealed that "agents of the intelligence branches of the United States Government, particularly the CIA, have posed as anthropologists" while conducting intelligence operations abroad, and that some American anthropologists "have been full- or part-time employees of the United States intelligence agencies including the CIA especially, either directly, or through grants from certain foundations with questionable sources of income, or as employees of private research organizations." (Quoted in *Science,* vol. 154, December 23, 1966, p. 1525.)

into the instrument of a security agency which is internationally known as the instigator of dictatorial coups."[13]

In order to mend its relationships with the academic
community, the Department of Defense (DoD) asked the
Defense Science Board to convene a panel of distinguished
scientists to review the Pentagon's social and behavioral
research program. The panel, chaired by S. Rains Wallace
of the American Institutes for Research, met at the National Academy of Science's Mount Hope, Massachusetts,
farm for ten days in July 1967. Members of this panel
included, in addition to Wallace, Dr. Peter Dorner of the
Council of Economic Advisers, Dr. Harold Guetzkow of
Northwestern University, Michael Pearce of the RAND
Corporation, Dr. A. Kimball Romney of Harvard University, Dr. Roger Russell of Indiana University, and Dr.
Eugene Webb of Stanford University. In their final report,
issued the following November, the panelists concluded:

The DoD mission now embraces problems and responsibilities
which have not previously been assigned to a military establishment. It has been properly stated that the DoD must now
wage not only warfare but "peacefare," as well. Pacification
assistance and the battle of ideas are major segments of the
DoD responsibility. The social and behavioral sciences constitute the unique resource for support of these new requirements
and must be vigorously pursued if our operations are to be
effective.[14]

The panel recognized, however, that attainment of this goal
was hampered by the reluctance of some academicians to
work for the Pentagon; they suggested, therefore, that the
Defense Department help establish a multiagency body to
sponsor sensitive foreign-area studies.*

* Although the panel did not spell out what it meant by waging
"peacefare," it is worth remembering that our war against the rural
population of Vietnam, involving the massive use of chemical
defoliants, antipersonnel weapons, and napalm, is usually summarized as a program for "bringing peace to the countryside."

This "peacefare" argument did not silence skeptical members of the Congress, who continued to press for a withdrawal of Pentagon support for social science research. The most outspoken critic of military software research is Senator J. William Fulbright, chairman of the influential Foreign Relations Committee. In May 1968, Fulbright's committee reopened the Camelot controversy in a series of hearings on Pentagon-financed foreign affairs research. In questioning a witness, Director of Defense Research and Engineering John S. Foster, Jr., Fulbright referred to the DSB panel's statement of "peacefare" cited above. The resulting interchange, as recorded in the transcript of the hearings, contains the essence of both Fulbright's position and the Pentagon's justification for sponsoring social science research:

The Chairman [Senator Fulbright].   I wondered if you could be more specific to explain your concept of the Department's role in waging peacefare. What do you mean by that?

Dr. Foster.   I mean by that, Mr. Chairman, that one of the best ways to avoid a war is to keep the peace. One of the best ways to keep the peace is to understand the mechanisms that can maintain stability in a country. . . .

The Chairman.   Normally I would have thought this was the responsibility of the State Department. . . . I thought the decisions as to what kind of action we took in the Dominican Republic or Lebanon and so on was a civilian decision to be made by the President in consultation with the Department of State. . . .

I would not have thought the President would expect you to advise him on the psychological, cultural and ideological background of a country. . . . It rather puzzles me that the Department [of Defense] now feels that the whole gamut of factors affecting a country's life is part of its responsibility to know about.

Dr. Foster.   Mr. Chairman, I think it is very clear from the situation we have going on now in Southeast Asia that the political, economic and cultural activities of a nation are intimately intertwined with military affairs.[15]

Both Fulbright and Foster have campaigned vigorously—in the press, in the academic community, and in Senate committee rooms—to line up support for their respective points of view.*

Despite the furor produced by Camelot, Pentagon spending on social science research has increased steadily since the project was terminated. In his testimony before the Fulbright Committee and the Senate Armed Services Committee, Dr. Foster revealed that Defense Department outlays for social and behavioral research programs had risen from $34 million in fiscal 1966 (which began on July 1, 1965, one week before Camelot was canceled) to a projected $48.6 million in fiscal 1970. Under pressure from Congress, however, the Pentagon has reduced its support of foreign area research and policy planning studies from a high of $17.2 million in fiscal 1967 to an estimated $13.3 million in 1970.[16] (See Appendix C for a breakdown of Pentagon expenditures on behavioral and social sciences research.)

In further testimony before the Senate Armed Services Committee on May 14, 1970, Foster described the Pentagon's modified policy on foreign affairs research as follows:

The [Department of Defense] strongly supports foreign area social science research efforts as a key national need. But national security affairs today are too complex and too critical for any single agency to assume the burden of providing all of the studies necessary to clarify our thinking and consider alter-

* Among those converted to Fulbright's perspective is Senate Majority Leader Mike Mansfield, who successfully pushed through an amendment to the fiscal 1970 Defense appropriation bill requiring the Pentagon to certify that every research project it sponsors has "a direct and apparent relationship to a specific military function or operation." As of this writing, Secretary of Defense Melvin Laird and Director of Defense Research and Engineering Foster are trying to line up industry and university support for repeal of Mansfield's amendment, known as Section 203.

natives to current policy. We do not intend to expand our activity. We have encouraged other parts of the Executive Branch to increase their activity. And we may decrease our support of work on problems of multiagency interest as other agencies do more.

In keeping with the recommendations of the DSB panel on social and behavioral research, the Defense Department has attempted to transfer sensitive foreign area studies to nonmilitary agencies, particularly the State Department and the Department of Health, Education and Welfare. (The Pentagon even offered the State Department $400,000 to start its own research program in this area.) Considering the present temper of Congress, it is likely that the Defense Department will increasingly be forced to resort to this kind of maneuver.

COUNTERINSURGENCY
RESEARCH SINCE CAMELOT

The disclosures concerning Project Camelot had, as we have seen, many repercussions here and abroad; these did not, however, include the termination of Camelot-type research. As a result of the relentless probing by Senator Fulbright, the Defense Department has been compelled to make public the details of its social science research program—revealing, beyond a doubt, that it has continued to sponsor research whose aim is identical to that of Project Camelot.[17] "It was Project Camelot which was canceled," former Army research chief General William W. Dick, Jr., told a Congressional committee in 1965. "This does not mean that we have backed off in any way from the objectives that Project Camelot was designed to meet."[18]

Project Camelot had two basic tasks: first, the identification of phenomena that precede the outbreak of insurrectionary violence, and second, the evaluation of various courses of action that could be taken by a regime in power to head off or control such conflicts. When the project ran into trouble, the Pentagon found it prudent to break up Camelot's functions into many discrete research tasks, which were then distributed to several universities and think tanks. "Although Camelot is dead under that name," Professor Ralph L. Beals of UCLA told the American Anthropological Association, "in a sense it has only gone underground. Similar types of projects have been conducted and are being planned under different names and through other kinds of agencies."[19] Most social science research projects sponsored by the Defense Department since 1965 have been related to one of the two Camelot tasks: they are concerned either with the social factors that generate insurgent behavior or with the development of strategies for government intervention at various stages of an insurgent uprising.

When SORO was reconstituted as the Center for Research in Social Systems in 1966, many of the original Project Camelot subtasks found their way back into the hands of the very people who were to have performed them under Camelot itself. An examination of the CRESS *Work Program for Fiscal Year 1967* reveals several projects whose orientation is clearly similar to that of Camelot. One study, entitled "A Survey and Formalization of Theories and Propositions Relevant to Revolutionary Social Processes," was designed to "produce a codified and readily retrievable system of knowledge, facts and theory relevant to revolutionary potential and related social processes."[20] If one cuts through the intentionally obtuse jargon used by CRESS researchers, one finds that we are dealing with the first of Camelot's two major tasks. Another CRESS project, "The Development of Analytic Models of Social Processes," was designed to "develop a prototype simulation of a society undergoing rapid political, social, or economic change in order to . . . create a test environment for assessing the impact of alternative political, economic, or military actions taken within or with respect to such societies."[21] In other words, we have Camelot task No. 2.

As the war in Vietnam increased in intensity, the United States became increasingly concerned with the sociological and psychological characteristics of guerrilla organizations. In particular, the Pentagon sought to identify the factors that led peasants in underdeveloped societies to give their loyalty to an underground political organization at the risk of their lives. In this way, it was hoped that the United States would be able to develop mechanisms for breaking down these patterns of loyalty and securing popular support for our client governments. A continuing CRESS study of "The Human Factors Considerations of Undergrounds in Insurgencies" was undertaken because "it is vital to U.S. defense interests, particularly those of the U.S. Army, to have as complete an understanding as possible about the nature of undergrounds—their origins, membership, organization, missions, strategies, methods of action, and relationships to other elements of the total revolutionary movement, such as guerrilla units."[22] The RAND Corporation was subsequently commissioned by the Office of the Assistant Secretary of Defense for International Security Affairs (OASD/ISA) and ARPA to conduct a series of classified studies of "Viet Cong Motivation and Morale." These studies were based on exhaustive interviews with captives and defectors conducted by a RAND field team in South Vietnam. According to General John W. Vogt, Director of the Policy Planning Staff of OASD/ISA, "The idea here was for us to get some idea of what was making the Vietcong tick. Why did the Vietcong soldier decide he wanted to fight on their side rather than go over to the legitimate government in Vietnam?"[23] Vogt went on to say that such research "gives the policymaker here in Washington—and that is the area in which I am working all the time, the question of coming up with political and military policy—it gives the policymaker a better feel for the kind of problem he is wrestling with."[24]

The second category of counterinsurgency software research is oriented toward the solution of paramilitary problems through the projection of historical or predictive "models" that delineate the stages of insurgency and probable outcome of various government countermeasures at each of these stages. The most extensive program of research on the application of social systems modeling to the problem of countering insurgency was undertaken in 1965 by Abt Associates of Cambridge, Massachusetts. In response to a request from the Advanced Research Projects Agency, Abt developed several counterinsurgency games, in which human players represented insurgents, villagers, and government troops in simulated exercises of various counterinsurgency strategies. These games included AGILE-COIN, a counterguerrilla game; URB-COIN, an urban counterinsurgency game; and POLITICA, a "countersubversion and counterconspiracy game." In a theoretical discussion of this mode of analysis, Abt researcher Holly J. Kinley elucidated:

The study of insurgency involves consideration of a great many complicated variables interacting with each other. Clearly the insurgency process involves an intricate web of political, military and economic factors whose parameters and interactions are known intermittently and imprecisely at best.

In circumstances where a process so little understood and so complex is to be analyzed, it is often fruitful to proceed by means of modeling and simulation. A model may be defined as a simplified representation of a process (usually a complicated process), and a simulation as the exercise or operation of that model. By these definitions a simulation presupposes the existence of a model, and implies that the model's variables are given particular (though not necessarily precisely known) values for the purpose. The model may then be exercised, that is, the simulation may be carried out, using human players (a manual game), or an electronic computer (a computer simulation), or a combination of both. . . .[25]

In exercises of the Abt games, it was found that excessive use of military force by either belligerent would lead to defeat if the loyalty of villagers had not been assured beforehand. While this finding is hardly surprising, it inspired the Pentagon and the Central Intelligence Agency to develop teams of government workers (called Revolutionary Development Cadres) who were sent to rural hamlets in South Vietnam in an effort to gain popular support for the Saigon regime.[26]

"Model building" and related exercises require a great quantity of historical data on actual instances of insurgent and counterinsurgent warfare. Not surprisingly, the Pentagon has shown particular interest in the experiences of the European powers that fought antiguerrilla wars against liberation movements in their colonial possessions in Africa and Asia following World War II. In the early 1960's, the Defense Department commissioned a series of studies on the Algerian war of independence and the guerrilla war in Malaya. As part of this effort, RAND prepared reports on such subjects as *Antiguerrilla Intelligence in Malaya, Resettlement and Food Control in Malaya 1948–60*, and *Pacification in Algeria 1956–58*, and the Research Analysis Corporation contributed a study of *Helicopter Operations in the French-Algerian War*. These earlier struggles for national liberation anticipated many of the features of the present conflict in Southeast Asia, and the Pentagon strategists have studied them carefully to develop tactics for the U.S. war effort in Vietnam. It is well known, for instance, that the Strategic Hamlet Program and related pacification measures were based on the British resettlement effort in Malaya.[27]

RESEARCH ON
MINORITIES AND ELITES

As noted in Chapter 1, a major objective of U.S. counter-insurgency strategy is to mobilize certain elements of foreign populations for the struggle against national liberation movements in their own or neighboring countries. The Military Assistance Program, the foreign aid program, import subsidies, and similar programs are all designed to create client subgroups in each Third World country that can be compelled to supply troops for American-led counterguerrilla operations. This process has been particularly pronounced in South Vietnam, where U.S. aid has created a new Westernized bureaucracy in Saigon to replace the Mandarin aristocracy and the French colonial civil service.[28] The United States has also attempted on various occasions to obtain the cooperation of various minority groups in a target population which, for various historical, economic, or political reasons, are alienated from the majority group and thus vulnerable to U.S. psychological operations. In Vietnam, for instance, we have recruited montagnard tribesmen and other ethnic minority groups for CIA-financed mercenary armies (see Chapter 11).

Before the process of mercenarization can begin, the American foreign policy apparatus must have complete data on the history, religion, culture, and social composition of a given society in order to select the appropriate levers for cooptation. This work involves the production of anthropological and sociological studies of the social underpinnings of the target culture—the values, social relations, and communications institutions that lend themselves to external manipulation. In particular, the Pentagon seeks to know which subgroups in the population can most readily be made to serve U.S. interests. Such research, which usually falls under the headings of elite or minority studies, is routinely performed by academic social scientists in the normal course of their work; it has only been necessary for the Pentagon to channel this research in the desired direction by awarding substantial contracts for investigations of a target culture, and to maintain a clearinghouse—the Center for Research in Social Systems—for the collection, storage, and retrieval of such information.

Because of its pivotal role in U.S. counterinsurgency planning, the social grouping of greatest interest to Washington is the officer class of the native armed forces. The Pentagon must know if the indigenous military can be persuaded to engage in combat against guerrilla movements, if they will accept the strategic leadership of their American "advisers," and if they are capable of performing a "modernizing" role in their society by introducing new technological and managerial skills. The need for such research was first highlighted by Lucian Pye of MIT's Center for International Studies in his 1961 paper on "Military Development in the New Countries." Pye, whose paper was prepared for the Smithsonian Institution's series on *Social Science Research and National Security*, argued that because of the superior organizational capabilities of Third World armies *vis-à-vis* the civilian population, it is often necessary for the military to assume a "tutelage" role during periods of internal disequilibrium and to "operate even as the prime institution of government" in threatened areas. "In order to evaluate more fully the potentialities of armies in providing political tutelage," he commented, "it is necessary to have further research into the social composition of the officer classes in transitional societies." On the basis of such research, "it should be possible to forecast the degree to which particular armies are likely to take a leading role in guiding national development."[29]

The first organization to sponsor research on the "tutelage role" of Third World armies was the RAND Corporation, which in 1962 published a series of papers on *The Role of the Military in Underdeveloped Countries*. Several noted social scientists, particularly John J. Johnson of Stanford University and Morris Janowitz of the University of Chicago, continued work in this field until the Center for Research in Social Systems assumed responsibility for coordinating all such research in 1964. Through a continuing study of "The Changing Roles of the Military in Developing Nations," CRESS seeks to "develop knowledge about the changing nature of the political, social, economic, and cultural roles and functions of military establishments in the contemporary world." The emphasis of the project, according to a CRESS prospectus, "is placed upon the relationship of military roles to processes of social change."[30]

Much of the CRESS work on military elites is performed "in house" by the Center's own researchers; in order to obtain the assistance of university scholars, however, the Army authorized CRESS to award subcontracts to selected universities for participation in this project. The largest subcontract was awarded to the University of Chicago's Center for Social Organization Studies, for the preparation of a series of "Studies in Military Sociology." Under the leadership of Morris Janowitz, the Chicago team studied military elites in Africa, the Middle East, and Asia. Products of this work include *Public Order and the Military in Africa,* by Henry Eisen; *Political Development and the Role of the Military in Modern Egypt,* by Lou Cantori; and *The Chinese Warlords System, 1916 to 1928,* by Hsi-hseng Chi.

Additional studies of foreign military elites are being conducted by several private research organizations. Guy J. Pauker of the RAND Corporation holds an Air Force contract for research on "The Role of the Military in Indonesia." In response to an inquiry from Senator Fulbright, this RAND project was described as "an analysis in support of Air Force plans and intelligence of the role of the military in the developing political, economic, and defense structure of Indonesia, and the probable role of Indonesia in the larger context of U.S. security interests in Southeast Asia."[31] At the same time, Amos Perlmutter of

Operations and Policy Research, Inc.—a private research organization based in Washington, D.C.—is engaged in a study of "The Political Functions of the Military in the Middle East and North Africa." Perlmutter's study, which is being financed by the Air Force Office of Scientific Research, is designed to provide an "improved understanding of the role of foreign military forces in the stabilization of the Middle East."[32] It is easy to determine why the Pentagon would be interested in studies of the political role of the military in these areas: in Indonesia, the military junta that overthrew the leftist regime of President Sukarno still rules under virtual martial law in vast areas of the island confederation, while many of the Arab states are ruled by military chieftains whose allegiance to or defiance of American policies may have far-reaching consequences for the whole region.

Studies of foreign military elites are supplemented by research on other social strata—students, technocrats, entrepreneurs, the traditional oligarchy—which play a pivotal role in underdeveloped societies. In planning long-range strategy, the U.S. foreign policy establishment seeks to identify the social groupings which, for political, ideological, or pecuniary reasons, can be expected to advance American interests in an area, and which groups might adopt an anti-American stance. Operationally, Washington needs to know how pro-U.S. elements can be maneuvered into a paramount position in the society. Several universities and think tanks are prepared to supply this kind of information: in 1960, for instance, Joel M. Halpern of the RAND Corporation completed a study of *The Lao Elite,* in which it was argued that "an understanding of the cultural attitudes and social values of the elite might aid in the development of a group compatible with Western interests and values."[33]

As one would expect, American policymakers have a particular interest in the attitudes and motivations of the various non-Communist groups that compete for power in the Saigon government. The Agency for International Development has provided the Asia Society of New York City a substantial fund for research on Southeast Asian affairs: some of this money has been used to finance studies of Vietnamese elites by selected university scholars. Under this program, Wesley Fishel of Michigan State University received $11,000 in May 1969 for research on "The Changing Composition of the Political Elite in South Vietnam." Fishel, who once headed the Michigan State University Advisory Group in Saigon, explained that this project constituted "a study of the South Vietnamese elections of 1966–67, compared with the elections of 1956, 1959, 1961 and 1963, to test the hypothesis that politically important and statistically significant changes have occurred in the composition of the political elite."[34] A similar grant was made in June 1969 to Allan E. Goodman of Harvard University for research on "South Vietnam's Emerging Elites." According to Goodman, this study was to focus on "the role of the 1967 Lower House [of the Saigon legislature] as an emerging political institution, and on its membership as an emerging elite."[35]

Groups at the other extreme of the social spectrum—ethnic, religious, and national minorities—are also the subject of Pentagon-sponsored investigation. Here too, the objective is to identify social formations within a country that can be employed to advance America's strategic interests. In particular, the Defense Department seeks to know if, and on what basis, a particular group or tribe can be mobilized into a mercenary force or otherwise aid U.S. counterinsurgency operations. At the same time, Washington must determine whether an oppressed minority will be likely to join an insurgent movement if its grievances are not redressed by the regime in power.*

* The Pentagon's interest in such research is summarized by the Research Analysis Corporation in a report on *The Mobilization and Utilization of Minority Groups for Counterinsurgency:*

Recent counterinsurgent operations in Southeast Asia have

The Department of Defense can easily obtain most of the information it requires on minority groups from the literature of scholarly anthropological research. The Cultural Information Analysis Center (CINFAC) of the Center for Research in Social Systems maintains an up-to-date computerized index to all anthropological studies produced in the United States, including Ph.D. dissertations, conference papers, and field reports. Studies of military significance are duplicated and distributed by the Defense Documentation Center. Most of the time, the authors of these studies are totally unaware that their research is being used to plan military operations. Since Camelot, however, there has been considerable controversy and introspection within the academic community on the propriety of accepting Pentagon funds for research on foreign cultures even when the results can be published openly.[36]

Only when vital gaps exist in academia's knowledge of strategically located minority peoples has the Pentagon found it necessary to sponsor original research in this field. As one would expect, the minorities of greatest interest to Washington are the tribes inhabiting the upland regions of central Indochina. As Gerald C. Hickey put it in a RAND Corporation study of minority groups in South Vietnam:

The society of the Indochinese peninsula may be divided roughly into two major segments: the people of the plains,

---

pointed up the importance of tribal and other minority groups in underdeveloped countries susceptible to communist-inspired insurgency. Such groups, because of either (1) a history of hostility between them and the dominant ethnic group; (2) their location in remote areas and consequently their lack of close contact with the national government and its representatives; or (3) the fact that they occupy terrain of strategic importance both to insurgent and government forces; or (4) a combination of these reasons, will probably constitute primary targets for subversion in future communist wars of "national liberation." (*Technical Abstract Bulletin*, June 15, 1967.)

valleys and deltas, who have been strongly influenced by the civilizations of India and China, and the inhabitants of the highlands who have remained far more aloof, and about whom even today very little is known.[37]

In order to add to our limited store of knowledge of these peoples, Hickey studied the settlement pattern, social organization, and religious beliefs and practices of the major South Vietnamese highland groups—the Rhade, Jarai, Mnong, Stieng, Bahnar, and Sedang.

Since the outbreak of guerrilla warfare in northern Thailand, the highland peoples of that country, particularly the Meo, have come under rigorous Pentagon scrutiny. Peter Braestrup of *The New York Times* reported from Bangkok in 1967 that a third of all Defense Department funds spent on research in Thailand was devoted to environmental and behavioral studies. "The old formula for successful counterinsurgency used to be 10 troops for every guerrilla," one researcher was quoted as saying; "now the formula is ten anthropologists for each guerrilla." Braestrup reported that several teams of American anthropologists had moved into highland communities to study the customs and beliefs of key tribal groups.[38] One such study, *Social Structure and Shifting Agriculture: The White Meo,* was conducted by George A. Binney of the Wildlife Institute, Washington, D.C., over a three-year period. Ultimately all this information was collated by the Joint Thai-U.S. Military Research and Development Center in Bangkok and published in 1969 as the *Meo Handbook.* According to the handbook's authors, this document is "designed to furnish information useful to individuals or organizations dealing with the Meo tribes."[39] Since 1967, the major "organizations" dealing with the Meo tribes have been the Royal Thai Army and the Thai Provincial Police.

As in the case of elite studies, the principal responsibility for coordinating research on Southeast Asian minorities has been assumed by the Center for Research in Social

Systems. In February 1966, CRESS published a basic guide to *Minority Groups in the Republic of Vietnam*, distributed to military personnel as Department of the Army Pamphlet No. 550-105. According to CRESS, this study "was designed to be useful to military and other personnel who need a convenient compilation of basic facts about the social, economic and political institutions and practices of minority groups in the republic of Vietnam."[40] CRESS subsequently initiated a comprehensive program of research on the customs and social organization of "militarily significant" minority groups in South Vietnam. Typical reports issued under this program include *Customs and Taboos of Selected Tribes Residing Along the Western Border of the Republic of Vietnam* (1967), *The Nung of Vietnam* (1966), and *Brief Notes on the Tahoi, Pacoh and Phuong of the Republic of Vietnam* (1966).[41] These studies and others like them have been immensely valuable to the CIA and Special Forces cadres responsible for recruiting, training, and commanding the mercenary tribesmen of the Civilian Irregular Defense Groups in South Vietnam, the Armée Clandestine in Laos, and similar groups elsewhere in Asia.

SOCIAL SYSTEMS ENGINEERING

The net effect of the historical research and model-building described above, coupled with events in Vietnam, has been a collapse of confidence in America's ability to counter revolutionary movements on an ideological level. Rather than acknowledge the political nature of the insurgent battlefield, the academic strategists would have us view insurgency as a "system," a mechanical process that is subject to external manipulation. From this perspective, it is not necessary to win the "hearts and minds" of the peasantry but only—through bribery and/or intimidation —to secure their withdrawal from the insurgent movement.

In one of the first presentations of this position, Charles Wolf, Jr., of the RAND Corporation suggested: "The main concern of [counter-] insurgency efforts should be to influence the behavior and action of the populace rather than their loyalties and attitudes. The leadership of countries in which insurgent movements appear can do much to influence the behavior and actions of the populace that make the operation of the insurgent system substantially more difficult." In other words, it does not matter if the people in a village have voted to support the Revolution; it only matters that—through police surveillance, crop spraying, saturation bombing, and other measures—you can deter them from making any "inputs" into the "insurgent system"—i.e., from providing the guerrillas with food, intelligence, and other forms of *concrete* support. In determining whether a specific counterinsurgency program should be implemented, according to Wolf, "The primary consideration should be whether the proposed measure is likely to increase the cost and difficulties of insurgent organizations rather than whether it wins popular loyalty and support."[42]

The systems engineering approach to counterinsurgency usually incorporates the three-phased sequence of insurgent warfare devised by Mao Tse-tung during his guerrilla campaign against the Japanese. In the first stage of the Maoist model, insurgent bands limit themselves to assassinations, ambushes, and other small-scale military actions designed to undermine the authority of the established government without exposing the fledgling guerrilla movement to destruction. In the second stage, the insurgents attempt to create a clandestine governmental apparatus that can win the loyalty of the populace while whittling away at the authority of the government. In the final stage, the guerrillas take the offensive against the now isolated government troops in an effort to seize control of the country as a whole. The counterinsurgent's response to this scenario is to identify the "inputs" available to a government at each stage of an insurgent uprising that will most effectively prevent its progress to the next stage.* Similarly, the counterinsurgent seeks to identify the measures that can best counteract the insurgents' own inputs into the system. Thus at the first stage of an insurgency, government inputs can include civic-action projects designed to reduce the peasant's hostility toward the government, and increased police and military patrols that prevent the guerrillas from making contact with the peasants. In the second stage, the government can institute a resources-control program in order to intercept supplies intended for the guerrillas, and can mount periodic "search and destroy" missions to drive the guerrillas away from friendly villages. In the final stage, when the government has lost the support of the countryside, no inputs remain except the bombs and shells which make the cultivation of crops, and all other normal human activity, impossible in the "free fire zones" that surround government fortresses. This approach to counterinsurgency is eloquently summarized

* The "input/output" approach to counterinsurgency has inspired some social scientists to seek a statistical method for rating the effectiveness of alternative military strategies. In 1968, D. M. Condit and Bert Cooper of CRESS, authors of a three-volume study of 57 postwar counterinsurgencies, began work on an Army-financed analysis of strategic characteristics of revolutionary warfare. The objective of this study, according to CRESS, "is to discover whether any strategic considerations were critical to the outcome of past cases of internal conflict." In order to isolate such considerations, Condit and Cooper prepared a set of 195 questions concerning aspects of insurgent and counterinsurgent warfare that were to be answered for each of the 57 conflicts previously studied. Afterward, a statistical tabulation of the answers would be made in order to determine if any correlation existed between the success or failure of strategies employed in the 57 cases. These findings would then be used to develop a set of "critical characteristics" of revolutionary conflict that would allow the counterinsurgent to select military options with some degree of confidence in their efficacy. (CRESS *Work Program, Fiscal Year 1969*, Washington, D.C., 1968, pp. 44–5.)

in a research proposal submitted to the Defense Department in 1967 by the American Institutes for Research:

The struggle between an established government and subversive or insurgent forces involves three different types of operations. The first is to make inputs into the social system that will gain the active support of an ever-increasing proportion of the local population. Threats, promises, ideological appeals, and tangible benefits are the kinds of inputs that are most frequently used. The second is to reduce or interdict the flow of the competing inputs being made by the opposing side by installing anti-infiltration devices, cutting communication lines, assassinating key spokesmen, strengthening retaliatory mechanisms, and similar preventative measures. The third is to counteract the political successes already achieved by groups committed to the "wrong" side. This typically involves direct military confrontation.[43]

In succeeding chapters, we will discover how the United States government has mobilized its resources and those of its client governments to make the prescribed inputs into the various insurgent systems that have threatened American hegemony in the Third World. That this response to revolution has in fact represented a retreat from the "real battlefield" of politics is acknowledged by the Pentagon's chief for Vietnam-oriented research, Leonard Sullivan, Jr., who wrote:

Who is the guerrilla? He is simply the local dissident or the local zealot. He is willing to commit acts of violence in order to change his lot and that of future generations. The threshold of his violence is a fine balance between the strength of his discontent and his view of the consequences of his violence. We should be able to change an insurgent's threshold of violence by adjusting both sides of the balance. We can lower his level of discontent by peaceful action, and we can raise the apparent deterrent by suitable military or police presence—and technology can probably help on both sides.[44]

Part Two

THE
TECHNOLOGICAL
WAR

Chapter 5

THE COUNTER-INSURGENCY RESEARCH NETWORK

To a considerable extent, the Kennedy Administration's initial optimism regarding the ability of the United States to triumph on any insurgent battlefield was based on the conviction that American scientific and technological knowhow would overcome every advantage normally accorded the guerrilla. As the first step in his effort to establish an effective counterinsurgency capability within the armed forces, Secretary McNamara directed the nation's research and development apparatus to study every aspect of limited warfare and to come up with suggestions for changes in military organization and tactics. To expedite this process, McNamara and his aides created an informal network of institutes, think tanks, and laboratories devoted to counterinsurgency research similar to the existing network for nuclear warfare studies. New "in-house" Pentagon agencies were created for the development and testing of limited warfare materiel, and a select group of universities and think tanks were given lucrative contracts for theoretical investigations of limited warfare strategy. In this chapter, we will identify the in-house organizations that make up the counterinsurgency research network, and describe the programs that were established to meet the research needs of our forces in Vietnam.

In order to weld the R&D community into a reliable instrument of national defense policy, it was first necessary to centralize research management functions in the Office of the Director of Defense Research and Engineering (ODDRE) in much the same way that overall Defense management functions were centralized in the Office of the Secretary of Defense. Prior to the McNamara incumbency, each of the military services maintained an autonomous research apparatus consisting of in-house laboratories, subsidized think tanks, and favored R&D contractors. To preserve their favored status within these networks, most researchers adopted the ideology and outlook of the service with which they were associated; the result, predictably, was that Army scientists produced weapons and strategy for one kind of war, while Navy and Air Force scientists planned for other kinds of wars. Since none of the services attached much importance to low-intensity warfare in underveloped areas, few scientists or strategists concerned themselves with the problem of such warfare unitl the late 1950's.

When the first Sputnik space satellite was launched by the Soviet Union in the spring of 1957, Congress was no longer willing to tolerate the disunity that prevailed in the nation's military R&D community. To assure American technological superiority in defense-related fields, new authority for the centralization of research management functions was granted in the Department of Defense Reorganization Act of 1958. To enhance the status of ODDRE, the Director of Defense Research and Engineering was made the third highest officer in the Pentagon (outranked only by the Secretary of Defense and his Deputy), and vested with the authority to "supervise all research and engineering activities in the Department." The operative powers granted the Director under the 1958 act include control over all R&D disbursements. This budgetary authority extends to the research programs of the separate services; thus the Director is empowered "to approve, modify, or disapprove programs and projects of the military departments and of the other Defense agencies to eliminate unpromising or unnecessarily duplicative programs."[1] The 1958 act also authorized ODDRE to establish its own in-house research organization, the Advanced Research Projects Agency, described below.

Although Defense Secretaries McElroy and Gates made some moves toward implementation of the Reorganization Act, it was not until McNamara took office that ODDRE assumed full control over the Pentagon R&D apparatus. The current Director of Defense Research and Engineering, John S. Foster, Jr., sits at the pinnacle of the world's largest military research apparatus. As head of ODDRE, he is both chief scientific adviser to the Secretary of Defense and the Pentagon's top research administrator. By directly supervising the activities of the Pentagon's own in-house laboratories, and by controlling the assignment of defense research contracts to universities, think tanks, and private industry, the Director effectively sets policy for the nation's scientific and technical community.

RESEARCH PRIORITIES

Despite McNamara's early emphasis on counterinsurgency research, the United States was inadequately prepared for the challenge it faced in Vietnam. Equipment designed for optimal performance in the temperate climate of Central Europe frequently failed to function in the humid jungles of Southeast Asia. The massive firepower of our artillery was often wasted because the jungle canopy provided concealment from even the most sophisticated "target acquisition" devices. Jet bombers designed to carry nuclear weapons deep into Soviet territory were unable to block North Vietnam's primitive supply system. Most discouraging, the much-publicized campaign to "pacify" the countryside succeeded only in inflaming the population further against our client regime in Saigon. Not surprisingly, the greatest weakness in U.S. strategy was our failure to allow for the widespread popular support enjoyed by the insurgent National Liberation Front. The Pentagon's chief for Vietnam-oriented research, Leonard Sullivan, Jr., later recalled:

We entered this war fully and beautifully equipped to fight either an all-out nuclear conflict or World War II over again. But then we found that Vietnam is a new war. . . .

At the time we undertook to help the South Vietnamese, I do not think we fully realized how difficult it would be to fight an enemy so closely interwoven with our allies. It is a war without front lines, a war where you can seldom distinguish friend from foe—except by the actions of the foe.[2]

As the foe in Vietnam secured control of ever-larger sections of the countryside, the Defense Department committed an increasingly larger share of its research and development budget to the study of counterguerrilla warfare. The extent of Pentagon spending on Vietnam-oriented R&D is illustrated by Table 3, prepared by the Deputy Director of Defense Research and Engineering for Southeast Asia Matters.

While total defense R&D spending increased by only 5 percent between 1964 and 1969, Vietnam-oriented research increased by 700 percent. Although most of these funds have been used for the development of fairly sophisticated items of military hardware—such as helicopter gunships and aerial surveillance systems—a significant

Table 3

R&D SPENDING FOR VIETNAM

(Dollars in millions)

Year	Total Defense R&D appropriation	Southeast Asia R&D spending
1964	7,635	100
1965	6,997	200
1966	7,553	370
1967	7,954	680
1968	8,002	780
1969 (estimated)	8,000	800

Source: Leonard Sullivan, Jr., "Research and Development for Vietnam," *Science and Technology* (October 1968), p. 33.

portion has been devoted to research in the social sciences. In a 1965 report on *Behavioral, Political and Operational Research Programs on Counterinsurgency Supported by the Department of Defense*, the Institute for Defense Analyses reported that the Pentagon was spending more than $10 million annually on such programs, and that the trend was for greater spending in this area. Much of this "software" research was designed to provide U.S. commanders with an understanding of the political tactics of the insurgents and to develop tests that would make it possible "to distinguish friend from foe."[3]

In a 1967 report to the House Committee on Armed Services on "R&D Support of the War in Southeast Asia," ODDRE chief Foster identified four areas in which research work had been concentrated: *interdiction,* or the air war against enemy supply routes in Laos, Cambodia, and North Vietnam; *counterinfiltration,* measures to prevent the enemy from penetrating "secure" areas of South Vietnam; *search and destroy,* the large-unit actions undertaken by our ground forces to destroy the enemy's "main force units" and their "base areas" (i.e., the villages loyal to the guerrillas); and *pacification and nation building,* the efforts extended to counteract the political effectiveness of the National Liberation Front in the countryside and to maintain the stability of the "indigenous government" in Saigon.[4]

At first, most of the Vietnam R&D program was devoted to "quick-fix" programs designed to adapt basic Armed Forces materiel to the environmental conditions encountered in Southeast Asia. It was discovered, for instance, that standard Army radios lost most of their effective operating range in the humid jungle; as a result, the Pentagon spent several million dollars in a crash program to develop new radios "optimized" for jungle transmission. The Kennedy brain trust originally gave equal priority to the development of noncombative programs—such as rural development, institution building, and civic action—but the failure of each successive pacification scheme has induced the military establishment to emphasize technological measures for controlling insurgency. Consequently, as the war progressed, the Pentagon allocated a greater share of its research funds to the development of totally new kinds of equipment which could be used experimentally in Vietnam but which will not find their way into the Army inventory on a large scale until after the present conflict is terminated. In this sense, Vietnam has always been thought of as a "laboratory" for the testing of new conventional war technologies. In the 1967 report to the House Armed Services Committee mentioned above, Dr. Foster stated:

We feel a strong obligation to learn as much as possible from our participation in this strange and difficult war. Though we have never fought one quite like it, this conflict may be typical of future struggles in which we might, sad to say, become involved. I am anxious to identify any possible shortcomings in our military capability in Southeast Asia, and take whatever steps we can to improve those capabilities as soon as possible.[5]

THE COUNTERINSURGENCY
LABORATORIES

When Robert S. McNamara assumed office as Secretary of
Defense, there was not a single agency within the Department that was responsible for research on counterinsurgency. One of his first concerns, therefore, was to establish
a chain of laboratories that would concentrate on the
various problems of counterguerrilla warfare. Within a
year, the four agencies described below had been organized
or expanded to serve as the nucleus of a counterinsurgency
research network.

The Advanced Research Projects Agency (ARPA) is an elite
organization of civilian scientists who work directly under
the Director of Defense Research and Engineering. Established in 1958 to coordinate Pentagon-sponsored research
on ballistic missile warfare and nuclear test detection,
ARPA has since been given added responsibility for research in the areas of counterinsurgency, computer technology, and the social sciences. According to Dr.
Eberhardt Rechtin, the Agency's former director, "The
establishment of ARPA was a recognition of the fact that
a Department of Defense R&D program based only on
assigned roles and missions of the services could lead to
serious interservice or triservice gaps in our overall defense technology, particularly in an era of rapid technological change." In precluding "sputniklike surprises,"
he asserted, "ARPA's role is to conduct high-risk R&D of
a revolutionary nature in areas where defense technology in the United States appears to be falling behind or in areas where we cannot afford the risk of falling
behind."[16]

Under existing Defense Department protocol, ARPA is
authorized to work on advanced technology projects not

clearly within the purview of a specific military department, on basic research in the fields of materials science and human behavior, and on short-term or "quick-fix" projects directly related to the war effort in Southeast Asia. Normally, ARPA staff members perform the initial conceptualization of a project, and then turn over developmental work to one of the service laboratories or to outside R&D contractors. In recent years, ARPA's budget has ranged between $225 and $250 million annually.[7]

ARPA is commanded by a civilian Director, who also holds the rank of Deputy Director of Defense Research and Engineering. From 1961 to 1963 the Director was Jack P. Ruina, and from 1963 to 1965 Robert L. Sproull. Both men have since assumed high posts in the academic community —Ruina is Vice-President for Special Laboratories at MIT, and Sproull is Vice-President and Provost of the University of Rochester. The current Director, Dr. Stephen J. Lukasik, was Director of the Computer Center at the Stevens Institute of Technology before joining the ARPA staff in 1966.

ARPA's elite status within the Pentagon R&D community has enabled it to attract many outstanding scientists from universities and industry. Citing this concentration of scientific talent, Secretary McNamara in 1962 directed ARPA to initiate a vanguard effort to utilize the new techniques of systems analysis and operations research in the development of tactics for counterinsurgency warfare in underdeveloped areas. At his instruction, the Remote Area Conflict Office was established within ARPA to administer a continuing counterinsurgency research program with the code name Project Agile. Although its budget of $25 million a year is small in comparison with other Pentagon R&D programs, Agile has played a decisive role by "opening up" many of the limited warfare technologies described in subsequent chapters. Furthermore, Agile has the primary responsibility for the development of materiel for foreign troops and mercenaries under U.S. command (see Chapter 8).

The U.S. Air Force **Armament Development and Test Center (ADTC)** is responsible for developing, testing, and acquiring non-nuclear munitions for limited warfare and counterinsurgency. "Aircraft systems, subsystems, allied equipment, guns, bombs, rockets, targets and drones, . . . all are tested and evaluated on [ADTC's] eight test ranges, eight auxiliary airfields, and the large Eglin Gulf Test Range." Originally designated the Air Proving Ground Center, ADTC houses a giant laboratory for testing aircraft components and weapons systems under extreme climatic conditions. In addition, ADTC provides technical support for the Air Force portion of the Pentagon's chemical and biological warfare test program.[8]

A component of the Air Force Systems Command, ADTC is based at Eglin Air Force Base, Florida, the largest airbase in the continental United States. Other agencies located at Eglin include the Air Force Armament Laboratory (AFATL) and the Tactical Air Command's Special Operations Force, both of which work closely with ADTC in the development of weapons and tactics for counterguerrilla warfare. As the research arm of ADTC, the Armament Lab conducts "exploratory and advanced development of non-nuclear air armament, including bombs, fuses, aircraft guns, rockets, air-delivered mines, dispenser and cluster munitions, [and] pyrotechnic weapons."[9]

It is interesting—and revealing—to note that the prominent role currently played by AFATL in Defense R&D work is a direct consequence of the shift in Defense priorities. In its analysis of AFATL, McGraw-Hills' DMS *Market Intelligence Report* comments:

Previously, with the emphasis on nuclear ordnance and strategic systems, the efforts at the Armaments Lab were minimal. With the emphasis switched to conventional ordnance dropped from high speed aircraft, and with the requirements for . . . the various types of weapons required for tropical environments, [AFATL] has grown in size and importance in the Air Force's developmental activities. . . . As the leading Air Force laboratory for ballistic studies, and analyses on lethality, vulnerability and weapons effects, the Armament Laboratory has been deeply involved in responding to Air Force requirements stemming from the Vietnam conflict.

Among the products of the collaboration between ADTC, AFATL, and the Special Operations Force is Puff the Magic Dragon, a C-47 transport plane converted into an aerial gunship armed with rapid-fire Gatling machine guns. (Puff and other antipersonnel weapons systems designed by AFATL are credited with a large share of the Vietcong —and civilian—casualties in Vietnam.) AFATL was also responsible for development of "interdiction" techniques for the Igloo White bombing campaign against enemy supply routes in Laos (see Chapter 7).

The Combat Developments Command (CDC) was established in 1962 in order to fill the "doctrinal gap" that developed after World War II between existing Army capabilities and the kinds of combat situations we would actually have to face in the contemporary world. According to Lieutenant General George I. Forsythe, the organization's former commander, CDC "provides the detailed blueprints which determine how the Army will fight, how it will be organized, and how it will be equipped in all future time frames and environments."[10] As part of this effort, CDC prepares multiple "threat studies" that evaluate current or projected conflict situations and the anticipated capabilities of potential enemies as well as the possible physical environments to be faced.

CDC component agencies include the Institute of Land Combat (ILC) in Alexandria, Virginia, and the Institute of Systems Analysis (ISA) at Fort Belvoir, Virginia. These organizations are composed of civilian scientists and Army officers who prepare blueprints for the "Army of the Future" on the basis of anticipated developments in weapons technology and the projected world situation. ILC is responsible for the conceptualization of future ground-warfare weapons systems, while ISA employs the proposed systems in computer-assisted war games to measure their potential military effectiveness.* Those ideas which score well in the war games are then tried out under simulated battlefield conditions by the 3,400 men of the 194th Armored Brigade at the CDC Experimentation Command's Hunter Liggett Reservation at Fort Ord, California.

CDC's principal achievement to date has been the conceptualization and preliminary organization of the air cavalry division. Since the tactics of airmobile warfare

---

* As an "Advanced Concepts Organization," the Institute of Land Combat is now engaged in the development of a "Land Combat System for the Army in the 1990's." In the remarkable passage quoted below, *Army Research and Development Newsmagazine* (August–September 1969) revealed how this process has been systematized and routinized:

> [ILC's] Environments and Threats Directorate (ETD), with the assistance of ITAG [the Intelligence Threat Analysis Group of the Office of the Assistant Chief of Staff for Intelligence], prepares the Conflict Situations and Army Tasks Study. World, regional and country environments are projected into the time period 1985–1995.
>
> Potential Conflict Forecasts (PCF) are evolved from this projection, including country against country, bloc against country, bloc against bloc.
>
> From analyses of these projects, the ETD identifies Plausible Conflict Situations (PCS) which may result in U.S. Army involvement. The PCS are then grouped by level of conflict into Representative Conflict Situations (RCS). . . .
>
> From the FCS, the ETD derives tasks which the Army in the field must be able to perform in the 1990's. . . .
>
> With input concerning Army tasks . . . the Conceptual Design Directorate [of ILC] will develop visualizations of combat systems to accomplish Army tasks in the 1990's. . . .
>
> The conceptual designs, with recommendations for adoption, then will be submitted to the Department of the Army for final determination, which is expected by mid-1972.

had not been fully developed when the 1st Cavalry Division entered combat in 1965, the Vietnam battlefield became, according to former CDC commander Harry Kinnard, "a laboratory for research as communications, maintenance, fire-control, support, and supply techniques were tried, modified, and tried again, all in the presence of the enemy."[11]

On the basis of its Vietnam experiments, CDC is now planning American strategy for the limited wars of the 1970's, 1980's, and 1990's. As part of this effort, CDC personnel are currently studying new battlefield vehicles (including heavy-lift helicopters and air-cushioned patrol craft), advanced battlefield-surveillance systems, and computerized tactical-data systems.[12]

The Limited War Laboratory (LWL) was established in 1962 to provide "a centralized research and development activity with a quick-reaction capability for meeting Army operational requirements relating to limited war." The Lab's mission, then, is to develop specialized counterinsurgency hardware on a crash basis. Since most of the day-to-day work of counterinsurgency is performed by the foot soldier, LWL activities are geared to the problems of infantryman and his basic combat vehicle, the helicopter.[13]

LWL's principal responsibility has been the solution of problems encountered by our troops in Southeast Asia. The Lab is frequently asked to modify or redesign essential Army equipment that was found to be unusable in Vietnam's tropical climate. An estimated 90 percent of all LWL projects are oriented toward the Vietnam battlefield; by the end of 1970, the Lab had produced more than a hundred items that were already being used by our soldiers there. LWL products include such items as leech repellent, an airborne floating platform for the 105mm howitzer (for use in the Mekong Delta), foliage-penetrating radars, and a Long-Range Patrol Food Packet (a 1,100-calorie meal in a ten-ounce packet).

In January 1970, the Limited War Laboratory's mission was broadened to include work on problems faced by U.S. ground troops in *any* combat environment, and its name was accordingly changed to Land War Laboratory (still LWL). The Lab's work force of 124 civilian scientists and twenty military officers will continue to be stationed at the Aberdeen (Maryland) Proving Ground.[14]

RESEARCH ON
ENVIRONMENTAL EXTREMES

The counterinsurgency R&D activities described above are augmented by an intensive program of research on "environmental extremes"—natural phenomena (temperature, humidity, altitude, etc.) that can impair the effectiveness of combat forces. In explaining the need for such research, three Pentagon scientists wrote: "With the U.S. Army's current global commitments, entailing rapid movement of forces, the soldier may find himself fighting in the humid tropics today, and the desert or cold regions tomorrow."[15] They note that certain remote and inhospitable areas, including the Himalayas and the Arctic, have assumed considerable strategic importance because of their location on the borders of the Soviet Union and Communist China. Furthermore, many of the underdeveloped nations of Africa, Asia, and Latin America encompass vast jungle and desert areas. In Vietnam we have learned that men and equipment that can be relied upon to perform respectably in temperate zones can easily be defeated by harsh and unfamiliar environments. Since the American soldier cannot be permitted "the luxury of coming in out of the cold, getting away from the heat, coming down off the mountain, or stopping whatever he is doing simply because he is tired and uncomfortable," it is necessary that special attention "be given to the problems associated with the development of a capability to operate and survive in such areas."[16]

As one would assume, the environment of greatest concern to the Pentagon today is the jungle and marsh areas of Southeast Asia. In an assessment of environmental stresses associated with such regions, the Army reports that "the humid tropics, comprising about 20 percent of the world's land area, present a challenge to the soldier because of the debilitating heat and humidity, tropical diseases and unsanitary conditions to which he has little or no built-in immunity." Compounding these factors "are the dense evergreen rain forests . . . in which target acquisition movement and communications are problems." To augment the soldier's ability to function in such areas, "improved jungle boots, tropical clothing and sleeping systems, and special tropical rations are being developed." Research aimed at improving communications and surveillance in the jungle is also underway. In addition, elaborate studies of "off-the-road mobility" in rice paddies and canal complexes, involving experimental "marginal terrain vehicles," have been undertaken in the United States, Panama, and Thailand.[17]

Desert areas, which make up approximately 19 percent of the earth's land surface, occupy strategic territory in North Africa, the Middle East, and Central Asia. Similar areas in the American Southwest are being used to test new clothing, equipment, and food in an effort to "develop an effective desert fighting man."[18]

Throughout history, mountainous regions have been a favorite haunt of partisan and guerrilla bands. Since World War II, such areas have been used to advantage by insurgent groups in Cuba, Algeria, Cyprus, Jordan, Yemen, Kashmir, Tibet, Vietnam, Thailand, and Laos. In addition, "Such terrain occupies the whole southern frontier of Communist power from Central Europe to Vietnam." Since U.S. counterinsurgency doctrine calls for the denial of all natural sanctuaries to enemy forces, the Army has given considerable attention to the problems of combat operations at high altitude.[19]

Fundamental research on these environmental systems usually involves the collection of great quantities of data in many scientific disciplines (including meteorology, geology, botany, soil study, and hydrology) in outdoor settings that have been carefully selected as representative of the particular environment being studied. Often, however, the Pentagon will be denied access to regions of strategic interest; in such cases, normal procedure calls for the selection of an alternative site in friendly territory that exhibits conditions analogous to those in the restricted area. This practice explains the Army's support of seemingly harmless environmental studies in areas far removed from any current battlefield. Thus, in an effort to accumulate data about climatic conditions in Vietnam, the United States established a "tropical environment data base" at Fort Clayton in the Panama Canal Zone and conducted field studies at sites in Colombia, Puerto Rico, Hawaii, and Thailand. A striking example of this practice is the Army's recent upsurge of interest in mountain environment studies. The Pentagon is particularly interested in factors that affect military operations at the altitudes common in the Himalayas (which form the western border of China). In order to obtain information of this sort, the Army has engaged in the following activities:

—Sponsored environmental surveys undertaken by the University of Colorado in selected valleys, basins, and adjacent mountains along U.S. Route 40 in western Colorado and eastern Utah. These surveys provide "fairly detailed observations of many militarily significant aspects of the landscapes of several distinctive regions there, comparable to certain regions of Eurasia."[20]

—Helped maintain the "world's highest research station" at the 17,600-foot level of Mount Logan in the Yukon Territory of Canada. This project, sponsored jointly with the Canadian armed forces and the Arctic Institute of North America, is intended to provide information on physiological stresses and other factors "associated with activities in similar high altitudes in other parts of the world, such as the Himalayan Mountains in India."[21]

—Conducted military maneuvers above the 11,500-foot level of Mount Evans, Colorado, in order to "evaluate the effects of 'thin atmosphere' on performance and health." The Mount Evans exercise, a part of the Advanced Research Projects Agency's High Terrestrial Altitude Research Program, involved some two hundred soldiers of the 3rd Special Forces Group.[22]

—Studied the performance of Chinese Nationalist troops during maneuvers at high altitude conducted by the U.S.-financed Cold Weather and Mountain Training Center on Taiwan.[23]

Research on environmental extremes is the responsibility of a network of relatively obscure Army agencies, most of which were established during the Kennedy Administration.

The Cold Regions Research and Engineering Laboratory (CRREL) was created in 1961 by combining the Army Construction and Frosts Effects Laboratory and the Snow, Ice and Permafrost Research Establishment. A component of the Army Corps of Engineers, CRREL performs basic and applied research design to improve Pentagon capabilities for operations in perennially snow- and ice-covered regions. The Lab also conducts mountain environment studies and has participated in the Mount Logan project described above. Located in Hanover, New Hampshire, CRREL draws many of its civilian staff members from nearby Dartmouth College.[24]

The Earth Sciences Laboratory (ESL) of the U.S. Army Corps of Engineers, Ft. Belvoir, Virginia, is responsible for the collection, analysis, and dissemination of environmental data on areas of interest to military planners. As part of its work for the Corps of Engineers, ESL uses geographic data "in establishing realistic requirements for the design, testing and issue of [Army] equipment." In conjunction with other Army laboratories, ESL has been involved in the development of new jungle boots, tropical uniforms, lightweight tents, and other basic equipment for use in Vietnam.[25]

In order to obtain a more precise knowledge of the jungle environment, ESL in 1966 established a series of field laboratories in Thailand. This effort, known as Project TREND (Tropical Environment Data), was designed "to collect quantitative data on natural factors affecting the soldier, materiel and operations in two types of tropical forest environment." The first laboratory was located in a dry evergreen forest a hundred miles northeast of Bangkok, and the second field station was to have been situated in a tropical rain-forest region; both sites were chosen because they exhibited characteristics similar to those encountered in large parts of Cambodia, Laos, and Vietnam as well as Thailand. According to an Army report, "The TREND plan calls for simultaneous acquisition of data in various earth science disciplines at different points, vertically and horizontally, and in various time frames (diurnally, monthly, seasonally, and annually) in an outdoor laboratory carefully selected as representative of the particular environment studied."[26] Although the Army did not specify what uses it had in mind for these data, previous studies of this sort have been used to improve jungle communications, to develop counterinfiltration devices, and to test infrared detection sets (see Chapters 7 and 8).

The U.S. Army Institute of Environmental Medicine (USA-RIEM) is concerned with the effects of extreme environmental conditions on the combat effectiveness of American soldiers. When the Institute was founded in 1961, it was given the mission of conducting "basic and applied research to determine how heat, cold, high terrestrial altitude, and work affect the soldier's life processes, his performance, and his health. The goal is to understand the complex effects of climatic stresses on the human body, the body's defenses, and the technique, equipment, and procedures best calculated to make the soldier operationally effective to an optimal degree." The Institute's facilities include a variety of "environmental chambers" used for measuring the effects of "a wide variety of simulated environmental extremes" on volunteer subjects. Located at the Army's Natick Laboratories, USARIEM employs many scientists from universities in the area, and cosponsors research at the Harvard Medical School, Boston City Hospital, Boston University Medical School, and Peter Bent Brigham Hospital in Roxbury, Massachusetts.[27]

R&D IN VIETNAM

Research can proceed just so far in the laboratory; then it becomes necessary to try out a new concept under "real world" conditions. This principle is as true of counterinsurgency research as of any other kind, and by the early 1960's the Pentagon found it necessary to establish test centers in an area where it would be possible to try out new weapons and tactics against live targets. Vietnam—we now know—was selected for this purpose in 1962. One cannot help recalling Maxwell Taylor's 1963 statement, "Here we have a going laboratory where we see subversive insurgency . . . being applied in all its forms." Speaking on behalf of the Joint Chiefs of Staff, Taylor asserted that the Pentagon "recognized the importance of the area as a laboratory," and had already sent "teams out there looking at the equipment requirements of this kind of guerrilla warfare."[28]

The first military research teams to arrive in Vietnam were associated with the Army Concept Team in Vietnam (ACTIV) and the ARPA R&D Field Unit, Vietnam (RDFU-V), both of which were activated in 1962. Initially, these units were primarily involved in the development of materiel for the South Vietnamese armed forces and only incidentally with the equipment requirements of our own troops. Thus the lightweight M-16 rifle, now the Army's standard individual weapon, was originally intended for use by Vietnamese soldiers (see Chapter 8). By 1964, however, Vietnam could no longer be considered a secure "laboratory" in which American personnel could test out their ideas with impunity. Instead, it was a new theater of war in which our indigenous counterinsurgency apparatus, the South Vietnamese Army, was being threatened with extinction. When it became obvious that massive numbers of U.S. troops would be required to preserve the Saigon regime, the orientation of these field units shifted to U.S. needs. At the same time, the Navy and Air Force established their own in-country research teams: the Naval R&D Unit, Vietnam (NRDU-V) and the Air Force Test Unit, Vietnam (AFTU-V). Finally, in order to assure some measure of coordination among these test programs, the Pentagon in 1964 consolidated all Vietnam R&D units into the Joint Research and Test Activity (JRATA).[29]

The creation and subsequent expansion of JRATA suggests the extent to which Vietnam has become both a major challenge to the U.S. military on its own terms and a testing ground for future counterguerrilla wars. JRATA's primary responsibility, of course, is to check out equipment that is urgently needed to overcome problems encountered in *this* war. JRATA has a small staff of civilian scientists and military personnel, most of whom are stationed at the headquarters of the U.S. Military Assistance Command (MACV) in Saigon; tests of new equipment, however, are performed by regular combat units in the field. As one JRATA official put it, "We don't test out here, we use." Thus equipment that goes to JRATA must be proved out as completely as possible in the United States. "If you give me something as a substitute for my rifle," the same official insisted, "it had better be as good as my rifle. My life is at stake." At the same time, however, JRATA is responsible for the collection of environmental data that will be used in the design of the next "generation" of counterinsurgency weapons.[30]

As we have seen, Vietnam-oriented R&D spending now accounts for approximately 10 percent of the Pentagon's total research budget. The majority of this money is channeled through Project PROVOST (Priority Research and Development Objectives for Vietnam Operations Support), a high-level Pentagon management operation designed to speed delivery of new items to the battlefield. Most funds for PROVOST activities are supplied by the Defense Emergency Fund, a special account established in 1950 "to enable the Secretary of Defense to meet unforeseen research, development, test, and evaluation needs which are of such urgency that funding is deemed necessary before the next appropriation becomes available."

A responsibility of the Office of the Director of Defense Research and Engineering, PROVOST is run by John S. Foster's Deputy for Southeast Asian Matters, Leonard Sullivan, Jr. In essence, PROVOST is "an administrative procedure through which high-priority activities are financed and pushed to early completion." Normally, a particular project is selected for PROVOST financing after a formal "requirement" has been transmitted from MACV and approval has been given by a steering committee consisting of the director of ARPA and representatives from the services at the flag-officer level. PROVOST projects, which have highest priority in the R&D field at this time, are defined as "those projects of critical need in the Southeast

Asian effort that can be accomplished in 18 months or less."[31]

PROVOST projects that require considerable exploratory development are farmed out to the various service R&D agencies, particularly the Land War Laboratory and the Armament Development and Test Center. Among the 150 or so items that followed this route before being sent to Vietnam are the E-63 Personnel Detector ("people sniffer"), the AN/PRR-9 and AN/PRT-4 squad radio sets, and the AC-47 gunship (Puff the Magic Dragon). Occasionally PROVOST requirements are fulfilled by adapting commercial "off-the-shelf" items to military use, such as the application of a Sears, Roebuck orchard blower to fill tunnels with CS riot gas. All products developed with PROVOST funds are tailored for use in Vietnam; nevertheless, many of these devices are being designed with post-Vietnam contingencies in mind. In a statement prepared for transmittal to the Senate, Sullivan reported:

Almost *all* of these new equipments have operational utility beyond Southeast Asia and will become part of our post-war standard equipment. Hence our efforts contribute not only to our combat capabilities in Southeast Asia, but to the combat potential of our future tactical forces, which have for many years received lesser priority than our strategic forces.[32]

In their periodic budget messages to Congress, the Pentagon's R&D officials have consistently argued that American technology can overcome the organizational and political advantages of a popularly backed national liberation movement. Thus in testimony to the Armed Services Committee, Dr. Foster claimed that in a limited war environment,

Technology can make difficult tasks easier. It can provide greater flexibility in the exercise of military power by firepower or mobility. It can help to provide the discrimination or selectivity to permit us to attack and neutralize the identified enemy while leaving the innocent and uncommitted untouched. It can permit our forces to know where the enemy is and what he is doing by day or night. Such measures go far to even the manpower odds which historically have favored the insurgent.[33]

America's brand-new technology, according to Foster's Deputy for Southeast Asian Matters, "has had a very significant, *if not decisive,* effect on the outcome" of "several discrete battles of this war." (Emphasis added.) Nevertheless, Sullivan continued, "we will find no single device that will have the climactic importance that the tank had in World War I or the atom bomb had in World War II."[34] Indeed, there is ample evidence that even within the Pentagon there are those who are skeptical of the potential of technology—by itself—to guarantee an American victory in struggles against a fully developed "people's army" of the kind we face in Vietnam. In a message to Congress dated August 8, 1969, Sullivan acknowledged that as of that date,

We still have many problems without adequate solutions—solutions that will be needed as long as we are in Vietnam. . . . Solutions that should be incorporated into our post-war General Purpose [i.e., non-nuclear] forces as soon as we can perfect them—to reduce the chances of our military being belittled again.

During the current "lull" for instance . . . our casualties (deaths) are very high from enemy mines and boobytraps, and from rockets and mortars (exact figures are classified). We still have no adequate, practical means for deterring either. We still frequently cannot "find the enemy" in the jungles before he finds us. We still cannot adequately monitor and "track" infiltration across the borders from Cambodia and Laos. We frequently expend massive amounts of ordnance to kill a small target because we cannot find it accurately.[35]

What Sullivan seems incapable of understanding, however, is that when an insurgent movement has mobilized the whole population of a country for a full-scale people's war, no combination of brand-new technology (short of nuclear annihilation) will bring stability to the countryside.* We can presume, therefore, that Sullivan's colleagues are still seeking some foolproof device for finding the enemy and tracking his movements.

* Nowhere, perhaps, is this more clearly documented than in the secret Pentagon history of the Vietnam war, first made public by *The New York Times* in 1971. In an evaluation of Operation Rolling Thunder (the air war against North Vietnam), the study concludes that persistent attacks on the enemy's supply routes had no measurable effect on North Vietnam's capacity to deliver supplies to the guerrillas in the South. By 1966, the study notes, Secretary McNamara had become "painfully aware of [the bombing campaign's] inability to pinch off infiltration to the South and had seen no evidence of its ability to break Hanoi's will, demoralize its population or bring it to the negotiation table."

Chapter 6

STRATEGIC MOBILITY AND INTERVENTION
—The Doctrine of Rapid Deployment

When American military advisers were first assigned to South Vietnamese combat units, few people foresaw the long, costly, and inconclusive conflict that was to follow. Although always considered a "limited" war—one in which America's vital strategic interests were not threatened— Vietnam has produced more American casualties than any other foreign war except for World Wars I and II, and has aroused greater public opposition than all previous foreign wars. While U.S. defense policy calls for the maintenance of sufficient forces for participation in several simultaneous limited wars, few contemporary observers would suggest that the Administration could embark upon another Vietnam and remain in office. Whatever the military situation, we are not psychologically, politically, or economically equipped to engage in any more drawn-out interventions of the Vietnam type.

One of the few people who accurately foresaw the consequences of American involvement in Vietnam was Che

Guevara, who left Cuba in 1965 to tour insurgent battle-fields around the world. After several years of self-imposed silence, Che surfaced in 1967 through a message sent to the executive secretariat of the Organization of Solidarity of the Peoples of Africa, Asia, and Latin America. In an analysis of the Vietnam conflict, Che wrote: "The largest of all imperialist powers feels in its own guts the bleeding inflicted by a poor and underdeveloped country; its fabulous economy feels the strain of the war effort." American imperialism "is bogging down in Vietnam," Che observed, and he reasoned that it could be destroyed if the United States were drawn into several Vietnams simultaneously. As a final watchword to fellow revolutionaries around the world, Che, who was soon to die in Bolivia in pursuit of the goals he enunciated here, enjoined them: "Create two, three . . . many Vietnams!"[1]

Secretary McNamara, who was fully cognizant of the threat of many Vietnams, concluded that the way to avoid more Vietnams was to destroy incipient guerrilla organizations at the earliest possible moment, before they had an opportunity to build up strong popular support. If this strategy was to be successful, he argued, it would be necessary for the United States to apply maximum pressure against an insurgent force as soon as it was detected, rather than waiting, as we did in Vietnam, until our client forces were at the point of collapse. On the eve of the 1965 U.S. intervention in the Dominican Republic, McNamara told Congress that since "the first few weeks of a limited war conflict are usually the most critical," it follows that "the ability to concentrate our military power in a matter of days rather than weeks can make an enormous difference in the total force ultimately required, and in some cases could serve to halt aggression before it really gets started."[2]

Traditionally, imperial powers have obtained the necessary forces for rapid deployment against insurgents by maintaining strong garrisons in each colonial territory. The

American public, however, has been loath to support the economic burden of large overseas forces, while in many countries such garrisons have become the focus of anti-American sentiment. In a discussion of possible American responses to the threat of "many Vietnams," McNamara indicated that we have two principal choices: "Either we can station numbers of men and quantities of equipment and supplies overseas near all potential trouble spots, or we can maintain a much smaller force in a central reserve in the United States and deploy it rapidly where needed." Since the maintenance of large overseas forces is both costly and politically detrimental, McNamara argued that of these alternatives, establishing "a mobile 'fire brigade' reserve, centrally located . . . and ready for quick deployment to any threatened area in the world is, basically, a more economical and flexible use of our military forces."[3] Backed by a responsive Congress eager to bring American G.I.'s back from strange lands, McNamara's concept of a mobile fire brigade and his rapid deployment strategy have become principal components of U.S. military policy.

STRATEGIC AIRLIFT— GARRISONS IN ABSENTIA

McNamara's solution to the problem of global defense against revolution clearly presupposed the availability of an adequate fleet of transport planes to carry the "fire brigade" where needed quickly enough to be decisive in a crisis. But when he took office in 1961, the new Secretary of Defense discovered that the United States had less than one-third of the estimated number of planes required for implementation of the rapid deployment strategy. One study concluded that with existing aircraft it would take the Military Air Transport Service twenty-six days to move a full Army division to the Far East—hardly the rapidity envisioned by McNamara.[4] Nevertheless, in order to test the validity of the new strategy and to determine requirements for an expanded air transport capability, the Pentagon went ahead with massive airlift exercises involving thousands of troops and hundreds of planes.

The first major demonstration of the rapid deployment strategy occurred in October 1963, when, as part of Operation Big Lift, the Military Air Transport Service airlifted 16,000 U.S. troops—the entire 2nd Armored Division—from Fort Hood, Texas, to Ramstein, West Germany, in seventy-two hours. Big Lift utilized two hundred aircraft—mostly propeller-driven C-124 Globemasters—working on an around-the-clock basis to complete the exercise. Even though the operation broke all existing records for large-scale troop deployment, it exposed many weaknesses in our airlift capability. To begin with, the 2nd Armored's tanks, trucks, and artillery could not be carried by plane and had in fact been "pre-positioned" in Germany. Furthermore, the C-124's lacked the speed, range, and payload to make such an operation practical in emergencies—one Army official commented that Big Lift was "a jet-age concept geared to the pace of a piston-engine fleet."[5] McNamara accordingly ordered the Pentagon's systems analysts to determine the optimum mix of air transports, fast ships, and other hardware needed to provide the United States with an adequate airlift and sealift capability. At the same time, he invited the aerospace research community to come up with radically new designs for giant transport aircraft.

The Pentagon received the first significant addition to its air transport fleet in October 1964, when the Lockheed Aircraft Corporation delivered the initial batch of C-141 StarLifter aircraft. The C-141 was the first pure jet designed from the start as a military cargo transport. With four Pratt & Whitney TF-33 turbofan engines, the StarLifter can carry 154 troops or 70,000 pounds of cargo a distance of 4,080 miles without refueling. Originally, the Pentagon had planned to acquire some 400 C-141's, but in 1965 Secretary McNamara reduced the planned C-141 fleet to 284 aircraft deployed in 14 squadrons. When the last StarLifter was delivered in February 1968, the Defense Department had spent nearly $2 billion in this first stage of its effort to expand the U.S. airlift capability.[6] Even this sum was soon to be dwarfed when the second stage got underway.

The C-141 StarLifter, while incorporating several technical innovations designed to speed the handling of cargo, did not represent any striking advances in aeronautical design. Although larger and faster than earlier, propeller-driven transports, it could not carry heavy or bulky equipment like tanks and helicopters. On the basis of the Big Lift evaluations, Secretary McNamara determined that the military establishment required an entirely new kind of airplane—a giant transport aircraft that could carry every item of equipment that an Army division needed in the field. Early in 1964, the military research apparatus began work on a new transport, known first as the CX-HLS Heavy Lift System (the "C" stands for cargo, and the "X" for experimental). By mid-1965, the Pentagon was ready to award a contract for development and production of the plane, formally designated the C-5A Galaxy.

The C-5A jet transport is the world's largest and most powerful airplane. Powered by four General Electric TF-39 turbofan engines rated at 41,000 pounds thrust each, the Galaxy can carry a maximum payload of 265,000 pounds—almost four times as much as the C-141. With a full payload, the Galaxy can fly a distance of 2,875 nautical miles without refueling; with 100,000 pounds of cargo it can travel up to 6,325 miles.[7] In order to provide laymen with some sense of the plane's giant size, Senator Barry Goldwater told the Senate on December 16, 1969, that "the C-5A could easily accommodate 67 Cadillacs, or six Greyhound buses, or 1,000 people, or 88 Volkswagens." The C-5A is large enough and powerful enough to carry two of the Army's M60 heavy tanks or a double row of trucks and howitzers. The Galaxy's passenger compartment can ac-

commodate eighty combat troops, while the cargo compartment can be refitted in an emergency to carry another six
hundred. Former Air Force Secretary Eugene Zuckert
estimated that only five C-5A's would have been required
to deliver the same payload carried by a fleet of 142 cargo
planes during the Berlin Airlift of 1948.[8] When (and if) all
the 81 C-5A's now on order join the Military Airlift Command's transport fleet, the United States will possess ten
times the airlift capacity it had in 1961.*

The C-5A has other unique features besides a tremendous cargo capacity. Unlike commercial cargo planes,
the Galaxy does not have to operate out of modern air-
ports with long, hard-surfaced runways but can land on
short and relatively primitive airstrips. Once on the
ground, it can "kneel" down to truck-bay level by partially
retracting its landing gear, thus obviating the need for
elaborate cargo-handling equipment. These features are
"of considerable importance," McNamara said in 1965,
since Pentagon studies demonstrated that "unless troops
and equipment can be routinely delivered well forward

---

* The first operational C-5A was delivered to Charleston Air Force
Base, South Carolina, on June 6, 1970. An additional sixty-four Galaxies were scheduled to be operational by the end of fiscal year
1972, and the remaning fifteen in fiscal 1973. Ultimately, two C-5A
squadrons will be stationed at Travis Air Force Base, California,
and one each at Dover Air Force Base, Delaware, and the Charleston
Air Force Base.

All C-5A's, as well as the C-141 and other long-range transport
aircraft, are under the operational authority of the Military Airlift
Command (MAC), successor to the Military Air Transport Service.
With over three hundrd cargo planes, most of them jets, MAC is
one of the largest air carriers in the world. MAC responsibilities
include aerial delivery of combat forces and their equipment in
emergencies, resupply of already deployed troops, and maintenance
of a logistical "pipeline" for supply of U.S. bases and garrisons
abroad. MAC's mission also includes supervision of the Civil Reserve Air Fleet (CRAF), a backstop force of civilian aircraft which
would be mobilized in an emergency for military logistics functions.

in the theater of operations, many of the advantages of airlift would be lost."[9]

When the first Galaxy rolled off the assembly line on March 2, 1968, President Johnson and various other dignitaries were on hand to mark the event. Not surprisingly, much fanfare was inspired by the plane's enormous size. Many journalists noted, for instance, that at 246 feet the C-5A was some 40 feet longer than the Wright brothers' first plane. But Johnson realized that the C-5A was more than just a big plane—in his brief dedication, the President pointed out that the Galaxy represented an entirely new strategy for intervention. "For the first time," he asserted, "our fighting men will be able to travel with their equipment to any spot on the globe where we might be forced to stand—rapidly and more efficiently than ever."[10]

At the very moment that the President was lauding the new supertransport in Georgia, Air Force officials in Washington were desperately seeking ways to cover up C-5A cost estimates, which showed an overrun of $1 billion over the original target cost of $3.4 billion. The Pentagon managed to keep the exploding C-5A costs secret for another six months, during which time the estimated overrun grew to $2 billion. When the public finally did learn of the mammoth cost increase, the C-5A program became the focus of the most intense Congressional challenge to the military-industrial complex since the onset of the Cold War.[11] Senator William Proxmire, who led the attack on the C-5A contract, told the Senate in 1969: "We are witnessing perhaps the greatest financial fiasco, in terms of the dollar amounts involved, in the history of Air Force procurement."[12]

The C-5A fiasco had its beginning in October 1965, when the Lockheed Aircraft Corporation received the prime contract for airframe production after underbidding its competitors for the job, Douglas Aircraft (now McDonnell-Douglas) and the Boeing Company. The multibillion-dollar contract was awarded to Lockheed despite the finding of an Air Force Source Selection Board that Boeing's proposal was superior in its technical aspects.[13] Lockheed proposed to build 120 of the aircraft for $1.9 billion; the jet engines, supplied by General Electric, and other expenses brought the target cost of the whole program up to $3.4 billion.[14]

By April 1968, when the first C-5A was being readied for its maiden flight, the C-5A Systems Program Office (SPO) in the Pentagon calculated that escalating costs at Lockheed's Marietta, Georgia, plant would produce a cost overrun of $1 billion on the 120-plane program. Worried that public disclosure of its estimate would seriously undermine public confidence in Lockheed stock, the SPO restricted circulation of its finding to a handful of top Air Force officials, who promptly clamped a tight security classification on the data.[15] SPO Director Colonel Kenneth N. Beckman later told a House subcommittee that his civilian superiors—Robert H. Charles, Assistant Secretary of the Air Force for Installations and Logistics, and Robert N. Anthony, former Defense Department Controller—had ordered that the overrun be concealed on the basis that "the nature of the estimates were such that if publicly disclosed might put Lockheed's position in the stock market in jeopardy."[16] Finally, on November 13, 1968, A. E. Fitzgerald, a Deputy Assistant Secretary of the Air Force for Management Systems, testified before a subcommittee of the Joint Economic Committee that Lockheed's production costs on the first C-5A run of fifty-eight aircraft were running at twice the planned rate, bringing the cost of the whole program to an estimated $5.2 billion, or nearly $2 billion more than the target price.[17] (Fitzgerald was subsequently dismissed from his job for making the C-5A data public.)

Originally, the Air Force had planned to acquire 120 Galaxies, but its contract with Lockheed specified that procurement proceed in two stages. Work on the first fifty-eight C-5A's was well under way by January 16, 1969, when the Air Force announced that it had notified Lockheed to begin work on another twenty-three aircraft from the second production run. This decision activated a unique provision of the C-5A contract known officially as the "repricing formula" and unofficially as the "golden handshake." In essence, it enabled the contractor to receive a higher price for the second batch of planes if he sustained significant losses in production of the first batch. Since the contract specified that the higher the losses on the first production run, the greater the price increase on the second, the golden handshake operated as a reverse incentive, encouraging Lockheed to be more wasteful during production of the first C-5A's in order to reap huge profits later.

The Fitzgerald disclosure and subsequent Congressional investigations identified the C-5A program in the public mind as an expensive boondoggle, and provoked increasingly strident demands that the program be terminated. In order to pacify critics of the supertransport, the Air Force announced in November 1969 that it would limit procurement of the C-5A to the eighty-one aircraft already on order.

The cost of the reduced C-5A program was subsequently estimated at $4.6 billion, or $1.2 billion more than the original $3.4 billion target price for 120 aircraft.[18] Since Pentagon liability to Lockheed under the C-5A contract amounts to only some $3.8 billion, the Defense Department has had to work out an emergency financing agreement with the aircraft firm to keep the project alive. In a settlement proposed by Deputy Secretary of Defense David Packard in December 1970, Lockheed agreed to assume a $200-million "fixed loss" on the C-5A with the Pentagon making up the difference.[19]

In addition to financial problems, the C-5A program has experienced serious technical difficulties almost from the moment production began in 1966. Many of these difficulties can be traced to Lockheed's 1965 decision to modify its original airframe design in order to overcome the technical advantage of the competitive Boeing design. Once it received the C-5A contract, Lockheed was obliged to undertake extensive redesign work to accommodate the airframe modifications while remaining within contract specifications. Apparently this work was never satisfactorily completed, for on July 14, 1969, a test version of the C-5A developed a wing crack during static load tests at a point well below the aircraft's specified load. As a result of the wing failure, the Air Force ordered Lockheed to install wing braces on all completed C-5A's and to build additional braces into each wing under construction. Subsequently, a blue-ribbon technical panel headed by Dr. Raymond L. Bisplinghoff of MIT reported that the wing fix proposed by Lockheed was inadequate and that the wing would have to be substantially redesigned. By 1971, these fixes had already added $28 million to the cost of the program.

In April 1971, Senator Proxmire charged that a study conducted by the General Accounting Office (GAO) of the first fifteen C-5A's delivered by Lockheed uncovered an average of 127 deficiencies per aircraft. Defects cited in the GAO report, he specified, included faulty landing gear, braking system, throttle, radar, navigational equipment, and avionics. Proxmire further charged that the Air Force had accepted the planes from Lockheed even though it knew them to be defective. Six months later, in October 1971, the Air Force grounded the entire working fleet of forty-one C-5A's when a jet engine fell off a Galaxy undergoing engine runup prior to takeoff. Subsequent checks uncovered flaws in the engine mounts which had to be repaired before the fleet was taken off grounded status.

The Pentagon's behavior in these events, copiously chronicled in the press over the past few years, reveals a consistent pattern of evasion and subterfuge designed to protect a favored contractor. "It is clear," Proxmire stated in 1970, "that we have been and are dealing with a highly organized and deliberate concealment and evasion of facts by the Pentagon." Evidence of this practice was so overwhelming, he noted, "that the purpose of the Pentagon's evasion and deception is showing through. Clearly, they are putting the immediate financial welfare of a giant, favored contractor ahead of the interests of the hard-pressed taxpayers."[20]

Lockheed probably received the C-5A contract in the first place, according to James G. Phillips of *Congressional Quarterly*, "for the sole reason of keeping the company in business."[21] The lucrative C-5A contract did more than keep Lockheed alive—it propelled the company into first place among the Pentagon's principal contractors, with total payments of $2.04 billion in fiscal 1969 and $1.84 billion in 1970.[22] During the life of the C-5A contract, the Pentagon was virtually Lockheed's only customer, with military projects accounting for nearly 90 percent of the company's sales.[23] As we have seen, when the C-5A program developed technical and financial difficulties, Air Force officials reportedly kept silent in order to protect Lockheed's standing on the stock market. And when the company finally ran out of money with which to complete production of the C-5A, the Pentagon supplied three-quarters of a billion dollars in order to keep the project afloat; by that time, according to *New York Times* correspondent Neil Sheehan, Lockheed's liquidity crisis had grown so acute that rescue of the C-5A had become "synonymous" with salvation of the corporation itself.[24]

In retrospect, it appears that the furor over government spending on the C-5A has had the unfortunate effect of obscuring the military *function* of the plane itself. Opponents of the program, including Senator Proxmire, tended to concentrate on the financial arrangements involved and avoided discussion of strategic issues. Only a handful of proponents of the transport, in fact, understood the significance of the C-5A for long-term U.S. defense strategy. The C-5A is nothing more nor less than a machine for intervention, and this fact was not lost upon the hawks who backed the aircraft in the Senate. Thus George Murphy, in a 1970 speech, explained that the C-5A

was designed to satisfy the requirement rapidly to deploy fully equipped Army troops anywhere in the world, without the need for intermediate servicing stops, or without the need for sophisticated airport facilities when they arrived at their destination. *We can carry an army, fully equipped and ready for operation, with great speed to any place in the world.* . . . The C-5A represents a major step forward in improving our capability for global military deployment in support of our national interests, while reducing our dependence on overseas bases. It insures that Army units being deployed will be accompanied by all their heavy equipment and will arrive in minimum time as a fully effective force, ready to go into operation immediately.[25] (Emphasis added.)

The C-5A is particularly valuable, according to Senator Barry Goldwater, as a means of implementing the Nixon Doctrine strategy of reducing U.S. troop deployments abroad while maintaining an effective intervention capability. It is clear, he observed, that despite withdrawals of some U.S. forces from Asia we will continue to "defend our national interests wherever they may be threatened." In the Nixon era, therefore, "the ability to deploy our general purpose forces rapidly will be even more important in the future than it has been in the past."[26]

Although the entire C-5A complement of four squadrons will not be operational until 1972 or later, the Pentagon has already been testing the new intervention strategy made possible by expanded U.S. airlift capabilities. In January 1969, more than 12,000 Army troops were airlifted from bases in the United States to the Seventh Army training center at Grafenwoehr in central Bavaria, twenty-three miles west of the Czech border. The troops, elements of the 24th Infantry Division that had originally been stationed in West Germany and then later recalled to the

United States as an economy measure, picked up their heavy equipment in Germany before participating in NATO field maneuvers. The airlift exercise, known as REFORGER I (for REdeployment of FORces from GERmany), was intended as a demonstration of America's ability to reinforce its European armies in the event of a Soviet attack.[27]

Because of budgetary limitations, REFORGER I was not designed to test *rapid* deployment techniques: the airlift operation, involving twenty-three C-133 transports and eighty-five C-141 jets, took two weeks to complete and was preceded by months of planning. Army spokesmen emphasized, however, that in an emergency the troops would be airlifted at a much faster rate.[28] In a second test of the new strategy, REFORGER II, 11,000 troops from the 1st Infantry Division were airlifted from the United States to Germany in seven days. As in the first test, the airlifted troops engaged in field exercises with West German forces and other American troops permanently stationed in Germany. REFORGER II, which took place in October 1970, required 144 trips by C-141's and 12 by C-133's; the same job, according to one Pentagon official, could have been performed by about 25 C-5A's.[29]

Even more prophetic than the REFORGER tests, perhaps, were two recent airlift operations in the Far East. In March 1969, some 2,500 soldiers of the crack 82nd Airborne Division were flown 8,500 miles from their regular quarters at Fort Bragg, North Carolina, to a training area in South Korea. (The 82nd Airborne is usually the first unit called upon to perform the role of a "fire brigade" in crisis situations.) Only seventy-two hours after their departure from Fort Bragg, the paratroopers were dropped over a training area some forty miles south of Seoul, where they joined South Korean forces in counterguerrilla exercises. (The trip was originally planned to take only thirty-one hours, but a snowstorm in Korea caused a twenty-five-hour layover in Okinawa.) According to Pentagon officials, the exercise, known as Focus Retina, was designed "to test the rapid reaction capability of the United States-based Strike Command forces to deploy in the Pacific Command ready for tactical employment." For the handful of journalists who covered the exercise, it was obvious that Focus Retina was intended to convince Seoul that the United States will defend the present regime even when most U.S. soldiers are withdrawn from their permanent garrisons in South Korea.[30] This message was repeated two years later, in March 1971, when once again troops from the 82nd Airborne were airlifted to South Korea. The new exercise, dubbed Operation Vault, involved an even larger force than Focus Retina. Like the earlier test, Vault was a "quick-reaction" exercise designed to demonstrate America's ability to move U.S.-based units long distances and have them ready for immediate action.[31]

Sometime in the near future, the Pentagon will conduct its first airlift exercise using the C-5A supertransport. When that day comes, the United States will have realized Robert McNamara's vision of "a mobile 'fire brigade' reserve, centrally located . . . and ready for quick-deployment to any threatened area in the world." The quick-deployment strategy, made possible by new advances in aircraft technology, will enable the United States to abandon many overseas bases while retaining the option of employing its troops whenever it deems intervention necessary.* Although originally a facet of President Kennedy's "Flexible Response" strategy, the fire-brigade concept—best described as garrisons in absentia—has been incorporated in its entirety into the Nixon Doctrine.

---

* One Pentagon official has been quoted as saying that acquisition of the C-5A "will mean that an Army division in Kansas is just as much in the front lines as one in Germany." With eighty operational C-5A's, the Pentagon reportedly can airlift some 15,000 Army troops with nearly all their heavy equipment to Europe in less than forty-eight hours. (Berkeley Rice, *The C-5A Scandal*, Boston, 1971, p. 3.)

STRATEGIC SEALIFT—
FLOATING GARRISONS

The C-5A was never intended to meet America's strategic
mobility needs by itself; as envisioned by McNamara, our
capability for intervention abroad was to be composed of
a combination of airlift and sealift forces. As the seagoing
equivalent of the C-5A, McNamara proposed development
of a floating arsenal that could be rushed to trouble spots to
"marry up" with troops being flown in on jet transports.
Such vessels, to be known as Fast Deployment Logistics
(FDL) ships, would be stationed in strategic waters around
the world. In an emergency, the FDL's would steam up to
the nearest friendly port or, if necessary, unload their cargo
"over the beach" using helicopters and amphibious
lighters.[32]

McNamara originally proposed an FDL fleet of thirty
vessels, each of which would carry 8,000 to 10,000 short
tons of supplies. Representative equipment to be carried
included heavy tanks, armored personnel carriers, and
trucks and artillery as well as "consumables" like ammunition and rations. The approved FDL design called for the
use of CH-54A Flying Crane helicopters to lift light- and
medium-weight cargo directly onto the beach, while heavy
equipment would be carried by LARC-60 amphibious
lighters. Modern cargo-handling equipment, including ship-
board computers, would enable the FDL to unload its
entire cargo in twenty hours. In this manner, a fleet of
only twelve FDL's could bring up enough equipment and
supplies to outfit an entire infantry division in less than a
week. Acquisition of the FDL was crucial, McNamara
argued, because "all of our studies show that the length of
a war, as well as the size of the force ultimately required
to terminate it favorably, are importantly influenced by
how fast we can bring the full weight of our military
power to bear on the situation."[33]

The thirty-ship FDL fleet was originally expected to cost $1.41 billion, or about $47 million per vessel. An initial outlay of $68 million was provided by Congress in the fiscal 1966 budget to begin work on two of the ships, but this money was transferred to Vietnam war accounts before construction could be initiated. The Pentagon requested $178.6 million in fiscal 1968 for five vessels and $183.6 million in 1969 for four, but both requests were turned down by the Congress. In 1970 the Defense Department reduced its planned fleet to fifteen FDL's, and requested $187 million to begin work on the first three—each of which would now cost about $62 million. When Congress refused to vote funds for the FDL in the 1970 budget, the Pentagon abandoned all plans to build the vessel.[34]

The FDL ran into trouble for a number of reasons, each of which was probably enough to kill the controversial project. In the first place, McNamara planned to turn over construction of the vessels to the aerospace industry in an effort to modernize the American shipbuilding industry—and thus incurred the enmity of commercial shipyards (competitors for the FDL contract included the General Dynamics Corporation, Litton Industries, and the ubiquitous Lockheed). Secondly, the FDL's would be kept stationary with their military cargo and therefore could not be used to provide work for the floundering maritime industry.[35] The ship's greatest handicap, however, was its association with the inconclusive war in Vietnam: even ardent advocates of the C-5A viewed the FDL as a symbol of the lingering and unpopular conflict in Southeast Asia. Critics of the vessel, including the late Senator Richard B. Russell, charged that acquisition of the FDL would enhance the President's power to intervene in future crises without consulting Congress. In an extraordinary 1967 address to the Senate, Russell reported that the Senate Armed Services Committee, which he headed with uncompromisingly hawkish vigor, was "concerned about the possible creation of an impression that the United States has

assumed the function of policing the world and that it can
be thought to be at least considering intervention in any
kind of strife or commotion occurring in any of the nations
of the world."[36] Although President Johnson retained the
FDL in his final (1970) budget, the new Administration
evidently decided that the wisest course was to abandon
the whole project and to move ahead with a more attractive intervention vessel, the LHA.

The LHA—General Purpose Amphibious Assault Ship
or Landing Helicopter Assault Ship—is the first Navy
vessel designed specifically for helicopter-assisted amphibious landings. Each LHA will carry a two-thousand-man
Marine landing force with its supplies and heavy equipment, plus scores of troop-carrying helicopters and amphibious vehicles. Like the FDL, the LHA will be stationed
near potential trouble spots so that it can begin landing
troops hours after the outbreak of a revolution. As large as
an *Essex*-class aircraft carrier, the LHA will combine the
functions of four existing vessels: the Amphibious Assault
Ship (LPH), the Amphibious Transport Dock (LPD), the
Amphibious Cargo Ship (LKA), and the Dock Landing Ship
(LSD).[37]

Development of the LHA presupposes the existence of
contingency plans for future "over the beach" amphibious
assaults. While some Defense analysts argue that development of the helicopter and other advances in military
technology obviate the need for amphibious forces, the
Pentagon argues that impending withdrawals of U.S. garrisons abroad render the need for such forces greater than
ever. Thus in a 1969 interview, Marine Corps Commandant General Leonard H. Chapman asserted: "It is
obvious that we must increasingly rely on going back
across the oceans; quite likely to land on a hostile shore
against a determined enemy. And if that time comes there
will be only one way to go ashore and the Marine/Navy
team must execute these operations." With the adoption
or rapid deployment doctrine, he added, "The future holds

not a lessening but a growing requirement for amphibious or Marine type landing forces."[38]

Although General Chapman's comments seem reminiscent of the island battles of World War II, it is clear that in acquiring the LHA the Pentagon has more contemporary contingencies in mind: "The vessel's boosters," reported the Washington *Post* in 1969, "speak enthusiastically of how it could have simplified U.S. operations in Lebanon and the Dominican Republic in recent years, or how it could be used against Cuba."[39] Although the stated mission of the LHA is to deliver troops and associated equipment by aerial and over-the-beach assault, classified Pentagon documents reportedly indicate that "show of force" is a "contingent task."[40] The LHA is, in fact, a floating garrison that will perform all the functions of intimidation and coercion usually associated with an earlier epoch of gunboat diplomacy. Present plans call for the first five LHA's to be stationed in the Caribbean and the Mediterranean, where they will be available for rapid U.S. intervention in any one of a number of foreseeable crisis situations.

When the LHA program was first announced, the Navy planned to build nine of the vessels for a total cost of about $1 billion. Litton Industries was awarded a $153 million contract for construction of the first LHA in 1969 after building a new multimillion-dollar automated shipyard in Pascagoula, Mississippi (the home state of Senator John Stennis, Chairman of the influential Senate Armed Services Committee and an ardent supporter of the LHA program). The first LHA was to have been built for $153 million, and the follow-on ships for an average of $122 million each. By 1970, the cost of the first LHA had jumped to an estimated $185 million and the subsequent ships to about $140 million each.[41] In 1971, with only three of the ships actually under construction, the Navy decided to cut the planned LHA fleet back to five vessels.[42] LHA I is expected to join the active fleet in 1973, and the other four ships in succeeding years.

INSTANT AIRPOWER—
THE BARE BASE CONCEPT

By 1966, with new additions to the airlift and sealift fleets already planned or under construction, the United States was well on its way toward acquisition of the rapid deployment capability envisioned by Secretary McNamara when he assumed office in 1961. All that was lacking from this package, he realized, was a mobile air base comparable to the mobile garrisons represented by new transport aircraft and assault ships. In order to provide the Tactical Air Command (TAC) with the same kind of mobility afforded the Army and Marines by the C-5A and LHA, McNamara introduced the "Bare Base" concept—otherwise known as "the instant air base"—which enables the Air Force to convert an unimproved or abandoned airstrip anywhere in the world into a fully equipped fighter base in a matter of hours. All that is needed for deployment of a fighter squadron abroad is a suitable "Bare Base"—an airstrip with taxiway, parking ramps, and access to a supply of fresh water. Everything else needed to keep the squadron airborne—including runway lights, control tower, power generators, maintenance shops, barracks, kitchens, latrines, and a chapel—can be shipped from the United States in transport aircraft.[43]

Development of the instant air base began in 1966 with the award of a research contract to the Boeing Company for work on an "advanced Bare Base support study."[44] As drawn up by Boeing, the Bare Base system will comprise a set of air-transportable containers that will open up to become shelters and aircraft hangars upon delivery to the base site. The container-shelters, made of lightweight metals and plastics, would come equipped with all the tools and mechanical systems associated with the function to be performed by the shelter. When the United States decides to intervene in a future crisis, the air base kit will be loaded onto C-130 and C-141 transport aircraft and flown to a suitable airstrip in secure territory. (The Air Force reportedly has a catalogue of some fourteen hundred airstrips around the world that can be used with the Bare Base system.) Seventy-two hours after the first construction crew arrives at the chosen location, F-4 fighter-bombers will be flown in and combat operations undertaken. When the crisis is over, the equipment will be demounted and flown back to a storehouse in the United States, where it will be ready for use in the next intervention. "With fast reacting tactical air power," TAC commander General William W. Momyer commented in 1970, "forces and facilities can be immediately deployed to critical areas for the time needed, then recalled." As an integral element of the Pentagon's rapid deployment strategy, the Bare Base system "will not only reduce constant dispersal costs but . . . will allow a larger portion of our tactical air units to be based in the continental United States."[45]

In March 1969, the Pentagon approved spending $8.5 million to provide one TAC fighter squadron, the 336th, with a complete set of "instant airbase" supplies. The full kit, when finally assembled, included the following items of equipment:

—Sixty-six expandable container-shelters constructed on an aluminum frame with polyurethane-filled aluminum siding. All shop equipment and supplies are shipped inside the units when they are in their shipping configuration. Once erected in the field, the shelters serve as maintenance shops, communications center, administrative offices, chapel, etc.
—Three aircraft hangars, 58 feet wide by 80 feet long, which can be set up in 160 man-hours. Two of these hangars (each of which can house two F-4 fighters when erected) can be carried in a single C-130 Hercules transport.

—Twenty-four personnel shelters 13 feet wide, 33 feet long, and 8 feet high. These shelters will house 11 men under normal conditions and up to 20 men in an emergency. The shelter comes in a compact package that opens up accordion-style to enclose an area eleven times greater than the shipping container.

—Four kitchens, each of which can prepare 250 meals an hour. Since all wiring, lighting, and other operating systems are preinstalled, the kitchen shelter can be erected and put in operation by a four-man crew within two hours of delivery.

—One AN/TSW-7 Transportable Control Tower with a complete set of UHF and VHF radio transmitters and receivers.

—One set of portable airfield-lighting devices, including approach, runway, and taxiway lights as well as glide-angle indicator and beacon. The runway lights unfold to illuminate an airstrip up to 9,000 feet long.

—Ten portable latrine facilities, each completely equipped with lavatories, showers, and toilets for 125 men.[46]

In a review of the instant air base concept, *Ordnance* magazine presented this scenario for deployment of the Bare Base kit in future emergencies:

Plans to erect an instant air base call for the first wave of transport aircraft to carry in heavy construction equipment, earthmovers, and engineers. Preceding their arrival, a site-development team will have arrived to lay out the base as close to the general plan as terrain actually permits.

The site-development team . . . will lay out locations for runways, roads, barracks, offices, power and water plants, munitions depots, and maintenance facilities.

Coded flags and markers are used to lay out these areas. These will be matched with precoded labels on the equipment in the air-transportable package.

When the site-development team completes its task, the

heavy construction engineering team moves in to smooth out terrain as needed and to cut facility access roads. As the instant air base equipment arrives, this team unloads the aircraft and takes the equipment, bit by bit, to its designated area.

At these areas, light construction engineering teams pull open, unfold, and erect the buildings. In less than 8 hours, the deployed tactical fighter unit will be conducting operations from the new base.[47]

If the airstrip surface is unsatisfactory, according to *Ordnance,* a membrane of neoprene-coated nylon can be applied to the runway in just a few hours.

The prototype Bare Base kit was first tested in October 1969 by the 336th Tactical Fighter Squadron from Seymour Johnson Air Force Base, North Carolina. The test, known as Coronet Bare, utilized the unimproved airstrip at North Field, South Carolina. Over 350 sorties (single flights) by C-130 aircraft were required to ship the test equipment to North Field, but Air Force engineers had the base in operation some seventy-two hours after initiation of the exercise.[48] Apparently the Pentagon was satisfied with the outcome of Coronet Bare, for in 1970 the decision was made to equip three more Tactical Air Command squadrons—one each from MacDill Air Force Base, Florida, Myrtle Air Force Base, South Carolina, and George Air Force Base, California—with a Bare Base capability. Completion of this program, known as Harvest Bare, is expected to cost $20 million by 1973.[49]

Acquisition of the instant air-base system will enable the Pentagon to provide its mobile fire brigade with the tactical airpower considered essential for control of the battlefield. In future interventions, troops flown in on the C-5A transport or delivered over the beach by the LHA floating garrison will find a tactical fighter base already under construction in the combat zone. Thus even if outnumbered by domestic insurgents, the expeditionary forces will be able to count on the support of bomb- and napalm-laden tactical fighters. The only opposition to the instant air-base program has come from the Navy, whose senior officers reportedly view the Bare Base system as a threat to the continued importance and prestige of the aircraft carrier.

Although entirely the creation of Robert S. McNamara, the fire brigade concept has been incorporated in its entirety into the defense strategy of the Nixon Administration. As the President has made clear, the planned withdrawals of U.S. troops from the Far East do not presage any lessening of our determination to control the destiny of that part of the world. While the nuclear-armed ICBM has become the deterrent to nuclear attack on the United States, the rapid deployment capability represented by the C-5A, LHA, and instant air base has become the deterrent to guerrilla attack on any of our dependencies. The Nixon Doctrine response to the threat of many Vietnams is thus identical to that of McNamara. In the following summary of current Pentagon doctrine, provided by Air Force Deputy Chief of Staff Lieutenant General George S. Boylan, the influence of McNamara is unmistakable:

The basic concept underlying strategic deployment consideration since 1965 has been based on a minimal overseas military presence coupled with the demonstrated ability to move appropriate ground and air forces rapidly to actual or potential contingency areas. The strategy is based on the premise that the capability for rapid deployment of combat forces is part of our deterrent posture and can provide an effective response to aggression and that *an early response in strength can minimize the intensity of conflict.*[50] (Emphasis added.)

Chapter 7

"THE ELECTRONIC BATTLEFIELD"
—Counterguerrilla Surveillance and Detection

A guerrilla attacks small enemy units when it is to his advantage but seeks to avoid engagements when threatened by superior enemy forces. This type of warfare is generally most effective in tropical, mountainous, or wilderness regions where conventional military forces and mechanized equipment cannot operate effectively. In order to compensate for his inferiority in manpower and firepower, the guerrilla must learn to take maximum advantage of his natural surroundings, to achieve surprise when attacking, and to find sanctuary when in retreat.

For counterguerrilla forces, on the other hand, nature is an enemy that must be overcome before the insurgent movement itself can be extinguished. Forward camps must be secured against surprise attacks, patrols must be protected from ambush, and methods must be devised to locate the guerrilla's hidden sanctuaries. The United States, seeking to find technological solutions to this challenge, has created the science of remote sensing and its component technologies of counterguerrilla surveillance and counterinfiltration. Since the outbreak of the Vietnam war, the design of mechanical systems (or "sensors") for the detection and surveillance of guerrilla forces has become a major objective of counterinsurgency planning in the United States.

In a 1969 address to the Association of the United States Army, former Vietnam Commander General William C. Westmoreland spoke of the urgency with which Pentagon scientists had searched for new detection devices: "The enemy we face in Vietnam is naturally elusive and cunning in his use of the dense jungle for concealment." American troops, on the other hand, had an abundance of firepower and mobility, but were often unable to locate the enemy; the United States had become, he recalled, "a giant without eyes." In order to overcome our blindness in Vietnam, "since 1965 a principal thrust of our experimentation, adaptation, and development in tactics, techniques, and technology has been toward improvement in our capability to find the enemy."[1]

In order to speed the development of guerrilla detection systems, in 1966 Secretary McNamara created a high-level Pentagon agency, the Defense Communications Planning Group (DCPG), to coordinate all research in this field.[2] According to the current (1971) Director of the Defense Communications Planning Group, Army General John R. Deane, Jr., "DCPG has been given unique and unprecedented management tools in terms of authority, organizational arrangements and resources." In testimony to a special subcommittee of the Senate Armed Services Committee, Deane described these "tools" as follows:

The Director, DCPG, reports directly to the Secretary of Defense, and has direct access to the Secretary for broad policy and funding decisions. . . .

The Director, DCPG, has decision authority and responsibility, within broad DoD guidance, over all aspects of system implementation: concept formulation, design, development, test, requirements analysis, procurement, and distribution. Another way of saying this is that DCPG cognizance over systems and equipment extends "from the cradle to the grave. . . ."

DCPG is authorized use of the highest industrial priority to expedite its development and procurement efforts. This speeds up our work by putting us at the head of the line for materials, facilities, and contracting.[3]

This authority is backed by abundant Pentagon funding. All DCPG projects benefit, according to Deane, from "the streamlined, expedited manner in which DCPG's financial requirements are handled by the Department of Defense."[4]

Since 1966, DCPG has spent a total of $1.68 billion on research, procurement, and emplacement of electronic sensors and antipersonnel munitions.* Of this amount, about

Table 4

**DEFENSE COMMUNICATIONS
PLANNING GROUP EXPENDITURES**

(By fiscal year; dollars in millions)

Budget category	1967	1968	1969	1970	1971	Five-year Total
Research & Development	51.6	88.8	66.5	41.2	45.0	293.1
Procurement	250.2	300.2	301.6	117.3	203.7	1,173.0
Operations, Maintenance, and Construction	28.2	35.0	43.6	54.5	53.2	214.5
Total	330.0	424.0	411.7	213.0	301.9	1,680.6

Source: U.S. Senate Armed Services Committee, Electronic Battlefield Subcommittee, *Investigation Into Electronic Battlefield Program, Hearings,* 91st Congress, 2d Session, 1971, p. 17.

* In March 1971, DCPG was renamed the Defense Special Projects Group and given broader responsibilities for coordination of multiservice research projects. In January, DCPG had already lost direct control over the air-monitored sensor system in Laos (Operation Igloo White) to the Air Force.

a third ($538 million) was used for the purchase of mines
and explosives used in conjunction with counterinfiltration
programs in Southeast Asia.[5] The breakdown of DCPG
spending in Table 4 was presented to a Senate subcommittee in 1970 by General Deane. These figures do not represent total Pentagon spending on surveillance equipment;
each of the services has its own programs of sensor research, not all of whose activities are monitored by the
DCPG. Using various industry sources, Senator William
Proxmire estimated in 1970 that more than $2 billion had
been spent on sensors and related equipment during fiscal
years 1967–71.[6]

DCPG does not conduct research on its own but allo-
cates funds to each of the services and to other Defense
agencies for this purpose. Sensor research is a major task
of Project Agile, the counterinsurgency research program
of the Advanced Research Projects Agency (see Chapter 8).
During hearings on the Pentagon budget for fiscal year
1968, Dr. Charles M. Herzfeld, then Director of ARPA,
testified:

The ARPA reconnaissance systems and detector programs are
now concentrated on the problem of detecting and locating
insurgent forces, and their basing and logistic systems. The
guerrilla techniques characteristic of insurgent operations require a complementary mix of ground-based and airborne
equipment which will allow our forces to find and fix small
groups of personnel at night and in the jungle environment
typical of Southeast Asia.[7]

Dr. Herzfeld reported that the detection systems under
investigation were based on seismic, magnetic, acoustic,
thermal, optical, and olfactory phenomena. All these systems are designed to detect the "signature" of hostile
ground forces by registering their motion, the metal they
carry, the sounds they make, or the heat or odors given off
by their bodies.

"A sensor-aided combat surveillance system," General

Deane told a Senate subcommittee, "consists basically of the following common components: detection devices, called sensors, which pick up the movement of vehicles or troops; a communications link (usually radio) from the sensor to a 'readout' device; the 'readout' device, which receives sensor transmissions and shows when each sensor is picking up a target; and display and processing equipment to assist in counting the targets and in determining their direction and rate of movement."[8] This chapter will consider two families of sensor systems: first, airborne units used by "hunter-killer" teams to search for dispersed guerrilla units over large areas; and second, fixed units spread in a regular pattern around an encampment or along a border to warn of approaching enemy troops.

HUNTER-KILLERS

One of the biggest problems faced by U.S. forces in South Vietnam is the task of locating enemy strongholds or troop concentrations in the tropical jungle. "Too often battles were not fought," General Westmoreland reported, "because the enemy could not be found or because, after initial contact, he had slipped elusively into the jungle."[9] In order to deny guerrillas their sanctuary in the dense jungle, the Advanced Research Projects Agency initiated a multimillion-dollar research program on airborne surveillance systems that could penetrate the jungle canopy to locate guerrilla units.

Airborne personnel detectors are normally utilized by "hunter-killer" teams consisting of low-flying helicopters or spotter aircraft accompanied by helicopter gunships or regular bombers. The Associated Press in 1970 described how such tactics were being used in the defense of Saigon:

A light, bubble-top observation helicopter is to fly at treetop level seeking out North Vietnamese and Vietcong positions and supply stockpiles. A Cobra [AH-1 helicopter] gunship armed with rockets and machine guns is to fly above the observation aircraft. Should the observation helicopter draw fire or spot an enemy concentration, Cobra gunships are to be called in to attack.[10]

The observation aircraft used in this kind of operation usually carry one of the two operational detection systems—olfactronic and infrared—that have been developed for this purpose. The history of these systems is discussed below.

Olfactronic Detectors

The science of olfactronics (the mechanical analysis of odor) was originally developed as an adjunct to the food-processing industry: since marketers want the canned and packaged foods they sell to have a pleasant smell when opened, it was necessary for the industry to design mechanical aids for the analysis and classification of odors. One of the institutions that has specialized in this kind of research is the Illinois Institute of Technology Research Institute (IITRI) of Chicago, an outgrowth of the Institute of Technology founded by meat-packer Philip Danforth Armour in 1892. In order to support its research on "the chemistry and processing of food ingredients and natural foodstuffs," the Institute has established an Olfactronics and Odor Sciences Center "to focus IITRI capabilities in the field of odor classification, characterization, control, modification and measurement." Under Pentagon sponsorship, these "capabilities" have been applied to the search for counterguerrilla detection systems: instruments developed to classify the odors of foodstuffs have been used to identify the odors produced by the human body—through respiration, perspiration, excretion, etc.—and to serve as models for devices that could detect such "chemical signatures" from the air.

In 1964, IITRI received an Army contract for research on "Detection and Identification of Chemical Signatures." This project was described in Pentagon documents as an investigation of "human airborne chemical signatures." The study, conducted by Boguslaw K. Krotoszynski and Andrew Dravnieks, was also designed to distinguish the "signatures" of blacks, whites, and Indians.[11] Dravnieks later collaborated with scientists from the Battelle Memorial Institute of Columbus, Ohio, in the preparation of a *State-of-the-Art Study on Chemical and Biological Detection of Humans by Sensing Natural Exudates.* According to Battelle, this report discussed "the detection of humans by acquisition and sensing of natural human exudates and effluvia, either vaporous or particulate."[12] (The Pentagon can go to great lengths to avoid mentioning bodily functions by their common names!)

In 1966, the Army Limited War Laboratory (LWL) commissioned Booz-Allen Applied Research, Inc., of Chicago to design an operational olfactronic detector utilizing the technology developed at IITRI and Battelle. Booz-Allen came up with a device known as the E-63 Manpack Personnel Detector, which originally was designed to be slung over the shoulders of an infantryman.[13] Since, however, a backpack detector would have to be carried into shooting distance of a guerrilla hideout before it would detect anything, LWL converted the E-63 to helicopter installation. The Army then awarded the General Electric Company a contract to manufacture the device, now designated the XM-2 Concealed Personnel Detector Aircraft-Mounted—universally known in Vietnam as the "people-sniffer."[14]

Asked to describe the people-sniffer, one American officer responded that it "looks like a Hoover vacuum cleaner" and "functions in much the same manner but it is, of course, painted Army green." The device is mounted in a helicopter with its intake tube attached to one of the external runners. (A more advanced version, the XM-3, is integrally mounted in the helicopter chassis.) Like a vacuum cleaner scooping up dust, the detector sucks in air as the helicopter flies over guerrilla-infested areas, and measures the percentage of ammonia present to determine if human beings are nearby.[15] (Ammonia is one of the elements naturally emitted by the human body.) Some detectors are also calibrated to measure the quantity of condensation nuclei present (these are minute particles, usually of carbon, given off by cooking fires and internal-combustion engines).

Flying in a sniffer helicopter is a dangerous mission, since to be effective the helicopter must fly "contour" just above the ground or at treetop level. Often the helicopters are shot at before the detector has time to register the presence of humans. For this reason, the hunter helicopters are always accompanied by killer gunships to provide covering fire. When the sniffer indicates the presence of people, the hunter aircraft often ascends to a thousand feet and drops a tear-gas container that scatters 264 small canisters over an area the size of a football field. "If there are some enemy troops down there," one officer explained, "then most of the time the gas will cause them to move around a little. We always have a second copter in right behind the sniffer helicopter to pick up signs of movement. If movement is reported we seal off the area quickly."[16]

The people-sniffer has a number of limitations: it cannot, for instance, distinguish between ammonia emitted by men and women, or by humans and water buffaloes. It also cannot tell whether one person or five hundred are hiding, and whether they are civilians or guerrillas. In Vietnam, the United States has discovered that the sniffer is not effective in heavily wooded areas where the operator cannot verify high meter readings with a visual check. Since the people-sniffer cannot tell the difference between soldiers and civilians, it is more than likely that the device has caused the death of many noncombatants, including women and children. A detector that could prevent such mistakes "would be welcome," an Associated Press correspondent commented in 1967, "but that is not the way the war is fought today." War Zone C (along the Cambodia border) and other large areas of South Vietnam, he added, "have been designated 'free bombing zones.' Anything that moves there is regarded fair game. Previous high readings on the 'people-sniffer' have brought B-52 raids from Guam into the area."[17]

One soldier has commented, "When the Army comes up with a model that will tell us the difference between the goodies and the baddies, then the 'people-sniffer' will win the war for us."[18] Since there is no scientific evidence that progovernment Vietnamese ("goodies") smell different from Vietcong guerrillas ("baddies"), it is unlikely that such a device will ever be developed .

Infrared Detectors

In its search for operational counterguerrilla surveillance systems, the Pentagon has systematically investigated the potential application of space-age technologies to counterinsurgency. One of the conspicuous payoffs of this approach is the development of infrared detection systems. The Defense Department was originally interested in infrared sensors for use in antimissile defense: missile reentry vehicles, upon entering the earth's atmosphere, produce a great deal of heat from air friction and can therefore be tracked by heat-sensitive infrared detectors. Using the same reasoning, Pentagon scientists determined that infrared sensors could detect unusual sources of heat on the ground—including campfires, vehicles, and even man himself. The Army's former Chief of Research and Development, General Austin W. Betts, told a Congressional committee in 1970 that "the sensors being developed for far-infrared sensing can discriminate between targets *having less than one degree temperature difference with their background.*"[19] (Emphasis added.) Since "all warm bodies radiate far-infrared energy," it is possible to develop sensors that can distinguish between a living human body and the cooler ground environment around it. Since such sensors are sensitive to thermal radiation rather than visible light, they can be used at night and on cloudy days without any loss of precision.[20]

When the Pentagon recognized the potential utility of infrared sensors in counterguerrilla operations, it naturally turned to the country's leading performer of infrared surveillance research, the University of Michigan's Institute of Science and Technology, to come up with an operational detection system. A major portion of Project Michigan, the Institute's continuing contract with the Department of Defense, is concerned with infrared detection of missile reentry vehicles.[21] Michigan has also studied the application of infrared surveillance techniques to ground warfare: as early as 1962, Michigan published a secret report on *Infrared Combat Surveillance and Target Acquisition Equipment for Use in Expeditionary Operations of the Marine Landing Forces* as part of "Subproject 2" of Project Michigan.[22]

In 1964 the University of Michigan and the Cornell Aeronautical Laboratory received a joint $2 million to $3 million contract from the Advanced Research Projects Agency to study the application of infrared reconnaissance technology to counterguerrilla surveillance in Southeast Asia. Officially known as Project AMPIRT (ARPA Multiband Photographic and Infrared Reconnaissance Test), this effort brought several teams of university scientists to Thailand for simulated counterinsurgency operations. According to Pentagon documents, the objective of Project AMPIRT was "to study the use of multiband aerial photographic and full spectrum infrared sensors in detecting target clues in a counterinsurgency environment."[23] Under this project, four field trips were made to Thailand to test the equipment and techniques that had been developed in

the United States under realistic battlefield conditions.*
During the first trip, which took place in January, February, and March 1965,

Airborne infrared imagery and associated ground data were
obtained for various sites, including a canal, a rubber plantation,
a forest, a river bank mangrove, limestone caves, and an area
near the Malaysian border. All but the cave site contained
concentrations of targets simulating actual and potential activities. *These targets included both military and civilian personnel*
and such manmade indicators as excavations, structures, and
cooking fires.[24] (Emphasis added.)

The second and third AMPIRT field trips, held in the
summer and fall of 1965, were intended to determine the
effect of seasonal conditions on airborne surveillance of
"insurgency-type targets";[25] a final trip, held in November
1965, was somewhat less experimental: it involved "an
infrared and photographic search for Communist-terrorist
camps in Southern Thailand."[26]

---

* As part of Project AMPIRT, Michigan scientists explored the use
of commercial infrared photographic equipment in counterguerrilla
surveillance operations. The Bendix Corporation of Ann Arbor (con-
veniently located near the Michigan campus) sells high-quality
infrared cameras to companies that engage in aerial survey work,
such as the Aero Services Division of Litton Industries. (Customers
for these services normally include mineral and oil companies, as
well as government agencies, seeking precise information on the
ecological and geological characteristics of wilderness areas.) Homer
Jensen, a physicist at Litton, describes the operation of their airborne Bendix infrared camera as follows:

> A mirror mounted at an angle on the aircraft's bottom reflects
> infrared rays from the ground into a horizontally-mounted tele-
> scope. These infrared rays, which measure the ground surface
> temperature and thus the composition of the terrain below, are
> then reflected into a heat sensitive cell, or sensor, which pro-
> duces an electrical output. This electrical output is then sent
> through a glow lamp and finally is converted to an image on
> photographic film. (Quoted in *The New York Times*, April 14,
> 1968.)

By 1966, the Department of Defense decided that Michigan's experience in infrared surveillance technology was sufficiently advanced to permit the transition from theory to practice. Under Project Agile, Michigan was given a million-dollar contract to develop a "Joint Thailand-U.S. Aerial Reconnaissance Laboratory" for use in counter-guerrilla surveillance missions. Using knowledge gained through Project AMPIRT, a team of Michigan scientists headed by Joseph Morgan outfitted a Thai C-47 airplane for aerial reconnaissance work. At the same time, some thirty officers of the Royal Thai military were given training in surveillance techniques at Michigan's Ann Arbor campus and at the Thai-U.S. Military Research and Development Center in Bangkok.[27] According to George Zissis, head of Michigan's Infrared Physics Lab, the aerial laboratory has "aided the Thais in pinpointing and determining the extent of Communist cells in northern Thailand." Clearly, the flying "laboratory" engaged in what can properly be termed *applied* research: for when its infrared sensors spot a suspicious campfire, Royal Thai soldiers are immediately rushed in to fight the guerrillas. Zissis claims that the project has already demonstrated its value: "Generally the Thais are doing a darn good job. We feel proud of our students."[28]

Utilizing the results of Michigan's work on infrared sensing in 1965, Texas Instruments, Inc., of Dallas, developed an experimental surveillance system, the AN/AAS-10 Infrared Detection Set. Early in 1966 the company was commissioned by the Pentagon to test the new device in areas of the United States that approximated the climate and topography of South Vietnam. During February and March of that year, TI conducted a "Remote Sensing Survey of Areas in Central Coastal Louisiana." According to Pentagon reports, airborne tests of the AAS-10 over "simulated Vietnamese villages and targets in a wooded semi-tropical environment" produced "imagery of high quality and great detail."[29] With experience gained from the AAS-

10 tests, TI began work on a more advanced system, the AN/AAS-24 Infrared Surveillance System. The Army awarded TI $7.1 million for work on the advanced device in early 1968, and several subsequent awards in the millions, for production of some fifty sets for the OV-1D Mohawk observation aircraft.[30] The AAS-24 is a highly sophisticated surveillance system that displays terrain images on a cockpit TV screen so that targets can be identified by the pilot while still in flight.

A similar detection system, the AN/AAS-14 Airborne Infrared Reconnaissance Sensor, is manufactured by HRB-Singer, Inc., of State College, Pennsylvania. Some two hundred units of the AAS-14 will be produced at an estimated $12 million for mounting in the OV-1C aircraft.[31]

Such "real time" (immediate-usage) infrared detectors will also be installed in attack helicopters now under development. Under the Army's Southeast Asia Multiple Sensor Armament System Helicopter (SMASH) program, the Aerojet-General division of the General Tire and Rubber Company has produced some ten test models of the AN/AAQ-5 Forward-Looking Infrared (FLIR) Control System at an estimated cost of $12 million.[32]

Airborne infrared reconnaissance systems are widely used by American forces in Southeast Asia, and have been adopted by other governments for counterguerrilla operations elsewhere. One of the most dramatic instances of the use of infrared sensors in counterinsurgency operations occurred in Bolivia during the hunt for Che Guevara. Early in 1967, the U.S. intelligence services began to receive reports of a fresh outbreak of guerrilla activity in southern Bolivia that did not bear the "trademark" of known Bolivian insurgents. Ultimately convinced that Guevara had finally surfaced after several years of wandering, the CIA assembled a special team of counterinsurgency experts to supervise the Bolivian Army's offensive against the new guerrilla organization.[33] This team included a group of sixteen men from the 8th U.S. Special Forces who left Fort Gulick in the Panama Canal Zone on April 29, 1967, to provide on-the-spot training in counterguerrilla operations to a handpicked group of Bolivian Rangers (see Chapter 10 for more on the 8th Special Forces). The Green Beret unit, headed by Major Ralph W. "Pappy" Shelton, was aided by a team of experts in communications, intelligence, and reconnaissance work, who undertook the job of locating Che's group in the Bolivian *selva* (jungle).[34] Although the Special Forces' training activities are openly acknowledged by the Pentagon, these intelligence activities have for the most part been kept secret; it is only through careful research that the outline of this story can be pieced together...

Sometime in 1966, Mark Hurd Aerial Surveys, Inc., of Minneapolis, Minnesota, and Goleta, California (near the Van Nuys Airport), received a contract from the U.S. Agency for International Development to "provide aerial photographs of approximately 23,500 square miles of Southern Bolivia."[35] The contract, worth $100,000, was not confirmed until the following year, when the campaign against Che was at its peak. Dean Hansen, a vice-president of the company, later reported that the survey was conducted from June to November of 1967, and that it encompassed the Rio Grande Valley area of south-central Bolivia. The company's aircraft—World War II P-38 and AT-11 planes that had been modified for survey work—operated from an airfield near the city of Cochabamba, on the edge of the guerrilla zone, while the project was in progress.[36]

It is now known that the Mark Hurd survey operation included infrared reconnaissance work. In a 1968 telephone interview, Hansen acknowledged that his firm used infrared cameras in their survey work, and that the exposed film was turned over to U.S. officers for processing and further use. Aerial photographs produced in this manner could be used to locate the guerrillas' campsites and to plot their movements. Armed with this kind of information, the Green Berets were able to position their Bolivian counterparts on the flanks of Che's line of march. On October 8, 1967, Ranger Company A encountered a guerrilla force in a wooded ravine near the Rio Grande River. Although outnumbered and outgunned, the guerrillas put up fierce resistance until overwhelmed; when the Rangers finally collected their prisoners, they found that they had captured Che Guevara himself—the world's most famous guerrilla. Worried that if allowed to live, Che would become a rallying point for dissident peasants and miners, the Bolivian high command ordered his assassination twenty-four hours later.[37]

COUNTERINFILTRATION: FROM "THE ELECTRONIC FENCE" TO "THE ELECTRONIC BATTLEFIELD"

By far the greatest emphasis of the sensor program, especially in the last five years, has been placed on the development of intrusion alarms and other border-security devices that can be used to track enemy movements across a given defense perimeter. Research on the use of sensors for the detection of intruders was initially undertaken in Vietnam as part of the Strategic Hamlet Program—President Ngo Dinh Diem's abortive attempt to relocate Vietnamese peasants in isolated compounds under military surveillance. Since this program was designed to restrict contact between the guerrillas and the population and to prevent peasants from becoming guerrillas at night, a considerable effort was made to develop intrusion-detection systems that could alert government troops to unauthorized movement into or out of the hamlets. In 1962 the Institute for Defense Analyses received a contract from the Advanced Research Projects Agency for work on a "Village Protection Systems Study." This effort, known as Project Vigil, was designed to develop simple intrusion alarms that could be used in the hamlet program.[38]

The original Strategic Hamlet Program collapsed long before IDA's system could be put to use; with the arrival in Vietnam of U.S. combat troops, however, such systems were needed to protect the many outposts and bases established in the countryside—all vulnerable to surprise enemy assaults at night. In order to offer our troops some assurance that they would be forewarned of guerrilla attacks, ARPA stepped up its support of research on intrusion detectors in the United States and at Project Agile laboratories in Vietnam and Thailand. As the ground war intensified, this program was also geared to the development of counterinfiltration systems that could be used to curtail the movement of men and supplies from North Vietnam to the South, and from the guerrillas' rear areas to their units in the field. When the air war against the North was suspended in 1968, the American bombing effort was shifted to enemy supply routes in southern Laos and air-dropped intrusion detectors became the main source of data on vehicle traffic along the Ho Chi Minh Trail.

The ARPA counterinfiltration research program began in the spring of 1964, when several universities and aerospace companies received substantial contract awards for work on related aspects of the study. The principal contractors on this project included the Stanford Research Institute (SRI), the Atlantic Research Corporation, the University of Michigan's Institute of Science and Technology, and MIT's Lincoln Laboratory, each of which has enjoyed a long association with ARPA as performers of military research. The SRI project, known as Project SEASURE (SouthEast Asia SUrveillance REsearch), was concerned with seismic and magnetic detection systems. Atlantic Research and Michigan worked jointly on a program of "Acoustic and Seismic Research," while MIT studied moving-target indicator radars. These four technologies—

acoustic, seismic, magnetic, and electromagnetic—form the basis of all counterinfiltration systems now in use.*

The ARPA programs were well underway by mid-1966 when the Jason Division of the Institute for Defense Analyses held a secret summer convocation to study the strategic implications of sensor development. Jason is an elite group of university scientists who meet weekends and summers to work on advanced projects for the Department of Defense (see Chapter 3). According to the secret Pentagon history of the Vietnam war, in March 1966 Professors George R. Kistiakowsky of Harvard and Jerrold R. Zacharias of MIT suggested to Secretary McNamara that they convene a group of academic scientists under Jason auspices to review the air war against North Vietnam and to investigate possible alternatives to the bombing strategy. McNamara, who at that time was under heavy pressure from the Joint Chiefs of Staff to authorize another escalation of the air war and to speed the development of U.S. ground troops in South Vietnam, heartily endorsed the convocation plan and asked Zacharias to make the necessary arrangements.[39] In a memorandum to Assistant Secre-

---

* A fifth system that was tested by the Pentagon and ultimately rejected utilized bedbugs and other "man-seeking arthropods" to warn of approaching humans. Under Project Bedbug, the Army's Limited War Laboratory experimented with such techniques in the mid-1960's. William Beecher of *The New York Times,* who visited the LWL in 1968, provided this description of the proposed system: since bedbugs "let out a yowl of excitement when they sense the presence of food, specifically including human flesh, the lab created a bedbug carrier fitted with a sound amplification device. . . . When a bug-bearing patrol approaches an enemy ambush, the members of the patrol would be forewarned by the happy cries of the animals upon sensing a meal up ahead." ("Way Out Weapons," *The New York Times Magazine,* March 24, 1968). Project Bedbug was abandoned when it was found that the insects became excited when they were moved around in the carrier and thus were too busy to notify their patrons of an approaching ambush.

tary of Defense John T. McNaughton, who was appointed to supervise the meeting, McNamara specifically instructed the scientists to look into the feasibility of "a fence across the infiltration trails, warning systems, reconnaissance (especially night) methods, night vision devices, defoliation techniques and area-denial weapons."[40] (According to the Pentagon Papers, McNamara got the idea for an anti-infiltration barrier from Professor Roger Fisher of the Harvard Law School, who on January 3, 1966, submitted a proposal for such a scheme.[41])

The Jason meetings, held in Wellesley, Massachusetts, during June, July, and August of 1966, were attended by forty-seven scientists representing "the cream of the scholarly community in technical fields." The scientists' report, "Effects of U.S. Bombing on North Vietnam's Ability to Support Military Operations in South Vietnam," was sent to McNamara on August 29, 1966, and reportedly had "a powerful and perhaps decisive influence" on his thinking.[42] The Jason study was subsequently incorporated into the Pentagon history and later made public by *The New York Times* on July 2, 1971. According to the published text of the report, the Jason scientists concluded: "As of July 1966 the U.S. bombing of North Vietnam had had no measurable direct effect on Hanoi's ability to mount and support military operations in the South at the current level." They argued, moreover, that since North Vietnam was basically an agricultural country with little industry and a primitive but flexible transportation system, and since most of its war supplies came from abroad, no conceivable intensification of the bombing campaign could be expected to reduce Hanoi's ability to continue its logistical support of the guerrillas in the South.* As an alternative to

---

* Because of the strong impact this study apparently had on McNamara's thinking and the strong language employed, it is worth including its major finding. The Jason scientists noted that an escalation of the air war, including attacks on Haiphong harbor, might make it more difficult for Hanoi to move supplies through

the air war, the scientists recommended construction of a barrier across the southern edge of the Demilitarized Zone (DMZ) in South Vietnam and stretching across the Laotian panhandle to a point on the Mekong River. The proposed barrier was to be composed of widely scattered antipersonnel mines known as Gravel and an air-supported antitruck system using assorted detection devices to pinpoint targets for conventional airstrikes. The air-supported barrier was to be supplemented by a manned "fence" along the DMZ itself. Although the Jason report warned that the North Vietnamese could be expected to develop various countermeasures to the barrier as time went on, it argued that such a scheme would ultimately be more effective in stopping enemy infiltration and supply operations than the bombing campaign against the North.

The Pentagon Papers note that Secretary McNamara was "strongly and favorably impressed" by the Jason proposals, and disposed to move quickly toward their implementation. Although he was not able to get White House backing for a reduction of the air war, McNamara was able to begin work on the barrier project. On September 15,

------

the "logistic funnel" to the National Liberation Front forces in the South. Nevertheless they concluded that:

> The low volume of supplies required, the demonstrated effectiveness of the countermeasures already undertaken by Hanoi, the alternative options that the NVN (North Vietnam) transportation network provides and the level of aid the USSR and China seem prepared to provide . . . make it quite unlikely that Hanoi's capability to function as a logistic funnel would be seriously impaired. Our past experience also indicates that an intensified air campaign in NVN probably would not prevent Hanoi from infiltrating men into the South at the present or a higher rate, if it chooses. Furthermore, there would appear to be no basis for assuming that the damage that could be inflicted by an intensified air offensive would impose such demands on the North Vietnamese labor force that Hanoi would be unable to continue and expand its recruitment and training of military forces for the insurgency in the South.

1966—less than a month after he received the Jason report —McNamara established the Defense Communications Planning Group to oversee the anti-infiltration scheme.[43] Work on the barrier began in late 1966, with an initial appropriation of $330 million for fiscal 1967 (July 1, 1966– June 30, 1967).[44] It was not, however, until September 1967 —nearly a year after DCPG was formed—that the public learned of the scheme. On September 7, 1967, McNamara announced at a Pentagon press conference that the United States would construct a barrier across the DMZ consisting of materials that would range from "barbed wire to highly sophisticated devices." Citing the need for extreme secrecy, McNamara did not identify the "highly sophisticated devices" that were to be employed, nor did he reveal that the barrier would extend into Laos.[45]

Ever since McNamara's 1967 announcement of the anti-infiltration barrier, also called the "electronic fence," there has been much confusion and misunderstanding as to what was really involved in this scheme. As General Deane of DCPG made clear in his 1970 Congressional testimony, the barrier project actually encompassed two distinct concepts: first, a series of manned fortifications and artillery firing points along the DMZ itself, and second, an air-supported system in Laos.

The first scheme, code-named Dyemaker/Muscle Shoals by the Pentagon, was described by General Deane as a "fixed barrier" which was to "combine sensors to detect enemy intrusions, physical obstacles to impede and canalize enemy movements, and tactical troop units operating from strong points or fortified bases, to strike at infiltrators by fire and ground action."[46] This scheme, which is what the public knew of as the McNamara Wall, was never fully implemented. As originally conceived, it would have required the deployment of hundreds of thousands of American and South Vietnamese troops in static positions along the DMZ. Ultimately, the U.S. Command in Saigon determined that the concentration of so many troops in one area would be extraordinarily wasteful and could lead to a disaster of Dien Bien Phu proportions. Seven months after the plan was announced to the public, a journalist who visited the DMZ reported that work on the barrier had come to a halt and that "plans to construct the line appeared to be dying quietly."[47] It was not until 1969, however, that the Pentagon acknowledged that the fixed-barrier scheme had been abandoned.

The second scheme proposed by Jason, an air-supported anti-infiltration system in Laos, has been in continuous operation since December 1967. According to General Deane, this system works as follows:

Acoustic and seismic sensors are dropped by aircraft along roads and trails. Truck or troop movements detected by these sensors are usually relayed through [other] aircraft for readout in a fixed installation using computerized equipment. . . .

Skilled target analysts in the fixed installation . . . then pass target information to the activity controlling strike aircraft such as the F-4 fighter-bomber. Because sensor locations are known, lucrative targets may be struck immediately, or information derived from the sensors may be used to establish enemy movements as a basis for preplanned strikes, such as B-52 strikes.[48]

Additional information on the operation of this system was provided by the "Special Assistant for Sensor Exploitation" of the Air Force, Brigadier General William John Evans. Before a Senate subcommittee, General Evans testified that the air-supported system, code-named Igloo White by the Pentagon, was activated in late 1967 and expanded in 1968 after the interruption of bombing in North Vietnam. Elements of the system, according to Evans, include (1) the F-4 Phantom jets used to deliver air-dropped sensors along truck routes in Laos; (2) an EC-121R relay aircraft in "'orbit" over the sensor fields that "receives the radio frequency transmissions from the sensors, and retransmits this information to the ground facility for processing";* and (3) the ground facility, or Infiltration Surveillance Center (ISC), whose IBM 360-65 computer receives the sensor data and then "produces a printout depicting activations of the sensors."† The IBM printout is used by intelligence personnel to allocate strike aircraft (F-4's and B-52's) for bombing missions in Laos.[49] By 1971, the Igloo White operation had become a major component of U.S. military strategy in the expanded Indochina war and

* Under a program known as Pave Eagle, the Air Force is trying to develop a pilotless "drone" aircraft to perform the relay functions of the EC-121R Constellations, which must orbit for hours over enemy-held territory in constant reach of antiaircraft fire. Approximately $4 million was budgeted in fiscal 1971 for Pave Eagle experiments, which currently employ the Beech Debonair single-engine, propeller-driven aircraft (designated the QU-22B by the Air Force).

† The Infiltration Surveillance Center, described as the "nerve center" of the Igloo White program, is located at Nakhon Phanom Air Base in northeast Thailand, where most air strikes against the Ho Chi Minh Trail originate. Target data provided by the computers at ISC can be forwarded immediately to an Airborne Battlefield Command and Control Center (ABCCC), a C-130E aircraft with multiple radio links to U.S. air bases and tactical bomber squadrons, or it can be used to develop a statistical analysis of enemy supply operations to identify targets for preplanned strikes by B-52 strategic bombers.

The ISC is a costly permanent installation and thus cannot be moved around on the battlefield in response to changing military situations. For this reason, the Air Force is developing a mobile sensor processing center, the Deployable Automatic Relay Terminal (DART). This air-transportable unit can pick up sensor data from relay aircraft and produce a printout of sensor activations, but it lacks the computer storage capability of the ISC and thus cannot develop statistical analyses. An unspecified number of DART's are deployed in South Vietnam, and one reportedly monitors sensors guarding infiltration trails leading into the I Corps Area (northern South Vietnam). A more advanced mobile processing center, the Sensor Reporting Post (SRP), is undergoing tests at Eglin Air Force Base, Florida.

a cornerstone of the Vietnamization program.* American strategists in Southeast Asia report that unless the flow of men and materiel into the war zone is curtailed, there is not even a glimmer of hope that the Saigon army can survive an American troop withdrawal.[50]

Although the concept of a fixed barrier along South Vietnam's borders has been abandoned by the Pentagon,

---

* Only the "target acquisition" (i.e., intelligence-gathering) phases of Igloo White are described here. On the other side of the coin, of course, is the actual attack phase or the "interdiction" campaign. Interdiction attacks, sometimes known as "Commando Bolt" operations, are conducted by F-4 Phantoms and B-57G bombers stationed at airfields in South Vietnam and Thailand, and from Navy A-6 fighters flown from aircraft carriers on "Yankee Station" in the Tonkin Gulf. A high percentage of "truck kills" are also credited to the AC-119 and AC-130 gunships participating in Commando Bolt operations.

When attacking trucks and enemy logistics personnel, these aircraft employ a whole new family of munitions that have been specifically designed as antitruck or antipersonnel weapons. Most of these munitions consist of a dispenser unit, or "mother bomb," that scatters the submunitions, or "bomblets," over a wide area; the bomblets themselves can contain ordinary explosives, various incendiary mixtures, or riot gases. Typical munitions used in Commando Bolt operations include WAAPM, a wide-area antipersonnel mine system composed of spherical bomblets; the XM41 Gravel Mine, which contains many small packets filled with explosives powerful enough to blow a man's foot off; the BLU-66 fragmentation bomblet; the BLU-52 chemical bomb, a standard fire-bomb case filled with 270 pounds of CS riot gas; the M-36 incendiary cluster bomb, composed of 182 magnesium bomblets; Dragontooth, an area-denial munition composed of many small arrowhead-shaped mines; the CBU-24 and CBU-49 antitruck fragmentation bombs; and a 2000-ton laser-guided bomb. (For further information on Commando Bolt aircraft and munitions, see U.S. Senate, Committee on Armed Services, Preparedness Investigating Subcommittee, *Investigation Into Electronic Battlefield Program, Hearings,* 91st Congress, 2d Session, 1971, pp. 128–69. For data on the development and production of antipersonnel munitions, see NARMIC, *The Weapons of Counterinsurgency,* Philadelphia, American Friends Service Committee, 1970.)

the use of intrusion detectors in counterinfiltration systems has not. The "wall," in fact, served as a kind of Manhattan Project for sensor development. One Pentagon official commented: "While that scheme did not work as well as some people hoped, many of the highly sophisticated devices that were developed for that program have been very successful, opening the way to a quantum jump in our ability to monitor even the most rugged border anywhere in the world."[51] William Beecher of *The New York Times* reported in February 1970 that the Pentagon was studying a plan "to provide enough modern sensing devices so that South Vietnam could seal its entire 900-mile border against sizeable enemy infiltration." The Pentagon plan, according to Beecher, involved the emplacement of up to $1 billion worth of sensors along the frontier and the expansion of South Vietnam's border armies.[52] Although there has been no formal announcement of such a plan, journalists who visited the border regions after the U.S. invasion of Cambodia were told that "hundreds of sensors of various types . . . were left behind by American troops when they pulled out of Cambodia June 30th to pinpoint targets for U.S. B-52 heavy bombers and smaller fighter-bombers."[53]

Another line of sensors and radar posts was established just inside Vietnamese territory: "Without the fanfare given the line conceived by Defense Secretary McNamara back in 1967," one journalist reported, "the Americans have created a similar line by dotting the frontier with sensors, radar, infra-red searchlights and other 'spook' devices." The main portion of this new line was reported to have been established in the Mekong Delta frontier area, between the Gulf of Thailand and Chau Doc, with a thinner screen extending northward. A visitor to this "Delta line" in 1970 wrote: "In Special Forces camps and isolated towers along the frontier sightless Americans in cut-off fatigue trousers sit through each muggy night reading the beeps, loudspeaker screeches and squiggly green radar lines of their strangelove machines." Radar sightings, according to the visitor, "almost immediately bring a barrage of 105-mm. howitzer shells from guns manned by South Vietnamese," while "air strikes are used deeper in Cambodia."[54]

It is now clear that sensor devices have become a standard item of battlefield equipment for all U.S. troops in Southeast Asia.* "Virtually every U.S. ground combat unit in South Vietnam," General Deane told a Senate investigating committee, "is now applying sensors to detect the enemy."[55] Army officers talk enthusiastically of "instrumenting the battlefield" by planting detection devices along all trails thought to be used by the enemy. This use of intrusion detectors to collect combat intelligence data over the entire theater of war has led to the concept of the "electronic battlefield" (the Army calls it the Remotely Monitored Battlefield Sensors System, or REMBASS). General Deane provided this example of expanded sensor activity in 1970:

Suppose we have a U.S. infantry unit responsible for securing a given area of operation (AO). This unit emplaces sensors at known locations along trails leading into or near its AO. If the sensors detect an enemy column moving along a trail, this information is received by a readout equipment operator, and he can . . . determine the size of the force, direction in which it is moving, and the speed, and he passes this information on to his commander.[56]

With this information, and with his knowledge of the terrain and weather, the commander makes his decision: "attack by artillery fire, an ambush, or whatever means is

---

* The "McNamara wall" also served as a model for similar counterinfiltration systems being installed in Korea. Under Project Agile, the Pentagon has developed sensor systems for implementation along the southern edge of the Demilitarized Zone between North and South Korea. The Korean barrier, equipped with surveillance radars and other secret devices, is designed to halt the infiltration of North Korean saboteurs and political agents into the South.

appropriate." As the director of the Pentagon agency responsible for management of the sensor program, General
Deane was naturally eager to emphasize the smooth and
efficient operation of such detection systems. Under questioning, however, he was forced to acknowledge that the
use of sensors does present some serious problems: first,
no device has yet been developed that can distinguish
between friendly soldiers and the enemy or between civilians and combatants; second, the sensors cannot be used
in or near cities or other population centers where normal
foot and vehicle traffic provides natural camouflage for
enemy movements.[57] The highly sophisticated sensor devices are also expensive and easily damaged. According
to Deane, the average sensor now in use in Vietnam costs
$1,800 to obtain and survives for only forty-five days in the
field—which means that the sensor operation cost (exclusive of manpower expenditures) is $40 a day.[58]

In a dispatch published July 10, 1970, the nationally syn-
dicated columnist Jack Anderson disclosed (presumably on
the basis of inside information), that sensors dropped along
the Ho Chi Minh Trail have often proved to be found
defective or useless. Most of these devices, he reported,
"landed with such a jar that they never worked at all.
Others picked up jungle noises of interest to no one except
nature lovers. . . . Even the hardiest of the detection devices seldom continued to transmit their mysterious sounds
for more than six or seven days." Anderson estimated that
the total cost of what he calls "the great electronic boondoggle" is closer to $4 billion than the $2 billion estimated
by Senator Proxmire. The added funds, he charged, "have
been hidden under innocuous titles in the budgets of the
three armed services."

Even though new "third generation" devices will reportedly cost less ($921 on the average), the sensor pro-
gram will still involve an investment of billions of dollars
in the next few years, and the most persistent critic of

spiraling Electronic Battlefield expenditures, Senator William Proxmire, estimates that the total cost of the program may grow to $20 billion within a decade. "The most shocking fact about the electronic battlefield," he told the Senate on July 6, 1970, "is that it has never been directly authorized by Congress. The program has never been subjected to public hearings or a detailed review." Proxmire also complained of the extreme vulnerability of such devices to malfunction due to the rough treatment they normally receive. Finally, he charged that sensors and associated munitions constitute an "indiscriminate weapon" because they cannot distinguish between enemy soldiers and civilians.

COUNTERINFILTRATION SYSTEMS

Since the Pentagon continues to place great faith in the ability of sensor devices to offer the United States some advantage in an expanded Southeast Asian war, it should be no surprise that all details of sensor operation are classified. Despite this restriction, it is possible to get some idea of the mechanisms involved. On the basis of research reports, Congressional hearings, and press accounts, the following picture of U.S. counterinfiltration systems has been developed.

Acoustic Detectors record the sounds produced by human or vehicular activity in a given area. An acoustical sentry system normally employs several outlying microphones monitored continuously by operators listening for abnormal sounds. As in the case of underwater acoustical systems (sonar), the operator must be able to distinguish between ordinary background noise and the sounds created by enemy intruders.

Basic research on acoustical detection systems was performed by the Atlantic Research Corporation and the Willow Run Laboratory (WRL) of Michigan's Institute of Science and Technology working under a joint contract from the Advanced Research Projects Agency. Using Thailand as an outdoor laboratory, teams of Americans "seeded" the countryside with microphones to test the utility of acoustical devices in counterinfiltration systems.[59] By planting microphones in fourteen sites in Thailand, David E. Willis of WRL explained in 1967, "we determined the natural variation in background noise level for different environments." One application of this information, Willis elaborated, would be to "plant these devices around a troop encampment," since once "the men know background noises they can detect intruders."[60]

The Army's Limited War Laboratory also experimented with acoustical counterinfiltration systems. William Beecher of *The New York Times* was told by former LWL commander Colonel R. W. McEvoy in 1968 that "we're working on noises the human ear can't pick up. Many are ultrasonic." Beecher reported that LWL personnel were developing sensors that could detect the sounds made by a man's shirt rubbing against his jacket, or by the movement of grass as he walks through the jungle.[61] LWL's work in this area was also discussed by the Army's Deputy Chief of Staff for Logistics, Major General H. S. Miley, Jr., during hearings on the fiscal 1969 Defense budget. "The Limited War Laboratory," he reported, "has developed an ultrasonic receiver and transmitter which can serve as a short range intrusion detector. . . . The receiver operates by translating ultrasonic sounds into audible tones. Typical sounds that can be detected are those produced by people walking on grass, the snapping of twigs, or the cocking of a weapon."[62]

The Navy's background in the acoustical detection of underwater craft has also been put to use in the development of counterguerrilla systems. The head of sensor operations for the Navy, Rear Admiral William H. House, told a Senate subcommittee in 1970: "The Navy has been involved in the development, production, and operational use of expendable sensors (sonabuoys, bathythermograph, and others) for many years. It was only natural, then, that the Navy should be called upon to lend its expertise to the early development of the land application of this technology."[63] As part of its participation in the Defense Communications Planning Group's air-supported detection system (the Igloo White program), the Navy converted an acoustic submarine detection buoy (Sonabuoy) into an air-dropped counterinfiltration device known as an Acoubuoy (acoustic buoy). Two kinds of Acoubuoy are used: one comes equipped with a camouflaged parachute and is intended to be suspended from trees; the other is spiked at the bottom and is designed for ground implantation.[64] These devices, manufactured by the Hazeltine Corporation of Little Neck, New York, and the Magnavox plant in Urbana, Illinois, contain microphones and radio transmitters to convey the sounds they pick up to relay aircraft orbiting overhead.

Seismic Detectors register the "pressure wave" produced in the earth's surface layer by a walking person or a vehicle in motion. In a typical sentry system, seismic detectors called geophones are buried in the ground along jungle trails in the vicinity of a base or camp site; the sensors are joined by wire or radio to a readout device that produces a visual display and/or audio tone when the geophones are activated.

Seismic detection systems were first tested in Thailand in 1964 as part of ARPA's counterinfiltration research program. Under SRI's umbrella contract for an "Investigation of Counterguerrilla Surveillance Processes," Norman E. Goldstein issued a report in 1966 on *Seismic Intruder Detection Tests* that was concerned with "the detection range of a portable seismometer in a low-noise environment . . . in connection with the evaluation of search techniques for use in counterinsurgency operations in Thailand."[65] Subsequent field tests by Atlantic Research and Willow Run at fourteen sites in Thailand established that "the seismic detection of intrusion yields a range two to five times the range of acoustic detection."[66] On the basis of these tests, Rowland H. McLaughlin of WRL in 1967 completed a secret report in which "the design and specifications for a proposed seismic intrusion detector of versatile characteristics are discussed."[67]

In April 1967, the Army's former Chief of Research and Development, General Betts, told a House committee that a seismic device manufactured by Texas Instruments, the AN/PSR-1 anti-intrusion set, "is a standard U.S. Marine Corps item now in use in Vietnam." General Betts described the PSR-1 as follows: "The system consists of four geophones, or pick-up devices which can be buried, and a control unit which can be remoted by field wire up to one mile. It produces an audio tone when it detects movement. This geophone will detect personnel movement from 20 to 100 meters, depending on the type of soil, and vehicular movement from 200 to 500 meters."[68] An Army version of the PSR-1, the Patrol Seismic Intrusion Detector (PSID), costs about $300 and is normally used by small patrols as a sentry device when camped in the jungle. Over 7,000 PSID's were deployed in Vietnam through June 1971, at an estimated cost of over $2 million.

General John M. Wright, Jr., Comptroller of the Army and former commander of the 101st Airborne Division in Vietnam, told Congressmen investigating the electronic battlefield program that the PSID "was one sensor in which I was particularly interested." Each battalion of the 101st, he said, was provided with twelve PSID's.

I tried to remove the mystery from this [device] and to have each trooper feel as familiar with it as he is with his rifle or a can of C-rations. He didn't have to understand how or why it worked. All he needed to know was that he had a thing small enough to carry in his pocket and that when his platoon stopped somewhere in the jungle for even a short time, he put this thing out on the trail 25 or 50 meters away from his position and have the benefit of an always alert scout . . . who would give warning of an enemy approach.[69]

Other seismic intrusion detectors (identified by the suffix "SID") that have been developed for this purpose are the MINISID, MICROSID, and DSID. The MINISID is a hand-implemented system composed of a geophone, a radio transmitter, and a readout device known as a Portatale; it is usually used in conjunction with the MAGID magnetic device (see below). The MICROSID is a smaller device that can be carried in the ammunition pouch of a soldier on patrol. The DSID—disposable seismic intrusion detector—is a small device that is not recoverable after emplacement. Air-dropped seismic intrusion detectors (ADSID's) form the "mainstay" of the Igloo White counterinfiltration system in Laos; these dart-shaped sensors are designed to be buried for most of their length (a plantlike camouflaged antenna is all that remains aboveground).[70] Seismic sensors of the kind used in Southeast Asia are produced by Texas Instruments, RCA, and the Sandia Corp.[71]

Magnetic Detectors indicate the presence of an unusual concentration of ferromagnetic metals. Magnetic sensors owe their utility to the obvious fact that any supply of metals in a jungle wilderness is cause for suspicion. Army counterinfiltration experts are reportedly interested in this approach because "the magnetic sensor provides positive identification of metal—something an infiltrating guerrilla is almost certain to have on his person."[72]

Before a magnetic sensor can be used to detect manmade metal objects, it is necessary to map out the natural magnetic field background in a search area. In 1965, scientists from the Stanford Research Institute used a rubidium-vapor magnetometer to measure magnetic field variations in a number of locations in Thailand. In a report on *The Magnetic Field Around a Magnetized Object*, J. Krebbers of SRI developed a formula that would "permit the prediction of the changes in the earth's magnetic field" that would be caused by a ferromagnetic object placed just above or below the ground.[73] SRI subsequently reported that the Varian rubidium-vapor magnetometer could be used to detect weapons buried in tunnels or otherwise hidden by insurgent forces.[74]

Magnetic intrusion detectors (MAGID's) have also been developed for counterinfiltration purposes. According to General Deane of DCPG, a hand-emplaced MAGID can be plugged into a Portatale readout device to report when rifles or other metal objects are being brought near a campsite.[75]

Surveillance Radars are designed to detect moving targets, including foot soldiers and vehicles, in the vicinity of a camp site or border zone. These devices, known as moving target indicator (MTI) radars, operate on the Doppler principle as follows: "A beam of energy is transmitted at a certain frequency, and the radar compares the frequency transmitted with the frequency returned as an echo from a target. If the object is stationary the frequency will be the same as transmitted; if the object is moving the return frequency will be slightly different. This difference is presented to the radar operator as both a visible and audible signal."[76] Before using such a device in battle, an operator must learn to distinguish the signals produced by men, animals, and vehicles.

Two types of MTI radars are now in use in Vietnam: the AN/TPS-25 wide-area surveillance radar and the AN/PPS-5 and PPS-6 Manpack Surveillance Radars. The TPS-25 was introduced in 1959 as a field-artillery target acquisition radar but has since been converted to counterinfiltration purposes. It can locate a truck at 18,280 meters and a moving man at 4,500 meters. The Tipsy 25, as it is known, is normally used in a semifixed position and requires electrical line of sight into the area of interest. The Marine Corps has had four of the sets in use in Vietnam, including one at Dong Ha near the DMZ that has a line of sight all the way to the North Vietnamese border. The PPS-5, manufactured by Cutler-Hammer, Inc., of Deer Park, New York, is a smaller radar used at the company level for base security and related counterinfiltration duties. Weighing only ninety-five pounds, the PPS-5 system consists of a disk-shaped antenna mounted on a tripod, a transmitter-receiver, and two silver-zinc batteries for power. Moving targets are indicated to the operator through a headset by an audio tone superimposed on background noise, or visually on a radar display scope.* According to General Betts, the PPS-5 can detect a walking man to 5,000 meters and a quarter-ton truck to 10,000 meters range.[77] The PPS-6 is a lighter version of the PPS-5 produced by the General Instrument Corporation of Hicksville, New York.[78]

American troops in Vietnam have encountered two basic difficulties with the TPS-25, PPS-5, and PPS-6 that preclude their use in jungle patrol work: both weigh too much to be easily carried by a foot patrol, and both have poor

---

* A journalist who witnessed the use of a PPS-5 for surveillance in Vietnam sent this report in 1969:

> The American soldier crouched attentively in front of the radar screen waits for the distinctive blip that might signal men on the move in the night-darkened rice paddies of South Vietnam.
>
> The blip, when it comes, is shaped rather like a tiny spruce tree. It moves so slowly that it seems to be standing still.
>
> The operator cranks his dials to bring a reference marker in line with the blip and then dons a pair of earphones to make the final, or auditory, evaluation of the signal. . . .
>
> A group of men make a sound that can only be described as a "whoosh, whoosh, whoosh" generated by their moving arms and legs. The background noise of swaying trees gives a steady, low, roaring sound like rushing water. (*The New York Times*, May 24, 1969.)

foliage-penetration properties. In order to overcome these deficiencies, the Advanced Research Projects Agency commissioned MIT's Lincoln Laboratory to develop a lightweight foliage-penetration surveillance radar. During an investigation of MIT's relationship with its "Special Laboratories," the director of Lincoln, Dr. Milton Clauser, testified that "on a personal appeal from Johnny Foster" (Dr. John S. Foster, Jr., Director of Defense Research and Engineering), Lincoln agreed to "help some of the people in Vietnam" by working on foliage-penetration MTI radars. In response to this appeal, Lincoln developed an MTI radar which can be "put up in the center of a Special Forces camp or some soldier camp and it could then act as a sentinel to any moving target, moving things as small as a person moving at very, very slow speeds, as slow as one can walk, even when one is crouching."[79]

An MTI radar of the sort identified by Dr. Clauser was described to a Congressional subcommittee during the 1970 investigation of the counterinfiltration program. The Army's manager for sensor programs, Major General William B. Fulton, reported: "We have been testing a radar, [weighing] 18 pounds, in a radar development effort to produce a radar to support offensive operations at small unit level. This device, the AN/PPS-14, is a lightweight foliage penetration radar that can give very fine, short range protection to a patrol or an outpost by being able to look through foliage." According to General Fulton, the PPS-14 was being tested in Vietnam.[80] Other lightweight radars being considered as replacements for the PPS-5 and PPS-6 include RCA's AN/PPS-9 Portable Tactical Radar and General Dynamics' AN/PPS-10 Combat Surveillance Radar. Both the PPS-9 and PPS-10 weigh about ten pounds and utilize solid-state components and printed circuitry.[81]

Night-vision Devices are designed to deny freedom of movement to the guerrilla at night. Although not precisely sensor devices, they play a key role in counterinfiltration systems by illuminating trails and roads at night when most infiltration and surprise attacks take place. Present night-vision devices were developed on a crash basis only after U.S. troops were sent to Vietnam; McGraw-Hill's Defense Marketing Service reports that some $372 million was spent on development and procurement of such equipment between 1966 and 1971.[82]

According to General Betts, "Four technological areas continue to be investigated for application to night-vision systems: visible light, near infrared, far infrared, and image intensification." Visible-light systems are conventional searchlights and flares. Near-infrared systems utilize that portion of the electromagnetic spectrum which is adjacent to the longer wavelength end of the visible spectrum (since most objects do not emit near-infrared radiation, it is necessary to illuminate the target with near-infrared light before it can be detected by infrared viewers). Far-infrared techniques, in contrast, allow for passive viewing since all warm bodies emit far-infrared energy. Image intensification is also a passive viewing system, in that available light energy (moonlight or starlight) is amplified fifty thousand to eighty thousand times to produce a visible image.[83] Image-intensification devices convert weak light rays into photoelectron beams that are amplified and flashed on a phosphor-coated screen; in order to obtain the high amplification desired, several of these intensifiers are connected in a series, or "cascade," through the techniques of fiberoptics.[84]

A great many searchlights, flare systems, viewers, and combinations of these have been introduced into the Army's night-vision inventory. Several slow-flying cargo planes have been equipped with visible-light and infrared (IR) searchlights, IR viewers, and flare-delivery systems to serve as an aerial light platform that can hover over a guerrilla battlefield at night. Image-intensification devices that have been used in Vietnam include the AN/PVS-2 individual weapon-mounted Starlight Scope, the AN/TVS-2 Crew-Served Weapons Sight for use with machine guns and mortars, and the tripod-mounted AN/TVS-4 Medium Range Night Observation Device. The Army has also developed electronic binoculars that employ the image-intensification technique.[85]

Under a crash program known as SEA NITEOPS, or Southeast Asia Night Operations, the Army is developing a number of sensor-equipped helicopter gunships for night combat missions. The Hughes Aircraft Company has a multimillion-dollar contract to outfit some forty UH-1C Iroquois helicopters with night-vision devices; the modified UH-1C, known as INFANT (Iroquois Night Fighter and Night Tracker), carries low-light-level television (LLLTV), visible and IR searchlights, and forward-looking infrared viewers (FLIR). INFANT is to be followed by SMASH, the Southeast Asia Multiple Sensor Armament System Helicopter. Mounted on the AH-1G HueyCobra helicopter gunship, the SMASH system will include a forward-looking infrared viewer and a forward-looking fire-control radar (probably of the moving-target indicator type).[86]

The Air Force equivalent of the Army's SEA NITEOPS, Project Shed Light, is designed to equip tactical aircraft, gunships, and reconnaissance planes with a night vision capability. Most of this effort has concentrated on the development of airborne LLLTV, FLIR, and image-intensification devices, and laser target-designator systems. Air Force night-vision R&D programs (usually designated by the code name "Pave") currently underway include:

—Pave Knife, an $8.4 million program to equip the F-4D Phantom jet with an LLLTV target acquisition and laser illuminating system designed by the Philco-Ford Corporation. Nighttime targets detected by the LLLTV are illuminated by the laser designator for destruction by a remote-controlled laser-guided bomb or missile. A more advanced version of this system, Pave Lance, will include LLLTV, FLIR, and laser target designators in an integrated package.

—Pave Nail, a $13 million program designed to modify the North American Rockwell OV-10 Bronco observation aircraft for nighttime forward air-control missions. Equipment to be installed includes a Varo stabilized night-periscope sight, a Westinghouse LLL-TV system, and a laser rangefinder/illuminator. The fourteen OV-10's modified in this fashion will be used for Igloo White bombing missions in Laos.

—Pave Moon, a secret program to equip A-6 and B-57G bombers with moving-target indicator radars and other night-vision devices. Pave Moon aircraft are reportedly used in the Igloo White program for anti-truck operations.[87]

In addition to these and other Pave programs, the Air Force is spending an estimated $22 million to convert fifty-two C-119 cargo planes into night-fighting gunships for use in Southeast Asia.* The conversion project, to be performed by Fairchild-Hiller's Aircraft Service Division in Saint Augustine, Florida, involves installation of forward-looking radars and FLIR detection sets, assorted night-vision devices, and a General Precision analog gun-

---

* Air Force gunships, reconverted cargo planes outfitted with cannon and high-rate-of-fire miniguns, are described as "the Air Force's most efficient truck-killers on the Ho Chi Minh trail." On February 3, 1971, the Department of Defense authorized release of motion-picture film of an AC-119 gunship in action over Laos. According to *Armed Forces Journal*, the film showed an Air Force crew member operating an LLLTV camera. "Observers at the Pentagon saw a green reproduction of the ground below with a light level comparable to early morning or late evening. An NVA [North Vietnamese] truck speeding down a Laotian road was clearly observed. Seconds later it disappeared in a burst of exploding 20mm. cannon shells fired from the AC-119's four 'Vulcan' cannon." (George Weiss, "Battle for Control of Ho Chi Minh Trail," *Armed Forces Journal*, February 15, 1971, p. 22.)

fire-control computer to direct fire of the plane's miniguns and 20mm cannon.[88]

THE AUTOMATED BATTLEFIELD

The urgency with which the Pentagon has pursued the various sensor programs described above is a direct result of the failure of conventional counterguerrilla tactics in Vietnam. The hundreds of "search and destroy" missions that crisscrossed the countryside in the first years of the war all came to the same end: high American casualties, increased popular disaffection toward the Saigon regime, and no detectable reduction in enemy capabilities. With rising domestic opposition to the American involvement in Southeast Asia, the Pentagon has come under increasing White House pressure to avoid costly ground engagements in order to reduce American casualty figures. Under President Nixon's "Vietnamization" program, American ground combat troops are to be withdrawn from Vietnam while the utilization of U.S. aircraft and artillery is to be increased. This strategy, sometimes summarized as "firepower, not manpower," has naturally presupposed the increased use of detection devices to locate "lucrative" targets for the bombers, gunships, and cannon that have replaced ground troops as the mainstay of jungle warfare. The former commander of the 25th Infantry Division in Vietnam, Major General Ellis W. Williamson, described this philosophy to a Senate subcommittee in 1970:

We are making unusual efforts to avoid having the American young man stand toe-to-toe, eyeball to eyeball, or even rifle-to-rifle against the enemy that may outnumber him on the battlefield. We are trying to fight the enemy with our bullets instead of the bodies of our young men—"firepower, not manpower."[89]

Electronic sensors were never designed to replace the infantryman, only to make his job easier and somewhat safer. With increased dependence on sensors, however, the ordinary foot soldier is spending more and more of his time watching radarscopes and listening for the sounds of enemy intruders. Every time more sensors are plugged into an existing counterinfiltration system, the job of monitoring the expanding series of readout devices requires more concentration and intellectual effort. Some Pentagon officials complain that the explosion in sensor use has provided the military with *too much* information. Thus, Lieutenant General George S. Boylan, Deputy Chief of Staff for Air Force Programs and Resources, has said that "our capacity to obtain information is continuing to increase more rapidly than our ability to reduce it to usable intelligence."[90]

Since human beings fatigue easily and are known to make errors of judgment, the Pentagon has decided to develop battlefield computers to process the vast quantities of data produced by sensor systems. This plan actually led to the idea of automating the entire theater of war, sending most of the troops home and allowing the machines to do the fighting. This concept of an "automated battlefield" was first presented to the public in 1969 by Army Chief of Staff William C. Westmoreland in an extraordinary speech to the Association of the U. S. Army. "Comparing the past few years of progress with a forecast of the future," he began, "produces one conclusion: we are on the threshold of an entirely new battlefield concept." With the introduction of advanced sensors, communications systems, and automatic data-processing equipment, it will no longer be necessary to devote large numbers of troops to the task of finding and engaging the enemy:

On the battlefield of the future, enemy forces will be located, tracked, and targeted almost instantaneously through the use of data links, computer-assisted intelligence evaluation, and automatic fire control. With first round kill probabilities approaching certainty, and with surveillance devices that can continually track the enemy, the need for large forces to fix the opposition physically will be less important.[91]

Westmoreland emphasized that he was not treating his audience to some kind of personal fantasy: "With cooperative effort," he prophesied, "no more than 10 years should separate us from the automated battlefield." Much of the groundwork, in fact, has already been laid. "Currently, we have hundreds of surveillance, target acquisition and night observation and information processing systems either in being, in development, or in engineering." The task now, he indicated, is "to incorporate all these devices into an integrated land combat system." In order to ensure that Army doctrine would be modified to account for the explosion in technological knowledge, General Westmoreland established a project office at the Department of the Army Staff level—the Systems Manager for Surveillance, Target Acquisition and Night Observation (STANO)—to coordinate all automated battlefield programs.

The STANO office, which was activated July 15, 1969, is responsible for planning and monitoring the integration of sensor capabilities into the Army under central control. Basically, the project has two main functions: to bring first-generation sensor systems into general Army use, and to begin development and integration of more highly sophisticated second-generation sensors and data-processing equipment for the "Army of the future." According to former Chief of Research and Development General Betts, "The STANO program was established to insure that all battlefield reconnaissance and surveillance activities are coordinated and that the end product of these activities is an upgrading of our capacity to find the enemy and to use our available firepower to the maximum."[92] By integrating advances in surveillance, communications, and data processing, the STANO office will preside over the development of an "Integrated Battlefield Control System" (IBCS), the Army's designation for the automated battlefield.

In fiscal 1971, the STANO Systems Manager was given a budget of $234 million to support sensor research programs and to obtain operational devices for Army units in the field.[93] Of the $44 million provided for R&D activities, some $4 million was to be spent by Project MASSTER (Mobile Army Sensor Systems, Test Evaluation and Review) on field tests of commercial and experimental automated battlefield systems. Located at Fort Hood, Texas, MASSTER is described as "a unique, operationally oriented, materiel and concept test activity . . . to postulate, evaluate and shape the organization of the future Army."[94] A somewhat simpler picture of MASSTER's function was provided by Lieutenant General John Norton of the Army Combat Developments Command, who explained that the project was organized "to provide the Army with an expanded and accelerated capability to evaluate from the soldier's point of view the merits and weaknesses of proposed hardware."[95] By testing new systems in full-scale field exercises, MASSTER will determine which proposed systems or concepts are ready for introduction onto the battlefield.*

The IBCS concept as now visualized calls for the integration of surveillance devices into an automated weapons system that not only monitors the sensor subsystems for signs of enemy activity but also searches a computerized data bank for information on the location of friendly and enemy forces in order to determine the appropriate coun-

---

* Senior Army officials, according to *Armed Forces Journal*, "give Project MASSTER number two priority, following only the Vietnam war." Although fiscal 1971 expenditures were set at only $4 million, the Army expects to spend $60 to $70 million on the project over the next five years. ("Army Unveils Project MASSTER," *Armed Forces Journal*, May 19, 1970.)

termeasure.* The hardware currently being developed to perform these functions is composed of the Automatic Data System for the Army in the Field (ADSAF), a computer-assisted command-and-control system that will coordinate maneuverable forces by applying automatic data processing to the interrelated functions of fire–control, intelligence, operations, logistics, and personnel. The four related but separate systems included in ADSAF are the Tactical Fire Direction System (TACFIRE), the Combat Service Support System (CSSS), the Tactical Operations System (TOS), and the Division Tactical Operations System (DIVTOS).[96]

The main effort within ADSAF has been devoted to TACFIRE, a central computer with interlinked terminals in each artillery battalion. TACFIRE is being developed jointly by Litton Industries, RCA, and the Stanford Research Institute, with the central unit to consist of a Litton 3050M militarized computer. Through fiscal 1970, more than $50 million had been spent on development and procurement of the system. While the initial estimate for research and development was $59.9 million, the total cost is now expected to surpass $100 million. The Army plans

---

* Army research officials, interviewed by Drew Middleton of *The New York Times,* have given this sketch of IBCS operation on a hypothetical battlefield:

An enemy column on foot and in vehicles is on the move. A wide variety of detection devices reports the movement from the enemy's sector. The information is received at combat headquarters and fed into a computer along with information from other areas of the battlefield.

The computer then tells the combat commander, for example, whether the column is entering his area and requires artillery fire or whether it is headed for another sector of the battlefield. The commander will not have to wait while intelligence officers correlate all the information. He can act at once. ("Army Is Developing Battlefield Computers and Detection Devices," *The New York Times,* October 27, 1970).

to equip all of its active field-artillery cannon and howitzer battalions with TACFIRE by 1974.[97]

The CSSS is a mobile, air-transportable command center, consisting of four thirty-five-foot trailer vans, with one van for each of the following: an IBM 360-40 central processor; an IBM 2314 direct-access storage system; communications equipment; and punch-card equipment. CSSS will provide Army forces in the field with a computer-supported logistic, personnel, and administrative system. IBM has constructed five prototype systems, at a cost of $19 million, that are undergoing tests prior to integration with TACFIRE. CSSS is expected to be fully functional by mid-1971, and to be operational at all active Army divisional and corps headquarters by the end of 1976.[98]

The function of TOS is to support staff intelligence and operations functions by collecting, processing, and displaying information on enemy and friendly dispositions. The Control Data Corporation produced the first experimental TOS in 1966 for $4.4 million; it was sent to Germany for field tests conducted by the Seventh Army. Both TACFIRE and TOS will be installed at Fort Hood as part of Project MASSTER so that the whole system can be integrated and used in tests of new components.[99]

DIVTOS development was initiated in fiscal 1969 to satisfy an Army requirement for a simplified TOS for immediate use in Southeast Asia. According to the Pentagon, DIVTOS "will consist of computers and appropriate displays at the division and brigade levels, input/output devices down to battalions, and handheld input devices for use by companies, patrols, sensor monitoring stations, radar sites, and other surveillance and target acquisition sites." This elaborate system is needed in Southeast Asia "because of the inability of the present system to expeditiously process large volumes of information obtained through patrols, the expanded use of sensors, and other surveillance and target acquisition means."[100] Research and development work on DIVTOS cost $9.8 million during fiscal 1969, and the Army programmed an undisclosed amount for fiscal 1970 and 1971 to develop prototype models.[101]

Where is all this headed? General Westmoreland, in his memorable speech to the Army Association, provided this vision of the future:

I see battlefields or combat areas that are under 24 hour real or near real time surveillance of all types.

I see battlefields on which we can destroy anything we locate through instant communications and the almost instantaneous application of highly lethal firepower.

In summary, I see an Army built around an integrated area control system that exploits the advanced technology of communications, sensors, fire direction, and the required automatic data processing.[102]

The Integrated Battlefield Control System will not, according to Army spokesmen, remove human judgment from the decision-making process. "Our IBCS of tomorrow," General Norton told a Senate subcommittee in 1970, "will not automate the battlefield or make automatons out of soldiers. . . . The decision logic process will rest with the professional soldier." The decision of when to bomb and when not to bomb will still be made, according to Norton, by commanders "who will assess the information and properly react to this information in a judicious manner."[103] On the basis of American performance in Vietnam, however, it is difficult to have much confidence in the "judicious manner" of American commanders. In fact, any analysis of the Pentagon's response to Vietnam cannot help but impress one with the desperation with which the military has sought technological solutions to the social and political challenges of revolutionary warfare. All of the sensors, bombers, and computers at Washington's disposal have not won popular support for the U.S.-backed regime in Saigon, nor have they persuaded the Vietcong guerrilla to abandon his struggle for independence and national self-fulfillment. One can understand, then, why the Pentagon looks to a future more promising than the present. The man responsible for all Vietnam-oriented Defense Department research, Leonard Sullivan, Jr., took comfort in this assessment of sensor technology in 1968:

These developments open up some very exciting horizons as to what we can do five or ten years from now: When one realizes that we can detect anything that perspires, moves, carries metal, makes a noise, or is hotter or colder than its surroundings, one begins to see the potential. This is the beginning of instrumentation of the entire battlefield. Eventually, we will be able to tell when anybody shoots, what he is shooting at, and where he is shooting from. You begin to get a "Year 2000" vision of an electronic map with little lights that flash for different kinds of activity. This is what we require for this "porous" war, where the friendly and the enemy are all mixed together.[104]

Part Three

THE
MERCENARY
WAR

Chapter 8

THE
SCIENCE OF
MERCENARIZATION
—Project Agile in Asia

Counterinsurgency has become the focus of United States military planning only within the past decade; the problem it is intended to overcome, however, is centuries old. Every imperium has been faced with the task of finding enough troops to maintain hegemony over colonial territories without overtaxing the financial and manpower resources of the mother country. The occupation army of an imperial power is always outnumbered by the indigenous population of a colony; when a liberation movement has secured the active support of sufficient numbers of people in a country to offset the technological advantage of the occupying forces, colonialism is doomed. Similarly, when several colonies revolt simultaneously—thus tying up all of the forces available to the mother country—the empire as a whole is threatened with collapse. The function of counterinsurgency planning, then, is to perpetuate imperial control with a minimum allocation of the military strength of the homeland.

Like all imperial powers of the past, the United States has found it necessary to employ mercenaries in order to maintain a favorable balance of power in its colonial territories. A primary objective of U.S. foreign policy, in fact, is to install client regimes in many countries that can be compelled to supply native troops for America's counterinsurgency mission. U.S. foreign aid programs, import subsidies, and military grants are all designed to create in each country privileged strata dependent upon continued American beneficence for their prosperity. When such a group acquires control of the national government, the United States government ultimately exercises the power of sovereignty. Since the ruling junta remains dependent upon U.S. aid even when in control of the governmental apparatus (in order to finance development projects and meet military payrolls), Washington can insist that such regimes provide troops for combat against insurgents in the same or neighboring countries. It is in Vietnam that one can witness the process of mercenarization carried to the fullest extent: American funds have been used to pay the expenses of Korean, Thai, and Philippine troops in addition to the million-man army of the Saigon regime.[1] The same mechanisms can be discerned elsewhere in Southeast Asia, and in Africa and Latin America. In some areas of the Third World, the United States has mobilized entire peoples—usually minority tribes inhabiting strategic border regions—to obtain mercenaries for U.S.-led counterguerrilla operations.

As noted in Chapter 4, the process of mercenarization usually entails the collection of data on the social composition of target populations. Once the Pentagon has identified the social strata most suitable for recruitment into mercenary armies, a new set of research tasks emerges. In Vietnam, the Department of Defense (DoD) discovered that the strategy of employing indigenous troops in counterinsurgency operations creates certain problems not encountered in conventional operations against an external enemy. In the first place, the employment of such troops against their own countrymen—in situations where soldiers often oppose members of their own village, or even of their own family—raised serious questions of motivation and morale. Secondly, the equipment that was initially supplied to these troops—surplus World War II rifles, artillery, and vehicles—was not suitable for rigorous use in a jungle or mountain environment. When McNamara took office in 1961, he discovered that these problems were not under the purview of any of the regular military research agencies. In order to develop a research and development program for our mercenary armies similar to the R&D program for the American armies, McNamara established a top-secret, continuing program of counterinsurgency research known as Project Agile.

According to a 1967 memorandum issued by the Director of Defense Research and Engineering, Project Agile is responsible for "research and development supporting the DoD's operations in remote areas, associated with the problems of actual or potential limited or subversive wars involving allied or friendly nations in such areas."[3] Operating on an annual budget of $20 million to $30 million, Agile is administered by the Overseas Defense Research office of the Advanced Research Projects Agency. In common with other ARPA projects (see Chapter 5), Agile is required to work on problems not being considered by any of the service-oriented laboratories, and on "high-risk" speculative solutions to new problems. In a 1968 appearance before the House Subcommittee on Defense Appropriations, Director of Defense Research and Engineering John S. Foster, Jr., described Project Agile as:

A broad program in applied research and development through which ARPA examines problems of multiservice and multigovernment interest and application in the fields of counterinsurgency and limited conflict. It provides friendly nations of the developing areas with better ways of organizing their own resources to counter insurgent threats. . . . Agile's systems R&D is intended to provide a basis of knowledge, techniques and technology from which to draw "blueprints" for deterring insurgency in its early stages.[4]

Agile's task of strengthening the counterinsurgency capabilities of client governments so as to reduce the need for direct U.S. intervention is further spelled out in a 1968 ARPA memo governing the "rationale and purposes" of the project:

[Agile will] conduct R&D programs for systems to provide improvements in allied nations' capability to meet the threat [of insurgency], and DoD capability to assist them in doing so with the particular goal of minimizing U.S. operational involvement. In particular [it will] concentrate on such areas as counterinfiltration, local security, capability of small units in guerrilla warfare, and specialized systems for specific related purposes.[5]

Historically, Agile has concentrated on surveillance systems and related "electronic battlefield" devices to reduce the manpower requirements for counterguerrilla operations in remote areas (see Chapter 7), and on the modifications of basic infantry equipment for use in extreme environmental situations (see Chapter 5). Agile has also developed specialized equipment for non-Western troops when standard G.I. issue was inappropriate or inadequate. In the area of behavioral research, Agile has sponsored research on ethnic minorities living in strategic areas (for example, on the montagnards of South Vietnam), and on the development of strategic doctrine for the armies of our client governments.*

* In an effort to deter Congress from voting a cutback in the fiscal 1968 Agile program, Dr. Foster argued that money spent by Agile *now* would help prevent much more costly Vietnam-type interventions later by developing strategies for mercenary operations against insurgents. He told a Senate committee, "Agile's long-term R&D program is designed to create knowledge, techniques, and tech-

The Overseas Defense Research office in the Pentagon does not itself engage in research activities but enters into contracts with a select group of universities, think tanks, and aerospace corporations to perform this work. Agile contracts are not issued directly by the Advanced Research Projects Agency but are managed by the Army Missile Command, Redstone Arsenal, Alabama, which serves as "agent" for ARPA in this area. Agile funds are also used to maintain the Remote Area Conflict Information Center (RACIC) of the Battelle Memorial Institute in Columbus, Ohio, whose mission is to "collect, store and disseminate information concerning remote area conflict, emphasizing the physical and engineering sciences," and to "perform information center services for all participants in remote area conflict and Project Agile."[6]

In pursuance of its responsibilities, Agile is one of the few Defense R&D organizations authorized to establish field research programs abroad. Because of the sensitive nature of such work (particularly in light of the Project Camelot fiasco), Agile is allowed to operate only in countries where:

1. The U.S. armed forces are involved operationally in counterinsurgency war and require R&D support that cannot be provided by the services.

---

nology that will make 'another Vietnam' far less likely." In approaching this problem, he added, "Agile has planned to provide R&D support for improvement of local counterinsurgency capability through the U.S. DoD presence in a few countries. . . . [These] R&D efforts wil develop techniques for countersubversive warfare in the unique country environment, so that they can be applied by agencies with operational responsibility in those countries, and also serve as models for analogous efforts by the operating community (not Agile) in other countries." (U.S. Senate, Committee on Appropriations, *Department of Defense Appropriations for 1968, Hearings,* 1967, p. 103.) Foster did not identify the agencies with "operational responsibility" for such operations, but one can safely include the Department of Defense and the CIA in any such category.

2. An actual or potential insurgency exists or is threatened, and the United States has a firm alliance or
defense agreement with the country.
3. The United States considers the country to be of strategic importance.
4. The United States has friendly relations with the
country.
5. There are agreements providing for a U.S. defense
presence.
6. Local conditions are such that research is feasible and
welcome.[7]

At present, the project maintains field offices in Vietnam,
Korea, Thailand, and Iran. In the past, Agile also maintained an office in Lebanon and awarded contracts to outside agencies for research on insurgency problems in Latin
America. In order to pacify Congressional critics of such
work, however, ARPA announced that it would not authorize Agile operations outside the four countries named
above "except by explicit direction of the Secretary of
Defense."[8] Since Agile's budget was cut by Congress from
$30 million to $22 million in 1969, it is unlikely that the
project will be extended to new countries in the near
future. The Agile field units in Vietnam and Thailand continue to absorb the bulk of project funds, and will therefore be discussed in detail below.

AGILE/VIETNAM

Project Agile made its appearance in Saigon soon after the
Kennedy brain trust selected Vietnam as the laboratory
for field tests of the new U.S. counterinsurgency apparatus.
By the middle of 1962, when the U.S. military presence in
Vietnam was still limited to a few hundred advisers, Agile
scientists were already in the countryside testing new
weapons and communications equipment. The November

5, 1962, issue of *Newsweek* carried a story on this effort in which Robert C. Phelps, then head of Agile, explained that "what we hope to do is to adapt weapons to the peculiar needs of the locality and the kind of warfare the Vietnamese are fighting."[9]

Agile's Vietnam office, the Research and Development Field Unit-Vietnam (RDFU-V), is responsible to the Commander in Chief, U.S. Military Assistance Command, Vietnam (MACV). According to the Pentagon document governing Agile activities, this office is required to "support MACV by conducting requested or mutually agreed upon R&D efforts relative to the war and pacification efforts, including military hardware, analytical sciences, and systems research and engineering." Most of Agile's Vietnam work falls into the "quick-fix" category; RDFU-V was designed as an in-country test center where, according to *The New York Times*, "immediate needs are first identified and where test versions of new equipment can be initially tried out."[10] Early Project Agile contributions to the Vietnam war effort include the following:

AR-15. At the request of the CIA, in 1962 Agile shipped 60,000 Colt AR-15 high-velocity rifles to Vietnam for testing by Special Forces units under combat conditions. The AR-15, a lightweight aluminum-alloy weapon, became particularly popular with the small montagnard tribesmen recruited for mercenary units, who had difficulty carrying standard Army rifles. Although the AR-15 fires a bullet weighing only a third that of standard .30-caliber ammunition, it is fired with such velocity that it seems "to explode the target rather than punch a hole through it."[11] The shock of impact is so great that many victims die from what would normally be superficial wounds. On the basis of the Agile tests, the Army overcame its initial antipathy to the unorthodox AR-15 and obtained large quantities for Vietnam use.

During the My Lai murder trial of Lieutenant William L.

Calley, Army pathologist Major Charles D. Lane testified that bullets fired from the AR-15 have the same effect as the fragmenting dumdum bullets proscribed by international law. "Upon impact and penetration into the target source," Lane said, "the bullet fragments into a number of pieces . . . producing a great deal of soft tissue injury and bone fragmentation." Lane was asked to testify after studying "wound ballistics" in South Vietnam as part of an Army research team that conducted more than 550 postmortems. Shown pictures of the My Lai victims, he identified the wounds as probably having been caused by AR-15 fire. Lane indicated that there probably would be no difference in wounds caused by dumdum bullets.[12] Nevertheless, the AR-15 rifle, now known by its military designation as the M-16, is issued to all Vietnam-bound G.I.'s and to all mercenary and "allied" troops.

Jungle Radios. When the first teams of U.S. advisers accompanied their Vietnamese counterparts on jungle patrols, they discovered to their dismay that local magnetic and atmospheric communications reduced the effectiveness of the Army's standard radios to less than 10 percent of their rated capacity. Agile hurriedly sent some radio engineers into the countryside to find ways of improving the range and reliability of existing equipment. On the basis of these tests, the AN/PRC-25 backpack radio was modified for high-frequency transmission and a new aerial, the AN/PRC-10, was added. Specially constructed for jungle use, the modified radio weighs only ten pounds and is completely immersionproof when in a closed position.[13]

Hamlet Evaluation System. In an "internal war" of the Vietnam type, it is of crucial importance to know which villages are loyal to the government, which are contested, and which are loyal to the guerrillas. Yet at the onset of the war, no centralized network existed to collect, store, and process such information. Accordingly, in 1966, Agile sponsored an exploratory effort to apply the techniques of automatic data processing to the task of measuring the allegiances of every hamlet in South Vietnam. As a result of this study, a computer-assisted operation known as the Hamlet Evaluation System (HES) was established at MACV headquarters in Saigon. Each month, on the basis of questionnaires filled out by pacification officers in the countryside, Vietnam's 12,722 hamlets are awarded a grade of "A," "B," or "C" if reasonably secure and under government control, "D" or "E" if contested, and "VC" if under Vietcong control.* From this simple determination many

---

* According to MACV documents, the hamlets are coded as follows:

—"A" Hamlet: A superhamlet. Just about everything going right in both security and development.
—"B" Hamlet: High-grade hamlet. Effective twenty-four hour security. Adequate development. No VC presence or activity.
—"C" Hamlet: VC military control broken. Relatively secure day and night. Most of VC infrastructure identified. No overt VC incidents—VC taxation may continue. Economic improvement programs underway.
—"D" Hamlet: VC activities in vicinity reduced. There may be terrorism and taxation. Local security forces present. There is a beginning at hamlet education and welfare activity. Although contested, it is more in GVN [Government of Vietnam] than VC camp.
—"E" Hamlet: VC frequently enter or harass at night. VC infrastructure largely intact. GVN program just beginning. Strictly contested.
—"VC" Hamlet: Definitely under VC control. Local GVN officials and our advisers don't enter except on military operation. Most of population willingly or unwillingly supports VC.

This code was taken from the "HES Hamlet Plot" map dated December 31, 1967 (prepared on the eve of the 1968 Tet offensive), which indicated that 66.9 percent of the population was then under Saigon government control, 16.5 percent contested, and only 16.6 percent under Vietcong control. Understandably, the criteria used to code the hamlets later came under severe criticism from Congressional investigators, who discovered that U.S. advisers in the field were often put under pressure to give optimistic reports on

tactical decisions are derived: where to send armed pacification teams, where to spray crop-destroying chemicals,
where to station Special Police interrogation squads.[14]
And any hamlet that shows up as "VC" on the "HES
Hamlet Plot" automatically becomes a "free fire zone"
where, as in My Lai, U.S. troops are authorized to shoot
first and ask questions later.

Project Agile also worked on problems not directly related to military operations. *Newsweek* facetiously reported in 1962 that Agile's outstanding contribution to
date had been the development of new field rations for
Saigon troops: "The Vietnamese GI abhors U.S. K-rations
and the like, and vastly prefers to eat rice covered with a
pungent sauce called *nucmom*. The drippings taken from
salted raw fish fermented for weeks in huge wooden vats,
nucmom is not exactly a portable item. In fact, it eats
through tin cans as if it were sulphuric acid. Agile was
called in. Working with the Army Quartermaster Food
Container Institute in Chicago, it developed a new plastic
(polyethylene) container. According to Phelps, 'it works
fine.' "[15] *Newsweek* acknowledged that "plastic bags won't
win the fierce struggle for Vietnam," nor would the other
innovations described above. "But each in its own way
contributes to raising the fighting potential of the Vietnamese GI"—and thus reduces the burden on America's
own contingent of GI's.

A major responsibility of Agile's Vietnam operations is
the preparation of reports on the effectiveness of the
Saigon regime's programs for winning control of the
countryside. These studies have been used by the military

---

local hamlets so that MACV headquarters could notify Washington
of steady progress in the pacification program. (See *Stalemate in
Vietnam*, Report on a Study Mission to Vietnam by Senator Joseph
S. Clark, U.S. Senate Committee on Foreign Relations, February
1968.)

planners in MACV to modify or redesign the pacification programs that they have compelled the South Vietnamese government to undertake. Most of this work has been performed by a handful of think tanks operating under contract to the Advanced Research Projects Agency, Agile's parent organization. Such studies include:

Pacification. In 1966, William A. Nighswonger completed a study of *Rural Pacification in Vietnam* that was concerned "with the efforts of the Republic of Vietnam and its allies to establish peace in the rural areas of South Vietnam."[16] According to Nighswonger, "the focus of the study is the administration of counterinsurgency campaigns at the province level and below." The report includes a history of the successive campaigns to pacify the countryside, beginning with the 1954 civic-action programs of President Ngo Dinh Diem. On the basis of his experience as a pacification adviser in Quang Nam Province, Nighswonger warns that "the many personal and parochial interests that have threatened to divert the announced revolutionary ambitions of every South Vietnamese regime since Diem, make successful pacification a near impossibility." Nighswonger concludes with the recommendation that "more American pressure, skillfully and discreetly applied, at hundreds of pressure points, may be able to move the [Saigon] government towards its announced goals."[17] In order to increase American "leverage" *vis-à-vis* the Vietnamese bureaucracy, in 1967 the U.S. pacification apparatus was brought under military control and made a subordinate component of MACV, by then the most powerful institution in South Vietnam.[18]

Regional and Popular Forces. The Regional Forces (RF) and Popular Forces (PF) of South Vietnam are lightly armed and poorly trained militia units stationed in the same province (Regional Forces) or the same district (Popular Forces) from which they have been recruited. Despite

numerous reports that RF/PF forces often fade away when
NFL troops approach a village, current MACV doctrine
calls for a significant RF/PF role in the protection of government pacification workers stationed in recently "secured" villages. In order to evaluate the motivation and
morale of RF and PF soldiers, a group of social scientists
from the Simulmatics Corporation of Cambridge, Massachusetts, conducted a total of 868 interviews with members of Regional and Popular Forces, their wives, and
fellow villagers. In its report on *A Socio-Psychological
Study of Regional/Popular Forces in Vietnam,* Simulmatics concluded that RF/PF ineffectiveness could be
traced to "poor national identification and commitment to
mission due to the feelings expressed by the troops that
there is little official concern over their personal family
needs and welfare, that official decisions seem arbitrary
and unjust, that they are unable to have any impact on
local and national policy."[19] The Pentagon's reaction to
these findings has apparently been to increase U.S. supervision of the RF/PF units while reducing Saigon government control. In 1967, MACV launched a major program
to upgrade these units by supplying them with new weapons (including M-16 rifles), by providing additional training,
and through "greatly expanded U.S. advisory attention."[20]

VC Infrastructure. One of the most ambitious Agile projects
is the RAND Corporation study of "Viet Cong Motivation
and Morale." Since the project was initiated in 1964, RAND
scientists have "interviewed thousands of Vietcong," in
order to develop an understanding of the political motivation of National Liberation Front cadres and to construct
a model of the NLF underground—the Vietcong Infrastructure (VCI). Some of this work led to studies on the Chieu
Hoi ("Open Arms") program to induce defections from
the NLF, and on the preparation of propaganda materials
(see Chapter 4). The most recent product of the RAND
effort is a *VC Infrastructure Handbook,* published in En-

glish and Vietnamese and distributed to all Saigon government organizations concerned with identifying and eliminating the VCI. According to the former head of ARPA, Dr. Eberhardt Rechtin, this document is "a guidebook to the organization of the Vietcong. It addresses the problem of how do I tell a Vietcong from an uninvolved South Vietnamese?" Rechtin did not reveal any of the contents of the handbook but asserted that it was used by Vietnamese police officers to "root out" the NLF administrative apparatus in contested villages.[21] The book is being used as part of the Operation Phoenix anti-VCI program, which in 1969 produced an official count of 6,187 "VCI agents" assassinated by Saigon government paramilitary units (see Chapter 9).

Despite these efforts to find a formula for pacification of rural Vietnam, resistance to the Saigon regime continues to grow. Meanwhile, President Nixon's "Vietnamization" program calls for the shift of responsibility for pacification and rural security operations to South Vietnamese military and police forces despite many gloomy reports on the capacity of these forces to assume such a burden. It is not surprising, therefore, that Project Agile is still searching for means to upgrade the counterinsurgency capabilities of the Saigon government. Recent listings of Agile contracts include an award of $2.1 million to Pacific Technical Analysts of Honolulu for research on "the development and operational implementation of the pacification program in Vietnam," one of $40,000 to Greenwich International, Inc., of New York City for a 125-day study of "a system for evaluating the effectiveness of Republic of Vietnam Armed Forces," and another of $660,000 to the RAND Corporation for studies of pacification techniques.[22] Although details of these projects are a tightly kept secret, it is safe to assume that they follow the pattern of earlier studies described above.

AGILE/THAILAND

At the same time that a Project Agile field office was being opened in Saigon, another Agile office—the Research and Development Field Unit-Thailand (RDFU-T)—was activated in Bangkok. When established in the early 1960's, the two Agile units were distinguished by *Aviation Week* as follows:

—Vietnam is considered the "quick fix" area. ARPA approaches research problems here from a viewpoint of what it can do on an immediate basis, and solely for this country.
—Thailand is used to define and proof-test longer-term projects, not only for this country, but for others which are located near the electromagnetic equator.[23]

Thailand, in other words, was to be the sanctuary in which Agile's scientists could develop weapons and strategies for Vietnam-type wars without risking interference from the local population. Thailand's environment, explained Agile spokesman General Robert H. Wienecke, "is similar to Vietnam's—but nobody's shooting at you."[24]

In 1965, Thailand ceased to be a peaceful sanctuary when shooting broke out in the impoverished northeast. Under the banner of the Thai Patriotic Front, a small but hardy insurgent organization began attacking police posts and conducting propaganda meetings in rural villages. Two years later, Meo tribesmen in the northern provinces rebelled against the Thai government's efforts to change their way of life (which included the cultivation of the opium poppy). At the same time, the Malayan rebels living in the southernmost provinces of Thailand—remnants of the Malayan Races Liberation Army that fought the British for twelve years—began expanding their guerrilla organization and undermining government control of the border area.[25] These developments forced the Pentagon to reconsider the function of its Bangkok research facility. No longer isolated from the dynamics of revolutionary conflict, Agile was given the new task of planning the counterinsurgency campaign of the Royal Thai Government's "Communist Suppression Operations Command."

When the expanded Agile effort got underway in 1966, the situation in Thailand looked particularly propitious to Pentagon analysts: the insurgent zone was restricted to a well-defined geographic area, and the insurgent force was limited to a few hundred poorly armed guerrillas. And while in Vietnam the earliest American counterinsurgency strategies had been based on an inadequate and inaccurate knowledge of local conditions, in Thailand Agile had accumulated a "data base" of environmental and behavioral information that theoretically should have made it possible to avoid costly mistakes and delays. Since Agile enjoyed the close cooperation of the Royal Thai military, many Pentagon officials believed that the Thailand effort could prove to be a "showplace" for counterinsurgency planning and serve as a model for similar struggles elsewhere. This confidence can be discerned in the 1967 Congressional testimony of Charles M. Herzfeld, then head of ARPA, on the Agile program in Thailand.

Last year ARPA initiated a major R&D program to assist the Royal Thai Government and the U.S. Mission in Thailand in their effort to suppress the growing Communist insurgency in that country's northeast provinces. Under the rural security systems program, ARPA will marshal the R&D community to: (a) gather and collate critical information on the local geography, the way of life of the local people, and on their attitudes toward the Government; (b) to set up and help maintain current data files on insurgent incidents and operations, and on the many Government programs and activities undertaken for counterinsurgency purposes in the northeast; and (c) provide assistance in analyzing the effectiveness of various counterinsurgency programs. . . . *This program will mark the first time that R&D has been given a major role in supporting a counterinsurgency in a comprehensive way, from the earliest stages of the con-flict.*[26] (Emphasis added.)

To carry out this ambitious program, the Agile office in Thailand was provided with an annual budget of $10 million and a staff of some 150 anthropologists, sociologists, economists, and specialists in various military fields.[27] Although some military personnel are attached to the project, a majority of the staff are civilian researchers supplied by the RAND Corporation, Research Analysis Corporation, Stanford Research Institute, and other Agile contractors. Since one of Agile's functions is to develop an indigenous research capability, the Bangkok office is known as the Joint Thai-U.S. Military Research and Development Center (MRDC), and is headed by a Thai officer.

Most Agile projects in Thailand were designed to amass the vast quantities of geographical, environmental, logistical, and political data required to plan government counterinsurgency operations. One begins to appreciate the extent of this effort by surveying a list of representative Project Agile studies:[28]

> *The Strategic Setting for Conflict in South Thailand,* by Russell F. Rhyne. Stanford Research Institute, 1965 (Confidential).
>
> *Supply Requirements for Royal Thai Government Deployment in Advanced Insurgency in Northeast Thailand,* by Angelo Giarratana. Research Analysis Corporation, 1965 (Confidential).
>
> *Quick Gaming Study of Force Objectives for the Royal Thai Army,* by Dorothy K. Clark and Charles V. Krebs. Research Analysis Corporation, 1964 (Secret).
>
> *Border Patrol Police Capabilities and Potentials for Counterinsurgency in Thailand,* by Dorothy K. Clark and Warren B. Stevens. Research Analysis Corporation, 1965 (Confidential).

Thailand Airfields and Airstrips: A Compilation of Physical, Climatic, and Facility Data, by J. A. Wilson and V. S. Dudley. RAND Corporation, 1967 (Secret).

Counterinsurgency Communications Requirements in Thailand, by York Lucci. Stanford Research Institute, 1966 (Confidential).

Preparation of these studies, in fact, constitutes the first step in the production of strategic war plans. Areas in which Agile planning was concentrated include:

Jungle Communications (Project SEACORE). One of Agile's first major tasks was the development of lightweight radios suitable for use in the tropical jungles of Southeast Asia. While the Agile office in Vietnam was concerned with the modification of existing equipment for immediate use, the office in Thailand was given the task of conducting basic research on jungle communications in order to provide data for the design of entirely new radios. The primary contractors for this effort, known as Project SEACORE (South East Asia COmmunications REsearch), were the Atlantic Research Corporation and the Stanford Research Institute, with Atlantic responsible for radio-signal measurements and Stanford for antenna studies. In order to determine the effects of the tropical environment on radio-signal propagation, Agile scientists established a test site at Pak Chong, in the Khao Yai National Park northeast of Bangkok. Propagation losses at various frequencies and with different antenna configurations were calculated at this site and compared with readings for open terrain in order to determine the optimum combination of performance characteristics. According to former ARPA Director Herzfeld, the technical reports issued by SEACORE contractors are now being used "by the scientific-industrial-government community in the design and development of new military communication equipment."[29]

Village Information Systems (VIST). When the insurgent movement first made its appearance in the northeastern provinces of Thailand, it rapidly became obvious to U.S. counterinsurgency planners that the central government in Bangkok knew next to nothing about the living conditions, grievances, and social structure of rural villages in that region. Since the Americans realized that to fight the guerrillas it would be necessary to deny them access to the resources of these villages, they immediately sought vast quantities of basic data on village characteristics. In 1965, Agile scientists completed a "Village Security Pilot Study" in northeast Thailand in which methodology was developed for the maintenance of a "village data base" containing information on the location, size, economy, leadership, population characteristics, and proximity to police posts and military bases of every village in the region.[30] Recognizing that such vast amounts of information could not be processed by conventional methods, ARPA awarded the Stanford Research Institute a multimillion-dollar contract to design a computerized "Village Information System" (VIST). According to SRI President Charles Anderson, this effort is aimed at the development of a "system for collecting, storing and retrieving in a form usable by the Royal Thai Government information about conditions and events in the villages and towns of Thailand." Anderson asserted that implementation of the VIST program would assist the Thai government in dealing with "civil disorder" and "subversive activity," as well as other "problems peculiar to a peasant society."[31] From this description, it is clear that VIST would have many of the same functions of the Agile-developed Hamlet Evaluation System in South Vietnam.

Police Capabilities. In Thailand, the major responsibility for low-level counterinsurgency is shared by the Provincial Police and the Border Patrol Police—both of which are paramilitary organizations outfitted with helicopters, mortars, machine guns, and other commodities provided by the Office of Public Safety (OPS) of the U.S. Agency for International Development (for more on OPS, see Chapter 9). Provincial Police (PP) units are deployed in village and district police posts throughout guerrilla-infested regions, where they are supposed to form the "first line of defense" against insurgent attacks; the Border Patrol Police (BPP), as one would expect, are concentrated along Thailand's borders (particularly those with Laos and Malaysia) and are entrusted with the task of preventing arms and other supplies from reaching Thai guerrillas from the outside.

Since the undermanned PP and BPP are dispersed in relatively small units over a vast area, U.S. counterinsurgency planners recognized that their effectiveness would be dependent to a considerable extent upon rapid communications between outpost and headquarters (if reinforcements were to be of any use). Consequently, Project Agile commissioned the Stanford Research Institute to study existing police communications in Thailand and to make recommendations for their improvement and expansion. SRI first constructed mathematical models to estimate the demands that would be placed on existing communications systems; on the basis of one such study, *Communications Traffic Requirements to Support Counterinsurgency Operations Against Medium-Level Insurgency in Thailand,* SRI researcher Angelo Gualtieri concluded that "both the Provincial Police and the Border Patrol Police communications systems would need substantial enlargement, in terms of message-carrying capacity, to be responsive to the needs of the postulated conditions."[32] Responsibility for expansion of the PP and BPP communications systems was then delegated to the Office of Public Safety, which has been spending more than $10 million a year to upgrade Thai police capabilities.

Insurgent Logistics. When the guerrilla war in Malaya ended in 1960, several thousand veterans of the Malayan Races Liberation Army established a chain of bases along the

Thailand-Malaysia border. In this inaccessible region, the
guerrillas were able to preserve intact their political apparatus and to begin recruiting new followers from the
Chinese and Muslim minority groups of southern Thailand.
Although not initially considered a threat to Thai security,
in 1965 this "Communist-Terrorist" (C-T) movement became the subject of an intensive Agile study conducted by
Stanford Research Institute personnel. The SRI effort was
apparently designed to develop information for future
counterinsurgency operations both against these particular
guerrillas and against similar groups that might appear
elsewhere in Asia. The focus of the SRI study was insurgent food production, logistics, stockpiling operations, and
other activities related to the survival of a guerrilla movement. From SRI documents, it is clear that the intention
here was to develop methods for destroying the guerrilla
supply system; thus a report on the *Communist Terrorist
Logistics System, Southern Thailand* notes: "The insurgent
logistics system is still one of the most vulnerable parts of
the C-T operation, and interdiction of this system appears
as likely to be a very effective operational means of forcing the C-T's out of their jungle camps into the open where
security forces may engage them on favorable terms."[33] In
Vietnam, "interdiction" has come to mean saturation
bombing, napalming, crop destruction, and all other forms
of firepower used to make the pursuit of normal life functions impossible in rebel areas; "interdiction" has also
been used to justify the devastation of Laos and Cambodia.
SRI's Thailand studies were explicitly designed to provide
models for interdiction operations against any insurgent
movement. Whether they will also be put to use in Thailand remains to be seen.

These studies, and others conducted by Project Agile,
constitute the basic input into the production of strategic
war plans. Commenting on Agile's Thailand operations in

1966, *Technology Week* predicted that "the collection of a mass of environmental and behavioral data on Thailand will put the U.S. in a much more knowledgeable position about that country, in contrast to our early understanding of conditions and customs in Vietnam, *should large-scale U.S. military intervention in Thailand ever be called for.*"[34] (Emphasis added.) As it turned out, American intervention in Thailand, when it occurred, did not involve combat troops but the corps of military advisers, Special Forces instructors, logistics and communications personnel, and other specialists responsible for managing a mercenary army in the field. While most of the 42,000 American troops in Thailand in 1971 were committed to the air war against Vietnamese, Cambodian, and Laotian insurgents, at least a third of them were involved in programs designed to upgrade the internal security capabilities of the Royal Thai Army. "After six centuries of agilely avoiding Asian and European imperialism," Zalin B. Grant wrote in 1969, "the Thais now nervously find themselves waist-deep in the big muddy of an uncertain American foreign policy. . . . For the past seven years the U.S. military has wormed its way into key areas of the Thai infrastructure—with men and money."[35] Some 17,000 Americans, according to Grant, were involved in military development projects in Thailand. When one remembers that no U.S. estimate of guerrilla strength in Thailand has ever placed the figure at over 5,000 men, the massive scale of the U.S. "advisory" intervention becomes even more pronounced.

In planning the Royal Thai Government's counterinsurgency campaign, Agile's strategists refined many practices and tactics that had already been tried and tested in Vietnam. Indeed, former ARPA Director Charles M. Herzfeld told the House Appropriations Committee in 1967 that the U.S. military aid effort in Thailand "takes full advantage of what the Defense Department has learned in Vietnam."[36] On the basis of these "lessons learned," the United States introduced the following programs in Thailand:

—The construction of a thousand new police stations in frontier areas, each of which will be manned by at least twenty members of the Provincial Police or the Border Patrol Police. Before being sent to guerrilla areas, these men receive six weeks of counterinsurgency training provided by U.S. Special Forces instructors at the Thai National Police Training Center at Hua Hin and at provincial training schools. Police radios, weapons, and vehicles are all provided by the Office of Public Safety of the U.S. Agency for International Development (AID).[37]

—The deployment of U.S. Army Engineer construction battalions in sensitive areas to build roads, wells, and irrigation canals as part of the military civic action program of the Royal Thai Army (RTA). Recognizing that "awareness and understanding on the part of Thai officials of the needs and aspirations of rural people . . . are essential to the solution of Thailand's security problem," AID provides funds, equipment, and training to the RTA Mobile Development Units that carry out civic action projects in rural areas.[38]

—The establishment of a thousand-man elite counter-guerrilla unit known as the Thai Special Forces Group. The men in this unit all receive counterinsurgency training at the U.S. Special Forces training center at Lopburi. According to the Washington *Star*, the U.S. Green Berets regularly accompany Thai Special Forces units on training exercises in guerrilla-infested areas.[39]

—The augmentation of the U.S. Military Assistance Program (MAP) in order to provide the "entire Thai army of slightly more than 100,000 men with M-16s as well as the latest machine guns, radios, and other standard light equipment."[40] For the past several years, MAP aid to Thailand has totaled more than $75 million annually, and is expected to rise in the 1970's.[41] According to *Army Digest*, recent new equipment delivered to the Thai military "includes M-41 tanks, M-16 rifles,

M-60 machine guns, M-79 grenade launchers, the VRC-12 family of radios, engineer construction equipment and OH-13 and UH-1H helicopters."[42]

In spite of all these measures, the U.S. counterinsurgency program in Thailand does not appear to be having any more success than in neighboring Vietnam. At the fourteenth annual meeting of the Southeast Asia Treaty Organization, held in Bangkok in September 1968, SEATO Secretary General Lieutenant General Jesus M. Vargas of the Philippines reported that insurgency and terrorism were on the increase in Thailand.[43] Seven months later, *New York Times* correspondent John Stirling reported: "A revolt among the Meo tribesmen of Thailand that flared up last November is still smoldering in the hills of the Phetchabun range extending from northeast Thailand into Laos." A police official told Stirling that the situation was still grave in Nan Loei and Phitsanulok Provinces, and that police reinforcements could not be withdrawn.[44] In November 1969, the U.S. Ambassador to Thailand, Leonard Unger, told the Senate Foreign Relations Committee that insurgent activity was increasing in all regions except the northeast, where U.S. counterinsurgency efforts had been concentrated. In the north, according to Unger, the insurgent force consisted of some 1,300 to 1,600 "aggressive, mobile, relatively well-trained and well led" Meo tribesmen. In the south, the Malayan Liberation Front units had "continued to expand their base areas in Thailand, developed a Malayan Communist Youth League of 2,500, increased their armed strength to 1,200-1,400 well-trained soldiers, and stepped up their propaganda and recruiting."[45] An even gloomier picture was painted at the January 1971 meeting of the International Congress of Orientalists, where Professor Richard C. Butwell of the American University in Washington, D.C., pointed to "low-level but escalating insurgencies" along the northern, northeastern, and southern borders of Thailand as part of a general pattern of rising revolutionary violence in Southeast Asia.[46]

Considering that the United States has been spending more than $100 million a year on counterinsurgency programs in Thailand since 1965 without measurable results, it is not hard to understand why the Advanced Research Projects Agency is no longer optimistic about the Project Agile effort in that country. Thus when the House Appropriations Committee challenged the usefulness of Agile's Thailand studies, the former head of ARPA, Dr. Rechtin, reported that "the results of past research have been mixed, with some projects (border zone security) paying off very well and the results of others (village security) not being implemented for a variety of nontechnical [i.e., political] reasons." At the present level of insurgency, Rechtin explained, "the core of the problem is the relationship of the Royal Thai Government to its people." While of primary concern to the Ambassador and his staff, "this government-to-people relationship is inherently so political that it has proven generally impractical as a field of ARPA research producing implemented results."[47] As a result, ARPA spending in Thailand was cut back from $10 million in fiscal 1969 to $4 million in 1970, and the emphasis changed from the "inherently political" aspects of counterrevolution to tried-and-true hardware items like surveillance and detection.[48] So much for the vision of Thailand as a "model counterinsurgency."

THE FUTURE OF AGILE

In its report on the fiscal year 1970 Defense budget, the House Appropriations Committee proposed a cut of $26 million in the ARPA appropriation, with most of the reduction to be applied against the Overseas Defense Research program (Project Agile). The committee noted that the General Accounting Office was conducting a review of

Agile operations, and that "preliminary analysis has indicated that a number of study projects have not been defense-related, have been of doubtful value, and in a few cases, useless and wasteful." The Director of Defense Research and Engineering was charged by the committee to "review the matters discussed as well as the overseas defense research program mission statement, which is all encompassing and permits almost any type of study effort, with a view of reducing it in scope and clearly delineating the purpose of this program."[49]

When ARPA Director Rechtin came before the House Appropriations Committee in 1970, he was already predisposed to accept the skeptical attitude of the Congressmen he faced. ARPA's "greatest single problem area," he acknowledged, "has unquestionably been overseas research in counterinsurgency." Such research "is not only technically difficult to accomplish, it also has strong social and political factors which influence whether the research results can be used." For this reason, "The total ARPA effort in overseas research in counterinsurgency has been steadily declining from a peak of $16.2 million in 1969 to $6.8 million in fiscal year 1971."[50] In response to the Appropriations Committee's call for a review of the Project Agile mission, Rechtin noted that "R&D on the relationship of the host country's government or military organization to the population will be minimized." Research conducted overseas would be cut back significantly, while "in the United States, R&D will continue on problems of border zone security, patrols as systems, and on documenting the lessons learned in counterinsurgency situations to date."[51]

The available information on the three major Agile projects identified by Rechtin signifies that the Pentagon's research establishment has indeed retreated from the avowedly political orientation of earlier counterinsurgency R&D efforts. Thus a description of the border-zone security project asserts: "Experience has demonstrated that much insurgency constituting a threat to international peace is supported from sources external to a country, with a flow of men and material across international boundaries."[52] This throwback to a simplistic view of insurgency must be a source of embarrassment to the professors and think-tank scientists who worked so hard to create a sophisticated, multidimensional approach to counterrevolution. Agile's future work in this area will be limited to the improvement of "intrusion detection sensors and subsystems" developed under earlier ARPA "Electronic Battlefield" programs (see Chapter 7).

Another Agile project, the Small Independent Action Forces (SIAF), is described as an effort "to apply the systems engineering methodology used in the design of complex weapons systems to the design of reconnaissance patrols." The idea here is to develop a mathematical model of the small patrol force and use it to test the effectiveness of proposed infantry weapons.[53] In defending this somewhat speculative approach to a complex problem, Senator Thomas J. McIntyre of New Hampshire told the Senate in 1969: "There is a great need for a systematic and integrated study of the independent action force—the patrol—with a view toward making this most hazardous, but vital, military operation a more effective and less risky venture."[54] A year later, Rechtin informed the House Appropriations Committee that the SIAF project had produced a "quantitative computerizable description" of patrol operations that by 1971 or so would be "useful to the services for evaluations of new sensors, weapons, and logistics as they affect patrol performance."[55] He did not, however, promise that they would make patrol operations in Vietnam any less hazardous.

William Beecher, who investigated the SIAF project in early 1971, reported in *The New York Times* for February 15, 1971:

The Pentagon is developing specialized weapons and tactics designed to enable a handful of soldiers to operate more effectively 10, 20 or even 100 miles behind enemy lines to collect intelligence or call in air strikes on well-camouflaged military installations.

The weapons include a portable laser device able to guide bombs to within a few feet of their target, an infrared scope that can pick up a foe's body heat in pitch darkness, a lightweight grenade that can be thrown the length of a football field and a jamproof rifle that fires 35 dartlike ['flechette'] bullets.

Another *Times* reporter, Drew Middleton, subsequently witnessed field tests of the SIAF concept at the Combat Development Command's Hunter Liggett Military Reservation near Fort Ord, California, and on April 25, 1971, reported that during the exercises, "six-man teams drawn from the Army's Special Forces, the reconnaissance units of the Marine Corps and the Navy's SEAL [Sea/Air/Land] organization . . . filtered through a rugged area of chaparral-covered hills to observe the actions of an 'aggressor force.' " Wire loops, set in the terrain, "sense and transmit the movements of the infiltrating team and of the aggressive force." This information, according to Middleton, is fed into computers that judge the effectiveness of infiltration techniques.

The third major Agile study currently underway, an analytic study of insurgency, represents a refinement of the input/output approach to counterinsurgency strategy discussed in Chapter 4. According to Dr. Rechtin, the purpose of this RAND study has been to:

Analyze insurgent conflicts as you would analyze nuclear conflicts; in other words, to try to show what the pluses and minuses, strengths and weaknesses are on both sides of a conflict, *endeavoring as best as you can to get the morality out of the equation* because there have been good revolutions put down by bad governments and bad revolutions brought down by good governments, and all kinds of combinations, and the concentration was on what are the tactics and what can you say.[56] (Emphasis added.)

Rechtin went on to concede that RAND "hasn't quite gotten it down to the point of writing equations and putting it on a computer in detail," but held out the hope that if we could only put morality out of the picture it might be possible to establish some formulas that would take all the uncertainty out of counterinsurgency. While this attitude is entirely consistent with a technological approach to counterrevolution (Rechtin, after all, is an expert in deep-space communication), it signified a total retreat from the political battlefield, where morality is a persuasive argument.

Chapter 9

"THE FIRST LINE
OF DEFENSE"

—Police Mercenaries

The by now familiar panacea for domestic ills, "law and order," has long been used to describe American objectives in the troubled areas of Africa, Asia, and Latin America. While the Federal government did not start aiding local police agencies in the United States until passage of the Omnibus Crime Control and Safe Streets Act in 1968, we have been supplying the police of selected underdeveloped nations with equipment, arms, and training since 1954. United States funds have been used to equip and train riot police in the Dominican Republic, to renovate and expand the South Vietnamese prison system, and to install a centralized police command post in Caracas, Venezuela. The Agency for International Development (AID) estimates that more than a million foreign policemen have received some training or supplies through the U.S. "Public Safety" Program—a figure that includes 100,000 Brazilian police and the entire 85,000-man National Police force of South Vietnam.[1]

U.S. foreign-aid programs in the Third World call for a modest acceleration of economic growth, to be achieved wherever possible through the normal profit-making activities of American corporations and lending institutions. It is obvious, however, that an atmosphere of insecurity and rebelliousness does not provide an attractive climate for investment. In the rapidly urbanizing nations of the Third World, civil disorders have become a common phenomenon as landless peasants stream to the cities in search of economic and cultural opportunities. Since most of these countries cannot satisfy the aspirations of these new city dwellers under present economic and social systems, built-up tensions are increasingly giving way to attacks on the status quo. During his spring 1969 tour of Latin America, Nelson Rockefeller had an opportunity to witness some of these disorders in person; in his report to the President, the Governor commented that "with urbanization in the Western Hemisphere has come crowded living conditions and a loss of living space in physical and psychological terms. . . . These sprawling urban areas of the hemisphere spawn restlessness and anger which are readily exploited by the varying forces that thrive on trouble."[2] Rockefeller warned that "radical revolutionary elements in the hemisphere [are] increasingly turning toward urban terrorism in their attempts to bring down the existing order."[3] This prediction has already been borne out in Brazil and Uruguay, where urban guerrillas have staged spectacular bank robberies and kidnappings.

Since the late 1950's, a paramount concern of American policymakers has been the preservation of social stability in Third World countries deemed favorable to U.S. trade and investment. In order to defeat rural guerrillas, the Military Assistance Program has been used to upgrade the counterinsurgency capabilities of Third World armies. And, on the premise that the police constitute the "first line of defense" against urban insurgency and subversion, the Agency for International Development has funneled American funds and supplies into the hands of Third World police forces.

During hearings on the foreign assistance appropriation for 1965, AID Administrator David Bell described the rationale behind U.S. police assistance programs as follows:

Maintenance of law and order including internal security is one of the fundamental responsibilities of government. . . .

Successful discharge of this responsibility is imperative if a nation is to establish and maintain the environment of stability and security so essential to economic, social, and political progress. . . .

Plainly, the United States has very great interests in the creation and maintenance of an atmosphere of law and order under humane, civil concepts and control. . . . When there is a need, technical assistance to the police of developing nations to meet their responsibilities promotes and protects these U.S. interests.[4]

The Public Safety Program is not large in comparison with the Military Assistance Program, but its supporters can muster some impressive arguments in its favor. Advocates of the Public Safety Program submit that the police, being interspersed among the population, are more effective than the military in controlling low-scale insurgency. According to former Administrator Bell, "The police are a most sensitive point of contact between government and people, close to the focal points of unrest, and more acceptable than the army as keepers of order over long periods of time. The police are frequently better trained and equipped than the military to deal with minor forms of violence, conspiracy and subversion."[5] A conspicuous feature of this argument is the belief (based on painful experience) that the military will overreact to an insurgent threat and thus alienate the civilian population. Thus, in testimony before the Senate Subcommittee on American

Republics Affairs, Professor David Burks of Indiana University commented:

I think we have to face a reality. The reality is that when insurgents appear, the governments will call upon the army to eliminate the insurgents. And, in most cases that I have examined, this was not too difficult to do. But there comes a point—and this came in Cuba in 1957 and 1958 when Castro was in the Sierra Maestra—there can come a point when the army cannot handle this kind of situation simply because the military establishment tends to use too much force, tends to use the wrong techniques and tends, therefore, to polarize the population and gradually force the majority of those who are politically active to support the revolutionary or insurgent force. . . . Whereas a civil police force . . . is with the people all the time carrying on the normal functions of control of or apprehension of ordinary or common criminals and can, therefore, move very quickly whenever an insurgent problem develops.[6]

A basic goal of any government threatened by revolution is, of course, to identify and neutralize the clandestine political apparatus of the insurgent opposition. The indigenous police force is uniquely suited for this function, it is argued, since "the police intelligence system adapted to rooting out the non-political criminal can easily turn its attention to the political criminal."[7] One of the most influential counterinsurgency strategists, Sir Robert Thompson, argues that "the best organization to be responsible for all internal security intelligence is the special branch [i.e., countersubversive unit] of the police force rather than any other organization. The police force is a state organization reaching out into every corner of the country and will have had long experience of close contact with the population."[8] Supporters of this position have come to the somewhat dubious conclusion that effective police work can often obviate the need for massive military intervention on the scale of Vietnam. In a 1965 address to graduates of the International Police Academy, General Maxwell Taylor spoke of the lessons he had learned in Southeast Asia:

The outstanding lesson is that we should never let another Vietnam-type situation arise again. We were too late in recognizing the extent of the subversive threat. We appreciate now that every young, emerging country must be constantly on the alert, watching for those symptoms which, if allowed to develop unrestrained, may eventually grow into a disastrous situation such as that in South Vietnam.[9]

Taylor told the foreign police officers that in Vietnam, "We have learned the need for a strong police force and a strong police intelligence organization to assist in identifying early the symptoms of an incipient subversive situation." When a nation seeks to protect itself from such symptoms, "the police is the first line of defense in this endeavor."

Supporters of the police-assistance program also point out that foreign police forces are considerably cheaper to maintain than military forces, since they do not require expensive "hardware" like planes, tanks, and artillery.

These arguments, advanced by men like Colonel Edward Lansdale of the CIA, received their most favorable response from President John F. Kennedy and his brother Robert, then Attorney General, in the early 1960's.* Presidential backing was responsible for a substantial expansion of the Public Safety Program in 1962, and for the centralization of all U.S. police-assistance activities in AID's Office of Public Safety (OPS). The State Department

---

* Undersecretary of State U. Alexis Johnson, who worked on police programs in the Kennedy Administration, told graduates of the International Police Academy in 1971 that when he "came into office in early 1961, President Kennedy took an immediate and personal interest in examining all of the programs in which the United States was cooperating with other governments in efforts to improve economic growth and political stability. He took a particular interest in our police programs, because it was his firm conviction . . . that the police forces are a basic element in resisting the threats posed by insurrection and internal subversion, themselves the enemies of the growth and stability he sought." (*Department of State Bulletin*, September 13, 1971, p. 280.)

memorandum establishing OPS, issued in November 1962, is noteworthy for its strong language. It declared that AID "vests the Office of Public Safety with primary responsibility and authority for public safety programs and gives that Office a series of powers and responsibilities which will enable it to act rapidly, vigorously, and effectively . . . powers greater than any other technical office or division of AID."[10] (These special powers will be discussed further below.) The two Kennedys also gave enthusiastic support to the creation of an Inter-American Police Academy in the Panama Canal Zone (later moved to Washington, D.C., and reorganized as the International Police Academy).[11]

OPS is empowered to assist Third World police organizations in three ways: (1) by providing instruction at the International Police Academy and other U.S. schools for senior police officers and technicians; (2) by stationing Public Safety Advisors abroad who dispense advice to local police commands and provide in-country training for rank-and-file policemen; and (3) by providing weapons, ammunition, radios, patrol cars, chemical munitions, and other commodities. AID spending on these programs in fiscal years 1961 through 1969 amounted to $236 million.[12] Annual spending on the Public Safety Program rose steadily from $10 million in fiscal 1961 to $54 million in fiscal 1968; in the past few years the program has been curtailed because of cuts in the AID budget, but it will probably rise again if the Administration's plan to switch the OPS appropriation to the Defense Department budget wins Congressional approval.*

* Although the legislative fate of President Nixon's foreign aid reorganization plan is uncertain, the Administration has asked Congress to support an expanded OPS program. Thus in its fiscal 1972 budget presentation to Congress, AID argued that the Public Safety program "can serve to prepare civil police forces to prevent the development of threats to internal order before they become explosive problems requiring military action." AID requested $26 million for OPS activities in fiscal 1972, an increase of $3 million over the fiscal 1971 appropriation. (U.S. Agency for International

Table 5

**AID PUBLIC SAFETY EXPENDITURES
BY REGION, 1961–9**

(In thousands of dollars)

Region	Fiscal 1969	Total, Fiscal 1961–9
East Asia	28,858	160,669
Latin America	3,931	43,630
Africa	1,105	19,155
Near East and South Asia	927	12,873
Worldwide, total	34,821	236,327

Source: U.S. Department of State, Agency for International Development, Statistics and Reports Division, *Operations Report,* Data as of June 30, 1961, June 30, 1962 . . . , June 30, 1969.

As can be seen from Table 5, about two-thirds of all Public Safety funds are committed to East Asia (including South Vietnam), with 20 percent going to Latin America and the remainder being divided between Africa, the Near East, and South Asia.

A country-by-country breakdown of Public Safety spending reveals that in each region OPS expenditures are concentrated in a handful of key countries, most of which have experienced or are now experiencing urban disorders or rural insurrections.

An example of this, and one of the largest OPS programs on record, is the case of Pakistan, where West Pakistani troops and police units were used in an effort to suppress the Bangladesh independence movement in East Pakistan. In justifying its request for $250,000 to fund this program in fiscal 1972, the Agency for International Development told Congress:

Pakistan has been, and is, experiencing serious difficulties and threats to its internal security which have served to inhibit

---

Development, *Program and Project Data Presentation to the Congress for Fiscal Year 1972,* Washington, D.C., 1971.)

economic and social development. . . . The geographic division of the country and the ethnic differences in its population have been contributory factors. . . .

Pakistan has been making a serious effort to build up the police as its first line of defense against threats to internal order. U.S. advisory assistance has emphasized the use of humane procedures in urban disturbance control and the police are now used as the primary force for this purpose.

There continues to be a need for Public Safety assistance for Pakistan . . . so the police may be enabled to perform effectively whatever internal security role given them by the Government of [West] Pakistan.[13]

In Table 6, the nations that have highest priority on police assistance funds are listed along with other data on the Public Safety Program in those countries. (See Appen-

Table 6

AID PUBLIC SAFETY OPERATIONS IN SELECTED COUNTRIES

Country	Expenditures (in thousands of dollars)		Personnel trained in the U.S., 1961–9	Public Safety Advisors stationed as of 6/30/68
	Fiscal 1969	Total, fiscal 1961–9		
Vietnam	19,647	64,180	267	200
Thailand	7,607	71,316	354	58
Brazil	862	7,416	455	17
Pakistan	735	7,583	106	6
Dominican Republic	435	3,116	122	15
Guatemala	411	2,482	243	2
Congo (Kinshasa)	378	3,133	79	5
Venezuela	331	2,627	517	10
Colombia	299	5,723	348	7
Jordan	185	2,365	52	5
Somali Republic	136	4,416	119	5

Source: U.S. Department of State, Agency for International Development, Statistics and Reports Division, *Operations Report,* Data as of June 30, 1961, June 30, 1962 . . . , June 30, 1969.

dix F for a complete breakdown of OPS expenditures.)

These funds are used to pay the salaries of Public Safety Advisors stationed abroad, the costs of training in the United States, and procurement of commodities delivered to the recipient country. The items most frequently included in the procurement program are riot-control munitions, small arms, vehicles, radios, and office supplies. Commodities shipped to Brazil in the past eleven years, according to a 1970 OPS press release, include: 36 patrol cars, 52 jeeps, 260 portable VHF radios, 800,000 rounds of .38 caliber pistol ammunition, 540 riot batons, 122 gas masks, 15,236 CN tear-gas grenades, 5,100 CS gas grenades, 20 fingerprint kits, and a $137,000 IBM information-processing system.

In fiscal 1967, three-fourths of the $40 million OPS budget was devoted to the procurement effort; a large part of the commodities thereby obtained, however, was shipped to Vietnam and Thailand, while in most countries training and advisory costs absorbed 50 percent or more of the OPS budget. In the Dominican Republic, for example, training and advisory expenses consumed about two-thirds of the OPS budget, and commodities the remaining third.[14]

OPS OVERSEAS OPERATIONS

An examination of the Public Safety programs in the countries for which documentation is available indicates that in each case AID has focused its efforts on certain key sectors of the police system—particularly training, management, intelligence, telecommunications, and riot control. Thus a description of OPS program objectives for East Asia (Thailand, Laos, Korea, and the Philippines) emphasizes:

Specifically, the Public Safety programs will focus on the development of key institutional elements, such as communications networks and training systems; on better administration and management leading to the effective use of resources; the improvement of rural paramilitary police ability to prevent and deal with guerrilla activities; the provision of effective police services at the hamlet level; the improvement of urban policing, including the humane control of civil disturbances and riots; and the development of the police ability to prevent the infiltration of enemy agents.[15]

Before any funds are committed to a given country, OPS conducts a survey of that nation's entire law-enforcement apparatus in order to determine how such funds should be spent. These surveys, ordinarily conducted by a two- or three-man team of OPS officers, include recommendations on how police agencies in the host country (particularly the paramilitary, antiriot, and intelligence units) can be made to operate more effectively. Not surprisingly, the emphasis in these reports is on the maintenance of public order and the elimination of revolutionary organizations—i.e., those aspects of police work which provide protection for U.S. business interests—rather than on the reform of brutal and corrupt police administrations. The awarding of OPS funds will often be made contingent on the agreement of the country involved to implement the recommendations made by the OPS team.[16]

The police assistance program in any given country is supervised and administered by the Public Safety Advisors attached to the AID mission in the U.S. embassy. As of June 30, 1968, there were 407 Public Safety Advisors serving abroad, of whom 200 were in Vietnam and 58 in Thailand.[17] In all other countries, the OPS staff did not exceed seventeen and in most cases was in the range of four or five men (see Appendix F). According to John George, a former Public Safety Advisor in Africa, these men "are in everyday contact with foreign police and government officials. Depending on the size and scope of the country program concerned, the advisors may be the purveyors of up to a score of separate police techniques, ranging from laboratory criminalistics and computer-assisted identification procedures to police public relations, traffic control, and routine street patrol for foot beats." Most advisers are middle-level or senior officers of domestic U.S. law-enforcement agencies, or men recruited from the FBI, CIA, Military Police, or the Special Forces.[18] Since OPS funds are usually granted with the proviso that management of key police functions be centralized in the headquarters of the national police force, the Public Safety Program naturally tends to enhance the influence of the resident OPS advisers, who ordinarily spend most of their time in the company of the top headquarters personnel.*

In providing this kind of assistance, OPS notes that most countries possess a unified "civil security service" which "in addition to regular police include[s] paramilitary units within civil police organizations and paramilitary forces such as gendarmeries, constabularies, and civil guards which perform police functions and have as their primary mission maintaining internal security." The AID police assistance program is designed to encompass all these functions; according to OPS:

Individual Public Safety programs, while varying from country to country, are focused in general on developing within the civil security forces a balance of (1) a capability for regular police operations, with (2) an investigative capability for detecting and identifying criminal and/or subversive individuals and organizations and neutralizing their activities, and with (3) a capability for controlling militant activities ranging from demonstrations, disorders, or riots through small-scale guerrilla operations.[19]

Obviously, when a country is experiencing a popular upheaval of some sort, OPS will be most concerned with

* In order to call attention to the role of American Public Safety Advisors in management of the repressive Uruguayan police apparatus, Tupamaro guerrillas kidnapped the chief OPS representative in Montevideo, Dan A. Mitrione, on July 31, 1970. When the guerrillas' demand for the release of a hundred political prisoners was not met, Mitrione was assassinated one week later.

developing the third function cited above. As noted in the 1962 State Department memo quoted earlier, OPS possesses unique powers not granted any other AID bureaus; these powers enable OPS to "act rapidly, vigorously and effectively" in aiding favored regimes threatened by popular uprisings. When a crisis develops in a foreign capital, Public Safety officials in Washington often work around the clock to speed critical supplies like tear gas and shotguns to the security forces of the beleaguered regime. Police weapons were rushed to Tunisia, for instance, in 1967 following the Arab-Israeli War and subsequent rioting in Tunisian cities. AID later told Congress that $250,000 had been spent by OPS to provide the Tunisian police with "radios, riot helmets, spotlights, teargas grenades, gas masks, shotguns and revolvers, and megaphones."[20]

In some countries, OPS has extended the definition of "civil security forces" to include paramilitary units of the regular army and private security agencies, particularly those which protect American overseas investments. Thus, a 1967 report on the Public Safety Program in Venezuela notes that "in recognition of the need for developing rural police capabilities, two public safety advisors (rural) have been assigned to work full time with the National Guard." These advisers worked jointly with the Military Assistance Advisory Group in providing training to the National Guard in counterinsurgency operations. The same report revealed that "the Chief and Deputy Chief Public Safety Advisors meet monthly with security officers of all major oil companies operating in the country and the security officer for the leading mining company. All aspects dealing with security and insurgency problems are discussed and unified action decided upon."[21]

The crucial role played by the Public Safety mission in countries threatened by revolution can perhaps best be seen in the Dominican Republic, which has received more than $3 million from OPS since 1962. Using the special emergency powers granted in its original State Department charter, OPS has twice initiated crash programs to develop a reliable riot-control force in the capital, Santo Domingo. The first such intervention occurred in 1962, during rioting that followed the assassination of the dictator Rafael Leonidas Trujillo and the establishment of a new government headed by Joaquín Balaguer. U.S. Ambassador John Bartlow Martin asked President Kennedy if he could arrange to send some policemen from the "Mexican squad" of the Los Angeles Police Department to Santo Domingo to help with riot-control training. According to Martin, "The President turned to Ralph Dungan, his staff member who handled Latin American affairs . . . and said, 'Ask Bobby if he can get him some help.' " Apparently the message got through to Attorney General Robert Kennedy, for "a week or two later two excellent Spanish-speaking Los Angeles detectives arrived in Santo Domingo. They trained the Dominican police in riot control, gave them nightsticks, tear gas, and gas masks, and white helmets—they became known as the Cascos Blancos, white helmets—and in a few weeks the [interim government] rewon the streets, thanks almost entirely to those two detectives."[22]

The U.S.-trained "Cascos Blancos" became so hated by the populace that in 1965 OPS was compelled to report that "this force was the subject of a severe and concentrated attack during the recent revolution which effectively eliminated the unit as a riot control force."[23] Once again, emergency measures were called for in order to restore government control of the streets. As reported by OPS,

In September and October 1965, USAID consultants confirmed the need for an accelerated program of training and commodity procurement for the police, and the reconstitution of the civil disturbance control force. Five Public Safety Advisors arrived in January, 1966, to begin an emergency civil disturbance control training course. Emergency procurement of gas masks, plastic shields, riot shotguns, ammunition and radio-equipped vehicles was effected.[24]

Within two years, after expenditures of well over a million dollars, OPS had begun retraining and resupplying the entire Dominican police force, and had organized two of five projected 180-man companies of riot police. This effort was supervised by an OPS team of fifteen advisers, of whom at least six were CIA agents.[25]

Additional indicators of the pivotal role of the Public Safety program in developing police training, communications, and management capabilities is indicated in OPS reports on Brazil, Colombia, and Venezuela.

—In AID's fiscal 1971 *Program and Project Data Presentations to the Congress,* OPS notes:

> Through December 1969, the Public Safety project in Brazil has assisted in training locally over 100,000 federal and state police personnel. Additionally, 523 persons received training in the United States. Major project accomplishments include: construction, equipping and development of curriculum, staff and faculty for the National Police Academy, National Telecommunications Center and National Institutes of Criminalistics and Identification.* All are functioning effectively in support of police departments throughout the country.[26]

* When the Public Safety Program was begun in 1960, Brazil's twenty-two states each had their own police force, but there was no national police force or central police command. Under the original Public Safety agreement with Brazil, a major goal of the OPS effort was to help establish a Federal police force with headquarters in the new capital of Brasilia. AID funds were subsequently used for the training of Federal police officers, and the establishment of a centralized police communications and intelligence apparatus. In 1968, a new agreement was signed with Brazil that called for the concentration of U.S. resources in the further development of the Federal police. Its purpose, according to a 1970 OPS press release, "was to develop the capacity of the Federal Police to assume an increasing share of the provision of training and technical services for the state level police forces." The success of this effort was later cited as the justification for termination of the Brazil Program in fiscal 1972.

—From June 4 to June 18, 1963, Public Safety Advisor Paul Katz toured Colombia inspecting the communications facilities of the National Police and the Administrative Department of Security (DAS—the notorious political police). In his *Republic of Colombia Police Communications Survey Report*, Katz noted that the internal security operations of both DAS and the police were hampered because each maintained their own inadequate communications systems. Since expansion of both networks would be costly and inefficient, Katz proposed that the two communications systems be merged and operated jointly. In order to obtain Colombian backing for this proposal, he recommended that any future OPS monetary assistance be made contingent on implementation of the merger. To sweeten this ultimatum, Katz promised the Colombians additional AID funds for the procurement of new radio equipment, training in the United States for Colombian radio technicians, and the stationing in Colombia of an OPS telecommunications adviser.[27] When the heads of the National Police and DAS had agreed to the merger proposal, OPS advanced several million dollars to establish a modern nationwide radio/teletype communications network.[28]

—Among the "program accomplishments" during his tour of duty, the Chief Public Safety Advisor to Venezuela reported:

In an effort to improve coordination among police agencies in the capital area, terrorists' prime and most sensitive target, the Public Safety Division urged the host country to accept the concept of a unified police command. Detailed recommendations for establishing this command were prepared, with full support from the Ambassador. . . . The President of the host country gave full support and per-

sonal attention to the plan. Initial resistance to the idea was
eventually overcome, and the unified operations center was
formally established in November 1963.[29]

AID officials insist that Public Safety assistance is "not
given to support dictatorships." But apparently there are
exceptions to this rule. Administrator David Bell told a
Senate committee in 1964 that "it is obviously not our
purpose or intent to assist a head of state who is repressive. On the other hand, we are working in a lot of countries where the governments are controlled by people who
have shortcomings."[30] Not wanting to embarrass AID or
any of the people we support who have "shortcomings,"
Bell did not mention names; nevertheless, he revealed
that:

Assistance to one country was completely stopped after a coup
and has been reinstated only recently on a reduced scale while
there is an evaluation of the country's performance on meeting
public safety requirements to create a reformed and civilian
controlled police force.

In another country, despite the limitations of the present government, it is considered desirable and proper to continue to
assist in the improvement of the efficiency of the civilian police
force to counteract the small amount of Communist-led terrorism and to make sure the police can confront and stop any
larger effort, if it should start.[31]

With the information provided by AID, it is hard to determine whether "Communist-led terrorism" does not in
fact connote an antigovernment movement enjoying widespread popular support. In fact, any number of Latin American countries ruled by military dictatorships could fit the
descriptions provided by Bell. Thus the United States maintains a substantial Public Safety Program in Brazil, despite
well-documented reports that political prisoners are routinely tortured by the police. In justifying continued OPS
aid to such regimes, Bell emphasized that "the police are a

strongly anti-Communist force right now. For that reason it is a very important force to us."[32] In view of the Cold War obsession shared by all U.S. police agencies, it is no surprise that these men should consider a modicum of (allegedly) Communist-led terrorism to be sufficient reason to subsidize the repressive apparatus of a totalitarian regime.

AID officials are fully aware that in many countries receiving OPS aid the police are regarded with suspicion and resentment by the local population because of a tradition of brutality and oppression. Since provocative police behavior frequently inspires antigovernment campaigns, an important aspect of the Public Safety training program is the effort to encourage "the development of responsible and humane police administration and judicial procedures." Students at the various OPS schools are advised to "stay out of politics" (i.e., to support whatever pro-U.S. regime happens to be in power), and are trained in the techniques of "nonlethal crowd control" (i.e., the massive use of riot gases). The main objective of this approach, according to OPS Director Byron Engle, is to prevent situations in which "an oppressive police force drives a deep wedge between the people and their government."[33] As a successful application of this philosophy, OPS cites the case of the Dominican Republic in 1965, where—after intensive training in the use of chemical agents—"police action against the Communists was so effective that the insurgents did not even end up with the body of a dead comrade to drag through the city in false martyrdom."[34]

PUBLIC SAFETY TRAINING

Of all the forms of police assistance provided by the United States, training, according to OPS, "has the most enduring effect." Although several other Western nations conduct police assistance programs in Third World countries (usually stemming from a colonial relationship), no country provides training on the scale of the U.S. Public Safety Program. Since the inception of this program after World War II, more than a million rank-and-file policemen have received some form of training from OPS instructors.[35] Such in-country training is provided by U.S. Public Safety Advisors, "who give technical advice, using training aids and equipment demonstrations; serve as guest instructors in the police academies and schools of the host country; and direct training in AID-sponsored special courses and seminars."[36] In addition, at least five thousand foreign police commanders and technicians have received advanced training in the United States, principally at the International Police Academy (IPA) in Washington, D.C.

Often described as the West Point of the international law enforcement community, IPA occupies a former streetcar barn in the Georgetown section of Washington. The Academy building, located adjacent to the campus of Georgetown University, houses two auditoriums, a gymnasium, library, classrooms, and one of the most modern rifle ranges in the country. These facilities were created when the building was remodeled for OPS use by O. Roy Chalk, whose D.C. Transit Company owns the building and rents it to AID for a reported $220,000 annually.[37]

As of January 1970, some 3,500 students had graduated from IPA or its predecessor, the Inter-American Police Academy. IPA's students are police officers of commissioned rank from Africa, Asia, the Middle East, and all Latin American countries except Haiti and Cuba. About 60 percent of the students enroll in a Spanish-language program known as the Inter-American Course. In addition to the basic IPA training program, another two thousand Third World police officers have been brought to the United States for "technical specialist training" at a number of government schools and other institutions. Such training includes a course in Questioned Document Examination offered by the Postal Service's Scientific Investigation Laboratory, a program in Maritime Law Enforcement conducted by the U.S. Coast Guard, and instruction in Penology and Corrections provided by Southern Illinois University.[38]

The basic program of studies at IPA itself includes a thirteen-week General Course for "officers of commissioned status with rank up to and including that of a major, or of equivalent civilian rank"; an Inter-American General Course for Latin Americans; and a Senior Course for "police executives of highest rank with Lieutenant Colonel minimum or with equivalent civilian ranks." OPS boasts that IPA graduates often attain high rank in the police establishments of their homelands. Among the men most often cited in this regard are Major General Vicente Huerta Celis, former director general of the Carabineros de Chile; Mohammed Abscir Mussa, commandant of the Somali police force; and Brigadier General Abdullah Rafie, deputy chief of the Jordanian National Police.[39]

The Senior Course, according to OPS literature, includes seminar-type study of such subjects as "Comparative police administration; police organization, management, operation, planning and research; public relations; communications; instructor training; crime prevention; investigation; firearms; counterinsurgency and countersubversion." The General Course provides lecture-type instruction on the same subjects, although here the emphasis is on field operations rather than management and logistics.[40] Students in both courses are given an extended tour of selected U.S. law enforcement agencies, including the FBI Academy and the Army Engineer School at Fort Belvoir, Virginia, where they witness a demonstration of chemical munitions and other riot-control devices. In addition, each class takes a three-day trip to the John F. Kennedy Special Warfare Center at Fort Bragg, North Carolina, for a series of briefings on "civil-military relationships in counterinsurgency operations and police support in unconventional warfare."[41]

Instruction at IPA is usually concluded with elaborate "war games" conducted in the Academy's Police Operations Control Center (POCC). A visitor to this facility described the training exercises as follows:

At the front of the POCC is a magnetic game board on which has been constructed the map of a mythical city, Rio Bravos, capital of the Republic of San Martin. Students elect officers who sit at a long, V-shaped desk in front of the board. Each has a phone and access to a teletype machine. From the control booth, faculty field commanders alert the students to a communist-inspired riot at the city's university, or to a bombing attempt by communist subversives from the hostile neighboring country, Maoland [sic]. The students deploy their forces on the board and plan strategies, much as they would from a real police control center.[42]

It should be obvious at this point that training at the International Police Academy includes not only the purveying of police skills and techniques but also indoctrination in the anti-Communist Cold War ideology of the American foreign policy apparatus. (It is not hard, for instance, to identify "Maoland" as Cuba and "Rio Bravos" as Caracas, Santo Domingo, or Panama City.) The U.S. police training program, like the military training program, is designed to establish a corps of officers in each Third World nation who, for ideological and/or opportunistic reasons, profess greater loyalty to their American counterparts than to their fellow countrymen. When IPA graduates resume their posts in their country's police forces, they continue to remain in contact with the Office of Public Safety, in the person of the resident Public Safety Advisor. By extending or withholding AID funds, the advisers are in a position to advance or retard the careers of senior police officers who seek OPS backing for the expansion or modernization of their commands. For these reasons, it is thus possible for a relatively modest program of police assistance (modest, that is, when measured against the Military Assistance Program) to exert a considerable degree of influence over the management of Third World police forces.

A CASE STUDY:
"PUBLIC SAFETY" IN VIETNAM

The Public Safety effort in South Vietnam is the largest and one of the oldest U.S. police assistance programs—half of AID's Public Safety Advisors and more than half of OPS's annual budget are committed to Vietnam operations. The Vietnam program began in 1955, when Michigan State University received a contract from the Foreign Operations Administration (AID's predecessor agency) to assemble a team of police experts to advise the government of Ngo Dinh Diem. The thirty-three advisers who served in the Police Division of the now famous Michigan State University Group (MSUG) supervised the reorganization of Vietnam's decrepit police system, provided training in a variety of police skills, delivered small arms and ammunition, and helped establish a modern records system for filing data on political suspects.[43]

The MSUG police program was taken over in 1959 by the Public Safety Division of the United States Operations Mission (USOM). In keeping with President Kennedy's call for increased counterinsurgency initiatives, the program was vastly expanded in 1962. Beginning with a staff of six in 1959, the OPS mission in Vietnam increased to 47 in 1963 and to 204 by 1968. Total AID support of the OPS program had reached $95,417,000 by the end of fiscal year 1968, and has continued at the rate of about $25 million a year (additional funds are supplied by the Department of Defense as part of Vietnam war appropriations). Reflecting the growing military orientation of the pacification program, on May 9, 1967, the Public Safety Division was brought under the control of the Military Assistance Command, Vietnam (MACV) as part of the Civil Operations and Revolutionary Development Support (CORDS) program.[44]

From the very start of the Vietnam conflict, the National Police (NP) of South Vietnam has been regarded by our government as a paramilitary force with certain responsibilities related to the overall counterinsurgency effort. In the foreword to an OPS manual on *The Police and Resources Control in Counter-Insurgency,* Chief Public Safety Advisor Frank E. Walton wrote: "The methods included in this text are emergency procedures not utilized in a normal peace-time situation. They are stringent, war-time measures designed to assist in defeating the enemy."[45] In order to upgrade the capacity of the Vietnamese police to carry out its wartime responsibilities, OPS supervised the consolidation of all regional, provincial, and specialized police agencies under the directorate of National Police in 1962, and subsequently prepared a "National Police Plan" for Vietnam in 1964. Under the plan, the NP grew from 19,000 men in 1963 to 52,000 by the end of 1965, 85,000 in 1969, and 100,000 by 1971.[46] To keep pace with this rapid growth, the plan provided for a vast increase in U.S. technical assistance, training, and commodity support. Public Safety Division aid and management has become so extensive, indeed, that the National Police might more properly be considered an extension of MACV than an indigenous institution.

The specific counterinsurgency functions performed by the police—resources control, identification, surveillance, and pacification—are spelled out in an OPS brochure on *The Role of Public Safety in Support of the National Police of Vietnam* and other AID documents.

Resources Control is defined by Public Safety Advisor E. H. Adkins, Jr., as "an effort to regulate the movement of selected resources, both human and material, in order to restrict the enemy's support or deprive him of it altogether."[47] As conceived by the British counterinsurgency expert Sir Robert Thompson, this program is designed to dry up the Maoist "sea" in which the guerrilla "fish" swim. In order to prevent the flow of supplies and people to and from villages loyal to the National Liberation Front, 7,700 members of the National Police currently man some 650 checkpoints at key locations on roadways and waterways, and operate mobile checkpoints on remote roads and trails. By 1969, more than 560,000 persons had been arrested in this program, of whom 38,000 were reported as "VC suspects."[48] And in 1970, AID reported that "resources control efforts resulted in 153,000 arrests, of which some 26,000 represented known or suspected VC, [while] confiscations included 2,000 weapons, 34,450 units of medicine/drugs and 1,000 tons of contraband foodstuffs."[49]

The National Identity Registration Program is "an integral part of the population and resources control program." Under a 1957 law, drawn up by MSUG, every Vietnamese fifteen years and older is required to register with the Saigon government and carry identification cards; anyone caught without the proper ID cards is considered a VC suspect and subject to imprisonment or worse. At the time of registration, a full set of fingerprints is obtained from each applicant, and information on his or her political beliefs is recorded. By the end of 1971, twelve million persons were to have been reached by this identification/registration program. "Once completed," AID asserts, "the identification system will provide for a national repository of fingerprints and photographs and biographical data. It will be one of the most complete national identification systems in the world, and one of the most badly needed."[50]

Surveillance of persons and organizations suspected of harboring antigovernment sentiments is the responsibility of the NP's Special Police Branch (SP). This agency is nothing more nor less than Vietnam's secret police; originally the Indochinese branch of the French *Sûreté,* the SP was known as the Vietnamese Bureau of Investigation during the Diem regime.[51] OPS documents state in uncharacteristically frank language that "SP agents penetrate subversive organizations," and "use intelligence collection, political data [and] dossiers compiled from census data . . . to separate the bad guys from the good."[52] AID has nothing to say about the criteria used to separate the "bad guys" from the "good guys"; anyone familiar with the Vietnamese scene knows, however, that the SP's major responsibility is surveillance of non-Communist groups that could pose a political challenge to the regime in power. Thus D. Gareth Porter, writing in *The Nation,* notes that "students, intellectuals, Buddhist monks and anyone who has been involved in political, social or educational activity, are the objects of special suspicion, and detailed dossiers are compiled for each individual from reports of plain-clothes men and informers who infiltrate every student, religious or social welfare group."[53] Persons who advocate negotiations with the NLF are routinely picked up by the Special Police and sentenced to stiff prison terms.

Pacification usually brings to mind "goodwill" projects like school construction and free medical care; in Vietnam, however, the paramount task of the U.S. pacification effort is the identification and neutralization of the local NLF administrative apparatus—in Pentagon nomenclature, the Viet Cong Infrastructure (VCI). The counterinfrastructure campaign was initiated by the CIA in July 1968 as the Phung Hoang program, better known by its English equivalent as Operation Phoenix. This program, incorporated into the Civil Operations and Revolutionary Development Support effort, is described by American officials as "a systematic effort at intelligence coordination and exploitation." In the *intelligence* phase, all allied intelligence services—including South Vietnam's Special Police Branch and

America's CIA and military intelligence organizations—
are supposed to pool the data they have collected (or
forcibly extracted) from informers and prisoners on the
identity of NLF cadres. In the *exploitation* phase of Phoenix, members of the paramilitary National Police Field
Forces, often assisted by the military or the CIA-controlled
mercenary units known as Provincial Reconnaissance
Units, make small-scale raids into contested areas to seize
or eliminate persons who have been identified by the intelligence services as VCI agents.[54] In testimony before the
Senate Foreign Relations Committee, the head of CORDS,
ex-CIA agent William E. Colby, stated that in 1969 a total
of 19,534 suspected VCI agents had been "neutralized"—
of this number 6,187 had been killed, 8,515 arrested, and
4,832 persuaded to join the Saigon side. By May 1971, 20,-
587 people had been killed under the Phoenix program.
Colby insisted that Phoenix did not constitute an "assassination" or "counterterror" operation, but acknowledged
that some "occasional abuses" of the program, including
political assassinations, had occurred.[55]

During Congressional hearings on the pacification program, as reported in *The New York Times* on August 3,
1971, two former U.S. military-intelligence agents told a
House Government Operations subcommittee that under
the Phoenix program Vietnamese civilians were indis-
criminately rounded up, tortured, and murdered by Americans in the effort to eliminate Vietcong cadres. K. Barton
Osborn, a former private in Vietnam and part-time employee of the CIA, told the committee that he knew of
hundreds of murders committed during his first fifteen
months in Vietnam in 1967 and 1968. None of the Vietnamese prisoners he had seen detained for questioning,
Osborn reported, had ever lived through their interroga-
tions. Another Phoenix agent, former First Lieutenant
Michael J. Uhl, repudiated the Pentagon's assertion that
only specific Vietcong leaders were attacked under the
program. Uhl insisted that most VCI suspects were cap-

tured during sweeping tactical operations and arbitrarily classified Vietcong agents.

In order to sustain these counterinsurgency activities, the United States provides the National Police with a steady flow of funds, supplies, technical assistance, and other resources. U.S. counterpart funds have been used to finance construction of the NP's High Command School, interrogation facilities, firearms ranges, training schools, ammunition reloading plant, Marine Police bases, and the central Saigon police garage.[56] Since each of the programs described above has swelled the ranks of "suspected VC," the Saigon government has found it necessary to greatly expand the country's already vast prison system. As prison management is considered a vital task of the overall police responsibility, the United States provided $1.6 million in 1968–69 for expansion or renovation of most of South Vietnam's 41 prisons and detention centers. OPS advisers work alongside Vietnamese prison officials in the Directorate of Corrections, and supervise the training of prison administrators. In order to "provide greater security from VC attacks," the U.S. financed the relocation of thousands of political prisoners from mainland jails to the prison island of Con Son, the site of the notorious "tiger cage" cells.[57] After two U.S. Congressmen visited the inhuman tiger cages in 1970, AID appropriated $400,000 for the construction of 288 new isolation cells at Con Son.[58]

One begins to appreciate the breadth of the OPS operation in Vietnam by examining AID's 1971 budget request— $13 million was sought to achieve the following "Project Targets" in the succeeding eighteen months:

Provision of commodity and advisory support for a police force of 108,000 men by the end of FY 1971; . . . assisting the National Identity Registration Program (NIRP) to register more than 12,000,000 persons 15 years of age and over by the end of 1971;

continuing to provide basic and specialized training for approximately 40,000 police annually; providing technical assistance to the police detention system including planning and supervision of the construction of facilities for an additional 8,000 inmates during 1970; and helping to achieve a major increase in the number of police presently working (6,000) at the village level.[59]

This presentation, it must be remembered, represents only programs under AID authority; missing from this prospectus are NP activities financed by the CIA and the Defense Department. As American forces are withdrawn from Vietnam and a greater share of the fighting is assumed by Saigon forces, U.S. assistance to the South Vietnamese National Police will be increased. In justifying a fiscal 1972 appropriation of $33 million for NP support (which includes $22 million in Pentagon funds), the Agency for International Development told Congress in 1971:

As one aspect of Vietnamization, the Vietnamese National Police are called upon to carry a progressively greater burden. They must share with the Vietnamese armed forces the burden of countering insurgency, and provide for daily peace and order —not only in the cities, but throughout the countryside. It is planned to increase police strength from about 100,000 at present to 124,000 during FY 1972 to allow assumption of a greater burden in the future. The U.S. plans to make commensurate assistance available.[60]

Pentagon funds are used to finance the activities of the paramilitary National Police Field Forces (NPFF), which by January 1969 constituted a small army of twelve thousand men organized into seventy-five companies. Because of the "military commonality" of their equipment, all commodities support to the NPFF is provided by the Department of Defense.[61] The extent of CIA contributions to the National Police is, of course, impossible to determine; it is known, however, that the CIA has been involved in modernizing Vietnam's secret police files since 1955, and is

deeply involved in management of the Phoenix program.[62]
One does not have to invoke the sinister image of the CIA,
however, to establish beyond a doubt that the United
States is intimately involved in every repressive and bar-
barous act perpetrated by the South Vietnamese police on
behalf of the Saigon regime.

Any honest assessment of the plight of the overwhelming
majority of people in the underdeveloped areas would
have to conclude that the conditions which give rise to
discontent and rebellion—poverty, unemployment and un-
deremployment, poor health care, etc.—are not disappear-
ing, and that consequently the need for abundant "civil
security forces" to protect American investments and
pro-American regimes will not disappear, either.* This,

* In studying the U.S. Public Safety Program abroad, one is sooner
or later struck by the extent to which the goals, doctrines, and
practices of this program have been adopted by authorities in the
United States as an answer to our own internal difficulties. AID
spokesmen have in fact made a determined effort to advise other
government officials of the domestic application of techniques
developed by OPS for use abroad. In September 1967, Public Safety
Director Byron Engle told the National Advisory Commission on
Civil Disorders (Kerner Commission) that "in working with police
in various countries . . . we have acquired a great deal of experience
in dealing with violence ranging from demonstrations and riots to
guerrilla warfare." Much of this experience, he asserted, "may be
helpful in the United States." Among the specific recommendations
made by Engle for the control of urban disorders were the massive
use of chemical munitions, stringently enforced curfews, and the
establishment of special tactical police units available on a twenty-
four-hour standby basis. Precisely the same recommendations were
made to President Johnson by former Pentagon aide Cyrus Vance,
and were later put into effect in Washington, D.C., when rioting
broke out following the death of Martin Luther King, Jr., in April
1968. And when, in the wake of this rioting, Congress passed the
Omnibus Crime Control and Safe Streets Act, a principal feature
of the Public Safety Program—U.S. government subsidization of the
training, arming, and modernization of local police forces—became
an established mechanism for domestic law enforcement.

at least, was the conclusion of Nelson Rockefeller following his 1969 Presidential Mission to Latin America. In his report to the President, Rockefeller warned: "At the present time . . . police forces of many countries have not been strengthened as population and great urban growth have taken place. Consequently they have become increasingly less capable of providing . . . the internal security that is their major function." In order to attain the necessary degree of stability, Rockefeller argued that "the United States should respond to requests for assistance of the police and security forces of the hemisphere nations by providing them with the essential tools to do their job." Specifically, he urged that the United States "meet reasonable requests from other hemisphere governments for trucks, jeeps, helicopters and like equipment to provide mobility . . . for radios, and other command control equipment for proper communications among the forces; and for small arms for security forces."[63]

The Governor of New York State is only one of many influential politicians who have argued for increased U.S. police assistance to the Third World. Since this posture is particularly attractive to the Nixon Administration (with its emphasis on the withdrawal of U.S. servicemen from overseas posts), it is safe to assume that the Public Safety Program will be assured of government support for a long time to come. While President Nixon has insisted that the United States does not want to be the world's policeman, he is quite willing to subsidize the world's police to do the job for us.

Chapter 10

THE
LATIN AMERICAN
MILITARY
—Mercenary
Statesmen

"We're going to lose Latin America," Rear Admiral Harold M. Briggs told the editors of *U.S. News & World Report* in 1961, "we're losing it right now."[1] Briggs, who had served as the Navy's Director of Pan-American Affairs, did not identify whom "we" were losing Latin America to— there really was no need for him to do so. Ever since Fidel Castro entered Havana at the head of a victorious guerrilla army, the U.S. establishment has been obsessed with what John Gerassi calls *The Great Fear*—the dread of a revolutionary movement that will sweep through Latin America and abolish the century-old system of exploitation that enriches American businesses at the expense of the rest of the hemisphere.[2] Between 1960 and 1970, the United States spent $1 billion to overcome insurgent threats to the existing order, but the Great Fear remains. Reporting to President Nixon on his 1969 fact-finding tour of Latin America, Governor Nelson A. Rockefeller warned:

Rising frustrations throughout the Western Hemisphere over poverty and political instability have led increasing numbers of people to pick the United States as a scapegoat and to seek out Marxist solutions to their socioeconomic problems. At the moment there is only one Castro among the 26 nations of the hemisphere; there could well be more in the future. And a Castro on the mainland, supported militarily and economically by the Communist world, would present the gravest kind of threat to the security of the Western Hemisphere and pose an extremely difficult problem for the United States.[3]

At a time when the Vietnam conflict was capturing most of the headlines, Rockefeller's warning did not elicit much public interest. Nevertheless, his findings and recommendations—many of which are discussed below—received considerable attention at the Pentagon and at the Panama headquarters of the U.S. Southern Command (SOUTH-COM), where high-ranking Defense strategists have quietly been developing plans for U.S. counterinsurgency operations in Latin America. Unlike current U.S. operations in Southeast Asia, our plans for Latin America do not envision a significant overt American military presence; the emphasis, in fact, is on low-cost, low-visibility assistance and training programs designed to upgrade the capacity of local forces to overcome guerrilla movements. Such programs are not, of course, limited to the Western Hemisphere—very much the same strategy is being pursued in Africa, the Near East, and South Asia. It is in Latin America, however, that this "low profile" approach has been developed most consistently and energetically. For this reason, it is instructive to examine the Pentagon's Latin American operations in some detail, always keeping in mind that similar operations are going on simultaneously in other parts of the Third World.

In his report to the President, Rockefeller provided eloquent testimony as to why the Great Fear was well founded: "Everywhere in the hemisphere, we see similar problems—problems of population and poverty, urbanization and unemployment, illiteracy and injustice, violence and disorder." In such a setting the abundant signs of prosperity enjoyed by a few become ever more provocative to the impoverished masses. Never again will the disadvantaged accept as inevitable the patterns of the past: "They want to share the privileges of progress. They want a better world for their children . . . their expectations have outrun performance. Their frustration is turning to a growing sense of injustice and disillusionment."[4]

The poverty and backwardness of the Third World will be overcome, in the establishmentarian view, only through the orderly processes of capitalist development. To be sure, the social changes wrought by piecemeal industrialization and rapid urbanization will engender some frustration and discontent, but these forces must be kept under control if the modernization process is to achieve its goals. There is, then, what Assistant Secretary of State for Inter-American Affairs Charles A. Meyer calls "a very close relationship between the prospects for achieving social and economic reform and development goals and a necessary level of internal security and stability."[5] American policy attempts to maintain this delicate balance by sponsoring limited reforms of trade and investment practices under the Alliance for Progress, while subsidizing the forces responsible for maintenance of internal security through the Military Assistance Program. Economic advancement and military security are seen therefore as being interdependent: "The goals of the Alliance," Secretary of Defense Robert S. McNamara once said, "can only be achieved within a framework of law and order."[6]

In the volatile atmosphere of a nation undergoing the process of modernization, Rockefeller argues, pluralistic forms of government are often incapable of maintaining the proper balance between development and stability. Few of the nations of Latin America, he believes, "have achieved the sufficiently advanced economic and social systems required to support a consistently democratic system."(For many of these societies, therefore, "the question is less one of democracy or a lack of it, than it is simply of *orderly ways of getting along.*" (Emphasis added.) In some countries, the armed forces have found it necessary to seize power in order to ensure the maintenance of public order. The United States, in Rockefeller's opinion, should forget "the philosophical disagreements it may have with particular regimes," and learn to live with the military strong men who now rule two-thirds of the Latin American republics. If we were to overcome our prejudices against military dictatorships, we would discover that "a new type of military man is coming to the fore and often becoming a major force for constructive social change in the American republics. Motivated by increasing impatience with corruption, inefficiency, and a stagnant political order, the new military man is prepared to adapt his authoritarian tradition to the goals of social and economic progress."[7]

The seemingly paradoxical view that professional soldiers can combine their "authoritarian tradition" with a movement toward "social and economic progress" can be traced to the argument, first advanced by a number of American social scientists in the late 1950's and early 1960's, that the disciplined structure of modern armies is an asset in underdeveloped countries where capable and efficient civilian institutions are slow to develop. An outstanding proponent of this theory is Lucian Pye, a professor of political science at the Massachusetts Institute of Technology; in a 1961 essay on "Armies in the Process of Political Modernization," Pye wrote:

In comparison to the efforts that have been expended in developing, say, civil administration and political parties, it still seems that modern armies are somewhat easier to create in transitional societies than most other forms of modern social structures. The most significant fact for our consideration is that the armies created by colonial administration and by the newly emergent countries have been consistently among the most modernized institutions in their society.[8]

In another essay, prepared for the Smithsonian Institution's series on Social Science Research and National Security, Pye carried this idea further:

The basic problem in most underdeveloped societies is the difficulty in creating effective organizations capable of sustaining all the activities basic to modern life. There generally is an imbalance in the development of organization with the result that whatever type of organization as is effectively developed is quickly called upon to perform functions generally associated with other organizations. . . .

That is to say that there is generally a high degree of substitutability of roles in transitional societies, and the more concrete and authoritarian organizations tend to assume the duties of the less explicitly structured organizations. . . . [In this situation] the military authorities often find that they are in control of one of the most effective general purpose organizations in the society and hence they may be called upon, or be compelled by events, to perform the duties of civil authorities.[9]

The underdeveloped countries should not, in Pye's view, "be deprived of the developmental value of the military organizations simply because the ideological basis of the military in advanced societies rejects the appropriateness of the military openly touching upon essentially civilian functions." This is even more true, he argues, "in countries faced with serious insurgency or subversion," where "it may be essential for the military to assume many civil affairs functions and operate *even as the prime institution of government* in certain regions."[10] (Emphasis added.)

Pye's arguments not only influenced the conclusion of Rockefeller's 1969 Latin American report; they have also become an integral part of U.S. defense policy in the hemisphere. Officially, the United States is pledged to

support the development of viable democratic governments throughout the region; yet, out of our fear of revolutionary upheavals, we have elected the Latin American
military as our chosen instruments for the maintenance
of the status quo, and provided them with the arms, training, and resources they require to perform this function.
Whenever any discrepancies occur between official policy
and the actual patterns of events, Pye's thesis is brought
in to bridge the gap. Thus Assistant Secretary of State
Meyer told the Senate Subcommittee on Western Hemisphere Affairs:

The continuance of inadequate and inequitable economic and
social structures which are vulnerable to subversion necessi-
tates the maintenance of the counterinsurgency capabilities of
Latin American forces in order that an internal atmosphere
conducive to social and economic progress can prevail. Our
training of small, mobile, rapid-reaction forces and our grant
materiel program geared to maintaining equipment for the support of such forces [under the Military Assistance Program]
play fundamental roles in this respect.[11]

Moreover, the argument that armies can play a positive
role in the development of their countries is, as we shall
see, a major tenet of the doctrine taught Latin American
officers at service schools in Panama and the United States.
Although ostensibly the function of these training programs is to foster a "democratic approach by the military
to their professional responsibilities," it cannot have escaped the attention of Latin American officers that we
would be willing to overcome our "philosophical disagreements" with authoritarian regimes if they would at least
profess to be carrying out some economic and social reforms. This tack, in any case, has been adopted by the
ruling military junta in Brazil to defend its suspension of
constitutional government and repression of political dissent: General Emilio Garrastazu Medici, the current President, has stated that the junta will remain in power "as

long as it is necessary for the implantation of the political, administrative, legal, social, and economic structures which can promote the integration of all Brazilians into a state of life that reaches at least the minimum level of well-being."[12]

THE CHANGING ROLE
OF MILITARY ASSISTANCE

The Military Assistance Program (MAP) is the principal agency through which the Pentagon determines the armament, organization, and strategic doctrine of the Latin American military establishment. The origins of this program, according to Professor Edwin Lieuwen of the University of New Mexico, "can be traced to World War II, when Washington, in order to counter the threat of Fascist and Nazi subversion, began to establish military missions."[13] Under the Lend-Lease Act of March 11, 1941, Latin American armies were supplied with arms and equipment in return for access to the region's strategic raw materials and the right to use certain air and naval bases. After the formal declaration of war in December 1941, the United States continued supplying weapons while Latin America provided temporary bases, stepped up production of strategic materials, and collaborated in antisubmarine warfare and other defense operations.[14]

Military aid to Latin America was suspended in the immediate postwar effort; as the Cold War intensified, however, the United States once again began supplying Latin America's armed forces with relatively modern tanks, planes, and ships. Under the Mutual Security Act of 1951, funds were made available for the modernization of Latin American armies in order to strengthen the hemisphere's defenses against external aggression. A country became eligible for these funds upon ratification of a bilateral mutual defense assistance pact with the United States.[15]

Such agreements were concluded with Ecuador, Cuba, Colombia, Peru, and Chile in 1952; with Brazil, the Dominican Republic, and Uruguay in 1953; with Nicaragua and Honduras in 1954; with Haiti and Guatemala in 1955; and with Bolivia in 1958.* As part of their contribution to the hemispheric defense effort, the MAP recipients pledged to supply the United States with minerals and other strategic raw materials needed for the production of military goods.†

The wording of these agreements, and all references made to them by public officials and the press upon their ratification, suggest that such pacts were viewed by Washington as being an integral part of the Cold War effort to contain Soviet Communism. Seen from this perspective, Latin America was expected to play a subordinate role to the United States, by providing a limited antisubmarine defense capability and as a supplier of certain strategic raw materials. This attitude was eloquently expressed by Sam Pope Brewer in a special article commissioned by *The New York Times,* in 1953: "Though it galls some South

* The United States also concluded an "Agreement relating to the furnishing of defense articles and services to Panama for the purpose of contributing to its internal security," and similar agreements with Costa Rica and El Salvador, in 1962. Special agreements were made with Paraguay in 1962, 1964, and 1966 for the provision of "civic action materials and services," and with Jamaica and Argentina for the delivery of military assistance goods and services in 1963 and 1964, respectively. (See U.S. Department of State, Treaty Affairs Staff, *Treaties in Force,* Washington, D.C., 1970.)

† Article VII of the agreement with Ecuador states: "In conformity with the principle of mutual aid . . . the Government of Ecuador agrees to facilitate the production and transfer to the Government of the United States of America for such period of time, in such quantities and upon such terms and conditions as may be agreed upon, of raw and semi-processed strategic materials required by the United States of America as a result of deficiencies or potential deficiencies in its own resources, and which may be available in Ecuador." (*Department of State Bulletin,* XXVI, March 3, 1952, pp. 336 ff.)

Americans who believe that power and prestige are measured only by industrialization, the fact is that South
America's value to hemisphere defense lies in geography
and raw materials rather than in great armies and the
industry to equip them. That state of affairs is bound to
continue for a long time."[16]

This outlook was reflected in Pentagon policy statements
on the Military Assistance Program. Throughout the 1950's,
the ostensible objective of aid to Latin America was to
strengthen the hemisphere's defenses against external (presumably Soviet) attack. Thus as recently as 1960, the major
goal of the assistance program was the development of a
strong antisubmarine capability. Charles H. Shuff, then
Acting Assistant Secretary of Defense, told a Congressional subcommittee in 1959 that "the most positive threat
to hemispheric security is submarine action in the Caribbean Sea and along the coast of Latin America."[17] Between
1951 and 1960, the United States supplied Latin America
with equipment worth some $500 million. Patrol ships,
reconnaissance aircraft, and other equipment used for antisubmarine operations constituted a large portion of this
largesse.

America's military aid policies came under intense review in 1959 and 1960 following the collapse, on New
Year's Day 1959, of the dictatorial regime of Fulgencio
Batista. The Cuban army had been one of the favored
recipients of American weapons and training: between
1951 and 1959, Cuba received more than $16 million in
modern arms while 521 Cuban officers had received advanced training at service schools in the United States or
the Panama Canal Zone.[18] Nevertheless, Batista's well-
supplied army was defeated by a poorly-equipped guerrilla
force that never exceeded several hundred men and
women. This extraordinary event, which took place when
maverick defense analysts had already begun to question
U.S. military policy, cast doubt upon the basic assumptions
of the Latin American aid program. In the final months of

the Eisenhower Administration, these "strategic revisionists" argued that the main threat to U.S. hegemony in the Third World was internal disorder rather than external attack, and that it was necessary, therefore, to equip local armies for the task of defeating armed revolutionaries. When the revisionists took power under Kennedy, the rationale for U.S. assistance underwent a rapid transformation; as noted by Lieuwen, "The basis for military aid to Latin America abruptly shifted from hemispheric defense to internal security, from the protection of coastlines and from antisubmarine warfare to defense against Castro-Communist guerrilla warfare."[19]

Funds for counterinsurgency training and equipment were first made available to Latin American armies in the fiscal year 1963 MAP program, and a year later the Director of Military Assistance, General Robert J. Wood, announced that "the primary purpose of the proposed fiscal year 1965 Military Assistance Program for Latin America is to counter the threat to the entire area by providing equipment and training which will bolster the internal security capabilities of the recipient countries."[20] During a 1967 Congressional review of the MAP program, Defense Secretary McNamara declared that the Pentagon's "primary objective in Latin America is to aid, where necessary, in the continued development of indigenous military and paramilitary forces capable of providing, in conjunction with the police and other security forces, the needed domestic security."[21]

Of the $45.5 million requested for grant aid to Latin America in fiscal 1968, the Defense Department proposed to spend $34.7 million, or 76 percent, on hardware and services related to counterinsurgency.[22] "The grant program," McNamara specified, "will provide no tanks, artillery, fighter aircraft, or combat ships. The emphasis is on vehicles and helicopters for internal mobility, communications equipment for better coordination of in-country security efforts, and spare parts for maintenance of existing inventories."[23] Among the items most frequently turned over to Latin American armies are jeeps, trucks, transport planes, river and coastal patrol boats, observation helicopters, and small arms. And while U.S. arms sales policies have been modified by the Nixon Administration, the MAP grant program is still aimed at improving the counterinsurgency capabilities of local forces. Thus MAP Director General Robert H. Warren told a Congressional committee in 1970 that the principal objective of the fiscal 1971 grant program was "to help Latin American nations maintain military and paramilitary forces capable of providing, with police forces, internal security essential to orderly political, social and economic development."[24]

Between 1950 and 1969, the United States provided Latin American armies with arms, training, and services worth $1,357 million. This amount includes $725 million in MAP grants, "excess" defense articles valued at $179 million, credit of $253 million toward the purchase of American arms, and naval vessels worth $200 million transferred under ship-loan legislation (see Appendix D). When the recipients of U.S. military assistance in Latin America are ranked by total aid received, it is apparent that the largest and most advanced countries are receiving the great bulk of such funds. (The one exception to this rule is Mexico, which for nationalistic reasons has traditionally shunned close military relations with the United States.) Thus Argentina, Brazil, Chile, Venezuela, and Peru, which together account for about 60 percent of the gross national product of Latin America, received $980 million in U.S. aid between 1950 and 1969, or 72 percent of the total MAP program in Latin America. When, however, these countries are ranked by the percentage of their total defense expenditures supplied by U.S. aid, a different pattern emerges. As can be seen in Table 7, the most favored Latin American recipients of U.S. aid, on a proportional basis, are the smaller and poorer nations of Central and South

Table 7

U.S. MILITARY AID AS A PERCENTAGE OF LATIN AMERICAN DEFENSE EXPENDITURES

(In rank order; dollars in millions)

Total defense expenditures, cumulative, 1964–7[a]		U.S. military aid, cumulative, fiscal 1964–7[b]		U.S. aid as a percentage of total defense expenditures	
Country	Amount	Country	Amount	Country	Percentage
Brazil	2,380	Brazil	50.3	Panama	32.5
Argentina	843	Peru	35.9	Bolivia	21.9
Venezuela	712	Colombia	31.2	Uruguay	18.0
Peru	367	Chile	31.1	Paraguay	17.0
Chile	321	Argentina	22.6	Ecuador	16.0
Colombia	302	Ecuador	16.0	Honduras	12.9
Dominican Rep.	133	Boliva	12.5	Guatemala	12.5
Ecuador	100	Uruguay	9.2	Colombia	10.2
Bolivia	57	Dominican Rep.	8.4	Peru	9.8
Guatemala	56	Guatemala	7.0	Chile	9.7
Uruguay	51	Paraguay	5.1	El Salvador	9.0
El Salvador	38	Venezuela	4.8	Dominican Rep.	6.3
Paraguay	30	Honduras	3.5	Argentina	2.7
Honduras	27	El Salvador	3.4	Brazil	2.1
Panama	4	Panama	1.3	Venezuela	0.6

[a] *Source:* U.S. Arms Control and Disarmament Agency, *World Military Expenditures 1969* (Washington, D.C., 1969), p. 18.
[b] *Source:* U.S. Department of Defense, *Military Assistance Facts* (Washington, D.C., 1969), pp. 16–19. (Includes grants and excess defense articles only.)

America. Not surprisingly, many of the proportionally largest handouts have gone to countries that have experienced guerrilla uprisings in the past decade—Bolivia, Panama, Uruguay, Guatemala.

Although the U.S. aid program has never constituted more than 5 percent of Latin America's annual defense expenditures (which, if Cuba is excluded, amounted to $2 billion in 1968), such assistance has accounted for as much as 50 percent of what the larger countries spend on arms acquisitions, and up to 90 percent of what many of the smaller countries spend.[25] United States aid, according to former SOUTHCOM commander General Robert W. Porter, Jr., "constitutes a very significant portion of the amount allocated [by Latin America] to force modernization."[26] In an evaluation of the MAP program, Joseph Novitski of *The New York Times* wrote in 1971 that between 1947 and 1967 (when such aid began to decline):

Most South American armed forces bore the stamp of United States influence. Military missions aided in training, organizing and purchasing to the point where the tactical doctrine, weapons, vehicles and often even the uniforms of any South American infantry outfit would have been familiar to a United States veteran of World War II or Korea. Parts and weapons, along with advanced training, always came from the United States during those 20 years.[27]

With a virtual monopoly in the supply of training, advice, and arms to Latin American armed forces, the United States was in a strong position to dictate the strategic orientation of these forces. The emphasis now given internal security and counterinsurgency by most Latin American armies is eloquent testimony to the exercise of this power by the United States.*

In 1967, Congressional liberals (backed by some fiscal conservatives) voted a number of restrictions to the mili-

---

* In a review of Latin American military developments during the 1960's, Colonel Thomas W. Flatley of the U.S. Army War College staff noted: "Current trends in military forces point toward the continued formation of light, mobile, rapid reaction-type units approximating battalion size. These forces are capable of giving the national command authorities the capability to move rapidly and decisively into a troubled area once it is identified, and to eliminate or suppress the insurrection. Inherent in the equipage of such type forces is the requirement for an adequate communications ability and support from a competent intelligence service. Both these capabilities have been strengthened and undoubtedly will continue to receive emphasis." ("Latin American Armed Forces in the 1960's— A Review," *Military Review*, April 1970, p. 16.)

tary aid program that have compelled the Pentagon to reduce MAP expenditures. Section 507(a) of the Foreign Assistance Act of 1968 limits grants of Defense articles (i.e., exclusive of training) to Latin America to $25 million annually. Under Section 33 of the Foreign Military Sales Act, the combined total of MAP grants and sales is limited to $75 million per fiscal year. Finally, Section 504(a) of the Foreign Assistance Act prohibits the government from furnishing "sophisticated weapons systems" to underdeveloped countries unless the President determines it is vital to national security. These restrictions, and the urgent need for MAP funds to bolster our allies in Southeast Asia, have forced a reduction in assistance to Latin America: from a high of $73 million in fiscal year 1968, U.S. grant aid dropped to $15.7 million in fiscal 1971. (Direct cash sales by the Pentagon in 1971 amounted to $13.8 million, and credit sales another $40 million, for a total aid package of $69.5 million.[28])

With the decline in arms aid to Latin America, the Pentagon has watched its influence with the local military establishments erode drastically. (Political factors, including the intensification of nationalist sentiments on the part of military leaders, have also played a part in this process; for example, in 1969 the highly nationalistic military government of Peru expelled the seventy-man United States military mission in Lima, and a year later the mission in Ecuador was expelled as a result of a dispute with the United States concerning fishing rights in Ecuador's coastal waters.) No longer is SOUTHCOM the arbiter of all changes in the doctrine, organization, and armament of Latin American armies. European arms producers, eager to establish new markets in the Western Hemisphere, have offered attractive credit arrangements on the sale of expensive hardware like tanks and supersonic jets. In order to regain some of our lost influence in Latin American defense councils, the Nixon Administration has been pressing for the lifting of all restrictions on U.S. aid programs in the region.

On May 5, 1971, the White House asked Congress to raise the ceiling on total arms aid to $150 million beginning in fiscal year 1972. At the same time, the President announced that he would exercise his option, allowed by Section 33(c) of the Foreign Military Sales Act, to waive the current $75 million ceiling on such aid. This move, according to Administration officials, was designed to enhance the Pentagon's capacity to negotiate with Latin American governments on the modernization of their armed forces. One official interviewed by *The New York Times* explained that "It's obvious you're going to lose influence with the Latin military if you don't furnish them equipment or let them buy it to replace the obsolete stuff they have on hand."[29]

A major reason given by the White House for its 1971 decision to waive the limit on arms aid to Latin America was the desire to increase *sales* of U.S. defense items to the region (as distinct from direct grants), thus reducing the unfavorable balance-of-payments deficit. Between 1950 and 1969, the nations of Latin America bought $342 million worth of weapons and other equipment from the U.S. Department of Defense (sales by private arms suppliers are not included in the Pentagon figures). The major buyers have been Argentina ($71 million), Brazil ($73 million), and Venezuela ($100 million).[30]

In order to keep the focus of hemispheric military concerns on the requirements of internal security, the United States has sought to dissuade Latin American governments from using scarce economic resources to obtain expensive, "sophisticated" weapons systems like supersonic jets, modern tanks, and naval vessels.* Pentagon spokesmen

---

* Although the United States has discouraged the purchase of modern jet aircraft by Latin American armies, there has been no such policy concerning the acquisition of propeller-driven fighters that have been refitted for counterguerrilla operations. Several such craft, P-51 Mustang fighters of World War II vintage, were acquired by Bolivia in 1968 from the Aero Sport Company of San Bernardino, California. Although ostensibly required for combat against guer-

point out that the Hemisphere is "protected against conventional military threats by the effective inter-American peacemaking machinery, by the Rio Treaty [Inter-American Treaty of Reciprocal Assistance] security guarantees, and by wide oceans."[31] These arguments, advanced by President Johnson at the Punta del Este Conference of April 1967, induced Latin American Presidents to affirm "their intention to limit military expenditure in proportion to the actual demands of national security . . . avoiding those expenditures that are not indispensable for the performance of the specific duties of the armed forces."[32] Within a few months of the conference, however, Peru announced that it would purchase sixteen Mirage V jet fighters from France at an estimated cost of $1.2 million each. Other Latin American nations soon followed suit by ordering comparable U.S. or European aircraft, thus nullifying the intent of the Punta del Este declaration.[33]

The desire of Latin American military establishments to acquire advanced weapons for prestige has created a serious dilemma for the United States. On the one hand, Washington seeks to deemphasize the traditional, external defense function of the military, while on the other it cannot afford to alienate the very group upon which it depends for implementation of counterinsurgency programs. Addressing himself to this problem following his 1969 tour, Nelson Rockefeller asserted:

The United States must face more forthrightly the fact that while the military in the other American nations are alert to the problems of internal security, they do not feel that this is their

---

rillas in remote areas, these Mustangs were used by the Bolivian military in 1971 to rout students occuping university buildings in La Paz as a protest against the ouster of President Juan José Torres. At least three high-explosive bombs were dropped on one building before army troops, loyal to the rightist regime headed by Colonel Hugo Banzer, assaulted the university and captured the student rebels. (*International Herald Tribune,* August 24, 1971.)

only role and responsibility. They are conscious of the more traditional role of a military establishment to defend the nation's territory, and they possess understandable professional pride which creates equally understandable desires for modern arms. . . . The result of all this is a natural resentment on the part of the military of other American nations when the United States refuses to sell modern items of equipment.[34]

Rockefeller suggested that many Latin American military leaders "see the United States acting to hold them back as second-class citizens" and are thus "becoming increasingly estranged from us at a time when their political role is on the rise." In order to not lose the loyalty of this all-important group, Rockefeller urged the President to seek the repeal of Congressional restrictions so as to "permit the United States to sell aircraft, ships and other major military equipment without aid cut penalties to the more developed nations of the hemisphere when these nations believe this equipment is necessary to protect their land, patrol their seacoasts and airspace, and otherwise maintain the morale of their forces and protect their sovereignty."[35]

Rockefeller's views are clearly shared by top officials of the Nixon Administration. Thus, in a 1969 statement to the Senate Subcommittee on Western Hemisphere Affairs, Assistant Secretary of States Charles A. Meyer reported that "Latin Americans have become puzzled and even suspicious of our motives. Strong nationalist resentment has arisen over what is seen as United States efforts to infringe on the sovereign rights of a country to determine its own military requirements." The time has now arrived, he observed, "when these nations consider that they cannot further delay their military modernization programs." While they would prefer to obtain U.S.-manufactured arms, Congressional restrictions against the sale of sophisticated weapons systems are forcing them to turn to more expensive European substitutes. Turning the Senators' arguments against them, Meyer concluded that "the long-term consequence of our paternalistic, even patronizing, restrictions will be the acquisition of more expensive items, higher maintenance costs, and greater diversion of financial resources from civilian purposes."[36] Backed by this kind of logic, the Defense Department has been putting pressure on Congress to remove the restrictions on weapons sales to Latin America, and to increase the appropriations for arms credits under the Foreign Military Sales program.

According to *The New York Times* for May 19, 1971, the Nixon Administration is planning a $30-million three-year program to sell tanks, howitzers, and armored personnel carriers to Brazil; a loan or credit sale of two destroyers to Argentina; and the sale of ground and air equipment, including transport and training planes, to Colombia, Venezuela, Uruguay, and Guatemala. It is also interesting to note that despite considerable U.S. discomfort with the socialist program of Chilean President Salvador Allende, the Pentagon has supplied $5 million in credits to Chile's armed forces for the purchase of U.S. arms.

United States assistance to the Latin American military has often provoked criticism in Congress, particularly when U.S.-supplied armies participate in illegal seizures of power and the installation of military regimes. In response to such criticism, former Defense Secretary McNamara revealed, "The essential role of the Latin American military as a stabilizing force outweighs any risks involved in providing military assistance for internal security purposes."[37] These arguments notwithstanding, Washington recognizes that continued assistance to the Latin American military establishment poses a serious problem for U.S. foreign policy, since the strengthening of the armed forces means strengthening the very institutions which are most closely associated with repression and dictatorship. Indeed, by 1960 it had become clear that our military policies were in danger of becoming counterproductive: American support of the military establishment incurred the antagonism of those Latin Americans who viewed the military as a major obstacle to social and economic progress. The Kennedy Administration, struggling with this problem in the early months of its incumbency, sought a solution in the arena of public relations: rather than curtail U.S. assistance to Latin American armies, we would seek to change public attitudes by refurbishing the image of the armed forces. If the military establishment could be converted, in the popular imagination, into an instrument of modernization and economic development, the contradiction in U.S. policy presumably would be resolved. The mechanism that could achieve this goal, Kennedy's advisers believed, was military civic action.

CIVIC ACTION

Military civic action is defined by the Department of Defense as "the use of preponderantly indigenous military forces on projects useful to the local population at all levels in such fields as education, training, public works, agriculture, transportation, communications, health, sanitation, and others contributing to economic and social development which would also serve to improve the standing of the military forces with the population."[38] The use of the military for internal development is not, of course, a new concept, as there are many precedents for such activity both in the United States and Latin America. The U.S. Army Corps of Engineers, for instance, has traditionally been active in the field of flood control and harbor design, while in many Latin American nations the armed forces are frequently employed in road-construction projects in frontier regions. The United States itself sponsored such activities in Latin America at the beginning of the century, during its sporadic military occupations of Caribbean and Central American countries.[39] It was only in the early 1960's, however, that civic action was elevated to its present status as one of the principal elements of U.S. counterinsurgency strategy in Latin America.

The Pentagon's counterinsurgency experts freely acknowledge that "the armed forces of some developing countries have been a major political force separate and apart from the people."[40] This condition is particularly pronounced in rural and wilderness areas, where government expenditures for education, health, and economic development are usually lowest. In Latin America, moreover, these areas are often characterized by great poverty and a highly unequal pattern of landownership, and so it is natural to expect that guerrilla movements will find it easy to take root here. The United States has learned in Vietnam that a guerrilla force is not easily crushed once it has secured widespread popular support, and that the use of indigenous troops for counterguerrilla operations in the countryside will more often than not inspire increased local resistance to the central government. Since Washington had already elected the Latin American military as the chosen instrument of U.S. policy in the hemisphere, it became imperative, in the Pentagon's view, that these armies extend the central government's authority to remote areas, and there engage in socially constructive projects designed to win the loyalty of the population.

Civic action is considered an appropriate use of Third World troops since "the most stable and modern organization in many developing nations is its military force." In remote and inaccessible areas, "the military forces are often the only governmental agency equipped and prepared to perform a much needed program in the socioeconomic field."[41] This hypothesis is clearly traceable to Lucian Pye's argument that the "armies created by colonial administration and by the newly emergent countries have consistently been among the most modernized institutions in their society," and that "the peculiar advantage of explicit lines of authority does give the military considerable advantages in becoming an effective organization in otherwise disorganized societies."[42] By treating some of the most obvious symptoms of rural poverty and neglect, civic action could reduce the discontent of the peasantry and at the same time project a more favorable image of the military.

The civic action concept, as it is presently understood, was first practiced in 1950 in the Philippines as part of Secretary of Defense (later President) Ramón Magsaysay's counterguerrilla campaign against the Huk movement (Hukbong Magpalaya Nang Bayan, or People's Liberation Army). In order to undercut the Huk's popular support, Magsaysay put an end to indiscriminate military terrorism and put much of the army to work on social projects— building schools and markets, repairing roads and bridges —while training small counterguerrilla units that fanned out into the countryside.[43] This effort, labeled Civic Action by the Philippine military, was closely observed by U.S. strategists, who employed the technique during the Korean War. Under the Armed Forces Assistance to Korea Program (AFAK), hundreds of schools, churches, medical facilities, orphanages, and the like were constructed by U.S. troops in South Korea.[44]

President Kennedy and other high-ranking members of his Administration eagerly embraced the civic action concept and incorporated it into their early policy statements. Kennedy's leading military adviser, General Maxwell Taylor, had launched the AFAK program while commanding the Eighth Army in Korea, and had become a strong proponent of the idea of using the military in development projects in underdeveloped areas. Taylor had seen many years of service in the Army Corps of Engineers, and his influence can be detected in Kennedy's many references to this organization as a model for the civic action program. Thus in his "Urgent National Needs" message to Congress on May 25, 1961, Kennedy stated: "Military assistance can, in addition to its military purposes, make a contribution to economic progress. The domestic works of our own Army Engineers are an example of the role which military forces in the emerging countries can play in village development, sanitation, and road building."[45] This argument was carried to an audience of Latin American military officers by Secretary of State Dean Rusk in 1962: "The United States Government would like to see Latin American armed forces increase their part in modernizing the basic facilities of all the American Republics. We believe they could borrow profitably from the long and honorable record of our own U.S. Army Corps of Engineers, in strengthening the civilian economy."[46]

The Defense Department had officially embraced the civic action concept as early as May 1960—but on the basis that any costs incurred by the program (other than training and advisory activities performed by U.S. personnel) would be borne by the host country. The first Civic Action Mobile Training Teams sent to Latin America reported, however, that in many countries no funds would be available for civic action. Consequently, on February 12, 1962, the President approved a funding formula which would release Department of Defense and Agency for Internatonal Development (AID) funds for such programs.[47]

In fiscal 1962, the first year in which U.S. funds were made available for civic action programs in Latin America, the Pentagon allocated $5.7 million for this purpose and the Agency for International Development another $3.3 million; most of this money went to Bolivia ($1.7 million), Brazil ($2.5 million), Ecuador ($1.8 million), and Peru ($1.2 million). The present tendency is for civic action funds to be distributed in smaller grants to a greater number of countries—in 1970, all but three of the Latin American nations received some funds for this purpose. Total Pentagon spending on the civic action program in Latin America since 1962 is enumerated in Table 8.

In addition to providing monetary assistance, the United

Table 8

U.S. MILITARY ASSISTANCE PROGRAM EXPENDITURES ON CIVIC ACTION PROJECTS IN LATIN AMERICA

Fiscal Years 1962–70

(Dollars in thousands)

Country	Expenditures	Country	Expenditures
Argentina	2,140	Honduras	792
Bolivia	2,918	Mexico	27
Brazil	11,266	Nicaragua	67
Chile	5,706	Panama	104
Colombia	5,728	Paraguay	4,394
Costa Rica	26	Peru	11,057
Dominican Republic	1,121	Uruguay	1,327
Ecuador	3,166	Venezuela	129
El Salvador	844	Regional	13
Guatemala	2,668	Total	53,493

Source: U.S. House of Representatives, Committee on Appropriations, Subcommittee, *Foreign Assistance and Related Agencies Appropriations For 1971, Hearings,* 91st Congress, 2d Session, 1970, Part 1, p. 420.

States helps initiate civic action projects by dispatching Civic Action Mobile Training Teams (CAMTT's) to the host country. Each team is composed of specialists in governmental administration, engineering, public health, sanitation, agriculture, and education. These teams tour the countryside in order to select target areas for civic action, and then draw up a country program that is within the capacity of the local armed forces. The CAMTT's also provide training and guidance for native military personnel, and in some instances provide technical assistance on actual projects. By 1965, such teams had visited most Latin American nations.[48]

A survey of civic action programs in Latin America by two North Americans associated with Ohio State University's Mershon Center for Education in National Security, Willard F. Barber and C. Neale Ronning, disclosed that in most countries the military favored "high-impact" projects intended to secure a rapid improvement in the public's opinion of the armed forces, rather than less visible projects that might have a long-range effect on the rural economy.[49] (Examples of the former are school construction and maintenance, literacy training, school hot-lunch programs, and medical and health programs, while the latter would include swamp drainage, forestry operations, and improvement of inland waterways.) At the Fourth Conference of the American Armies, held in July 1963, representatives of the Latin American military establishment reported that in ten countries the armed forces were building schools and churches, in eight they were conducting adult literacy campaigns, and in six they were engaged in housing construction.[50]

From what is known of the civic action program, it is not surprising that Barber and Ronning found that local populations did not express a sense of participation. They describe one study in which "it was found that the program in Bolivia had engineered no particular gratitude on the part of the civilian beneficiaries. Most of the civilians interviewed expressed suspicion as to the army's motives in engaging in civic action projects, especially when it was working under contract."[51] When, in 1966, the Center for Research in Social Systems began a study of "Criteria to Assess Military Civic Action Programs," it pointed out that "Supposedly these programs contribute to the social and economic development of the countries and improve the attitudes of the people toward their national governments and military forces. To date, there is no available scientific evidence that these civic action programs in fact achieve these ends."[52]

Although there is no evidence that the civic action program has actually contributed to the economic health of the countryside, the Pentagon's public relations officers have nevertheless used the program to justify their claims that the Latin American military has become committed to the long-range socioeconomic development of their countries. For instance, General Porter, in his 1967 testimony to the House Foreign Affairs Committee, complained that "Reference to the Latin American military still conjures up images of pompous, bemedaled men— 'caudillos' with little interest in or understanding of their peoples' problems and aspirations." Porter then quoted David Rockefeller to the effect that "this false concept does a disservice to many members of the armed forces in Latin America. The current generation of military leaders includes men of considerable sophistication in economic and social matters, and a sincere desire to improve the lot of the poor and quicken the pace of economic growth."[53]

The U.S. public-relations effort on behalf of the Latin American armed forces has been particularly well received in those nations ruled by military juntas. Many of the military officers who have seized state power in recent years are particularly enthusiastic supporters of the civic action program (the late René Barrientos of Bolivia is an outstanding example). Barber and Ronning discovered that in countries where the military traditionally plays a decisive political role, "The experienced observer of Latin America can detect in the speeches of its leaders and the publications issued by its defense departments the ideas and arguments advanced by United States spokesmen for civic action. The same ideology and the same phrases are utilized."[54] Thus the National Defense Minister of Colombia, General Alberto Ruiz Novoa, told an audience of Latin American military officers in 1963:

Besides accomplishing an effective program of assistance to the people, military civic action gains the support of the populace for the legitimate and rightful regime and for its armed forces. It also helps to prove the usefulness of the army and to counter the attacks of those who see in military expenditures only a useless drain of public funds.[55]

Many Latin American armies have launched well-publicized civic action programs in the interior of their country; but despite lavish subsidies provided by the United States, these programs do not seem to have had any significant effect on the miserable conditions in which most people of these regions live. In practice, many of the civic action projects backed by the United States are oriented more toward facilitating military operations in rural areas than to the improvement of social and economic conditions. The construction of roads and highways, for instance, is one of the most common forms of civic action activity. Ostensibly, such work is designed to improve integration of the countryside with the cities by extending government services to remote villages while allowing peasants to sell their products to a wider market. In reality, many road-building projects are intended to expedite government surveillance of potentially rebellious areas, and to enhance the mobility of military and paramilitary forces during actual outbreaks of guerrilla warfare.

TRAINING

Other than the supply of arms and equipment, the most important function of the U.S. military apparatus in Latin America is to provide training to indigenous military personnel. In fiscal 1971, $10 million or 62 percent of the MAP grant aid program was devoted to this purpose.[56] Training also constitutes the principal day-to-day activity of officers assigned to the seventeen U.S. military missions in Latin America. The high priority given to training activities was underscored by Defense Secretary McNamara in a 1962 appearance before the House Appropriations Committee:

Probably the greatest return on our military assistance investment comes from the training of selected officers and key specialists at our military schools and training centers in the United States and overseas. These students are handpicked by their countries to become instructors when they return home. They are the coming leaders, the men who will have the know-how and impart it to their forces. I need not dwell upon the value of having in positions of leadership men who have first-hand knowledge of how Americans do things and how they think. *It is beyond price to us to make such friends of such men."*[57] (Emphasis added.)

This estimate of the Latin American training programs is shared by the present Secretary of Defense, Melvin Laird, who once affirmed that MAP training is "one of the most important and successful programs we have had, not only in South America but in other places of the world."[58]

The United States provides three kinds of training for Latin American military personnel. These three programs were identified in 1967 by Vice Admiral L. C. Heinz, then Director of Military Assistance, as follows:

First, training in the United States, in which we bring students to this country for various types of training. . . .

Second, training in the Canal Zone. Students go to the Army School of the Americas and U.S. Air Force School in the Canal Zone for training. . . .

Finally, training includes mobile training teams which go to countries for particular purposes, from a few days to several months, depending upon the special training required.[59]

To these formal programs, one need only add the informal advisory function performed by the military attachés and mission personnel in each country to complete the picture of U.S. training activities in Latin America.*

---

* All U.S. training programs in Latin America are supervised by the Commander of the United States Forces Southern Command (SOUTHCOM), with headquarters at Quarry Heights in the Panama Canal Zone. With jurisdiction over all U.S. Army, Navy, and Air Force units stationed on the mainland of South and Central America

Between 1950 and 1969, the Defense Department provided training to 50,581 Latin American officers and enlisted men at schools in the United States and the Panama Canal Zone. A total of 22,059 men were trained in the period 1964–8 alone—a number equal to the total armed forces of El Salvador, Haiti, Honduras, and Nicaragua combined. A country-by-country breakdown of Latin American military personnel trained under MAP since 1950 is provided in Appendix E.

As one would expect, the countries with the largest armed forces had the greatest number of students trained under MAP programs. However, as in the case of MAP grants, when these countries are ranked on a proportional basis the reverse pattern emerges. As can be seen in Table 9, the countries with the greatest percentage of men trained have relatively small armed forces. Furthermore, of the six countries with the largest proportional training programs, five—Guatemala, Bolivia, the Dominican Republic, Venezuela, and Peru—have experienced serious insurgent challenges within the past decade.

United States training programs in Latin America have several related goals, most of which are clearly political. One objective of such programs is an improvement in the professional competence of indigenous troops; obviously, the better trained the Latin American military is, the less the likelihood that United States troops will have to be called in to save the situation for some favored regime. U.S. strategy also requires that the local military be *motivated* for the performance of internal security functions, which has not always been the case. Many Latin

---

(excluding Mexico), SOUTHCOM is one of the regional "unified commands" that reports directly to the Joint Chiefs of Staff. On February 14, 1971, *The New York Times* reported that President Nixon had decided to abolish SOUTHCOM and turn over its functions to the Atlantic Command, based at Norfolk, Virginia; six months later, however, Defense Secretary Laird announced that SOUTHCOM would remain in operation.

Table 9

**U.S. MILITARY TRAINING PROGRAM IN SELECTED
LATIN AMERICAN COUNTRIES, 1959–69**

(Countries listed in ranked order)

Total armed forces		Average annual number of military personnel programmed for training		Average percent of total armed forces programmed for training	
Country	Number	Country	Number	Country	Percent
Brazil	194,000	Brazil	580	Nicaragua	3.5
Argentina	120,000	Venezuela	380	Guatemala	2.6
Mexico	68,500	Argentina	370	Bolivia	1.7
Chile	60,000	Chile	370	Dominican	
Peru	54,650	Peru	370	Republic	1.4
Colombia	54,000	Colombia	330	Venezuela	1.2
Venezuela	30,500	Bolivia	260	Peru	0.65
Dominican		Dominican		Chile	0.62
Republic	19,300	Republic	260	Colombia	0.62
Bolivia	15,000	Nicaragua	260	Argentina	0.30
Guatemala	9,000	Guatemala	235	Brazil	0.30
Nicaragua	7,100	Mexico	60	Mexico	0.08

Source: Geoffrey Kemp, *Some Relationships Between U.S. Military Training In Latin America and Weapons Acquisition Patterns: 1959–1969* (Cambridge, Mass.: MIT Center for International Studies, 1970), p. 4.

American military officers would rather command elite units like jet fighter squadrons, naval flotillas, or armored brigades than slug it out with the guerrillas in long, unspectacular jungle campaigns. U.S. training programs are designed, therefore, to emphasize the importance of counterguerrilla operations (and to suggest, thereby, that the United States will reward those officers who make a good showing at this kind of warfare). [Another function of training programs is to accustom Latin American military personnel to the use of U.S.-made equipment—so that, upon returning to their countries, they will tend to purchase such equipment when outfitting their own armies [(thus further enriching U.S. arms manufacturers and contributing to a favorable balance of trade).

U.S. training is also intended, according to Pentagon doctrine, to foster "a constructive and democratic approach by the military to their professional responsibilities and to the solution of national problems."[60] One can only wonder what is said on this subject in the classroom, out of reach of prying newsmen and skeptical Congressmen; in any case, there is little evidence that U.S. efforts in this direction have had any effect whatsoever on the authoritarian designs of Latin American officers. (In fact, Pentagon emphasis on the "nation-building" role of the military has probably had the opposite effect.) In a 1967 report to a subcommittee of the Senate Foreign Relations Committee, Professor Lieuwen reported:

The recent wave of military interventions suggests that the U.S. training programs, the work of the missions, and the contact between United States and Latin American military men did little to improve military respect for civilian authority and constitutional processes. (Most of the Latin American military leaders who conducted the nine coups between 1962 and 1966 had been recipients of U.S. training.[61]

If one brings this accounting up to date, the evidence is even more compelling: coups in Panama, Bolivia, and Peru have all been led by men who received at least some training at Pentagon expense in the United States or the Canal Zone. In Peru, for example, ten of the twelve military officers holding cabinet posts in the present regim received at least some training in the United States.

The fact that so many military rulers received U.S. training was cited by Congressional critics of the MAP program in their successful effort to impose a limit on the number of foreign military personnel that can receive such training in any given year. Under Section 510 of the Foreign Assistance Act of 1970, the number of military trainees brought to the United States under MAP is limited to the number of foreign students attending classes here in the previous fiscal year under the Mutual Educational and Cultural Exchange Act of 1961 (Fulbright-Hays Act). Adoption of this measure has proved a strong blow against the current Administration, which seeks, as part of the "Nixon Doctrine" plan to reduce U.S. troop strength abroad, to upgrade the capabilities of Third World armies. Pentagon spokesmen have been outspoken in their opposition to the restriction and have seized every opportunity to argue for repeal of the measure. Thus, during hearings on the 1971 foreign aid appropriation, MAP director General Warren asserted that compliance with Section 510 "means that, at the very time we are asking our friends and allies to assume more responsibility for their own and the common defense, we must sharply curtail our efforts to enhance their professional skills and to increase their understanding of what we consider the role of the military in a democratic society."[62] In its effort to expand the training program, the Administration has the backing of Governor Nelson Rockefeller, who reported, after his 1969 tour of Latin American that: "In view of the growing subversion against hemisphere governments . . . it is essential that the training program which brings military and police personnel from the other hemisphere nations to the United States and to training centers in Panama be continued and strengthened."[63]

Considering the importance that has been accorded the MAP training program, it is appropriate at this point to provide a brief sketch of the schools in the United States and the Panama Canal Zone that have the largest attendance of Latin American personnel.

School of the Americas

The U.S. Army School of the Americas (USARSA), located at Fort Gulick in the Panama Canal Zone, is the major U.S. training institution for Latin American military personnel.

Founded in 1949 as the Army Caribbean School in Panama, it received its present name in 1963 when a new curriculum emphasizing training in counterinsurgency and civic action was introduced. All courses are given in Spanish; faculty and staff consist of U.S. Army personnel and guest lecturers from Latin American military organizations. In fiscal 1969, some 1,600 Latin American officers, cadets, and enlisted men attended courses at the School, bringing its cumulative number of graduates to more than 26,000.[64]

USARSA has four instructional divisions: the departments of Command, Combat Operations, Technical Operations, and Support Operations. The Department of Command, which provides instruction to high-ranking commanders and staff officers only, offers a forty-week course patterned after the Command and General Staff Course taken by prospective U.S. Army generals at Fort Leavenworth, Kansas. Courses taught by the Technical Operations and Support Operations departments, on the other hand, are intended primarily for specialists and enlisted men. Technical Operations provides training in communications, engineer, and maintenance specialties, while Support Operations involves training in military intelligence, military police, and medical and supply activities.

The Department of Combat Operations offers instruction to officers, cadets, and enlisted men. Students from military academies in eleven nations attend courses here in order to complete their training as candidate officers. Cadets and junior officers "are taught leadership roles for units assigned to irregular warfare, jungle operations, and combat engineer missions." The cadets also receive marksmanship training with assorted light weapons and participate in tactical field exercises. "Assaults, ambushes and patrols are carried out both day and night in the thick, insect-infected, obstacle-ridden rain forests bordering the Panama Canal." Cadets who study at the school for nineteen weeks or longer, according to a USARSA brochure, "complete a week-long maneuver known as the *Balboa Crossing* in which they trek across the isthmus from Pacific to Atlantic shores on a simulated search-and-destroy mission, putting into practice what they have learned about guerrilla warfare and jungle living."[65]

Fort Gulick boasts that alumni of the School "have risen to such key positions as Minister of Defense and Chief of Staff in Bolivia, Director of Mexico's War College, Minister of War and Chief of Staff in Colombia, Chief of Staff for Intelligence in Argentina and Under-Secretary of War in Chile." The Pentagon hopes, of course, that alumni of the School will endorse U.S. military policies for Latin America: according to *Army Digest*, "Training Latin Americans in U.S. military technical skills, leadership techniques and doctrine also paves the way for cooperation and support of U.S. Army missions, attachés, military assistance advisory groups and commissions operating in Latin America."[66]

Inter-American
Air Forces Academy

The Air Force equivalent of the Army School of the Americas is the Inter-American Air Forces Academy (IAAFA) at Albrook Air Base in the Canal Zone. IAAFA offers courses in aircraft maintenance, electronics, radio, instrument training and repair, engine and weapons mechanics, and other technical subjects. All courses are taught in Spanish by bilingual U.S. Air Force instructors and guest lecturers. During fiscal 1970, some 560 students from fourteen Latin American countries were graduated from IAAFA, bringing to nearly 10,000 the number graduated since classes began in 1943.

Unlike USARSA, most of the Academy's students are enlisted men. According to a Congressional study mission, "the greatest part of the Academy's efforts have been toward training fledgling airmen in the technical skills necessary to keep aircraft mechanically fit." Upon graduation, the student is essentially still an apprentice, although because of the scarcity of men with such skills in most of Latin America he will probably have to work on his own immediately upon graduation.[67]

Beginning in 1965, the Academy offered a course in Special Air Operations (i.e., counterinsurgency) jointly with the School of the Americas, the 605th Air Commandos, and the 24th Special Operations Wing. The course includes study of such activities as close air support on the battlefield, airlift supply operations for counterguerrilla forces, and airborne operations.[68]

Inter-American Defense College

The Inter-American Defense College (IADC) was established in 1962 as a senior service school similar to America's National War College, Great Britain's Imperial Defence College, and the NATO Defense College. In its founding statement, IADC was described as a "military institution of high-level studies, devoted to conducting courses in the Inter-American system and the political, social, economic, and military factors that constitute essential components of inter-American defense, in order to enhance the education of selected armed forces personnel and civilian government officials of the American republics for carrying out undertakings requiring international cooperation."[69] The College, located at Fort Lesley McNair in Washington, D.C., is a creation of the Inter-American Defense Board (IADB), which is composed of high-ranking military representatives of the twenty-two member nations of the Organization of American States.

The emphasis at IADC is on the quality, not quantity, of its students, who number about forty each year (each member nation of the IADB may send up to five students annually). Admission requirements include the rank of lieutenant colonel or above, graduation from an advanced command and staff college, and military experience at an advanced level. Instructors are senior military and government officers nominated by members of IADB, with final selection by the college director (always an American). As of June 1970, some 229 students had graduated from the college. According to IADC records, "Thirty-eight of the college alumni have attained flag rank," while "many past officials of the college have assumed other positions of great importance in their home countries."[70]

The nine-month course of study at IADC stresses Cold War ideology and the need for joint action against "Castro-Communist" subversion. Several sessions are devoted to the theory and practice of military civic action and related counterinsurgency activities. The course is usually concluded with strategic planning exercises involving the principles of collective defense.

Service Schools
in the United States

A total of 142 Army, Air Force, and Navy installations in the United States provide training for foreign military personnel under the MAP program. These include the Army Infantry School at Fort Benning, Georgia, the Command and General Staff College at Fort Leavenworth, Kansas, and the Army Chemical Corps School at Fort McClellan, Alabama.[71] Graduates of the U.S. service schools include Major General Juan Velasco Alvarado and Brigadier General Edgardo Mercado Jarrin, the President and Foreign Minister respectively of Peru; Major General Hernando Currea Cubides, Defense Minister and commanding general of the Colombian armed forces; and other prominent political figures.

Although precise figures on the numbers of Latin Americans attending each of these schools are not available, it is known that the Army has tailored the curricula at two of the schools to emphasize military operations in under-developed areas. These installations are the Special Warfare School at Fort Bragg, North Carolina, and the Civil Affairs and Military Government School at Fort Gordon, Georgia. The Special Warfare School (part of the John F. Kennedy Center for Military Assistance) offers courses on counterinsurgency operations, psychological warfare, and related subjects. Most of the students are U.S. military personnel who have been assigned to military missions or Special Forces units in Third World areas; however, several hundred Latin American officers have also received training at the school.[72] In 1963, Assistant Secretary of State Edwin Martin reported that Latin American military personel were receiving training at Fort Bragg "in riot control, counterguerrilla operations and tactics, intelligence and counter-intelligence, and other subjects which will contribute to the maintenance of public order."[73] The Civil Affairs School is the principal center in the United States for training in the administration of military civic action programs. As at the Special Warfare School, most students are U.S. Army, Navy, and Air Force officers who are under assignment to a military mission, mobile training team, or military assistance advisory group. The civic action course includes instruction in the theory of economic development, organization and logistics for civic action projects, and psychological operations in counter-insurgency.[74]

The formal training programs described above are supplemented by special in-country training programs organized on an ad hoc basis by mobile training teams (MTT's). These teams are usually composed of a handful of specialists in various military skills (small arms, vehicle maintenance, road construction, jungle warfare, etc.) who set up improvised courses wherever they are needed.

Although the MTT's may be made up of men from any of the services, one unit has this activity as its principal mission: the Eighth U.S. Army Special Forces, based at Fort Gulick in the Panama Canal Zone. Composed of some 1,100 officers and enlisted men, this unit regularly fields some two dozen MTT's of up to thirty men each that provide training in counterguerrilla tactics to selected Latin American combat units. Journalists who visit Fort Gulick are told that "the principal mission of the Special Forces is to advise, train and aid the Latin American military and paramilitary forces to conduct counterinsurgency activities, and to do so in support of the objectives of the United States of America within the framework of the Cold War."[75]

Since the formation of the Eighth Special Forces in 1962, Green Beret MTTs' have worked with the troops of every Latin American nation except Mexico, Cuba, and Haiti; according to official statistics, four hundred such MTT's were constituted between 1962 and 1968. Researchers at MIT's Center for International Studies have demonstrated that MTT activity always peaks when a country is threatened by an insurgent movement.[76] The most famous MTT operation is undoubtedly the counterinsurgency courses organized by Major Ralph W. "Pappy" Shelton in Bolivia in April 1967. Shelton's team of four officers and twelve enlisted men is credited with training the Ranger company that captured Ernesto Che Guevara in the Bolivian jungle on October 8 of that year. Special Forces personnel are not (officially) authorized to engage in combat operations in Latin America; most of the activities of the Green Berets are secret, however, and it is nearly impossible to keep track of their comings and goings. A former stringer for *Time* and *Life* with wide experience in Latin America, Andrew St. George, reported that by the end of 1962 Che's disciples and the Green Berets "were at each other's throats in a dozen countries. Thousands of anonymous combatants on both sides were killed in far-flung, merciless guerrilla battles. Among them died quite a few *yanquis* never mentioned in official dispatches."[77]

Advisory Missions

In-country training programs are the direct responsibility of the military missions, sometimes known as Military Assistance Advisory Groups (MAAG's), stationed in sixteen Latin American nations. The advisory missions range in size from five men in Costa Rica to ninety-two in Brazil; as of July 1, 1971, there were 505 officers, enlisted men, and civilian employees assigned to advisory groups in Latin America. Mission personnel normally maintain close working relations with the indigenous military establishment (in Brazil, for instance, the mission is known as the Joint U.S.-Brazil Military Command and has offices in the headquarters of the Brazilian Army Command) and administer the country's MAP program. U.S. advisers are also called upon to train native troops in the use of MAP-supplied equipment, and to teach at in-country military schools and academies. American instructors helped revise the curriculum of the Brazilian Army Command and General Staff School to provide greater emphasis on counterinsurgency training, while in Colombia the military group aided in the establishment of senior service academies.[78]

While the largest advisory missions are stationed in the countries with large military establishments, the highest ratio of advisers to total armed forces occurs in the countries with relatively small armies (see Table 10).

This pattern, which is consistent with the data on MAP grants and training, suggests that Pentagon influence is generally greatest in the smaller and poorer countries, which depend, to a great extent, on U.S. assistance to meet the equipment, training, and administrative needs of their

Table 10

**U.S. MILITARY ADVISER PATTERNS
IN SELECTED LATIN AMERICAN COUNTRIES**

(In rank order)

Country	Average number of U.S. advisers 1964–8	Country	Ratio of advisers to total armed forces
Brazil	109	Guatemala	1:300
Venezuela	82	Bolivia	1:306
Peru	68	Nicaragua	1:323
Colombia	60	Venezuela	1:372
Argentina	59	Dominican Republic	1:522
Bolivia	49	Peru	1:804
Chile	48	Colombia	1:900
Dominican Republic	37	Chile	1:1,250
Guatemala	30	Brazil	1:1,760
Nicaragua	22	Argentina	1:2,034

Source: Geoffrey Kemp, *Some Relationships Between U.S. Military Training In Latin America and Weapons Acquisition Patterns: 1959–1969* (Cambridge, Mass.: MIT Center for International Studies, 1970), p. 7.

armed forces. While there is no scientific way of testing this supposition, there is considerable evidence that the influence of U.S. advisers in many of the small (and not so small) Latin American countries is considerable. David Fairchild, who served as Assistant Program Officer in the AID mission in Santo Domingo from April 1966 to September 1967, stated in an interview that the Dominican military "is clearly sitting around waiting for MAAG to tell it what to do. And it is also clear that the president [of the Dominican Republic] has less power over the Dominican military than the MAAG does. The 65-man MAAG mission lives, eats, sleeps with those guys."[79] An American journalist who visited the headquarters of Colonel Carlos Arana Osorio in the Zacapa military zone of Guatemala in 1966 was told by a Special Forces Advisor that Arana, then commander of a counterguerrilla detachment, had established "a real good close relationship" with the U.S.

advisory staff and faithfully carried out their suggestions.[80] (Arana is now President of Guatemala.) A Congressional study group that visited Peru, Colombia, and Panama in 1970 found that the same kind of close relationship existed between the military of those countries and the U.S. advisory missions.[81]

Of the larger Latin American countries, U.S. influence is considered greatest in Brazil, where a military junta has ruled under martial law since 1964. Many Latin Americans believe that Brigadier General Vernon A. Walters, formerly a U.S. military attaché in Rio de Janeiro, was instrumental in organizing the 1964 coup that catapulted the late Marshal Humberto Castello Branco into power.[82] Notwithstanding some halfhearted State Department criticism of the military regime, relations between the U.S. advisory group and the Brazilian military have remained friendly and courteous. (This relationship is probably cemented by the $130 million in military assistance provided to the regime since it seized power.) A Congressional study group that visited Brazil in 1970 related that "U.S. military personnel report being welcome at all activities of the Brazilian Armed Forces. Their advice is often solicited on military problems and, at times, through personal contacts, individual U.S. representatives have been able to exert beneficial influence on authorities."[83] What kind of "beneficial influence" was exerted was not explained by the Congressmen, but it did not include a return to constitutional rule. There does not seem, in fact, to be any substantive political disagreements to divide the Brazilian military and their American advisers; the Congressional group gave this summary of statements made by U.S. advisory personnel:

Rather than dwell on the authoritarian aspects of the regime, they emphasize assertions by the Brazilian armed forces that they believe in, and support, representative democracy as an ideal and would return government to civilian control if this could be done without sacrifice to security and development.

This withdrawal from the political arena is not seen as occurring in the near future. For that reason they emphasize the continued importance of the military assistance training program as a means of exerting U.S. influence and retaining the current pro-U.S. attitude of the Brazilian armed forces. Possible disadvantages to U.S. interests in being so closely identified with an authoritarian regime are not seen as particularly important.[84]

Chapter 11

THE GREAT
SOUTH ASIAN WAR
—Mercenary Strategy
for the Endless War

In order to gain a world-historical perspective on the Vietnam war and on American strategy for the region, it is necessary to regard the current conflict as but one episode in a Great South Asian War which began almost immediately after the conclusion of World War II and which can be expected to continue through the 1970's, if not well beyond them. The Great War has already encompassed the Indochinese War of Independence (1946–54), the guerrilla war in Malaya (1948–60), civil wars in Vietnam, Laos, and Cambodia (continuing), guerrilla skirmishes in Thailand (continuing), and other armed struggles in Burma, Malaysia, the Philippines, and Indonesia. Combatants in these conflicts have included, in addition to troops of the countries named, the armies of Great Britain, France, Australia, New Zealand, South Korea, and, of course, the United States.[1]

These episodes constitute a common war not only because they occupy overlapping zones in a single theater of war but also because they spring from a common cause:

the determination of the advanced industrial nations of
the West—led by the United States—to intensify their control over the destinies of the underdeveloped lands of Asia.
The Western presence in Southeast Asia naturally constitutes a military and economic challenge to Communist
China, whose real or imagined influence has been a factor
in each of these struggles; it is not, however, the threat of
Chinese belligerence that lends unity to all these episodes,
but rather the determination of the region's peoples to secure a future that will be free of foreign control. Because
the nations of South Asia have been locked in a state of
permanent underdevelopment, and since national boundaries (which, more often than not, were established by European powers) do not always conform to the pattern of
ethnic distribution, these conflicts often take the form of
"insurgencies"—i.e., local struggles against centralized authority—and the response to them has been a succession of
"counterinsurgencies." Although such "limited wars" were
originally seen as occupying the opposite end of the military spectrum from "all out" (nuclear) war, in South Asia
we witness a counterinsurgency that threatens to become
unlimited in its destructiveness and duration.

At the end of World War II, the United States and its
Western European allies agreed to sanction the reestablish-
ment of each other's spheres of influence in Asia. The
United States, having conquered Japan, was to control the
northern and western Pacific (China, Korea, the Philippines, etc.), while France would remain dominant in Indochina and Britain in the Indian Ocean area (India, Burma,
Malaya, Singapore, etc.). The allies also apportioned responsibility for the maintenance of a defense perimeter,
corresponding to their colonial holdings, which encircled the
eastern half of Asia from Korea to Kashmir, and pledged to
come to one another's aid in the event that any point on
the perimeter came under heavy attack. This "gentlemen's
agreement" soon came to the test—the restoration of colonial regimes in South Asia (despite wartime promises of

independence) led to the outbreak of guerrilla warfare throughout the region. Several countries won their independence this way, where continued occupation would have been unprofitable (Burma) or beyond the capacity of the home economy (that of the Netherlands in the case of Indonesia). But in Southeast Asia proper, the imperial powers were prepared to engage in protracted counterguerrilla struggles in order to maintain their control of the area's resources. The guerrilla conflict in Malaya lasted twelve years before Britain (with the aid of Australia and Gurkha tribesmen) forced the last remnants of the Malayan Races Liberation Army across the border into Thailand. In Indochina, however, the occupying power—France —faced a more formidable foe. By 1950, confronted with a deteriorating military situation in Vietnam and growing discontent at home, France appealed to the United States to honor its commitment to help prevent a breach of the Asian defense perimeter. Although the United States had already deployed its troops in South Korea to protect the northern flank of the perimeter, it nevertheless agreed to supply France with arms and badly needed funds. (U.S. contributions to the French military effort in Indochina amounted to $2.6 billion, or 80 percent of the cost of the war.) Despite substantial U.S. aid, France was defeated on the battlefield and compelled to abandon its colonies in Indochina. With the withdrawal of French troops from Southeast Asia, a substantial military vacuum developed at the midpoint of the Asian defense perimeter. The United States, which until this time had considered Southeast Asia to be of secondary importance to its Pacific territories, quickly moved in to fill the breach.

The French colonial apparatus had not even completed its removal from Saigon when America's first paramilitary legions began arriving. In order to circumvent the Geneva Accords—which had prohibited the introduction of new weapons or foreign military personnel into Vietnam—the Michigan State University Group was established to provide a "cover" for the CIA team that armed and trained South Vietnamese President Ngo Dinh Diem's secret police and palace guard. The gradual intensification of U.S. military activity in Vietnam—from the arrival of the first Special Forces "advisers" to the deployment of a half-million-man army—is too familiar to need repeating here. Despite the well-publicized troop withdrawals from South Vietnam, U.S.-initiated military activity in Southeast Asia actually increased in 1970 and 1971, with most of this increment taking place in Laos and Cambodia. After the May 1970 invasion of Cambodia and the February 1971 incursion into Laos, it became obvious that the United States was no longer dealing with a local conflict but had precipitated a wider war that now envelops the entire Indochinese Peninsula.[2]

Even while fighting in Southeast Asia to maintain the Asian defense perimeter, the United States is preparing to extend its responsibility for security of the perimeter to still another region of South Asia: the Indian Ocean area. On January 16, 1968, Prime Minister Harold Wilson announced that his Labour Party government would withdraw all British troops stationed east of the Suez Canal by the end of 1971. This announcement produced dismay in Washington, where it has always been assumed that Great Britain could be counted upon to protect America's western flank in Asia. One American strategist, James D. Atkinson of Georgetown University, wrote that "for almost a century the vast Red Sea-Persian Gulf-Indian Ocean complex was an area of relative stability. This was so because . . . British forces were on hand throughout these sea spaces and able to respond quickly for any needed police actions."[3] With Britain no longer able to perform this police function, the Pentagon began making plans to assume responsibility for defense of the Indian Ocean area. Although the Conservative government headed by Prime Minister Edward Heath later announced that Britain would retain a small military force in South Asia, American defense preparations in the area—including the acquisition of new bases—are going ahead on schedule. The United States, long a Pacific power, is now on its way to becoming an Indian Ocean power.

THE GENESIS OF POLICY

America's tenacious involvement in the Vietnam conflict, which has survived widespread popular discontent at home and lack of success on the battlefield, has prompted many public figures to suggest that U.S. strategy in Asia is based on irrational principles. But military policies are never formulated in the absence of political and economic considerations, and these must be weighed before judgment is made on the soundness of any given strategy. An evaluation of America's long-term stake in the Pacific-Indian Ocean area suggests that the present conflict is not an isolated phenomenon but rather an integral component of U.S. strategy for domination in Asia. This long-term outlook is summed up in the concept of the "Pacific Basin" —a trade and investment complex that already rivals the Atlantic economy and is expected to surpass it in the decades ahead.[4] In order, then, to understand the factors that tend to perpetuate the Great South Asian War, it is necessary first to examine the role of the Pacific Basin and adjacent Indian Ocean areas in projected U.S. economic expansion.

The Pacific Basin, according to the business-minded *Forbes* magazine, "unites the western coasts of South and North America with Japan and the nations of the Orient and South Pacific, extending all the way to Australia." Among these nations, *Forbes* reported in 1970, "are to be found the fastest economic growth rates in the world and the most rapid increase in international trade."[5] On the basis of such reports, Bank of America President Rudolph A. Peterson told an audience of California industrialists,

"There is no more vast or rich area for resource development or trade growth in the world today than this immense region, and it is virtually our own back yard."[6]

By any set of indicators one could choose, it is evident that the Pacific Basin area has achieved parity with Latin America and Europe as an outlet for U.S. trade and investment. According to Commerce Department figures, U.S. trade with Asia and Oceania in 1969 amounted to $16.7 billion, compared with $9.1 billion in Latin America and $22.5 billion in Europe.[7] While trade with Japan (America's leading trading partner after Canada) accounts for a large bulk of U.S. commerce in the Pacific, our commercial relations with other Asian countries are becoming increasingly significant.[8] Direct U.S. investment in this area amounts to only $6.4 billion (comparable figures for Latin America and Europe are $13.8 billion and $21.6 billion respectively), but long-term development projects now underway—particularly in mining and electronics—signify that U.S. economic interest in the area will continue to grow.[9]

Without doubt, the most attractive field for U.S. investment in the area is the rapidly developing offshore oil-drilling industry in the western Pacific. Geological surveys undertaken by the United Nations Economic Commission for Asia and the Far East (ECAFE) and private Japanese and American companies have found signs of huge oil reserves along the continental shelf potentially rivaling those of the Persian Gulf area. The offshore reserves, in the view of many geologists, may extend along the entire eastern edge of Asia—from Korea across the East China Sea to Japan and Taiwan, along the coasts of Vietnam, Cambodia, and Thailand, and down the Malay Peninsula to the Indonesian Archipelago.[10] Significant oil discoveries in this area would be doubly enticing to American firms: first, because they would reduce dependence upon the increasingly nationalistic oil-producing states of the Middle East (which have been demanding a greater and greater share of profits realized from sales of the refined product), and secondly because such oil is expected to be low in sulfur content and thus easier to market in pollution-conscious American and Japan. When one calculates the fortunes that can be made from exploitation of such reserves, it is easy to see why American, Japanese, and European oil companies have been rushing to make bids on offshore exploration areas in waters off China, Southeast Asia, and Indonesia. *Fortune* reported in 1970 that "the quest off Indonesia and neighboring nations . . . is creating an atmosphere reminiscent of the Alaskan-Yukon gold rush."[11] At least twenty-two American and European companies are expected to bid for exploration rights off the coast of South Vietnam, while another six firms are already prospecting in the waters off Thailand.[12] Before the decade is over, if Board Chairman David Rockefeller of the Chase Manhattan Bank is to be believed, oil companies will have spent $35 billion in capital investment along the western rim of the Pacific.[13]

Although U.S. trade and investment in the Indian Ocean area has not increased as rapidly as in the Pacific, the region is a principal market for countries like Australia and Japan, whose economies, through a complex of joint ventures and multinational corporations, are becoming increasingly linked to that of the United States. The Indian Ocean itself has acquired considerable strategic importance (particularly since the closing of the Suez Canal) as a major sea route for the shipment of oil. Persian Gulf states currently supply 50 percent of the oil imports of Western Europe, 90 percent of Japan's, and 65 percent of Australia's; some of this oil is carried by pipeline to the Mediterranean, but the bulk of it goes by tanker through the Indian Ocean.[14] And with the development of new oil fields in the offshore regions of Indonesia and Southeast Asia, tanker traffic in the Indian Ocean probably will be increased substantially in coming decades.

In the view of most strategists, the Indian Ocean region has not even begun to realize its potential as an economic community. Rocco M. Paone, a Professor of Foreign Affairs at the U.S. Naval Academy, has termed this area the newest "heartland of the world" and provided this accounting of its assets:

The western portion of the Indian Ocean heartland includes much of the untapped mineral, agricultural, and forest resources of some of the most fertile regions of Africa. . . . Along the northwestern border is concentrated about 60 percent of the world's [known] oil reserves. The northern portion of this heartland includes the manpower resources of India, and, on its eastern and southeastern areas are located the enormous riches of the East Indies and the rapidly developing continent of Australia.[15]

From a strategic point of view, it also must be remembered that the Indian Ocean borders on the second, fifth, and sixth most populous nations in the world (India, Indonesia, and Pakistan, respectively), whose allegiance to the West is considered a major objective of United States policy. A socialist revolution in any of these countries would unalterably change the balance of power in the region and threaten the West's continued domination of Asia.* Paone believes that ⁺the nation that controls the

---

* In view of this assessment of the area's importance and potential wealth, it is easy to understand why the United States has become so disturbed by the presence of Soviet naval vessels in the Indian Ocean. Although the Soviet fleet has never encompassed more than twenty warships in these waters, its appearance in 1967 caused great alarm in Washington and other Western capitals. Citing statistics on the amount of oil carried by tankers through the Indian Ocean from Persian Gulf ports, the Center for Strategic and International Studies of Georgetown University warned in 1969 that "the strategic interests of the non-Communist world would be in grave jeopardy if freedom of movement in and out of the Gulf were curtailed or denied." (Quoted in *The New York Times,* January 19, 1969.) The Center's recommendation that the United States plan an increased naval presence in the area has received strong Pentagon endorsement. For the past few years, vessels from the Pacific Com-

[Indian] Ocean landmasses and waterways controls the new heartland of the world and can be dominant in shaping world politics.'

If American business interests have their way, the Pacific Basin countries will be allotted various roles in a regional division of labor with the United States running the whole show. This process might perhaps best be described as the "Latin Americanization" of South Asia— i.e., the stabilization of Asia's dependent status *vis-à-vis* the United States as a supplier of raw materials and cheap labor, and as a market for capital-intensive manufactured goods. As in South and Central America, the United States has encouraged the formation of free-trade zones to facilitate the penetration of Asian markets, and has cultivated partnerships with the more advanced nations in the area (particularly Australia and Japan) in order to exploit the resources of the whole region more efficiently. Because this strategy will doom South Asia to a condition of permanent underdevelopment, and most of its inhabitants (especially those in rural areas) to a condition of permanent impoverishment, conflict is inevitable. The revolutionary tide that swept through the colonial nations after World War II has not diminished with the attainment of nominal self-rule: everywhere in the Third World rebellious peasants are demanding that their economic subjugation come to an end. In Vietnam, the United States has learned at tremendous cost the bitter lesson that even poor farmers—when inspired by the promise of a better life for their children—can stop the most powerful armies in the world. It has become abundantly clear that American plans for the creation of a mercantile empire in South Asia will require the continued presence and intervention of U.S.

---

mand's Seventh Fleet have made periodic visits to the Indian Ocean. (A somewhat larger force, which included the aircraft carrier *Enterprise*, was dispatched during the Indian invasion of East Pakistan in 1971.)

troops (or native troops under American command) for as long as one can see into the future.

Evidently the military planners in the Pentagon realize the necessity for a continued U.S. presence, for despite promises of U.S. troop withdrawals from Asia following the cessation of hostilities in Vietnam, the Defense Department has made it quite clear that it will maintain a military establishment in the area for an indefinite period. Thus, in its annual budget report to Congress, the Pentagon stated in 1969 that it will "be necessary for the United States to continue some form of military presence in the region for some time," and that this "presence" will require "appropriate basing arrangements."[16]

Defense Secretary Melvin R. Laird has stated on many occasions that the United States will keep some kind of military apparatus in South Vietnam long after the termination of the present conflict. In a press conference held in Washington on October 16, 1969, Laird stated that we would maintain a "residual force" of several thousand military men for training and advisory duty after the fighting had ended. In another press conference, on April 12, 1971, he indicated that the Pentagon will station air and naval forces in Southeast Asia for an indefinite time. Laird emphasized that the Administration's Vietnamization program does *not* call for the withdrawal of *all* U.S. combat forces in Indochina: "To say that we would not have a presence in Asia [after Vietnam] under the strategy of realistic deterrence . . . would certainly be misleading."[17]

Nevertheless, popular disaffection with the Vietnam war in particular and with defense spending in general has created a serious problem for Pentagon officials: on the one hand, they recognize the need for a continued United States military presence in Asia to protect American investments, while on the other hand public resentment toward U.S. policy can force the government to reduce or withdraw its Asian garrisons. To resolve this dilemma, the Pentagon has evolved a multitiered formula for the use of mercenaries in future counterguerrilla operations. This scheme envisions a hierarchy of mercenary forces aided by the United States in the areas of logistics, communications, and air and naval support, made up of the following components:

Irregular Mercenaries. This category includes the primitive tribesmen and other minority groups that engage in clandestine operations for the CIA and other secret agencies of the U.S. government. Such "irregular" troops can be used behind enemy lines and in countries where direct U.S. participation is undesirable or illegal.

Regular Mercenaries. Most full-scale troop operations in Asia will be fought by the regular armed forces of America's client states, aided, where need be, by U.S. air and sea power. Such forces would be armed with American weapons, led by American-trained officers, and guided strategically by American advisers.

Elite Mercenaries. The professional armies of other Anglo-Saxon nations in the Pacific area—Australia and New Zealand—will be brought in where needed to buttress the conscript armies of our Asian clients.

The Mercenary-Support Infrastructure. In order to ensure that the various components of the mercenary apparatus work effectively, the United States—ultimately assisted by Japan—will maintain a support infrastructure in Asia to perform the logistical, communications, intelligence, and command functions that provide sustenance and direction to the whole system.

The substitution of mercenaries for American troops in counterinsurgency warfare has many advantages for the U.S. military establishment: domestic opposition to overseas operations is reduced because our involvement is less visible and less costly; opposition abroad is reduced because people are not confronted with the overt presence of our expeditionary forces; and finally, foreign troops cost the United States much less to maintain. These benefits were summed up by former Secretary of Defense Clark M. Clifford in an unusually candid statement to Congress on January 15, 1969: "Clearly, the overriding goal of our collective defense efforts in Asia must be to assist our allies in building a capability to defend themselves. *Besides costing substantially less* (an Asian soldier costs about 1/15th as much as his American counterpart), *there are compelling political and psychological advantages on both sides of the Pacific for such a policy.*"[18] (Emphasis added.)

This mercenary strategy was adopted with great enthusiasm by President Nixon, who has given it his own name. On July 25, 1969, at the Top of the Mar Hotel in Guam, the President told a group of hurriedly assembled newspapermen that thenceforth the United States would leave to its allies the primary defense role in Asia, while limiting itself to the necessary support functions. Although there was considerable confusion as to the precise meaning of the President's words (direct quotes were not permitted), the White House described the Guam message as "a major shift in U.S. foreign policy."[19] In order to assure textual consistency, the Guam Doctrine—later glorified as the Nixon Doctrine—was codified in these three propositions:

1. The United States will keep all its treaty commitments.
2. We shall provide a shield if a nuclear power threatens the freedom of a nation allied with us, or of a nation whose survival we consider vital to our security or to the security of the region as a whole.
3. In cases involving other types of aggression, we shall furnish military and economic assistance when requested and as appropriate. But we shall look to the nation directly threatened to assume the primary

responsibility of providing the manpower for its defense.[20]

Needless to say, it is the third principle of the Nixon Doctrine that has created the most controversy. Senate Majority Leader Mike Mansfield, who chose to amplify the Guam Doctrine in a formal report to the Senate, stated in 1969 that insofar as Asia is concerned, the policy meant that "The United States will maintain its treaty commitments, but it is anticipated that Asian nations will be able to handle their own defense problems, perhaps with some outside material assistance but without outside manpower. . . . The United States will avoid the creation of situations in which there is such great dependence on us that, inevitably, we become enmeshed in what are essentially Asian problems and conflicts."[21] It is now obvious, however, that the Pentagon never placed such a narrow interpretation on this proposition.* In testimony to the House Appropriations Committee, Secretary Laird described the Administration's mercenary strategy in Asia as follows:

The basic policy of decreasing direct U.S. military involvement cannot be successful unless we provide our friends and allies . . . with the material assistance necessary to insure the most effective possible contribution by the manpower they are willing and able to commit to their own and the common defense. Many of them simply do not command the resources or technical capabilities to assume greater responsibility for their own defense without such assistance. The challenging objectives of

---

* Upon his arrival in Canberra on January 10, 1970, Vice President Agnew—then on a tour of our Pacific allies—greeted Australian officials as follows:

> First, let me make it very clear that, despite a great deal of speculation and rumor, we are not withdrawing from Asia and the Pacific. We have said before, and I say it again today, that the United States will keep its treaty commitments. . . . As a Pacific power, we will remain in the Pacific. (*Department of State Bulletin*, February 23, 1970, p. 198.)

our new policy can, therefore, best be achieved when each partner does its share and contributes what it best can to the common effort. In the majority of cases, this means *indigenous manpower organized into properly equipped and well-trained armed forces with the help of materiel, training, technology and specialized military skills furnished by the United States.*[22] (Emphasis added.)

When doubts persisted about the meaning of "specialized military skills," Laird explained that "as has been stated repeatedly since the President enunciated the Nixon Doctrine in Guam in 1969, the United States would be and is prepared to provide material assistance and air and sea assistance to our allies and our friends in Asia."[23] This clarification, which was made during the catastrophic invasion of Laos early in 1971, represents the essence of American mercenary strategy in Asia. In the remainder of this chapter, we will examine the components of this strategy in detail.

IRREGULAR MERCENARIES

The lowest rank in the mercenary apparatus is held by the primitive tribesmen and minority peoples organized into commando groups under direct U.S. command. Although nominally part of the regular indigenous armed forces, such "irregular" units owe their primary loyalty to the CIA agents or Special Forces officers who supply their food, weapons, and pay. Mobilization of such mercenaries has a number of advantages to the United States: since the nomadic tribes of Southeast Asia normally wander across national boundaries, it is possible to send members of these tribes behind enemy lines without causing undue suspicion; they can also be used in sensitive missions without going through local army channels, and without implicating the United States; finally, their death in battle provokes no great concern on the part of the American public. Inevitably, however, the process of mercenarization causes a serious disruption in village life that in times of great stress leads to the collapse of the mercenary force itself.

The principal sources of mercenary irregulars in Southeast Asia are the tribal groupings that inhabit the highland areas of Vietnam, Cambodia, Thailand, and Laos. Ethnically different from the rice-growing peoples of the coastal and delta areas, the highlanders (or montagnards, as they are called by the French) have consistently remained aloof from the lowland societies and continue to worship animistic spirits. The lowland peoples (Laos, Thais, Khmers, and Vietnamese), for their part, regard the hill tribes with suspicion and contempt. (In Vietnam, the highlanders are referred to as *mo'i,* or savages, while in Laos they are known as *kha,* or slave.) Even under colonial rule, the lowland peoples continued to harass and exploit the highlanders, who thus remain alienated from the U.S.-backed "nationalist" regimes in Saigon, Vientiane, and Bangkok. For this reason, many hill tribes joined the insurgent forces after receiving assurances that they would be granted autonomy under a revolutionary government.[24] (To give credence to these promises, the insurgents can point to North Vietnam, where the highlanders have been granted nominal self-rule in regions where they constitute a majority of the population.[25]) The hill peoples are not a homogeneous group, however, and the United States has been able to exacerbate traditional tribal rivalries in order to obtain recruits for its mercenary armies. Other recruits have come from the national minorities that can be found throughout Southeast Asia as a result of border realignments brought about by conquest or colonial administration. Because of their antipathy to the central governments, these dissident peoples—the Meos, Lao Teung, and "Black Thais" in Laos, the Rhade, Nung, Khmers, and others in Vietnam—have formed temporary alliances with the American military while remaining independent of the national armed forces. Since they cannot grow enough crops to sustain themselves under present wartime conditions, these tribal and minority groupings have become progressively more dependent upon the United States for their very survival—their mercenary status, in other words, has become a permanent way of life.

Since 1960, the task of recruiting, training, and commanding mercenary irregulars in Southeast Asia has been the unique responsibility of the U.S. Special Forces. Up until then, however, the Green Berets had been entrusted with an entirely different mission: rather than perform the role of counterguerrillas, they were expected to serve as guerrillas themselves during an anticipated Soviet invasion of Western Europe. Former Special Forces Sergeant Donald Duncan, who joined the Green Berets in 1959, recalls that the "Special Forces' mission at its inception was to infiltrate trained guerrillas into foreign countries to teach indigenous populations how to mount insurrections against unpopular governments." The Russians, he was told, "were only waiting for an opportune moment to overrun Western Europe and push the Free World forces into the Atlantic." As soon as this invasion got underway, Special Forces units were to be parachuted behind enemy lines in Eastern Europe to organize anti-Soviet partisan units. The resulting insurrection would divert Russian troops from the front and make it easier for the allies to repel the invasion force.[26] This, at least, was the theory behind Special Forces planning; needless to say, no opportunity has arisen to test this concept under actual battlefield conditions.

In 1959, the role of the Special Forces was reversed: instead of operating as partisans behind enemy lines, the Green Berets would constitute a counterguerrilla strike force that could be sent to underdeveloped countries on short notice and, it was hoped, stave off the need for full-scale American intervention. Duncan recalls that this new function was rationalized as follows: "Who . . . is better qualified to fight guerrillas—conventional forces or men trained as guerrillas? Who can anticipate guerrilla moves better than someone thoroughly familiar with the psychology and doctrine of guerrilla warfare? . . . The best people to fight guerrillas are other guerrillas—anti-guerrillas."[27]

This argument, according to retired Air Force Colonel L. Fletcher Prouty, represented the thinking of CIA operative Colonel Edward Lansdale and his assistant Samuel Wilson. Prouty, who was working in the office of the Joint Chiefs of Staff at the time, remembers that Lansdale and Wilson went to Fort Bragg, headquarters of the Special Forces, to teach the new doctrine and to write texts on counterinsurgency.[28] Lansdale also sold John F. Kennedy and his brother Robert on the idea; for soon after taking office in 1961, the President requested a rapid buildup of Special Forces strength. "President Kennedy was very keen on the Green Berets," General Maxwell Taylor recalled in 1969, "and Bobby was sold on them, too."[29] With this kind of backing and a nationwide publicity campaign, Special Forces strength grew from 1,800 to 9,000 men and new units were established at Fort Bragg and in Okinawa and the Panama Canal Zone.

The first use of the Green Berets in their new role as organizers of indigenous counterguerrilla armies occurred in 1960 in Laos, when Special Forces units known as White Star teams were sent into the northern highlands to organize a mercenary force of Meo tribesmen. The mercenary units, which were to form the basis of the CIA's Armée Clandestine, engaged in hit-and-run attacks deep within Pathet Lao territory. The White Star operation was continued until July 1962, when Laos was neutralized under the Geneva Accords and the Special Forces were officially withdrawn; many of the Green Berets discarded their uniforms, however, and continued working with the Meos as civilian "contract employees" of the CIA.[30]

The Special Forces' big break came in 1961, when President Kennedy authorized their deployment in South Vietnam. Transferred to CIA jurisdiction for the interim, the Green Berets were given the task of organizing montagnard tribesmen and other minority groups into a mercenary force that could engage in operations deemed too sensitive for regular South Vietnamese troops. The mercenary forces, known as Civilian Irregular Defense Groups (CIDG's), were paid directly from CIA funds and operated independently of the Vietnamese Army command in Saigon. Numbering, at peak strength, some 45,000 men, the CIDG's conducted reconnaissance patrols along the Vietnamese border and in Laos and Cambodia, and attacked enemy villages, supply units, and small guerrilla forces.[31]

The CIDG mercenaries, their families and Special Forces advisers, and token South Vietnamese regulars all lived in a series of forts built opposite the border with Laos and Cambodia. At least sixty of these forts—like those at Longvei, Bu Prang, and Dakseang—were built at a reported cost of $3 million each. A journalist who visited the camp at Dakseang in 1970 described it as "a long rectangle of barbed wire, bunkers, sandbags and howitzers."[32] The montagnard warriors who inhabited the camp were sent out on patrols for seven days and then remained in camp for the next seven. Most reported that they joined the CIDG unit because of the higher pay they received from the Americans, and because of the maltreatment they received at the hands of regular South Vietnamese officers. Most visitors to such camps have been struck by the paternalistic attitude with which the Green Berets regard the montagnards (or "Yards," in Army slang) under their jurisdiction. "When they talk of the montagnards," one journalist wrote in 1970, "the Americans are fiercely possessive. They remind a visitor of the manner in which the British military once talked of the Gurkhas of Nepal."[33] Another journalist quoted Green Beret commander Colonel Michael Healy as saying, "We took them out of loincloths and put them into uniforms and now they are elite forces."[34] Now that the Green Berets have been withdrawn from Vietnam, the future of the montagnard troops is in question, since they will earn less under Saigon jurisdiction and many are afraid of the Vietnamese officers who are replacing the Americans.[35]

While the fate of the montagnard irregulars is still in doubt, the status of other CIDG mercenaries is a lot clearer: in May 1970, American-trained Khmer (ethnic Cambodian) commandos appeared in Phnompenh, the Cambodian capital, where they became the major strike force of Premier Lon Nol's rebel government. These units were composed of men from the Khmer Serai sect, opposed to the ousted Chief of State, Prince Norodom Sihanouk, and from the Khmer Kampuchea Krom minority living in the delta area of South Vietnam. When airlifted from Special Forces camps in Thailand and Vietnam to the Cambodian capital, these men brought with them their American weapons, uniforms, and radios. When the Khmer mercenaries were first flown to Phnompenh, an official at the American embassy there declared: "As far as we know these are ethnic Cambodians who wish to fight for the Cambodian Government, and were given permission by the South Vietnamese Government to leave Vietnam for this purpose." Journalists who witnessed their arrival reported that "the soldiers' uniforms are completely American, from boots right up to the cap, though some of them have been hurriedly issued with the cloth Cambodian Army beret." The men openly admitted that they were from the "Mike" forces, or mobile strike units, of the CIA's CIDG army.[36] An Associated Press correspondent who visited the Cambodian headquarters of this unit in May 1970 reported that their commander, Lieutenant Colonel Thach Thuong, used his powerful radio to confer with U.S. forces then operating in the "Parrot's Beak" area of eastern Cambodia. Colonel Thach, while nominally under the command of a Cambodian Army field officer, reportedly made no moves without first checking with his American liaison.[37]

The most elaborate U.S. mercenary organization in Southeast Asia is without doubt the Armée Clandestine in

Northern Laos—the "Secret Army" of highland tribesmen. Organized in 1961 by the White Star Green Beret teams, the Secret Army has grown to a force of 15,000 full-time troops and 40,000 part-time irregulars. Very little was known about this force until 1969, when a number of Western journalists began to investigate their activities. Henry Kamm of *The New York Times*, who first reported on Secret Army operations in detail, wrote in October 1969 that it is "armed, equipped, fed, paid, guided strategically and tactically, and often transported in and out of battle by the United States."[38]

Most Secret Army soldiers are Meo tribesmen or members of other tribal groupings that inhabit the mountains of northeastern Laos. The Meos are a nomadic people who emigrated to Indochina from southern China in the middle of the nineteenth century. As in Vietnam, the highland Meos are feared and distrusted by the lowland peoples, who have made no effort to integrate them into national life. For this reason, many hill tribes have made common cause with the insurgent Pathet Lao, who promised to help overcome the highlanders' isolation and poverty. The hill peoples of Laos are not united, however, and the United States has been able to pry away some tribes from Pathet Lao influence. (The nucleus of the Secret Army, for instance, is reportedly composed of a Meo clan that had feuded with another clan loyal to the Pathet Lao.[39]) This process has been abetted by the U.S. air war in Laos, which has made it nearly impossible to grow any crops in rebel-held zones—thus creating many refugees who have become mercenaries in order to obtain the basic necessities of life for themselves and their families.*

* In 1970 the Vientiane correspondent of the *Far Eastern Economic Review*, Hong Kong, gave this picture of the U.S. air war in northern Laos:

> For the past two years the U.S. has carried out one of the most sustained bombing campaigns in history against essen-

The Meo troops of the Secret Army are led by Major General Vang Pao, described by columnist Jack Anderson as "a foul-mouthed former sergeant in the French Army."[40] Although nominally responsible to the Laotian High Command in Vientiane, Vang Pao is for all purposes an independent warlord with his own army and a private American advisory and logistics apparatus. With undisputed leadership of the dissident Meo tribes, he follows no orders except his own and those which emanate from CIA headquarters in McLean, Virginia. Vang Pao normally avoids contact with newsmen, but in December 1969 he agreed to an interview with Peter R. Kann of the *Wall Street Journal.* Vang Pao showed up for the interview in "a fancy field uniform . . . bedecked by so many medals that he almost appears armor-plated." Kann gave this summary of their interchange:

Are U.S. jets bombing in Laos? he is asked. No, he says, though his voice is periodically drowned out by U.S. jets flying overhead. Are his troops armed with U.S.-made M-16 rifles? he is asked. No, he says, though the very men guarding him are carrying M-16s. Are U.S. helicopters supporting his war effort?

---

tially civilian targets in northeastern Laos. The area is a carpet of forest dotted by villages and a few towns. Refugees report that the bombing was primarily directed against their villages. Operating from Thai bases and from aircraft carriers, American jets have destroyed the great majority of villages and towns in the northeast. Severe casualties have been inflicted upon the inhabitants of the region, rice fields have been burned, and roads torn up. Refugees from the Plain of Jars report that they were bombed almost daily by American jets last year. They say they spent most of the past two years living in caves or holes. ("The Labyrinthine War," *Far Eastern Economic Review,* April 16, 1970.)

The U.S. air war, according to most reports, has produced the great majority of the 600,000 refugees at large today in Laos. (See T. D. Allman, "Support by U.S. Alters Laos War." *The New York Times,* October 1, 1969.)

he is asked. No, he says, though he boards a U.S. chopper after concluding the interview.[41]

Throughout most of the 1960's, the Secret Army was considered the most effective fighting force in Laos. During the air war against North Vietnam, Meo troops rescued American pilots who were downed behind enemy lines, defended U.S. radio beacons in rebel territory, and staged daring reconnaissance missions along the North Vietnamese border. Vang Pao's troops are also credited with the successful 1969 offensive that drove the Pathet Lao off the Plaine des Jarres.[42] Western visitors often contrast the impetuous fighting spirit of the Meos to the pacifist temperament of the ethnic Laos; thus the former U.S. Ambassador to Laos, William H. Sullivan, told a Senate subcommittee in 1969 that "the Lao are generally a gentle, peaceful people and would far rather live in peace than fight." The Meo, on the other hand, "have had a tradition of having to fight to defend themselves over the past 200 years. They are a somewhat more scrappy group."[43] Another reason given by Sullivan for the better performance of Meo troops was the higher pay they received as U.S. mercenaries: "Food allowances and incentive pay stimulate them to greater efficiency."[44] (Privates in the Royal Laotian Army receive the equivalent of $5 a month, while Secret Army troops often receive as much as $30 a month plus food supplies for their families.[45])

In order to feed, equip, train, and transport Vang Pao's irregular army, the United States has created an elaborate, covert military apparatus in Laos and Thailand. According to Colonel Peter T. Russell, Deputy Chief of the Joint U.S. Military Advisory Group in Thailand (JUSMAG-THAI), "the Geneva Agreements of 1962 required that all foreign troops—except a small French military training contingent—be withdrawn from Laos"; in order to continue support of pro-U.S. forces, therefore, "some special organizational and procedural arrangements were necessary."[46] The "special" arrangements devised by the U.S. to bypass the 1962 accords were spelled out in the Senate Foreign Relations subcommittee hearing, chaired by Stuart Symington, on United States Security Agreements and Commitments Abroad in 1969, and in a series of newspaper reports in the Western press.

The logistical and supply effort, according to Colonel Russell, is handled by the office of the Deputy Chief JUSMAGTHAI with headquarters at Udorn air base in northeastern Thailand. Supplies required by the Secret Army are shipped to the U.S. base at Sattahip on the Gulf of Siam, and then trucked to Udorn or other bases in Thailand and Laos.[47] The supplies are finally loaded on planes and helicopters owned by Air America and Continental Air Services for transshipment to isolated Meo campsites in the mountainous regions of northern Laos. In-country supervision of the supply operation is performed by the "Rural Development Annex" of the U.S. aid mission in Vientiane; this agency, although nominally run by civilians in the employ of Air America or the Agency for International Development, is staffed by "retired" military personnel under CIA jurisdiction.* Support of the Secret Army reportedly cost the United States $70 million in 1971.[48]

---

* The fact that the AID mission in Vientiane was being used as a cover for CIA mercenary-support operations was first reported by Jack Foisie of the Los Angeles *Times* on March 10, 1970. Foisie disclosed that CIA agents attached to AID's "Rural Development Annex" were supplying and training members of Vang Pao's Secret Army. Three months later, on June 8, AID Director John A. Hannah acknowledged on the Metromedia radio news program "Profile" that the AID mission was being used as a cover for CIA operations. (Foisie's disclosure should have come as no surprise to Hannah—in 1955, when he was president of Michigan State University, Hannah allowed the MSU advisory group in Saigon to be used as a cover for the CIA operatives who supervised the reorganization of South Vietnam's secret police.) Air America, although nominally a civilian-operated airline, is generally considered to be the air arm of the CIA. (See Richard Halloran, "Air America's Civilian Facade Gives it Latitude in East Asia," *The New York Times*, April 5, 1970.)

The nerve center of all Secret Army operations is the CIA base at Long Cheng on the southwestern edge of the strategic Plaine des Jarres. In addition to serving as General Vang Pao's headquarters, Long Cheng (also known as Long Tieng) houses the families of the Meo tribesmen who constitute the bulk of Secret Army personnel. Normally closed to journalists, the base was visited in February 1970 by three Western correspondents who had to slip past several Royal Laotian Army roadblocks in order to get in. Before being whisked away by CIA personnel, the reporters saw unmarked planes and helicopters land and take off at Long Cheng's 3,000-foot-long all-weather paved airstrip at the rate of one a minute; most of these planes were transport craft used to supply isolated Meo outposts in the mountains bordering the Plaine des Jarres. The airfield also housed T-28 fighter-bombers flown by Laotians but serviced by Americans and Filipinos. At least fifty Americans were reported to be stationed at the base—the CIA agents, former Green Berets, and Air America pilots who supply, train, finance, and direct the troops under General Vang Pao's command.[49]

Other foreign nationals at Long Cheng are Thai soldiers in Laotian uniform who man the base's artillery defenses, and South Vietnamese communications specialists. According to Senator J. William Fulbright (as reported in *The New York Times* on June 8, 1971), the United States has provided financial and material support to at least 4,800 Thai "volunteers" fighting in Laos under CIA command. In addition to two Thai battalions committed to the defense of Long Cheng, Thai troops have been sighted in the Plaine des Jarres and in the southern panhandle region. On June 8, 1971, the State Department acknowledged for the first time that U.S. funds were used to support the Thais in Laos, and asserted that such support (since it had been going on for several years) did not violate recent Congressional prohibitions on the use of American funds for support of "third country" mercenaries in Laos. By 1971, with the progressive deterioration of the Royal Laotian Army, these Thai troops were being called upon to assume an ever-increasing burden in defense of the Vientiane regime.

Although under seige by Pathet Lao troops since mid-1970, Vang Pao seems determined to hold onto Long Cheng at all costs, since its loss would undoubtedly weaken the morale of his troops as well as threaten his special relationship with the U.S. government. The General's concern for the morale of his troops is understandable, as the Meos' long service in the Secret Army has proved extremely costly to his tribe. Senator Edward M. Kennedy disclosed in 1970 that "estimates in the field suggest that up to 50 percent of these people—perhaps as many as 200,000 men, women and children—have already lost their lives in combat or from the hardships brought on by their service to our cause."[50] The loss of so many adult men has forced Vang Pao to recruit younger and younger men to serve in his army; Henry Kamm reported in 1970 that a fourth of all Secret Army soldiers were boys under sixteen, and many were only twelve or thirteen. The General himself requested that all noncombatants under his jurisdiction— some 50,000 women and children—be withdrawn from the battle zone and resettled in Sayaboury Province along the Thai border; since Meo soldiers usually will not fight if separated from their wives and children, the move will probably further reduce the effectiveness of what remains of the Secret Army. (All remaining civilians were evacuated from Long Cheng in December 1971, when the base came under renewed enemy attack.)

In this brief sketch of America's irregular mercenary armies in Southeast Asia, it has been possible only to identify some of the larger and better-known forces. While much attention has been focused on Vang Pao's Secret Army, very little is known to this day about other U.S. irregular mercenary units in Laos. In the southern panhandle region, for instance, commando teams known as Special Guerrilla Units make periodic forays into Pathet

Lao territory in order to collect intelligence on enemy movements along the Ho Chi Minh Trail. These units, often referred to as "trail watchers," are reportedly composed of Lao Teung tribesmen from the Bolovens Plateau of southern Laos. One commando force, which calls itself Tigers of the Jungle, is composed of at least 3,000 highlanders (many in their teens) and an unknown number of Green Beret officers. The Americans, based in Pakse and Savannakhet on the Mekong, often accompany the commandos on their reconnaissance missions.[51]

Available information suggests that only the most conspicuous features of the U.S. mercenary apparatus have been revealed (a force the size of General Vang Pao's Secret Army could not, after all, be hidden forever). Reports by Michael Morrow of Dispatch News International indicate that the United States has indirectly aided Burmese rebels seeking to overthrow the government of General Ne Win. According to Morrow, the Burmese insurgents —members of ousted Premier U Nu's National United Liberation Front—receive training at isolated camps in western Thailand. Although American and Thai officials refuse to acknowledge the presence of the rebels, it is understood that they have been granted permission to use the camps for this purpose. Morrow added that there is evidence that the CIA is providing some assistance to Karen and Shan tribesmen who are in revolt against the Ne Win regime. Morrow also reported that teams of Yao tribesmen from northern Laos periodically enter China to gather intelligence for the CIA.[52] It is reasonable to assume, therefore, that further disclosures on this vast mercenary operation will emerge as the Great South Asian War spreads.

"REGULAR" MERCENARIES

Ever since the triumph of the Chinese Revolution in 1949, United States policy has called for the maintenance of solidly anti-Communist regimes in key countries near main-land China. These nations—South Korea, South Vietnam, Taiwan, Laos, and Thailand—are expected to bear the brunt of any fighting with Chinese or "satellite" troops; at the present time, all are either engaged in combat opera-tions in Southeast Asia or exist at a technical state of war with a Communist neighbor. Because of their strategic location, the United States has not hesitated to use any means—up to and including armed force—to maintain pro-U.S. governments in each of these countries. This in-tervention includes a vast economic aid program designed to underwrite the costs of permanently militarized soci-eties; such aid today sustains the regimes of General Park Chung Hee in South Korea, Chiang Kai-shek in Taiwan, General Nguyen Van Thieu in South Vietnam, General Thanom Kittikachorn in Thailand, Prince Souvanna Phouma in Laos, and, since 1970, Lon Nol in Cambodia.

During the first postwar era, under Presidents Truman and Eisenhower, these countries were viewed as buffer states that would "contain" the expansion of Communist power. The principal architect of U.S. Cold War strategy, Secretary of State John Foster Dulles, hoped to turn these nations into impregnable fortresses that would be capable (with the necessary American backing) of stopping any further advances of Communist influence on the mainland of Asia. This strategy called for lavish gifts of U.S. arms, equipment, training, and monetary support in order to ensure a favorable balance of power on the periphery of Asia. In pursuit of this objective, the United States pro-vided more than $9.6 billion in military assistance to the five countries between 1945 and 1969, *exclusive* of Vietnam war support.

Under the Mutual Security Act of 1951 and subsequent legislation, South Korea and Nationalist China (Taiwan) are designated "forward defense countries" and have first call on all Military Assistance Programs (MAP) funds. In fiscal 1970, for instance, the four forward defense countries

(Korea, Taiwan, Greece, and Turkey) received 90 percent of the grant program. Between 1950 and 1970, total MAP grant aid to South Korea came to $2.9 billion, while Taiwan received $2.5 billion.[53] Military assistance to South Vietnam and Thailand had reached $1.5 billion and $600 million respectively by fiscal 1965, when all such aid to these countries was transferred to the regular Department of Defense budget; between 1965 and 1971, Pentagon support of the armies of Vietnam, Laos, and Thailand cost the United States $10.3 billion.[54] Even this largesse, however, does not represent the sum of U.S. payments to the defense establishments of these countries. Under Section 104(c) of the Food for Peace program (Public Law 480), foreign currencies generated by the delivery of surplus U.S. agricultural commodities can be used "to procure equipment, materials, facilities, and services for the common defense, including internal security." Asian beneficiaries of this program over the past twenty years include South Korea ($597.2 million), South Vietnam ($541.6 million), and Taiwan ($107 million).[55] These countries have also been invited to take what they want from a $17 billion stockpile of "excess" U.S. defense articles—items in good working order but no longer required by American troops.[56] Taiwan has already helped itself to equipment worth $517 million and South Korea to another $351 million.* No accounting has been made of the value of American goods turned over to the Saigon army under the Vietnamization

---

* In 1969 alone, the United States gave Taiwan the following items: equipment from a Nike Hercules missile battery that had been installed in Hawaii; more than 35 F-100 Super Sabre Jets, which are relatively old supersonic interceptors; more than 20 F-104 Starfighters, which are supersonic fighter planes still in use by the U.S. Air Force and the NATO countries; more than 30 C-119 "flying boxcars"; some 50 medium tanks; and about 120 howitzers. All together, this booty was valued at approximately $157 million. (John W. Finney, "Taiwan Secretly Given Millions in U.S. Arms in '69," *The New York Times,* March 29, 1970.)

program, but everyone agrees that the total will reach far into the billions. As of December 1970, the Vietnamese military had already received 700,000 M-16 rifles, 30,000 M-79 grenade launchers, more than 10,000 machine guns, some 4,000 mortars and 500 heavy artillery pieces, at least 1,200 tanks and armored personnel carriers, 20,000 radios, nearly 25,000 trucks and jeeps, 250 airplanes and helicopters, 800 small naval craft, and 60 bases with all their equipment. In fiscal 1972 alone, the Pentagon expects to spend $2.2 billion on support of our client armies in Southeast Asia.[57]

Besides providing arms and equipment, the United States has assumed responsibility for the training of its client armies. Almost the entire officer class of Korea, Taiwan, Vietnam, Laos, and Thailand has received its advanced education at American military schools or at in-country academies financed and directed by the United States. According to Pentagon statistics, 29,808 Korean, 23,453 Chinese Nationalist, 13,998 Vietnamese, 18,924 Thai, and an unspecified number of Laotian officers and specialists received instruction under the Military Assistance Program between 1950 and 1969.[58] Many top-ranking commanders of Asian armies are graduates of the U.S. Army Command and General Staff College at Fort Leavenworth or of one of 141 other military training centers in the United States. Upon returning to their own countries, these men often constitute the only sizable pool of skilled technicians in such fields as communications, vehicle maintenance, electronics, and all forms of engineering. In addition to learning technical skills, these men are indoctrinated in the abominations of communism and the merits of capitalism. Tours of such attractions as Disneyland, Colonial Williamsburg, and typical suburban tracts are designed to inculcate an appreciation for the American way of life and a consciousness of the rewards available to those who advance American interests in their own countries.[59]

The cumulative effect of U.S. military aid policies has

been to transform these small and relatively undeveloped countries into garrison states in which all national functions are subordinated to preparation for war. South Vietnam, South Korea, and Nationalist China maintain the fifth, sixth, and seventh largest standing armies in the world respectively, although none ranks high in population. Taiwan, with an army of 600,000 men and a population of less than 14 million, has the highest percentage of its population enrolled in the military of any nation not currently at war. Defense spending also consumes a large portion of the national budget and thus diverts scarce resources to unproductive uses. U.S. aid funds, moreover, comprise a significant portion of the foreign currency available to the governments of these countries in any given year. With control of the largest, wealthiest, and most "modernized" institutions in their societies, the military chieftains of these garrison states exercise undisputed hegemony over national life, suppressing all dissent with unmitigated ruthlessness.

With the appearance, in the early 1960's, of a popularly supported revolutionary movement in South Vietnam, it became obvious that the strategy of containment—which was intended to stop the spread of Communism through the buildup of conventional military fortifications—did not guarantee immunity from the outbreak of rebellion within. As a consequence, the military role of our client states shifted radically: instead of maintaining a static defense posture, these nations would now be compelled to furnish soldiers for active combat operations outside their homeland. At the prodding of the United States government, Thailand and South Korea both agreed to send substantial military contingents to South Vietnam to help defend the Saigon regime. Besides lessening the burden on U.S. troops, this move was cited as proof of "international support" for the U.S. intervention. On another level, the dispatch of Korean and Thai troops to Vietnam was seen as a way of providing advanced counterinsurgency training to troops that might ultimately require such skills for combat against insurgents in their own countries. (This outlook subsequently bore fruit when returning Thai troops were used to fight guerrillas in the embattled northeast, and Korean troops were used to hunt North Korean infiltrators and their sympathizers below the Demilitarized Zone.) Finally, when the Nixon Administration decided to expand the war by attacking rebel strongholds in Cambodia and Laos, such "third country" forces carried the brunt of the fighting.

The overseas use of client armies has proven to be extremely costly: besides the multibillion-dollar retainers already mentioned, the United States had to furnish additional funds and supplies before these countries would supply troops for Vietnam. These mercenary payments were first brought to the public's attention during the Symington subcommittee hearings on United States Security Agreements and Commitments Abroad. At the hearing on Thailand, it was revealed that the United States had agreed on November 9, 1967, to pay all costs of the Thai troops sent to Vietnam—including overseas pay allowances and "representation," or entertainment expenses— and to accelerate the modernization of forces remaining in Thailand.* While the total costs of this package were not

* Although the actual text of the agreement between the Royal Thai Government (RTG) and the United States regarding U.S. support for Thai troops sent to South Vietnam is classified information, the Department of State provided this summary in 1969:

> In early November 1967, the U.S. Government undertook to assist the RTG in sending a combat division to Vietnam and to maintain and improve the capability of the forces remaining in Thailand. It agreed to fully equip and provide logistic support for forces going to Vietnam; pay overseas allowances; assume costs of preparing and training—including logistics and transportation of the additional forces for Vietnam; pay mustering-out allowance and representation [entertainment] funds for units.
> The Thai were concerned that the dispatch of this force could weaken their security position at home. To avoid this,

made public, the Vietnam end of the operation was estimated at $50 million per year or $200 million as of the end
of 1969.[60] Data on compensation to Korea were even more
specific: according to State Department officials who testified at the inquiry, U.S. commitments to the Korean government included: payment of all expenses incurred by
Korean troops in Vietnam, procurement of military commodities in South Korea for United States troops in Southeast Asia, expanded work for Korean contractors in South
Vietnam, increased economic and military aid to the Seoul
regime, and assorted other premiums.[61] These terms were
spelled out in the so-called "Brown Memorandum" of
March 4, 1966, which coincided with the deployment of a
second Korean division to Vietnam. Since this agreement is
without parallel in American history, it is worth reproduc-
ing some of its provisions. Under "Military Assistance,"
the United States government, represented by Ambassador
Winthrop G. Brown, agreed:

To provide over the next few years substantial items of equipment for the modernization of Republic of Korea forces in
Korea.
To equip as necessary, and finance all additional *won* [Korean
currency] costs of, the additional forces deployed to the Republic of Vietnam.
To equip, provide for the training, and finance complete
replacement of the additional forces deployed to the Republic
of Vietnam.
To assume the cost of overseas allowances to these forces. . . .

---

the U.S. Government also agreed to accelerate the modernization of the Thai armed forces by increasing the military assistance programs for FY 68 and 69 by a total of $30 million. The
U.S. Government further agreed to assist the Thai with [their]
air defense problems by providing a battery of Hawk antiaircraft missiles. (U.S. Senate, Committee on Foreign Relations,
*United States Security Agreements and Commitments Abroad,
Hearings,* 91st Congress, 1st Session, 1969, Part 3, p. 657.)

Under "Economic Assistance," we promised:

To procure in Korea insofar as practicable requirements for supplies, services and equipment for Republic of Korea forces in the Republic of Vietnam and to direct to Korea selected types of procurement for United States and Republic of Vietnam forces. . . .

To procure in Korea . . . a substantial amount of goods being purchased by the Agency for International Development (A.I.D.) for use in its project programs for rural construction, pacification, relief, logistics, and so forth, in the Republic of Vietnam [and] to provide Korean contractors expanded opportunities to participate in construction projects undertaken by the United States Government and by American contractors in the Republic of Vietnam.

To provide . . . additional A.I.D. loans to support the economic development of the Republic of Korea.[62]

These expenditures, according to U.S. government statistics, added up to $927.5 million by December 21, 1969, and passed the billion mark shortly thereafter. Since most of the American dollars paid to Korean contractors and soldiers in Vietnam were sent to banks in Korea, U.S. war spending accounts for a large share—perhaps as much as 20 percent—of that country's foreign-currency revenue. Overseas allowances alone, which run from $1.25 a day for privates to $10 daily for a lieutenant general, were being remitted to Korea at the rate of $2 million a month.[63] This extraordinary influx of American dollars is considered to be largely responsible for South Korea's widely publicized economic "boom" of the late 1960's.[64]

In explaining the South Korean government's decision to supply troops for the Vietnam war, Ambassador William J. Porter told the Symington committee that "they desired to repay in this manner sacrifices that Americans and others had made for them in Korea in 1950."[65] Such generalizations, however, cannot withstand the scrutiny of a skeptic like Senator Fulbright; during the hearings on U.S. commitments abroad, the following interchange took place:

Senator Fulbright: Do you think the Korean forces would have been sent if we did not provide individual allowances to each soldier, which in some cases doubled their salaries?

Mr. Porter: I cannot say, sir. I cannot say. There was an economic burden.

Senator Fulbright: Wait a minute. You have already said you based your case on the fact that they were motivated by a very great desire to repay a debt to us.

Mr. Porter: Yes, sir.

Senator Fulbright: Then why would the allowances be paid? Why were they made, if that was their motive?

Mr. Porter: They didn't have the resources with which to support such a force overseas and to pay for all of its requirements."[66]

At the end of another such interchange, Fulbright cut in with the observation that "it does not really add up very well that this is a great gesture of self-sacrifice on the part of Korea to pay their obligation. They were simply making a good business deal at our request and urging."[67]

In utilizing client armies in Southeast Asia, the United States has not escaped the problems historically associated with the use of mercenary forces. There is, first of all, the problem of motivation and morale: it is understandably hard to go out into the jungle against expert guerrillas when one's only compensation is the $1.25 daily allowance paid by the United States Treasury—particularly when there's a lot more money to be made in black-market sales of U.S. PX items. The Thais and Koreans who serve in Vietnam at America's behest are paid in United States military script—paper certificates enabling them to make purchases at American post exchanges. One American journalist who investigated the Thai effort in South Vietnam reported in 1969 that until various currency-control procedures had been instituted, "on a typical morning at the main American post exchange in the Cholon section of Saigon, lines of Thai soldiers would wait at the checkout counters with baskets filled with tubes of toothpaste, cartons of cigarettes and tins of food." Usually, the journalist commented, "these items found their way to the black market."[68]

The Thai "Black Panther" Division has shown great reluctance to fight at all, while highly touted Korean troops are reportedly most effective when they face an "enemy" composed of women, old men, and children.* The South Vietnamese, who showed great enthusiasm for pillaging eastern Cambodia,† had no stomach for the fighting in east-

---

* The former director of a Pentagon-sponsored research project in Vietnam reported in 1970 that his interviewers turned up evidence in 1966 that South Korean forces murdered "hundreds" of South Vietnamese civilians. The researcher, A. Terry Rambo, also stated that a high-ranking officer of the U.S. command in Saigon ordered him to stop his investigation of the Korean atrocities and not to mention it in his reports. Rambo, then an employee of Human Science Research, Inc. (a private think tank located in McLean, Virginia), spent several months in Vietnam in 1966 to supervise a study of Vietnamese refugees commissioned by the Advanced Research Projects Agency. The study, designed to find out why refugees left their home villages, involved interviewing over 2,000 persons in Phuyen Province. In the course of interviewing, Rambo was told by the refugees that the Koreans stationed in Phuyen made a regular practice of killing civilians in villages suspected of harboring Vietcong guerrillas. "The principal kind of thing," he reported, "was when Korean troops passed a village and received sniper fire. They would stop and pull out people at random and shoot them in retaliation." Rambo estimated that such killings must have numbered in the hundreds: "For the Koreans," he said, "this was a deliberate, systematic policy." (Quoted in *The New York Times,* January 10, 1970.)

† Thus a correspondent for the *Wall Street Journal* who visited the Cambodian town of Kompong Speu after Vietcong guerrillas had been driven out by South Vietnamese infantrymen reported that the civilian population was "far from happy with their Vietnamese 'liberators.' " One resident, a middle-aged woman, showed the cor-

ern Laos when they were surrounded by crack North Vietnamese and Pathet Lao regulars. Furthermore, one characteristic of all mercenaries is that they quickly lose interest in a battle when their pay fails to come through. Thus when Uncle Sam was not able to provide extra pay for the Thai troops that had been mobilized for deployment to Cambodia in 1970, the Bangkok regime decided to limit their participation to a token force of border guards.[69] Present Congressional restrictions on the use of American funds to support "third country" troops in Cambodia severely restrict the Pentagon's ability to find "volunteers" to defend the Lon Nol regime. In campaigning against appropriation of U.S. funds for Thai and Vietnamese forces in Cambodia, Senator Fulbright alluded to these problems and declared to the Senate on June 26, 1970:

I believe it is time that we stop making mercenaries out of allies and allies out of mercenaries. We must prevent our money from distorting the ability of countries to determine their own national interests. We must stop deceiving ourselves as to what our own interests are in Cambodia and in all of Southeast Asia. The first step in this process should be to prevent Cambodia from becoming a profitable mercenary war for the Thais or anyone else.[70]

---

respondent her ruined house and declared, "These Vietnamese bandits, these pigs looted my house. They broke down my door. They came through the windows. They stole everything. Everything." The same story was true throughout the town: "Having liberated Kompong Speu, Vietnamese soldiers went on a wild looting spree, stealing nearly everything that could be carried away and smashing much that could not be." A Cambodian officer commented that, "The Vietcong came but left with nothing. The South Vietnamese came and took everything. Our people have more fear of the South Vietnamese than of the Vietcong." (*Wall Street Journal,* July 2, 1970.) The Cambodian government announced in September 1971 that it would hold talks with the Saigon government to secure the withdrawal of South Vietnamese troops, but as of the end of 1971, Vietnamese soldiers were still occupying much of eastern Cambodia.

Despite these setbacks, the Nixon Administration is determined to expand the use of regular force mercenaries in order to reduce public resistance to its Vietnam policies. This strategy is, in fact, the essence of the Nixon Doctrine. In order to obtain additional funds for the enlargement and modernization of client armies, Pentagon spokesmen have plagued Congress with requests for supplemental military-assistance appropriations. In presenting the Administration's argument, Secretary of Defense Laird told Congress in 1970:

Each nation must do its share and contribute what it can appropriately provide—manpower from many of our allies; technology, materiel, and specialized skills from the United States. In many cases, our allies are able and willing to provide the forces if we can contribute some of the needed weapons, and, in some circumstances, specialized military support.[71]

Laird insisted that increased military assistance expenditures were essential "if we are to honor our obligations, support our allies, and"—most important to the Congressmen—"reduce the likelihood of having to commit American ground combat units." This approach has met with some success. In the last days of 1970, Congress passed a $525 million supplemental military aid bill designed to expedite Nixon Doctrine programs in Asia. The aid measure, which incorporated the Cooper-Church Amendment barring use of U.S. troops in Cambodia, provided $255 million for the Lon Nol regime in Cambodia, $150 million for South Korea, $65 million for South Vietnam, $13 million for Indonesia, and smaller amounts to a number of other countries.[72] U.S. military-aid expenditures in fiscal 1971 totaled $5.2 billion—up 25 percent from 1970—and they are expected to rise again in 1972.[73] According to one high-ranking Pentagon official interviewed by *Armed Forces Journal*, "increased military assistance as a concomitant to the Nixon Doctrine seems inescapable to me."[74]

ELITE MERCENARIES—
THE ANGLO-SAXON ALLIANCE

Among the many Cold War alliances that the United States
has forged since World War II, there exists a clear but
unspoken differentiation between contracts of convenience
and contracts of conviction. While the State Department
may speak glowingly of U.S.-Vietnamese friendship, U.S.-
Korean friendship, or U.S.-Thai friendship, there are very
few countries which Washington trusts implicitly—trusts,
that is, with secret military information or access to the
inner circles of defense policy-making. The small group of
countries which do enjoy these privileges have two striking
characteristics in common: they are all former colonies of
Great Britain, and are all ruled by the white descendants of
European immigrants. At present, this select group includes Canada, Australia, and New Zealand; if the Pentagon had its way, and diplomatic considerations were set
aside, the Republic of South Africa would also be admitted
to this exclusive club. Military officers of these favored
countries routinely receive copies of secret U.S. intelligence reports, are kept informed of Pentagon work on
chemical and biological warfare and other secret projects,
and participate as equals in military strategy conferences.
In order to cement this working relationship further, the
Pentagon has initiated a program known as Project Mallard
to provide a "joint tactical international communication
system for the armies, navies and air forces of the United
States, United Kingdom, Canada and Australia."[75] Needless
to say, one does not share military communications channels with any but the closest allies.

Anglo-Saxon cooperation in the Pacific is guaranteed by
the ANZUS Pact (the Security Treaty Between Australia,
New Zealand, and the United States), which commits these
countries to come to each other's aid in the event of an
attack on any one of them or upon any of their Pacific de-

pendencies. Australia and New Zealand are further associated with the United States as members of the Southeast Asia Treaty Organization (the only Asian members are Pakistan, Thailand, and the Philippines, all heavily dependent upon U.S. military assistance). The strength of the ties that bind the military establishments of Australia and New Zealand to that of the United States is perhaps best shown by the fact that both countries supplied combat troops for the war in Vietnam despite widespread domestic opposition.* When Vice President Agnew arrived in Canberra during his January 1970 tour of Asia and the Pacific, he spoke warmly of Australia's contribution to the U.S. war effort in Korea and Vietnam. Australia, he promised, "will always have the unfailing support and loyal friendship of the United States of America."[76] In a subsequent press conference, the Vice President spoke of the "common English ancestry" of Australia and the United States.[77] Agnew was told by Prime Minister John G. Gorton, "You have never been more welcome than you are here in the capital of Australia."[78]

The close relations that have developed in recent years between the United States, Australia, and New Zealand are not just the product of a common language and cultural

---

* On August 18, 1971, Australia and New Zealand announced that their combat troops in South Vietnam would be withdrawn by the end of 1971. (Australia had 8,000 troops in Vietnam, organized into three infantry battalions and support elements, and New Zealand had a combat force of several hundred men.) The announcement came at a time of increasing popular disaffection with the Vietnam conflict; although there had always been some opposition to the war in these countries, antiwar sentiment reached a peak in July 1971, when publication of the Pentagon Papers established that Australia and New Zealand had been pressured into sending troops to Vietnam by Washington. Opposition Labour Party spokesmen in Canberra charged that Australian participation in the war effort constituted "payment of the premium" on America's pledge to defend Australia in case of attack. (The New York Times, August 22, 1971.)

heritage; they result from some very real policy considerations that make such cooperation attractive to all parties involved. The United States, as we have seen, seeks to replace its Asian forces with foreign troops whose loyalty to American objectives can be assured; Australia and New Zealand, for their part, must be assured of unhampered trade relations with, and sea routes to, the nations bordering the Pacific and Indian Oceans. Australia, moreover, is motivated by policies of racial exclusion. Like the whites of South Africa, Australians dread the southward migration patterns of colored peoples, and therefore are willing to provide military assistance to their northern neighbors (Australia provides such aid to Malaysia and Singapore, just as South Africa does to Rhodesia) in order to establish a buffer zone against further migrations. These racial considerations are not incompatible with U.S. policy, which seeks to maintain Western (i.e., white) hegemony in the Pacific-Indian Ocean area. Thus, in return for its promise to come to the assistance of Australia and New Zealand in any future emergencies, the United States has been invited to establish new military installations in those countries and can expect their help in the reconstitution of the Asian defense perimeter following the planned reduction in British strength.

As evidence of its support for America's Asian defense policy, the Canberra government went so far as to suggest that the United States would be welcome to establish new military bases on Australian territory. In an interview with the Sydney *Daily Mirror,* Prime Minister Gorton indicated that Australia would not refuse if the United States asked for base rights. "I would not take the initiative of inviting the United States to come and establish a base here," he told the interviewer, "but it would be a different thing if they came along and asked if they can do something which benefits them and us."[79] At a time when many countries are telling the United States to remove its bases on their territory, the United States could hardly fail to take advantage of Australia's friendly attitude. Since the mid-1960's, the United States has established several new bases in Australia and expanded others. At Pine Gap in Australia's largely unpopulated Northern Territory, the Advanced Research Projects Agency has constructed a multi-million-dollar satellite-monitoring station designed to warn of Chinese and Soviet missile launchings. Other defense communications stations are located at Nurrungar in South Australia and North West Cape in Western Australia.[80] The North West Cape facility, known as the Harold E. Holt Naval Communications Station, houses a powerful very-low-frequency (VLF) transmitter for communication with submerged Polaris submarines.[81]

The cooperation of Australia and New Zealand became particularly valuable to the United States in December 1971, when Great Britain completed withdrawal of most of its remaining forces in South Asia. Britain had been pledged to provide for the defense of the Federation of Malaysia (which incorporates the former colonies of Malaya, Sarawak, and North Borneo, now renamed Sabah) and the island state of Singapore. These two countries, whose combined armies can boast only 40,000 men and a handful of aircraft, are threatened by lingering guerrilla activity along the Thai border, by territorial disputes with the Philippines and Indonesia, and by internal racial unrest. Because of the strategic location of these countries and the high potential for conflict, the impending British withdrawal had compelled the United States to contemplate some police role in the area. Since, however, the stability of this area is considered vital to the security of Australia and New Zealand, the United States will be able to leave the primary defense role to its Anglo-Saxon allies. Australia and New Zealand will jointly maintain a battalion each at Singapore, with one company on rotation in Malaysia. They will each station a naval vessel in the area at all times, and Australia will keep two squadrons of Mirage jet aircraft at Butterworth, near the Thai border.

Australia has also promised to supply the Malaysian Air Force with ten Sabre jet fighters and the necessary maintenance equipment.[82]

While neither Australia nor New Zealand—with armies of 84,000 men and 13,000 men respectively—can be considered major military powers, their role in maintaining the Asian defense perimeter is not insignificant and renders the burden of the United States that much more manageable.

THE MERCENARY
SUPPORT INFRASTRUCTURE

The mercenary army envisioned by the United States for future Asian operations is, for all practical purposes, a ground-combat army. It lacks the logistical apparatus, communications network, and close air-support capability that are considered essential for highly mobile ground operations. These functions, under current Pentagon doctrine, are to be performed by the United States through its permanent mercenary-support infrastructure in Asia. Thus in the Pentagon's annual budget message to Congress, former Defense Secretary Clifford argued that while "there are no insuperable obstacles to the development of good local land forces capable of offering a credible deterrent to a Communist aggression, it is less likely . . . that our Asian allies, except for Japan, will have the economic strength in the foreseeable future to become self-sufficient in air and naval forces or in logistical support." The United States, therefore, "should remain prepared to provide such support where needed." According to Clifford, the continued American military presence would have to include "appropriate basing arrangements."[83]

What exactly is meant by "appropriate basing arrangements"? The Director of the Australian Institute of International Affairs, T. B. Millar, explains that "in naval or air terms, a base is normally considered to have substantial capacity to house, repair and supply ships or aircraft, and to defend itself or be defended against hostile attack." In the nineteenth century, overseas bases were considered primary instruments of colonial expansion, and the great imperial powers of Europe vied with one another for possession of naval bases commanding principal trade routes and for garrisons that controlled access to inland territories. Since World War II, however, "The European ex-imperial powers have disposed of most of their external bases because they have disposed of the empires which they were designed to protect."[84] The United States, on the other hand, has established its hegemony in many ex-colonial areas abandoned by the European powers, and has accordingly found it expedient to retain many of its overseas bases and even to acquire new "basing arrangements" in the Pacific and Indian Ocean areas.

Military bases come in several forms: logistics bases, to supply troops at the front; communications bases, to maintain contact with roving air and naval squadrons; headquarters bases, to exercise "command and control" functions over units in the field; rear-area bases, to house supply depots, reserve troops, and repair facilities. In the past two decades, the United States has acquired hundreds of new bases in Asia, has expanded existing facilities, and is currently acquiring sites for future bases. A Pentagon inventory of "major" overseas bases and installations lists 55 such facilities in Korea, 3 in Taiwan, 7 in Thailand, 6 in the Philippines, 25 on other Pacific islands, and 59 in South Vietnam.[85] While some of these facilities will be deactivated when the Vietnam conflict is terminated, many others will be needed for continued support of our mercenary apparatus in Asia.

Major logistics bases, capable of handling the largest supply ships in existence, have been established on the edge of Asia at Camranh Bay and Da Nang in South Vietnam and at Sattahip in Thailand. While these bases are

currently being used to funnel war materiel to the battlefields in Vietnam, Cambodia, and Laos, they will retain a
major strategic function—as forward staging points for
large-scale military operations—long after the cessation of
hostilities in Vietnam.[86] Such naval facilities are comple-
mented by U.S. air bases at Tan Son Nhut (Saigon) in
South Vietnam and U-Tapao and Khorat in Thailand.
These airfields are actually giant military complexes, with
adjacent supply depots, communications facilities, and living quarters. Like the naval bases, these installations will
continue to function as staging points for U.S. military
operations after the Vietnam conflict is settled. Large quantities of war supplies are to be stored there for use by
troops flown in on giant C-5A jet transports during future
crises.[87]

U.S. communications, command-and-control, and intelligence bases have been established throughout Southeast
Asia. The most important of these is MACV headquarters
(Military Assistance Command, Vietnam) at Tan Son Nhut
airport outside Saigon. From this complex of airstrips,
warehouses, and air-conditioned office buildings, General
Creighton W. Abrams directs all U.S. military operations
in South Vietnam. Tan Son Nhut is also the headquarters
of the Seventh U.S. Air Force, whose planes conduct most
of the tactical bombing missions in Vietnam and Laos.
Other bases, not as well known as Tan Son Nhut, oversee
U.S. mercenary operations in China, Burma, Thailand, Laos,
and Cambodia. The headquarters of the Fifth Special
Forces Group, located in the Vietnamese resort city of
Nhatrang, houses the CIA's B-57 Special Operations detachment that operates networks of native intelligence
agents throughout Southeast Asia.[88] The U.S. air base at
Ubon in northeastern Thailand accommodates the CIA station responsible for coordination of intelligence-gathering
missions along enemy supply lines in eastern Laos.[89] Military operations in northern Laos are directed from the
Combined Operations Center in Vientiane and the air base

at Udorn, across the Mekong in Thailand.[90] Closer to the fighting, the CIA's communications base at Long Cheng serves as headquarters of the U.S.-financed "Secret Army." While none of these makeshift bases can boast the elaborate facilities of Tan Son Nhut, they will continue to play an important role in any future conflict in which American officers command large numbers of native troops.

Hundreds, even thousands, of miles from the Vietnam battlefields lie the rear-area strategic bases whose activities are essential to the prosecution of the war. These bases include the huge supply and ammunition depots in Okinawa, Japan, and the Philippines; the Strategic Air Command airfields in Okinawa and Guam (which house the giant B-52 bombers used in Vietnam and Laos); and the Navy's repair and servicing facilities at Subic Bay in the Philippines. Without these key Pacific bases, the United States would be unable to sustain large-scale military operations on the mainland of Asia. The whole Nixon Doctrine concept, with its promise of air and sea support for our client armies, is predicated upon continued U.S. occupation of these facilities.

Of all American bases in the Pacific, none is more valuable or more important strategically than Okinawa. If the United States is ever forced to abandon all its bases in Asia, according to *U.S. News & World Report,* "the loss of Okinawa . . . will be most damaging." Here are the reasons it gave:

The U.S. has invested more than 1 billion dollars in the postwar years on what is probably the most elaborate multi-service military installation anywhere in the world.

Since the start of the Vietnam war, activity has increased tenfold. Okinawa, long the mainstay of U.S. defenses in the Western Pacific, has now become also a giant funnel through which much of the paraphernalia of war pours into South Vietnam and Southeast Asia.

U.S. money and imagination have turned the island—67 miles long and from 2½ to 19 miles wide—into one vast patchwork of military posts, airfields, an Army port, training camps and housing complexes. In all, there are 117 separate military installations on the one island.[91]

U.S. troops stationed on the island include the Third Marine Division (the first large American combat unit to be deployed in Vietnam), the First Special Forces Group, and assorted logistical, communications, and supply personnel.

Opposition to U.S. occupation of Okinawa emerged in 1969 as a major foreign policy dispute between Japan and the United States. Under the terms of the 1952 peace treaty with Japan, to whom the island had belonged, no time limit was set on U.S. occupation of Okinawa. The resurgence of nationalism in Japan, however, has led to the demand (also voiced by the Okinawans themselves) that the United States recognize Japanese sovereignty over the island. The question of reversion to Japanese control had already become a major issue by July 1969, when the accidental leakage of lethal nerve gas on the island threatened to provoke a serious rupture in U.S.-Japanese relations.[92] As a result of the gas incident, Premier Eisaku Sato pledged to make reversion the primary foreign policy objective of his administration.[93] In November, after three days of talks with President Nixon in Washington, Sato secured a pledge that Okinawa would be restored to Japanese rule by 1972; details of the reversion agreement were left to Secretary of State William P. Rogers and Japanese Foreign Minister Kiichi Aichi, who spent eighteen months drawing up a draft treaty. In a television-linked ceremony held in Washington and Tokyo on June 18, 1971, the United States agreed to turn over control of Okinawa to Japan in April 1972. Although the United States will remove the nuclear devices stored on the island, the draft treaty ensures that reversion of the island will not jeopardize supply operations for the Vietnam war. Okinawa will continue, therefore, to serve as a major logistics base for U.S. and allied forces in Asia.[94]

As soon as it became apparent that the status of our

bases on Okinawa might be altered, the Department of Defense ordered studies of potential fallback positions. From available information, it appears that the location presently favored by the Pentagon for such purposes is the Mariana Islands in the South Pacific. The Marianas— Guam, Saipan, Tinian, and Rota—are among the two thousand islands of Micronesia held by the United States under a United Nations trusteeship. Unlike all other U.N. trusteeships, the Micronesia agreement permits the United States to construct military bases there at its own discretion.* In the past three years, several high Pentagon officials have made secret trips to the Marianas to determine their suitability for new strategic bases. Recent visitors to the island, including Admiral U. S. Grant Sharp, former Pacific commander, and Lieutenant General Lewis W. Walt (before his retirement as Assistant Marine Commandant), reportedly examined "an extensive collection of maps showing the prime locations for airfields, naval bases and missile sites."[95] As early as 1967, *U.S. News & World Report* indicated that the Pentagon had begun drawing up plans for use of the islands as a "complex of troop-staging and logistics bases for conventional wars in Asia."[96]

Although the United States will continue to have the use of Okinawa as a logistics base, we are pledged to remove all strategic weapons from the island, including B-52

---

* Although America's occupation of Micronesia seems more secure than that of Okinawa, an independence movement is beginning in the trust territory that may ultimately frustrate the Pentagon's plans to use the islands as a basing complex. In 1970, the Congress of Micronesia turned down a proposal for the conversion of the territory into a permanent commonwealth of the United States, and proposed instead a relationship of "free association" that would allow the Micronesians to become independent at their own initiative. Although the islanders are divided by racial, ethnic, and cultural differences, the growing independence movement has won the support of a significant segment of the territory's population. (See: P. F. Kluge, "Will the U.S. Ever Let Micronesia Go?" *Wall Street Journal,* September 28, 1970.)

bombers. Since these aircraft have become a principal instrument of U.S. strategy in Southeast Asia, their relocation is a matter of great concern to the Pentagon. The Air Force has stationed B-52's at U-Tapao in Thailand on an interim basis since 1967, but in 1970 the United States sought permission from Thailand to keep the B-52's there permanently.[97] One alternative to Okinawa is Taiwan; the Air Force has already expanded its base on Taiwan to handle the giant bombers on an emergency basis, while the Taipei regime has extended other runways at its own expense in the hope that the United States will station B-52's there on a permanent basis (thus giving us a greater stake in Taiwan's independence).[98]

With its elaborate "basing arrangements" in Okinawa, Japan, Korea, Taiwan, Vietnam, Thailand, Micronesia, and the Philippines, the United States possesses the necessary infrastructure for support of large-scale troop operations on the eastern edge of Asia. In the Indian Ocean, however, there is no complex of bases comparable to those in the Pacific. In order to protect our expanding interests in the area and to compensate for planned British troop withdrawals, the Pentagon has quietly undertaken a search for new bases in the Indian Ocean that could be used to sustain military activities on the southern edge of Asia.

As the first step in development of a U.S. presence in the Indian Ocean, the Pentagon is building a series of communications bases to handle the anticipated increase in naval traffic. The communications station on Australia's North West Cape, now being outfitted with additional transmitters, will facilitate naval activity in the eastern waters of the Indian Ocean,[99] while a similar facility at Asmara in Ethiopia performs the same function in western waters. In order to extend secure radio coverage to the entire region, the Defense Department began construction in 1970 of a major communications facility on a British-owned atoll located near the geographic center of the Indian Ocean.[100] The island, Diego Garcia, is part of the Chagos group and is incorporated into the British Indian Ocean Territory; in an obscure 1967 agreement with Great Britain, the United States acquired the right to establish military installations in the area.[101] Citing its strategic location, U.S. Commander-in-Chief, Pacific, Admiral John S. McCain, Jr., commented, "As Malta is to the Mediterranean, Diego Garcia is to the Indian Ocean."[102]

With the Diego Garcia facility under construction, the Pentagon next seeks a major supply and repair base in or near the Indian Ocean comparable to that at Subic Bay in the Philippines. The Navy would like to gain access to the Republic of South Africa's Simonstown naval base, but present diplomatic considerations preclude such a solution. Under existing conditions, the most likely candidate for such a base is Singapore, where the elaborate complex of air and naval facilities constructed by the British will soon go up for sale. As soon as Harold Wilson announced that Britain would withdraw its forces from the Far East, the United States expressed an interest in acquiring the soon-to-be-vacated Singapore bases. In 1969, *The New York Times* reported that "United States warships call regularly at Singapore and admirals frequently tour the British installations."[103] The admirals must be pleased with what they see there, for on January 9, 1970, Vice President Agnew, then on a tour of America's Asian allies, told reporters in Singapore that the United States would enter into a "definite relationship" with the island state for use of the bases.[104] Such an agreement, according to the Vice President's staff, is to consist of contracts for repairs of U.S. ships and planes at the bases Britain will evacuate.

The costs of maintaining a mercenary apparatus on the scale of the American infrastructure in Asia are, of course, immense. No precise estimate is possible, since the Pentagon does not itemize its budget that way and the CIA doesn't publish a budget at all; nevertheless, it is possible to get some inkling of how high these costs must run from the fact that U.S. bases in Vietnam, Japan, Thailand, and Okinawa represent an investment of over $2.5 billion, while operating costs of the bases run to about $500 million a year in each country. Arms aid and logistical support to U.S. allies in Asia (including the combatants in Vietnam) come to about $4 billion to $5 billion per year—if Pentagon statistics are to be believed—and such spending is expected to increase in the years ahead. Air and naval support operations are even more costly: thus a single bombing run over Laos, flown by one B-52 bomber stationed on Guam, is estimated to cost $50,000—and there are more than a thousand B-52 sorties every month.[105] In order to ease the financial burden of mercenary operations in Asia, Washington hopes to persuade Japan to become our "partner" in maintaining the Asian defense perimeter.[106]

In 1967, Richard M. Nixon wrote in *Foreign Affairs* that "the natural momentum of Japan's growth, the industry of her people, and the advanced state of her economy must inevitably propel Japan into a more conspicuous position of leadership. . . . Along with [its] dramatic economic surge, Japan will surely want to play a greater role both diplomatically and militarily in maintaining the balance in Asia."[107] Two years later, with Nixon in the White House, the State Department began to sketch out the role it expected Japan to play in the stabilization of the area: Secretary William Rogers told a press conference on June 5, 1969, that as the United States withdraws its forces from the Far East, it would look to Japan to "assume a greater burden of economic aid and to provide additional security for that region."[108] Specifically, U.S. policy calls for Japan to play a significant role in the defense of South Korea and key Pacific islands (especially Okinawa), and gradually to assume partial responsibility for support of anti-Communist regimes in Southeast Asia. In any such partnership, Japan would be expected to help provide economic, logistical, communications, and training support—but not necessarily to commit ground combat troops (the Japanese soldier is even more hated and feared in Asia than the American soldier). Japan, in other words, would be invited to share America's position at the apex of the mercenary hierarchy.

During an eight-day visit to Japan—the first ever by an American Secretary of Defense—Melvin Laird told government officials that the United States expects them to take up a greater share of the defense burden in the Far East. Although Laird's presentation to the Japanese defense ministry was not made public, Takashi Oka of *The New York Times* gave this summary of his argument on July 12, 1971:

The United States is keeping up its nuclear umbrella, but you have to do more in the conventional field. We respect your no-war Constitution and do not require you to send troops abroad or to pay for the upkeep of American troops in Japan, but we do expect you to step up drastically your economic aid to the three Indochinese countries.

While Article IX of the postwar Japanese Constitution imposed by the United States outlaws the development of a significant warmaking capability, Japan's "Maritime Self-Defense Force" is considered the third most powerful naval force in the Pacific (after those of the United States and the Soviet Union), and its air force (with 1,500 aircraft) to be stronger than that of any other Asian nation.[109] Military spending, while constituting less than 1 percent of the nation's GNP, amounted to $1.6 billion in 1970 and is rising at a rate of over 15 percent a year; even if defense spending continues to represent only 1 percent of the GNP, by 1975 this would come to $2.4 billion at the current pace of economic growth (giving Japan the world's seventh highest defense budget, after the United States, the Soviet Union, Communist China, Britain, France, and West Germany). Many powerful voices in Japanese industry are demanding, moreover, that military spending increase to 1.5 percent of the GNP or more, and it is probable that the defense budget will increase even faster than at present.[110] Furthermore, with the third largest GNP in the world, and the second largest steel-producing capacity, Japan's economic potential for waging war is greater than that of any other nation in Asia.[111]

Although it is too early to predict how much of a role Japan will play in propping up the American military apparatus in Southeast Asia, it is certain that the rapid growth of Japanese investments in the area will constitute an increasing inducement to participate in future counter-insurgency struggles. Thus Yoichiro Makita, president of the powerful Mitsubishi Heavy Industries, argues: "Now that our GNP is third in the world, now that we are among the rich, we have to guard against burglars."[112] Something of this sort was obviously being contemplated in 1969, when a squadron of four Japanese warships sailed through the Strait of Malacca to Burma (visiting these waters for the first time since World War II) and participated in joint naval maneuvers with Australian and Malaysian vessels. The Strait is of particular strategic importance to Japan, since 90 percent of her oil comes by tanker through this narrow stretch of water. Several prominent Japanese politicians have spoken of the need to establish a military presence in the area, and it is likely that the growing Maritime Self-Defense Force will increase the frequency of its visits there.[113] Such predictions, in any case, lead U.S. officials to believe that time is on our side—that as Japan's stake in Southeast Asia grows, so will its willingness to share in the burden of defending the region against socialist revolution.

EPILOGUE

In the 1930's and 1940's, Mao Tse-tung formulated the strategy of "Protracted War" to guide his poorly equipped partisan forces to victory over the heavily armed troops of Japan. Mao's strategy called for the complete mobilization of the Chinese population in a slow, unrelenting war of attrition against the occupying power; in such a contest, he reasoned, a combination of small guerrilla victories, sabotage, passive resistance, and psychological warfare would count for more in the long run than conventional troop operations by "main-force" enemy units. This analysis allowed Mao to enlarge his area of operations to all of northern China by the end of World War II, and ultimately to defeat the American-supplied troops of Chiang Kai-shek.

The strategy of Protracted War was taken up in Indochina by General Nguyen Vo Giap, commander of the Viet Minh troops, who successfully used it to defeat the expeditionary forces of France in 1954. As modified for the particular conditions of Southeast Asia, this strategy was subsequently employed by the National Liberation Front and the Pathet Lao in their revolutionary struggle against the U.S.-installed governments in Saigon and Vientiane. When the American troops were brought in to rescue our client regimes, the same relentless tactics were used against us, too. Like Japan and France before us, the United States soon discovered that technological superiority does not assure success in a conflict in which time, determination, and commitment are the crucial factors. We have become bogged down in a protracted war with no hope of a conclusive victory, while at home the public has become increasingly vocal in its dissatisfaction with government policy.

Since the day he took office in early 1969, President Nixon has been searching for a formula which would permit the United States to survive a protracted war without loss of our Asian empire, and without incurring further upheavals at home. The present solution, as embodied in the Nixon Doctrine and the policy of Vietnamization, calls for large mercenary forces on the ground and massive numbers of American bombers and gunships in the air. This strategy provided Nixon with a breathing space during the first two years of his Administration: U.S. casualties were reduced, Vietnam war spending was cut significantly, and domestic opposition was muffled. But the President's mercenary strategy has not yet been put to the real test—how well will the mercenaries perform when they no longer can rely upon American ground troops to bail them out of threatening situations? And how long will the American public tolerate an endless war, even if the casualty rate is much lower? Most important, what will happen when the mercenaries finally realize that they are being used as cannon fodder by an absentee imperial power? Although it is much too early to answer these questions with any degree of certainty, the outcome of South Vietnam's 1971 "incursion" into Laos—in which half the invasion force was lost despite abundant U.S. air support—suggests that a mercenary strategy offers no long-term solution to the challenge of a protracted Peoples' War.

APPENDIXES

Appendix A
MEMBERS OF THE
DEFENSE SCIENCE BOARD,
1965–70

Name and Position	Years of membership in Defense Science Board			Membership in other military panels
	1965	1968	1970	
Agnew, Harold M., Director, Weapons Division, Los Alamos Scientific Lab		X	X	ASAP
Alpert, Daniel, Dean, Graduate College, University of Illinois		X	X	
Astin, Allen V., Director, National Bureau of Standards	X	X		
Biehl, Arthur T., Assoc. Dir. of Advanced Studies, Lawrence Radiation Lab			X	AFSAB
Bradbury, Norris E., Director, Los Alamos Scientific Lab		X	X	
Branscomb, Lewis M., Director, National Bureau of Standards			X	Jason
Brattain, Walter H., member of Technical Staff, Bell Telephone Labs	X			
Bucy, Fred J., Group Vice President, Texas Instruments, Inc.			X	
Cairns, Robert W., Vice President, Hercules, Inc.	X	X		
Curreri, Anthony R., Prof. of Surgery, Univ. of Wisconsin Medical Schools			X	ASAP

Continued

Name and Position	Defense Science Board			Other panels
	1965	1968	1970	
Dryden, Hugh L., Deputy Administrator, NASA	X			
Fink, Daniel J., General Mgr., Space Systems, General Electric Co.			X	
Flax, Alexander H., President, Institute for Defense Analyses			X	
Fubini, Eugene G., Vice President, IBM Corp.		X		AFSAB
Garwin, Richard L., IBM Watson Lab, Columbia University		X		Jason
Goldberg, Leo, Higgins Professor of Astronomy, Harvard University	X			
Goldberger, Marvin L., Palmer Physical Lab, Princeton University			X	Jason
Griggs, David T., Institute of Geophysics & Planetary Physics, UCLA	X	X	X	AFSAB, ASAP
Hafstad, Lawrence R., Chairman, General Advisory Comm., AEC	X	X		
Haggerty, Patrick E., Chairman, Texas Instruments, Inc.	X	X		
Haworth, Leland J., Director, National Science Foundation	X	X		
Heinemann, Edward H., Vice President for Engineering, General Dynamics Corp.			X	NRAC
Herzfeld, Charles M., Technical Director, Defense Space Group, IT&T			X	AFSAB

Continued

Name and Position	Defense Science Board			Other panels
	1965	1968	1970	
Lanier, Lyle H., Exec. Vice President and Provost, University of Illinois	X			
Larsen, Finn J., former Assistant Secretary of the Army	X			ASAP
Latter, Albert L., head, Physics Dept., RAND Corp.		X	X	AFSAB
Lewis, W. Deming, President, Lehigh University		X		NRAC
MacDonald, Gordon J. F., Vice Chancellor, Univ. of California, S. Barbara		X	X	
McCormack, James, Chairman, Communications Satellite Corp.	X	X		
McDonnell, Gerald M., Dept. of Radiology, Univ. of California Medical Center	X			AFSAB
McElroy, William G., Director, National Science Foundation			X	
McLucas, John L., President, The MITRE Corp.		X		
McMillan, William G., Senior Physicist, RAND Corp.	X		X	AFSAB, ASAP
Newell, Homer E., Associate Administrator, NASA		X	X	
Payne, Fred A., Vice President for Technical Operations, Martin-Marietta Corp.			X	
Perkins, Courtland D., Chmn., Dept. of Aerospace & Mech'l Sciences, Princeton Univ.			X	AFSAB

Continued

Name and Position	Defense Science Board			Other panels
	1965	1968	1970	
Phillips, Thomas L., President, Raytheon Co.	X	X	X	
Pool, Ithiel de Sola, Chairman, Political Science Dept., MIT		X	X	
Pratt, Perry W., Vice President & Chief Scientist, United Aircraft Corp.	X	X		
Puckett, Allen E., Exec. Vice President, Hughes Aircraft Co.	X			
Root, L. Eugene, President, Lockheed Missiles & Space Co.	X			
Schelling, Thomas C., Center for Int'l Affairs, Harvard University		X		
Seitz, Frederick, President, Rockefeller University	X	X	X	NRAC
Sheingold, Leonard S., Vice President, Sylvania Electronic Systems		X		AFSAB
Smith, Lloyd P., Vice President for Research, Philco Co.	X			
Sproull, Robert L., Vice President and Provost, University of Rochester		X	X	
Stever, H. Guyford, President, Carnegie-Mellon University	X	X		AFSAB
Suttle, Andrew D., Jr., Vice President for Research, Texas A&M Univ.	X		–	
Tape, Gerald F., President, Associated Universities, Inc.			X	

Continued

Name and Position	Defense Science Board			Other panels
	1965	1968	1970	
Vesper, Howard G., Chairman, General Advisory Committee, AEC			X	
Walker, Eric A., President, Pennsylvania State Univ.	X			NRAC
Watson, Kenneth M., Physics Dept., Univ. of California, Berkeley	X			Jason
Weber, Ernst, President, Polytechnic Institute of Brooklyn	X			
Wells, Edward G., Senior Vice President, Boeing Co.			X	
Wheelon, Albert D., Vice President, Hughes Aircraft Co.		X	X	

Abbreviations:

AFSAB: Air Force Scientific Advisory Board
ASAP: Army Scientific Advisory Panel
NRAC: Naval Research Advisory Committee

Appendix B
FEDERAL OBLIGATIONS
FOR RESEARCH
AND DEVELOPMENT, 1953–70

(Dollars in millions)

Fiscal Year	Total, All Agencies	Dept. of Defense	NASA	AEC	Total, DoD, NASA, AEC	Per cent, DoD, NASA, AEC	Total, Other Agencies	Per cent, Other
1953	2,168	1,632	79	250	1,961	90	207	10
1954	1,918	1,379	60	266	1,705	89	213	11
1955	2,252	1,668	64	294	2,026	90	226	10
1956	2,693	1,935	66	425	2,426	90	267	10
1957	3,176	2,149	83	531	2,763	87	413	13
1958	5,542	4,373	77	644	5,094	92	448	8
1959	7,363	5,480	300	925	6,705	91	658	9
1960	8,078	5,825	487	988	7,300	90	778	10
1961	9,606	6,688	905	1,063	8,656	90	950	10
1962	11,066	6,817	1,684	1,316	9,817	89	1,249	11
1963	13,650	7,373	3,434	1,399	12,206	89	1,444	11
1964	15,310	7,352	4,842	1,479	13,673	89	1,637	11
1965	15,731	6,865	5,482	1,540	13,887	88	1,844	12
1966	16,162	7,099	5,327	1,442	13,868	86	2,294	14
1967	17,149	8,136	4,988	1,485	14,609	85	2,540	15
1968	16,525	7,908	4,494	1,534	13,936	84	2,589	16
1969*	16,664	8,142	3,852	1,842	13,836	83	2,828	17
1970*	17,193	8,662	3,851	1,734	14,247	83	2,946	17

Source: U.S. National Science Foundation, *Federal Funds for Research, Development, and Other Scientific Activities, Fiscal Years 1968, 1969, and 1970* (Washington, D.C.: Government Printing Office, 1969). Data for previous years from earlier editions of this report.
*Estimated.

Appendix C
DEPARTMENT OF DEFENSE
OBLIGATIONS FOR BEHAVIORAL
AND SOCIAL SCIENCES RESEARCH
(In millions of dollars)

R&D Program	Fiscal Year				Request, fiscal year
	1966	1967	1968	1969	1970
(1) *Human performance:* Measuring individual physiological and psychological capabilities related to military operations	5.9	7.2	6.9	6.9	6.3
(2) *Manpower selection and training:* Methods to improve selection, classification, training, and use of military personnel	8.8	12.2	14.0	21.5	25.3
(3) *Human factors engineering:* Human component in a man/machine system	5.0	4.4	3.8	3.3	3.7
(4) *Cultural and social factors:* Relevant to training for overseas assignments, counterinsurgency, psychological operations, military assistance, and basic data inputs to policy planning	7.4	9.3	8.3	7.3	6.9
(5) *Policy planning studies:* Strategic planning in response to changing pattern of political and power alignments. Part of basis of threat analysis. Contingency planning, force structure, hardware, and R&D requirements	6.9	7.9	7.8	6.4	6.4
	34.0	41.0	40.8	45.4	48.6

Source: U.S. Senate, Committee on Foreign Relations, *Defense Department Sponsored Foreign Affairs Research, Hearings,* May 9, 1968, p. 7; and "Changes in Defense Department Support of Social Science Research," *FAR Horizons,* vol. II (September 1969), p. 2.

Appendix D

U.S. MILITARY ASSISTANCE PROGRAM EXPENDITURES BY COUNTRY, FISCAL YEARS 1950–69

(In millions of dollars)

Region and country	Military Assistance Program grant aid[a]	Credit extended for purchase of U.S. arms[b]	Value of naval vessels transferred[b]	Value of excess defense articles delivered[c]	Funds provided through "Food for Peace" program[b]	Total aid
East Asia, total	**10,036.2**	**281.1**	**377.9**	**1,356.8**	**1,177.6**	**13,229.6**
Australia	—	122.7	—	—	—	122.7
Burma	#	—	—	#	—	#
Cambodia	87.1	—	—	12.8	—	99.9
China, Republic of	2,490.4	87.5	72.2	481.8	106.8	3,238.7
Indochina (1950–4 only)	709.6	—	—	21.9	—	731.5
Indonesia	70.7	—	—	6.4	30.5	107.6
Japan	854.5	34.8	175.0	176.0	—	1,240.3
Korea	2,714.0	—	56.7	307.2	564.9	3,642.8
Laos	#	—	—	#	—	#
Malaysia	0.8	15.6	—	—	—	16.4
New Zealand	—	1.5	3.0	—	—	4.5
Philippines	392.3	—	60.3	65.6	9.4	527.6
Singapore	—	19.0	—	—	—	19.0
Thailand[d]	589.4	—	4.6	65.2	—	659.2

Vietnam, Republic of[d]	1,476.3	—	6.1	171.1	466.0	2,119.5
Region*	651.1	—	—	48.8	—	699.9
Near East & South Asia, total	**5,865.6**	**973.4**	**363.9**	**616.9**	**211.9**	**8,031.7**
Afghanistan	3.8	—	—	—	—	3.8
Ceylon	0.1	0.3	—	—	—	0.4
Greece	1,456.0	20.0	231.9[e]	186.4	11.3	1,905.6
India	#	#	#	#	—	#
Iran	805.1	504.1	—	60.0	10.5	1,379.7
Iraq	46.7	—	—	3.3	—	50.0
Jordan	52.0	#	—	12.0	—	64.0
Lebanon	9.0	—	—	0.3	—	9.3
Nepal	#	#	—	#	—	#
Pakistan	#	#	7.8	#	79.3	#
Saudi Arabia	34.6	#	—	1.9	—	#
Syria	0.1	—	—	—	—	0.1
Turkey	2,672.8	—	124.2[e]	307.3	110.9	3,215.2
UAR/Egypt	#	—	—	—	—	#
CENTO/region*	785.6	449.0	—	45.6	—	1,280.2
Latin America, total	**724.9**	**252.8**	**200.5**	**179.0**	—	**1,357.2**
Argentina	40.2	48.6	37.0	3.0	—	128.8
Bolivia	21.0	—	—	3.5	—	24.5
Brazil	213.3	72.7	57.1	82.5	—	425.6
Chile	89.4	20.1	29.9	23.6	—	163.0

Continued

Region and country	Grant aid	Credit sales	Ship loans	Excess items	Food for Peace	Total aid
Colombia	86.4	—	14.5	14.8	—	115.7
Costa Rica	1.8	—	—	0.1	—	1.9
Cuba^f	10.6	—	—	5.5	—	16.1
Dominican Republic	20.5	—	1.0	3.0	—	24.5
Ecuador	39.0	0.7	10.0	9.5	—	59.2
El Salvador	5.7	—	—	0.6	—	6.3
Guatemala	14.2	0.5	—	2.9	—	17.6
Haiti[9]	3.2	—	1.1	0.2	—	4.5
Honduras	7.0	—	—	1.3	—	8.3
Jamaica	1.1	—	—	**	—	1.1
Mexico	1.7	4.4	4.4	0.1	—	10.6
Nicaragua	11.0	—	—	0.6	—	11.6
Panama	3.0	—	—	**	—	3.0
Paraguay	8.0	0.2	1.4	1.6	—	11.2
Peru	84.8	20.1	32.8	18.5	—	156.2
Uruguay	39.4	0.3	0.1	7.4	—	47.2
Venezuela	8.6	85.2	11.3	0.3	—	105.4
Regional	15.1	—	—	—	—	15.1
Africa, total	**239.2**	**35.6**	**5.9**	**40.6**	**3.9**	**325.2**
Congo (Kinshasa)	21.9	—	—	5.3	3.9	31.1
Dahomey	0.1	—	—	—	—	0.1

Ethiopia	155.5	—	20.3	5.9	129.3	—
Ghana	0.1	—	0.1	—	0.1	—
Guinea	1.0	—	—	—	0.9	—
Ivory Coast	0.1	—	—	—	0.1	—
Liberia	8.0	—	0.2	—	6.7	1.1
Libya	17.1	—	1.9	—	15.2	—
Mali	3.0	—	0.2	—	2.8	—
Morocco	76.6	—	-1.6	—	35.3	29.7
Niger	0.1	—	—	—	0.1	—
Nigeria	1.5	—	—	—	1.2	0.3
Senegal	2.8	—	—	—	2.8	—
Sudan	2.2	—	—	—	0.7	1.5
Tunisia	25.6	—	1.0	—	21.6	3.0
Upper Volta	0.1	—	—	—	0.1	—
Regional	0.3	—	—	—	0.3	—
Europe & Canada, total	**15,481.7**	**9.9**	**758.7**	**308.6**	**14,231.0**	**133.5**
Austria	#	#	#	#	#	#
Belgium	1,264.3	—	18.9	—	1,237.6	7.8
Canada	13.1	—	—	13.1	—	—
Denmark	638.7	—	20.9	1.2	616.6	—
France	4,548.7	—	289.8	25.3	4,153.2	80.4
Germany (West)[h]	952.2	—	0.7	50.7	900.8	—
Italy	2,517.5	—	205.5	22.7	2,289.0	0.3
Luxembourg	8.4	—	0.2	—	8.2	—

Continued

Region and country	Grant aid	Credit sales	Ship loans	Excess items	Food for Peace	Total aid
Netherlands	1,217.0	2.2	21.3	44.0	—	1,284.5
Norway	888.2	—	5.9	44.0	—	938.1
Portugal	316.5	—	8.4	23.0	—	347.9
Spain	567.4	2.3	47.9	42.9	9.9	670.4
United Kingdom[h]	1,034.5	—	—	73.0	—	1,107.5
Yugoslavia	693.9	1.5	—	27.5	—	722.9
Region*	308.3	39.0	112.1	8.2	—	467.6
Non-Regional	2,753.1	112.2	—	312.7	—	3,178.0
Total	33,850.1	1,786.6	1,256.8	3,304.7	1,403.3	41,603.4

\# Classified data.

* Includes data for classified countries.

** Less than $50,000.

[a] Source: U.S. Department of Defense, Office of the Assistant Secretary of Defense for International Security Affairs, Military Assistance and Foreign Military Sales Facts (Washington, D.C., 1970).

[b] Source: U.S. Agency for International Development, Office of Statistics and Reports, U.S. Overseas Loans and Grants, July 1, 1945–June 30, 1969 (Washington, D.C., 1970).

[c] Source: U.S. Department of Defense, Office of the Assistant Secretary of Defense for International Security Affairs, Military Assistance Facts (Washington, D.C., 1969), and report cited above in note a. Data for 1950–68 represent original acquisition cost of the materials delivered; data for 1969 represent "utility value" of such items (roughly 30 percent of acquisition cost).

[d] Figures show the cumulative program through 1966 when military assistance to these countries was shifted to the regular Department of Defense appropriation.

[e] Includes so-called "Greek-Turkish Aid" of Truman Doctrine era.

[f] U.S. aid suspended fiscal 1961.

[g] No aid since fiscal 1964.

[h] No aid since fiscal 1965.

Appendix E
FOREIGN MILITARY PERSONNEL
TRAINED UNDER U.S. MILITARY ASSISTANCE PROGRAM,
FISCAL YEARS 1950–69[a]

Region	Country	Total students trained
East Asia	Cambodia	337
	China, Republic of	23,453
	Indochina (1950–4)	434
	Indonesia	2,995
	Japan	15,280
	Korea	29,808
	Malaysia	198
	Philippines	12,903
	Thailand	10,136
	Vietnam, Republic of	13,998
	Classified countries[b]	18,924
	East Asia, total	**128,466**
Near East &	Afghanistan	275
South Asia	Ceylon	24
	Greece	13,194
	India[c]	24
	Iran	9,885
	Iraq	404
	Jordan	419
	Lebanon	1,357
	Nepal[c]	11
	Pakistan[c]	60
	Saudi Arabia	1,200
	Syria	23
	Turkey	17,303
	Yemen	5
	Classified countries[d]	4,589
	Near East & South Asia, total	**48,773**
Europe	Austria[e]	39
	Belgium	5,198
	Denmark	4,710

Continued

Region	Country	Students trained
	France	14,342
	Germany	1,624
	Italy	9,363
	Luxembourg	176
	Netherlands	6,297
	Norway	5,532
	Portugal	2,627
	Spain	7,804
	United Kingdom	3,867
	Yugoslavia	844
	NATO Agencies	465
	Classified countries	383
	Europe, total	**63,271**
Africa	Congo (Kinshasa)	227
	Ethiopia	2,672
	Ghana	96
	Guinea	4
	Liberia	376
	Libya	453
	Mali	60
	Morocco	1,327
	Nigeria	321
	Senegal	12
	Sudan	126
	Tunisia	302
	Upper Volta	20
	Africa, total	**5,996**
Latin America	Argentina	2,603
	Bolivia	2,448
	Brazil	6,296
	Chile	3,975
	Colombia	4,353
	Costa Rica	529
	Cuba (1950–9)	521
	Dominican Republic	2,448
	Ecuador	4,044
	El Salvador	953

Continued

Region	Country	Students trained
	Guatemala	2,158
	Haiti	504
	Honduras	1,468
	Mexico	570
	Nicaragua	3,753
	Panama	3,020
	Paraguay	902
	Peru	4,723
	Uruguay	1,591
	Venezuela	3,722
	Latin America, total	**50,581**
Grand Total		**297,087**

aSource: U.S. Department of Defense, Office of the Assistant Secretary of Defense for International Security Affairs, *Military Assistance and Foreign Military Sales Facts* (Washington, D.C., 1970), p. 17. Includes students trained in the United States and at U.S. bases abroad.

b Includes Laos and Burma.

c Data for fiscal years 1967–9 only.

d Includes Israel and Egypt.

e Data for fiscal years 1966–9 only.

Appendix F

**AID PUBLIC SAFETY PROGRAM
EXPENDITURES & TRAINING BY COUNTRY,
FISCAL 1961-9**[a]

Region and country	Expenditures, Fiscal 1961-9 (in thousands of dollars)	Personnel trained in the U.S., Fiscal 1961-9	Public Safety Advisors abroad as of June 30, 1968[b]
East Asia, total	**160,669**	**1,082**	**276**
Burma	195	10	—
Cambodia	2,583	5	—
Indonesia	10,121	202	—
Korea	6,704	27	6
Laos[c]	3,184	40	4
Philippines	2,386	159	8
Thailand[c]	71,316	354	58
Vietnam[c]	64,180	267	200
Near East & South Asia, total	**12,873**	**638**	**14**
Greece	129	34	—
Iran	1,712	216	—
Jordan	2,365	52	5
Lebanon	149	15	—
Pakistan	7,583	106	6
Turkey	200	43	—
UAR/Egypt	312	97	—
Other/CENTO	379	75	3
Latin America, total	**43,630**	**3,166**	**90**
Argentina	120	81	—
Bolivia	1,598	98	3
Brazil	7,416	455	17
Chile	2,265	89	1
Colombia	5,723	348	7
Costa Rica	1,235	103	4
Dominican Republic	3,116	122	15
Ecuador	3,219	213	6
El Salvador	1,826	202	4
Guatemala	2,482	243	2
Guyana	955	34	2

Continued

Region and country	Expenditures	Training	Advisors
Honduras	1,188	60	2
Jamaica	451	34	2
Mexico	745	12	—
Panama	1,467	266	3
Peru	4,115	151	9
Uruguay	1,032	68	3
Venezuela	2,627	517	10
Other countries/Regional	2,050	70	—
Africa, total	**19,155**	**669**	**27**
Central African Republic	241	7	—
Chad	527	5	2
Congo (Kinshasa)	3,133	79	5
Dahomey	323	15	—
Ethiopia	2,875	109	2
Ivory Coast	743	4	1
Kenya	679	9	1
Liberia	2,752	87	3
Libya	444	22	—
Malagasy Republic	454	4	1
Niger	398	9	1
Rwanda	1,073	2	1
Somali Republic	4,416	119	5
Tunisia	640	83	1
Upper Volta	219	9	—
Other countries/Regional	238	98	4
Worldwide, total	**236,332**	**5,547**	**407**

[a] *Source:* U.S. Department of State, Agency for International Development, Statistics and Reports Division, *Operations Report,* Data as of June 30, 1961, June 30, 1962 . . . , June 30, 1969.

[b] *Source: Operations Report.* Data as of June 30, 1968.

[c] Additional commodity support provided by U.S. Department of Defense under Military Assistance Program and Vietnam war appropriations.

NOTES

INTRODUCTION

1. Critical studies of postwar American foreign policy include: William A. Williams, *The Tragedy of American Diplomacy* (New York: Delta Books, 1962); Gabriel Kolko, *The Politics of War* (New York: Random House, 1968) and *The Roots of American Foreign Policy* (Boston: Beacon Press, 1969); David Horowitz, *The Free World Colossus* (New York: Hill & Wang, 1965) and *The Corporations and the Cold War* (New York: Monthly Review Press, 1969); David Horowitz, ed., *Containment and Revolution* (Boston: Beacon Press, 1967); Carl Oglesby and Richard Schaull, *Containment and Change* (New York: Macmillan, 1967); and Richard J. Barnet, *Intervention and Revolution* (New York: New American Library, 1968).

2. The analysis presented here is based on pioneering studies of the economics of imperialism by Paul Baran, Paul Sweezy, Andre Gunder Frank, and Harry Magdoff. These studies include: Paul Baran, *The Political Economy of*

Growth, 2nd ed. (New York: Monthly Review Press, 1962);
Andre Gunder Frank, *Capitalism and Underdevelopment in
Latin America* (New York: Monthly Review Press, 1967)
and *Latin America: Underdevelopment or Revolution?*
(New York: Monthly Review Press, 1970); and Harry Mag-
doff, *The Age of Imperialism* (New York: Monthly Review
Press, 1969).

3. Cited in Williams, p. 17.

4. Cited in Gareth Stedman Jones, "The Specificity of U.S.
    Imperialism," *New Left Review* (March–April 1970), pp.
    80–1.

5. Magdoff, *The Age of Imperialism,* p. 183.

6. U.S. Congress, Joint Economic Committee, Subcommittee
    on Inter-American Economic Relationships, *Private Invest-
    ment in Latin America, Hearings,* January 14–16, 1964,
    cited in Edie Black, "The New Strategy in U.S. Invest-
    ments," *Viet-Report* (April–May 1968), p. 30.

7. Magdoff, *The Age of Imperialism,* pp. 182 *ff.*

8. *Ibid.,* pp. 50–1.

9. U.S. Senate, Committee on Interior and Insular Affairs,
    *Accessibility of Strategic and Critical Materials to the
    United States in Time of War and for Our Expanding
    Economy,* Report, July 9, 1954, cited in Kolko, *The Roots
    of American Foreign Policy,* p. 51.

10. *The Roots of American Foreign Policy,* pp. 52–3.

11. "Is Imperialism Really Necessary?" *Monthly Review*
     (November 1970), pp. 6–7.

12. *The Age of Imperialism,* p. 26.

13. "Modern Capitalism," *Monthly Review* (June 1971), p. 3.

14. Edward Boorstein, *The Economic Transformation of Cuba*
     (New York: Monthly Review Press, 1968), p. 236. See also
     the works by Andre Gunder Frank cited in note 2
     above.

15. See Kolko, *The Roots of American Foreign Policy,* pp.
     58–62.

16. See Black, "New Strategy," pp. 30–2.

17. See Hector Melo and Israel Yost, "Funding the Empire,"
     NACLA Newsletter, vol. 4 (April 1970), pp. 1–13.

18. "Address on the Sixth Anniversary of the Bay of Pigs
     Invasion," Havana, April 19, 1967, in Martin Kenner and

James Petras, eds., *Fidel Castro Speaks* (New York: Grove Press, 1970), p. 137.

19. *Ibid.*
20. Fidel Castro, "The Second Declaration of Havana," Feb. 4, 1962, in Kenner and Petras, pp. 105–6.
21. "The Theory and Fallacies of Counterinsurgency," *The Nation* (August 2, 1971), p. 76.
22. See Research Bibliography for a list of works on the strategy and tactics of revolutionary warfare.
23. See Kolko, *The Roots of American Foreign Policy*, Chapter 2, pp. 27–47. For further discussion of this topic, see also: C. Wright Mills, *The Power Elite* (New York: Oxford University Press, 1959); and G. William Domhoff, *Who Rules America* (Englewood Cliffs, N.J.: Prentice-Hall, 1967).
24. *The Age of Imperialism*, pp. 20–1.
25. "Instances of Use of U.S. Armed Forces Abroad, 1798–1945," *Congressional Record*, June 23, 1969, pp. S6955–8.
26. *The Essence of Security* (New York: Harper & Row, 1968), p. 149.
27. See Walt W. Rostow, "Guerrilla Warfare in Underdeveloped Areas," in T. N. Greene, ed., *The Guerrilla—And How to Fight Him* (New York: Praeger, 1962). See also Rostow's memoranda on the Vietnam war published in the Pentagon Papers.

CHAPTER 1:
FROM DETERRENCE TO COUNTERINSURGENCY

1. John S. Tompkins, *The Weapons of World War III* (Garden City, N.Y.: Doubleday, 1966), p. xii.
2. Robert E. Osgood, "The Reappraisal of Limited War," *Adelphi Papers*, 54 (February 1969), p. 44.
3. *Ibid.*
4. Maxwell D. Taylor, *The Uncertain Trumpet* (New York: Harper & Row, 1960), pp. 5–6.
5. *Ibid.*, pp. 6–7.
6. U.S. Senate, Committee on Foreign Relations, *The Foreign Aid Program*, Compilation of Studies and Surveys, 85th Congress, 1st Session (Washington, D.C.: U.S. Government Printing Office, 1957), p. 18.

7. Rockefeller Brothers Fund, *Prospect for America: The Rockefeller Panel Reports* (Garden City, N.Y.: Doubleday, 1961), pp. 111–12.

8. Rostow's views prior to his appointment are expressed in *The United States in the World Arena* (New York: Harper & Row, 1960).

9. Hilsman's views on counterguerrilla tactics are expressed in "Internal War: The New Communist Tactic," originally published in the January 1962 issue of the *Marine Corps Gazette*, and later included in T. N. Greene, ed., *The Guerrilla—And How to Fight Him* (New York: Praeger, 1962), pp. 22–36.

10. Osgood, *op. cit.*, p. 44.

11. General Maxwell D. Taylor, Address at Graduation Exercises, International Police Academy, Washington, D.C., U.S. Department of State press release, December 17, 1965. (Hereinafter cited as IPA Address.)

12. Roger Hilsman, *To Move a Nation* (Garden City, N.Y.: Doubleday, 1967), p. 415.

13. Cited in *ibid.*

14. Theodore Sorensen, *Kennedy* (New York: Harper & Row, 1965), p. 632.

15. Hilsman, *To Move a Nation*, p. 415.

16. Sorensen, p. 632.

17. *Ibid.*

18. *Ibid.* See also, L. Fletcher Prouty, "The Secret Team and the Games They Play," *Washington Monthly* (May 1970), pp. 16–17.

19. *Sorensen*, pp. 632–3.

20. *Ibid.*, p. 633.

21. Taylor, IPA Address.

22. U.S. House of Representatives, Committee on Appropriations, Subcommittee, *Department of Defense Appropriations for 1963, Hearings*, 87th Congress, 2d Session (Washington, D.C.: U.S. Government Printing Office, 1962), Part 2, pp. 49–50.

23. For background on the events leading up to the July 25 speech, see Sorensen, pp. 583–601.

24. The complete text of the July 25 speech, plus commentary and analysis, appeared in *The New York Times* on July 26, 1961.

25. See David Wise, "Capitol Hill to Hurry Up Arms and Men," New York *Herald Tribune* (July 27, 1961).

26. From the July 25, 1961, speech, as published in *The New York Times* on July 26. Further quotations from this speech are also taken from *The New York Times* text.

27. "Getting Back to the Fighting Soldier," New York *Herald Tribune* (July 28, 1961).

28. C. Neale Ronning and Willard F. Barber, *Internal Security and Military Power* (Columbus, Ohio: Ohio State University Press, 1966), pp. 95–6.

29. For background on Johnson's approach to the Vietnam war, see the analysis of the Pentagon's secret history of the war plus supporting documents in *The New York Times* (June 13, 14, and 15, 1971).

30. Nixon's approach to the Southeast Asian conflict is spelled out in Richard Nixon, *U.S. Foreign Policy for the 1970's,* a Report to the Congress, February 25, 1971 (Washington, D.C.: U.S. Government Printing Office, 1971).

31. Hilsman, *To Move a Nation,* pp. 419, 428.

32. *Ibid.,* pp. 420–4, 427–9, 440–4. See also Sorensen, pp. 652–61.

33. Hilsman, *To Move a Nation,* pp. 419, 427–39.

34. U.S. House of Representatives, Committee on Appropriations, Subcommittee, *Department of Defense Appropriations for 1964, Hearings,* 88th Congress, 1st Session (Washington, D.C.: U.S. Government Printing Office, 1963), Part 1, pp. 483–4.

35. Quoted in Hedrick Smith, "Pentagon Papers: Study Reports Kennedy Made 'Gamble' Into a 'Broad Commitment,' " *The New York Times* (July 1, 1971).

36. Excerpts from the memorandum were published in *The New York Times* on July 1, 1971. Further references to the McNamara-Rush memo are taken from this source.

37. Smith, *op. cit.*

38. Quoted in Smith, *op. cit.*

39. *Ibid.*

40. Osgood, *op. cit.,* p. 44.

41. National Security Action Memorandum 52 was published in *The New York Times* on July 1, 1971.

42. From the interdepartmental task force report on "A Pro-

gram for Action in South Vietnam," incorporated into National Security Action Memorandum 52 and later published in *The New York Times* on July 1, 1971.

43. See Smith, *op. cit.*
44. *Ibid.*
45. *Ibid.*
46. General Maxwell Taylor, Memorandum to Secretary of Defense Robert S. McNamara, January 22, 1964, "Vietnam and Southeast Asia," as published in *The New York Times* (June 13, 1971).

CHAPTER 2:
RESTRUCTURING THE PENTAGON

1. For background on this aspect of the Korean conflict, see J. Lawton Collins, "A Dismantled Army Goes to War," *Army* (December 1969), pp. 44–50, and, by the same author, *War in Peace Time* (Boston: Houghton Mifflin, 1969).
2. Roger Hilsman, *To Move a Nation* (Garden City, N.Y.: Doubleday, 1967), p. 128.
3. C. W. Borklund, *The Department of Defense* (New York: Praeger, 1968), p. 153.
4. *The Uncertain Trumpet* (New York: Harper & Row, 1960), p. 24. For background on American schemes for intervention in Dien Bien Phu, see Bernard B. Fall, *Hell in a Very Small Place* (Philadelphia: Lippincott, 1966).
5. *The New York Times* (June 27, 1958).
6. Henry A. Kissinger, *The Necessity for Choice* (Garden City, N.Y.: Doubleday, 1962), p. 98.
7. McNamara, p. 69.
8. *Ibid.,* p. 78.
9. U.S. House of Representatives, Committee on Appropriations, Subcommittee, *Department of Defense Appropriations for 1962, Hearings,* 87th Congress, 1st Session (Washington, D.C.: U.S. Government Printing Office, 1961), Part 3, pp. 18–9.
10. Quoted in C. W. Borklund, *Men of the Pentagon* (New York: Praeger, 1966), pp. 227–8.

11. *The Essence of Security*, p. 90.
12. Sol Stern, "The Defense Intellectuals," *Ramparts* (February 1967), p. 33.
13. For biographical sketches of McNamara, see: Borklund, *Men of the Pentagon*, pp. 206–8; and Jack Raymond, *Power at the Pentagon* (New York: Harper & Row, 1964), p. 282.
14. *The Essence of Security*, p. 87.
15. *Ibid.*, pp. 87–8.
16. *Ibid.*, p. x.
17. *Ibid.*, p. ix.
18. See Jack Raymond, "Mr. McNamara Remodels the Pentagon," *The Reporter* (January 18, 1962), pp. 31–5.
19. These centralization measures are described in Borklund, *Men of the Pentagon*, p. 215, and in Raymond, p. 293.
20. *The Essence of Security*, p. 88.
21. The best description of these measures appears in Alain C. Enthoven and K. Wayne Smith, *How Much Is Enough?* (New York: Harper & Row, 1971).
22. *The Essence of Security*, p. xii.
23. For background on these events, see Raymond, pp. 284–6.

CHAPTER 3:
THE SCIENTIFIC MERCENARIES

1. U.S. House of Representatives, Committee on Government Operations, *Conflicts Between the Federal Research Programs and the Nation's Goals for Higher Education*, Report, 89th Congress, 1st Session (Washington, D.C.: U.S. Government Printing Office, 1965), p. 16.
2. I first discussed the concept of a civilian research service in *The University-Military Complex* (New York: North American Congress on Latin America, 1969), and in "The Military Research Network," *The Nation* (October 12, 1970), pp. 327–32.
3. Albert Shapero, Kendall D. Moll, Robert A. Hemmes, and Richard P. Howell, *The Role of the University in Defense R&D* (Menlo Park, Cal.: Stanford Research Institute, 1966), p. 10. (Hereinafter cited as *The Role of the University*.)

4. Cited in The Role of the University, p. 14.

5. U.S. Senate, Committee on Aeronautics and Space Science, Scientists' Testimony on Space Goals, Hearings, 88th Congress, 1st Session, 1963. Cited in The Role of the University, p. 13.

6. National Science Foundation, Federal Support to Universities and Colleges, Fiscal Year 1967 (Washington, D.C.: U.S. Government Printing Office, 1969), p. 45.

7. National Science Foundation, Federal Funds for Research Development and Other Scientific Activities, Fiscal Years 1969, 1970, and 1971 (Washington, D.C.: U.S. Government Printing Office, 1970), p. 28.

8. Most research centers in the United States are identified in A. M. Palmer and A. T. Kruzas, eds., Research Centers Directory, 2d ed. (Detroit: Gale Research Co., 1966); and/or in William W. Buchanan, ed., Industrial Research Laboratories in the United States, 12th ed. (Washington, D.C.: Bowker Associates, 1965). Foreign affairs research centers are identified in the following publications of the Office of External Research of the U.S. Department of State: Research Centers on the Developing Areas (1964), Language and Area Study Programs in American Universities (1964), and University Centers of Foreign Affairs Research (1968).

9. This paper was later printed in U.S. House of Representatives, Committee on Government Operations, Conflicts Between the Federal Research Programs and the Nation's Goals for Higher Education, Responses from the Academic and Other Interested Communities . . ., 89th Congress, 1st Session (Washington, D.C.: U.S. Government Printing Office, 1965), p. 369.

10. U.S. Senate, Committee on Foreign Relations, Defense Department Sponsored Foreign Affairs Research, Hearings, 90th Congress, 2d Session (Washington, D.C.: U.S. Government Printing Office, 1968), Part 1, p. 7. (Hereinafter cited as Foreign Affairs Research.)

11. Albert Blumstein and Jesse Orlansky, Behavioral, Political and Operational Research Programs on Counterinsurgency Supported by the Department of Defense (Arlington, Va.: Institute for Defense Analyses, 1965), p. 16.

12. The basic source of information on CRESS activities is the *Work Program* published for each fiscal year. SORO/ CRESS was discussed at length during the hearings held by a subcommittee of the House Committee on Foreign Affairs in 1965 on *Behavioral Sciences and the National Security.* See also Judith Coburn, "University Contractors Cut Ties with CRESS, HumRRO . . . ," *Science,* vol. 164 (May 30, 1969), pp. 1039–41. CRESS is also discussed periodically in *Army Research and Development Newsmagazine,* and in the annual Congressional hearings on Department of Defense appropriations.

13. The basic source of information on HumRRO activities is the *Bibliography of HumRRO Publications,* updated periodically, and an annual *Work Program.* HumRRO projects are frequently described in *Army Research and Development Newsmagazine;* see, for example, "HumRRO Work Program Outlines Training Research" (January 1968), and, "HumRRO Unit 7 Copes with Problems of Countering Insurgency" (March 1968). See also Coburn, "University Contractors Cut Ties . . ."

14. The basic source of information on IDA activities is the Institute's *Annual Report.* See also Cathy McAffee, "IDA: The Academic Conscripts," *Viet-Report* (January 1968), pp. 8–12. IDA's clash with the student movement is described in D. S. Greenberg, "IDA—University-Sponsored Center Hit Hard by Assaults on Campus," *Science,* vol. 160 (May 17, 1968), pp. 744–8.

15. The basic source of information on RAND activities is the Corporation's *Annual Report.* The history and function of RAND is surveyed in Bruce L. Smith, *The RAND Corporation* (Cambridge, Mass.: Harvard University Press 1966). See also Sol Stern, "Who Thinks in a Tank?" *New York Times Magazine* (April 16, 1967), pp. 28 *ff.*

16. The basic source of information on RAC is the Corporation's descriptive brochure sent to prospective employees. RAC activities are occasionally described in *Army Research and Development Newsmagazine;* see, for example, "RAC Performs Army Operations Research, Systems Analysis" (June 1967), and "Research Analysis Corp. Work Program Lists 37 Army Projects" (December 1969). See

also the annual Congressional hearings on Defense Department appropriations.

17. Most of the information now available on SRI has been uncovered by activist researchers in the Stanford community. See, for example, David Ransom, "The Stanford Complex," *Viet-Report* (January 1968), pp. 22–5; and *SRI,* a pamphlet published by the April 3rd Movement at Stanford in 1969. See also, John Walsh, "Stanford Research Institute: Campus Turmoil Spurs Transition," *Science,* vol. 164 (May 23, 1969), pp. 933–6.

18. Cited in Brooke Nihart, "Science Advisory Boards: Bargain or Boondoggle?" *Armed Forces Journal* (March 7, 1970), p. 19.

19. Members of the principal science advisory boards were identified in the March 7, 1970, issue of *Armed Forces Journal.* The affiliations of the panelists is discussed in *The Role of the University,* pp. 43–53.

20. Nihart, p. 18.

21. U.S. Department of Defense, Office of the Director of Defense Research and Engineering, *Organization and Purpose of the Defense Science Board* (Washington, D.C., 1968).

22. *The Role of the University,* Table A-1. See also Nihart, pp. 18–24.

23. Institute for Defense Analyses, *Annual Report for 1964.*

24. Institute for Defense Analyses, *Annual Report for 1966.*

25. The minutes of the Thailand Study Group meeting were published in the April 2, 1970, issue of the *Student Mobilizer* (official publication of the Student Mobilization Committee to End the War in Vietnam), pp. 7–13.

26. These documents were published in *Student Mobilizer* (April 2, 1970), pp. 4–7.

27. Gayl D. Ness and L. A. Peter Gosling, "Suggestions on the Elaboration of a University Role in USOM," August 30, 1965. (Mimeographed paper in the files of the Academic Advisory Committee on Thailand, UCLA.)

28. This text is taken from the contract as renewed on September 1, 1968. The contract renewal, "Amendment No. 3 to the Contract Between the United States of America and the Regents of the University of California," is quoted in *Student Mobilizer* (April 2, 1970), p. 4.

29. From the contract renewal of September 1, 1968.
30. U.S. House of Representatives, Committee on Foreign Affairs, *Behavioral Sciences and the National Security, Hearings,* 89th Congress, 2d Session, 1966, Part 9, p. 15. (Hereinafter cited as *Behavioral Sciences and the National Security.*)

CHAPTER 4:
SOCIAL SYSTEMS ENGINEERING

1. Michael C. Conley, "The Military Value of Social Sciences in An Insurgent Environment," *Army Research and Development Newsmagazine* (November, 1966), p. 22.
2. *Ibid.*
3. *Ibid.,* p. 23.
4. *Behavioral Sciences and the National Security,* p. 72.
5. Defense Science Board, Subcommittee on Behavioral Sciences, *Research in the Department of Defense on Internal Conflict and Insurgency in the Developing Countries* (Washington, D.C.: Office of the Director of Defense Research and Engineering, 1965). The conclusions of this report are cited in *Behavioral Sciences and the National Security,* p. 72.
6. The quotations from the Institute for Defense Analyses are from Albert Blumstein and Jesse Orlansky, *Behavioral, Political and Operational Research Programs on Counterinsurgency Supported by the Department of Defense* (Arlington, Va.: Institute for Defense Analyses, 1965), p. 27.
7. *Behavioral Sciences and the National Security,* p. 20.
8. Testimony of Lieutenant General W. W. Dick, Jr., Chief of Research and Development, Department of the Army, in *Behavioral Sciences and the National Security,* p. 30. The origins and nature of Project Camelot are discussed at length in these hearings, and particularly on pp. 1–65.
9. Special Operations Research Office, The American University, Washington, D.C., press release, December 4, 1964. This document is included in Irving Louis Horowitz, ed., *The Rise and Fall of Project Camelot* (Cambridge, Mass.: MIT Press, 1967), pp. 47–9.

10. Special Operations Research Office, The American University, Washington, D.C., Working Paper, December 5, 1964. This document is reproduced in Horowitz, pp. 50–5.

11. See Irving Louis Horowitz, "The Rise and Fall of Project Camelot," the introductory essay in the book of the same title, pp. 3–44, for the best summary of the Camelot fiasco.

12. See the compilation of essays on Camelot in Horowitz, *The Rise and Fall of Project Camelot*. See also John Walsh, "Social Sciences: Cancellation of Camelot After Row in Chile Brings Research under Scrutiny," *Science,* Vol. 149 (September 10, 1965), pp. 1211–13; and, Elinor Langer, "Foreign Research: CIA Plus Camelot Equals Trouble for U.S. Scholars," *Science,* vol. 156 (June 23, 1967), pp. 1583–4.

13. Cited in Langer, p. 1584.

14. *Foreign Affairs Research,* Part I, p. 67.

15. *Ibid.,* pp. 16–8.

16. *Ibid.,* p. 7; see also "Changes in Defense Department Support of Social Science Research," *FAR Horizons* (September 1969), p. 2.

17. Data on Pentagon-sponsored social science research were published by Senator Fulbright in *Foreign Affairs Research,* Part 2, May 28, 1968, pp. 65–9, and in the *Congressional Record* for July 12, 1967 (pp. S9442–3), April 18, 1968 (pp. S4241–3), May 1, 1969 (pp. S4418–23), and August 11, 1969 (pp. S9623–8).

18. *Behavioral Sciences and the National Security,* p. 48.

19. Quoted in Bryce Nelson, "Anthropologists' Debate: Concern Over Future of Foreign Research," *Science,* vol. 154 (December 23, 1966), pp. 1525–6.

20. American University, Center for Research in Social Systems, *Work Program for Fiscal Year 1967* (Washington, D.C., 1966), p. 47. (Hereinafter cited as *CRESS Work Program 1967.*)

21. *Ibid.,* p. 25.

22. Andrew Molnar, *Undergrounds in Insurgent, Revolutionary, and Resistance Warfare* (Washington, D.C.: Special Operations Research Office, The American University, 1963), abstract.

23. *Behavioral Sciences and the National Security,* p. 80.

24. *Ibid.,* p. 82.

25. Holly J. Kinley, "Development of Strategies in a Simulation of Internal Revolutionary Conflict," *American Behavioral Scientist* (November 1966), pp. 5–6.

26. For background on the genesis of the Revolutionary Development program in South Vietnam, see Robert W. Komer, "Clear, Hold and Rebuild," *Army* (May 1970), pp. 16–24.

27. For background on the influence of the Malayan experience on America's Vietnam policy, see Roger Hilsman, *To Move a Nation* (Garden City, N.Y.: Doubleday, 1967), pp. 429–35.

28. For an excellent case study of the processes by which the United States creates a client regime, see Robert Scheer, *How the United States Got Involved in Vietnam* (Santa Barbara, Cal.: Center for the Study of Democratic Institutions, 1965). See also John McDermott, "Welfare Imperialism in Victnam," *The Nation* (July 25, 1966), pp. 76–88.

29. Lucian W. Pye, "Military Development in the New Countries" (Cambridge, Mass.: MIT Center for International Studies, 1962), pp. 29–34. (Mimeographed.)

30. *CRESS Work Program 1967,* p. 21.

31. *Congressional Record,* May 1, 1969, p. S4420.

32. *Ibid.*

33. *Selected RAND Abstracts,* vol. 1 (Santa Monica, Cal.: RAND Corporation, 1963), p. 109.

34. U.S. Department of State, Office of External Affairs, *Government Sponsored Research: International Affairs* (Washington, D.C.: U.S. Government Printing Office, 1970), p. 106.

35. *Ibid.*

36. See the essays compiled by Horowitz in *The Rise and Fall of Project Camelot.*

37. Gerald C. Hickey, *The Major Ethnic Groups of the South Vietnamese Highlands* (Santa Monica, Cal.: RAND Corporation, 1964), abstract.

38. Peter Braestrup, "Researchers Aid Thai Rebel Fight," *The New York Times* (March 20, 1967).

39. *Meo Handbook* (Bangkok: Military Research and Development Center, 1969), abstract.

40. U.S. House of Representatives, Committee on Appropriations, Subcommittee, *Department of Defense Appropriations for 1970, Hearings,* 91st Congress, 1st Session (Washington, D.C.: U.S. Government Printing Office, 1969), Part 5, p. 183.

41. *Ibid.,* pp. 183–6.

42. Charles Wolf, Jr., *Insurgency and Counterinsurgency: New Myths and Old Realities* (Santa Monica, Cal.: RAND Corporation, 1965), abstract.

43. American Institutes for Research, *Counterinsurgency in Thailand: The Impact of Economic, Social, and Political Action Programs,* p. 1. This document, identified as a "research and development proposal," was submitted to the Advanced Research Projects Agency in December 1967 and subsequently printed in a special issue of *Student Mobilizer* on April 2, 1970.

44. Leonard Sullivan, Jr., "Research and Development for Vietnam," *Science and Technology* (October 1968), p. 29.

CHAPTER 5:
THE COUNTERINSURGENCY RESEARCH NETWORK

1. C. W. Borklund, *The Department of Defense* (New York: Praeger, 1968), p. 70.

2. Leonard Sullivan, Jr., "Research and Development for Vietnam," *Science and Technology* (October 1968), p. 28.

3. Albert Blumstein and Jesse Orlansky, *Behavioral, Political and Operational Research Programs in Counterinsurgency Supported by the Department of Defense* (Arlington, Va.: Institute for Defense Analyses, 1965), p. 16.

4. "R&D Support of the War in Southeast Asia," memorandum inserted in U.S. House of Representatives, Committee on Armed Services, *Hearings on Military Posture,* 90th Congress, 1st Session (Washington, D.C.: U.S. Government Printing Office, 1967), pp. 1426–34.

5. *Ibid.,* p. 1425.

6. U.S. House of Representatives, Committee on Appropriations, Subcommittee, *Department of Defense Appropriations for 1971, Hearings,* 91st Congress, 2d Session (Washington, D.C.: U.S. Government Printing Office, 1970), Part 6, p. 734.

7. For background on ARPA, see "Brown Oversees all Military RDT&E," *Missiles and Rockets* (March 25, 1963), pp. 81–5; and DMS, Inc., "ARPA Analysis," *Aerospace Agencies* (Greenwich, Conn., 1970). (DMS, Inc. is the Defense Marketing Service of McGraw-Hill.)

8. For background on ADTC, see James Ferguson, "Technology—The Goal and the Challenge," *Defense Industry Bulletin* (May 1969), p. 29; "Armament Development Center," *Armed Forces Journal* (April 19, 1969), p. 24; and, DMS, Inc., "ADTC Analysis," *Aerospace Agencies* (Greenwich, Conn., 1970).

9. For background on AFATL, see, in addition to sources cited in note 8, Abner B. Martin, "Air Force Armament Laboratory—Putting the Weapon in the Weapon System," *Defense Industry Bulletin* (October 1969), pp. 14–6; and DMS, Inc., "ADL Analysis," *Aerospace Agencies* (Greenwich, Conn., 1970).

10. For background on CDC, see Harvey Ardman, "How Vietnam Tested U.S. Army Planning," *American Legion Magazine* (February 1970), pp. 10–13; Harvey W. O. Kinnard, "The Future Begins Today," *Ordnance* (September–October 1968), pp. 162–4; and DMS, Inc., "CDC Analysis," *Aerospace Agencies* (Greenwich, Conn., 1970).

11. Kinnard, p. 163.

12. For more on CDC current activities, see "CDC Studies Postwar Army," *Armed Forces Journal* (April 4, 1970); "CDC Systems Analysis Institute Evaluating Army of 1990's Concepts," *AR&DN** (April 1968); and, "DATA Gets Briefing on CDC from Lt./Gen. Forsythe," *DATA on Defense and Civil Systems* (December 1969), pp. 15–19.

13. For background on LWL, see Ardman, "How Vietnam Tested U.S. Army Planning"; William Beecher, "Way Out

* Abbreviation: *AR&DN = Army Research and Development Newsmagazine.*

Weapons," *New York Times Magazine* (March 24, 1968), pp. 49 *ff.*; John J. Juel, "Aberdeenites Like the Jingle of the Howitzers," *Potomac* [the Washington *Post*] (October 11, 1970), pp. 9 *ff.*; and DMS, Inc., "LWL Analysis," *Aerospace Agencies* (Greenwich, Conn., 1971).

14. "LWL Broadens R&D Scope with Revised Mission," *AR&DN* (January 1970).

15. F. P. de Percin, Leo Alpert, and Donald C. Hilton, "Army R&D Advancing Combat Capability in Environmental Extremes," *AR&DN* (January 1967), p. 22.

16. David E. Bass, "Research Institute of Environmental Medicine Aims at Protection of Soldier for Maximum Effectiveness," *AR&DN* (November 1969), p. 42.

17. de Percin, et al., pp. 22–3.

18. *Ibid.,* p. 23.

19. Will F. Thompson, "Military Significance of Mountain Environment Studies," *AR&DN* (May 1967), pp. 30–2.

20. *Ibid.,* p. 32.

21. For information on the Mount Logan project, see "Army Supports AINA Alaska Mountain Study," *AR&DN* (April 1968); and " 'World's Highest Research Station' Serving Army Interests," *AR&DN* (October 1968).

22. "Army Completes High Elevation Field Maneuver Appraisal," *AR&DN* (July–August 1967).

23. U.S. House of Representatives, Committee on Appropriations, *Foreign Assistance and Related Agencies Appropriations for 1970, Hearings,* 91st Congress, 1st Session (Washington, D.C.: U.S. Government Printing Office, 1969), Part 1, p. 797.

24. For background on CRREL, see "Army Research Office Marks 10th Year," *AR&DN* (April 1968), p. 47; and "Engineers Regain Control, Restore Name of CRREL," *AR&DN* (June–July, 1969), pp. 1, 6.

25. For background on ESL, see "Army Research Office Marks 10th Year," p. 45; and William C. Robinson, "Natick Earth Sciences Laboratory Reports Southeast Asia Environmental Research," *AR&DN* (March 1969).

26. Paul A. Blackford, "Project TREND—Environmental Research in Thailand," *AR&DN* (March 1967), pp. 2, 24–5.

27. For background on USARIEM, see David E. Bass, "Army

Environmental Research Broadens Combat Capability,"
AR&DN (January 1967), pp. 18–20; and, by the same au-
thor, "Research Institute of Environmental Medicine,"
AR&DN (November 1969), pp. 42–4.

28. U.S. House of Representatives, Committee on Appropriations, Subcommittee, *Department of Defense Appropriations for 1964, Hearings,* 88th Congress, 1st Session
(Washington, D.C.: U.S. Government Printing Office, 1963),
Part I, pp. 483–4.

29. For background on the Vietnam research units, see Luther
J. Carter, "Vietnam: Jungle Conflict Poses New R&D Prob-
lems," *Science,* vol. 152 (April 8, 1966), pp. 187–90; Law-
rence J. Curran and Heather M. David, "DOD, Services
Gear to Manage War," *Missiles and Rockets* (March 28,
1966), pp. 132–41; and J. Elmore Swenson, "The Army
Concept Team in Vietnam (ACTIV)," *U.S. Army Aviation
Digest* (July 1968).

30. Curran and David, p. 134.

31. See the statement of Leonard Sullivan, Jr., and supple-
mentary documentation, inserted into the *Congressional
Record,* August 11, 1969, pp. S9589–91.

32. *Ibid.*

33. "R&D Support of the War in Southeast Asia," p. 1426.

34. Sullivan, "Research and Development for Vietnam," p. 30.

35. From Sullivan's statement cited in note 31.

CHAPTER 6:
STRATEGIC MOBILITY AND INTERVENTION

1. Comandante Ernesto Che Guevara, Message to the Executive Secretariat of the Organization of Solidarity of the
Peoples of Africa, Asia and Latin America (OSPAAAL),
published as a "Special Supplement" to *Tricontinental,*
Havana, April 16, 1967.

2. U.S. Senate, Committee on Armed Services, *Military Procurement Authorizations, Fiscal Year 1966, Hearings,* 89th
Congress, 1st Session (Washington, D.C.: U.S. Government Printing Office, 1965), pp. 77, 120–1. (Hereinafter
cited as *Authorizations 1966.*)

3. *Ibid.,* p. 120.

4. John S. Tompkins, The Weapons of World War III (Garden City, N.Y.: Doubleday, 1966), p. 40.

5. See "Big Lift Tests Army, USAF Flexibilities," *Aviation Week & Space Technology* (October 28, 1963), pp. 26–7.

6. DMS, Inc., "Lockheed C-141," *Military Aircraft* (Greenwich, Conn., 1969).

7. U.S. House of Representatives, Committee on Appropriations, Subcommittee, *Department of Defense Appropriations for 1969, Hearings*, 90th Congress, 2d Session (Washington, D.C.: U.S. Government Printing Office, 1968), Part 3, p. 338.

8. *Authorizations 1966*, p. 954.

9. *Ibid.*, p. 121.

10. "President Views Biggest Airplane," *The New York Times* (March 3, 1968).

11. For background on the C-5A dispute, see James G. Phillips, "The Lockheed Scandal," *New Republic* (August 1, 1970), pp. 19–23; Berkeley Rice, "What Price Lockheed?" *New York Times Magazine* (May 9, 1971), pp. 24 *ff.*; Harold B. Meyers, "For Lockheed, Everything's Coming Up Unk-Unks," *Fortune* (August 1969), pp. 76 *ff.*; Members of Congress for Peace Through Law, *Report on Military Spending* (Washington, D.C., 1970); Democratic Study Group of the U.S. House of Representatives, "The Fiscal Year 1970 Defense Budget," inserted in *Congressional Record*, September 26, 1969, pp. E7877–88; Institute for Policy Studies, "Report of the National Security Summer Research Project," inserted in *Congressional Record*, November 6, 1969, pp. E9417–23; and DMS, Inc., "Lockheed C-5A," *Military Aircraft* (Greenwich, Conn., 1970).

12. *Congressional Record*, May 16, 1969, p. S5254.

13. Rice, p. 86.

14. Phillips, p. 20.

15. *Ibid.*, p. 22.

16. Quoted in Neil Sheehan, "Outgoing Pentagon Aide Calls C-5A Program the 'Best' Air Force Contract," *The New York Times* (May 3, 1969).

17. *Wall Street Journal* (November 20, 1968).

18. Neil Sheehan, "Lockheed Woes May Cost U.S. Public $600-Million," *The New York Times* (December 13, 1970).

19. "Lockheed Agrees to Accept Loss," *Armed Forces Journal* (March 1, 1971).

20. *Congressional Record*, August 20, 1970, p. S13836.

21. Phillips, p. 19.

22. *Wall Street Journal* (October 16, 1970).

23. Michael Getler, "Lockheed: Dilemma for United States," Washington *Post* (July 26, 1970).

24. Sheehan, "Lockheed Woes."

25. *Congressional Record*, August 18, 1970, p. S13577.

26. *Congressional Record*, August 13, 1970, p. S13417.

27. For background on REFORGER I, see William Beecher, "U.S. to Fly Men to Germany to Test Reinforcing," *The New York Times* (January 5, 1969); Ralph Blumenthal, "U.S. Flying 15,500 to Germany in Deployment Test," *The New York Times* (January 7, 1969); and Ralph Blumenthal, "Redeployed U.S. Troops Begin Exercise in Bavaria," *The New York Times* (January 30, 1969).

28. See Beecher, "U.S. to Fly Men to Germany."

29. "Dual-Basing Concept Tested in Reforger/Crested Cap II," *Armed Forces Journal* (September 21, 1970).

30. For background on Focus Retina, see David K. Willis, "U.S. Airlift Reassures Koreans," *Christian Science Monitor* (March 15, 1969); Philip Shabecoff, "Paratroops From the U.S. Leap in Korea War Game," *The New York Times* (March 18, 1969); and Philip Shabecoff, "Long-Distance Deployment of U.S. Troops for Airdrop in South Korea Stirs Seoul's Fear of Pullout," *The New York Times* (March 20, 1969).

31. See "Korea: Airborne Exercise," *Military Review* (January 1971), p. 99; and "Aerospace World," *Air Force* (April 1971), p. 14.

32. For background on the FDL, see Democratic Study Group, "1970 Defense Budget"; Leonard Rodberg and Derek Shearer, eds., *The Pentagon Watchers* (Garden City, N.Y.: Doubleday, 1970), pp. 202–14; and DMS, Inc., "FDL," *Ships/Vehicles/Ordnance* (Greenwich, Conn., 1969).

33. U.S. Department of Defense, *The Fiscal Year 1968–72*

Defense Program and 1968 Defense Budget (Washington, D.C.: U.S. Government Printing Office, 1967), p. 111.

34. See "After Six Years of Trying DOD Gives Up on the FDL," *Army* (March 1970).

35. See George C. Wilson, "Rough Sailing in Congress Seen for Pentagon Cargo Ship Program," Washington *Post* (January 15, 1967).

36. Quoted in John Herbers, "House Unit Backs Supply Ships Rejected Senate," *The New York Times* (April 27, 1967).

37. For background on the LHA, see Democratic Study Group, "1970 Defense Budget"; DMS, Inc., "LHA," in *Ships/ Vehicles/Ordnance* (Greenwich, Conn., 1970).

38. Quoted in Craig Powell, "Hostile Shores Must Still Be Taken," *Armed Forces Management* (March 1969), p. 36.

39. Richard Homan, "Navy Floats Dream Ship," Washington *Post* (June 29, 1969).

40. *Ibid.*

41. DMS, Inc., "LHA."

42. "Cutback in LHA Program," *Armed Forces Journal* (March 1, 1971).

43. For background on the Bare Base system, see "U.S. Developing Instant Air Bases," *The New York Times* (November 1, 1970); Cecil Brownlow, "USAF to Test Bare-Base Concept," *Aviation Week and Space Technology* (October 6, 1969), pp. 16–17; "Instant Air Base," *Ordnance* (March-April 1970), pp. 533–5; "Air Force to Test New Mobility Concept," *U.S./R&D* (November 1969), pp. 246–7; and DMS, Inc., "Bare Base," *Electronic Systems* (Greenwich, Conn., 1971).

44. DMS, Inc., "Bare Base."

45. Quoted in "U.S. Developing Instant Air Bases."

46. "Air Force to Test New Mobility Concept."

47. "Instant Air Base."

48. Brownlow, p. 16.

49. DMS, Inc., "Bare Base." See also "The Tactical Air Command," *Air Force* (May 1971), p. 88.

50. Quoted in Bruce Cossaboom, "America's Strategic Airlift Capability: A Risky Calculation," *Armed Forces Journal* (July 18, 1970), p. 18.

CHAPTER 7:
"THE ELECTRONIC BATTLEFIELD"

1. General William C. Westmoreland, Address at the Annual Luncheon of the Association of the United States Army, Washington, D.C., October 14, 1969. This speech was published in its entirety in the *Congressional Record* for October 16, 1969, pp. S12728–9. (Hereinafter cited as AUSA 1969 Address.)
2. For background on the DCPG, see U.S. Senate, Committee on Armed Services, Subcommittee, *Investigation into the Electronic Battlefield Program, Hearings,* 91st Congress, 2d Session (Washington, D.C.: U.S. Government Printing Office, 1971), pp. 3–38. These hearings, hereinafter cited as *Electronic Battlefield,* are one of the basic sources of information on U.S. sensor programs.
3. *Ibid.,* p. 5.
4. *Ibid.*
5. *Ibid.,* p. 15.
6. Proxmire's estimate was made in a speech on the Senate floor on July 6, 1970. The transcript of the speech appears in the *Congressional Record* of the same date, pp. S10545–7. In response to hostile comments made by Senator Barry M. Goldwater on July 7, 1970, in the Senate, Proxmire had an opportunity to extend his remarks on the "Electronic Battlefield" program on July 13 (see *Congressional Record,* July 13, 1970, pp. S11102–14).
7. U.S. House of Representatives, Committee on Appropriations, Subcommittee, *Department of Defense Appropriations for 1968, Hearings,* 90th Congress, 1st Session (Washington, D.C.: U.S. Government Printing Office, 1967), Part 3, pp. 176–7. (Hereinafter cited as *Defense Appropriations 1968.*)
8. *Electronic Battlefield,* p. 5.
9. Westmoreland, AUSA 1969 Address.
10. "New Copter Unit is Formed by U.S.," *The New York Times* (December 15, 1970).
11. *Technical Abstract Bulletin* (April 1, 1967). This semi-

monthly listing of contractor reports is published by the U.S. Department of Defense, Defense Documentation Center, Alexandria, Virginia.

12. *Technical Abstract Bulletin* (November 15, 1966).

13. Booz-Allen's reports on the development of the E-63 are abstracted in *Technical Abstract Bulletin* for April 15 and August 15, 1967.

14. For technical description of the XM-2, see Department of the Army, *Employment of Riot Control Agents, Flame, Smoke, Antiplant Agents, and Personnel Detectors in Counterguerrilla Operations,* Training Circular No. 3–16 (Washington, D.C., 1969), pp. 69–75.

15. Beverly Deepe, "Tactical Nose—'People Sniffer' Peers Beneath Vietnam Foliage," *Christian Science Monitor* (September 26, 1968).

16. Quoted in Gene Roberts, " 'People Sniffer' Follows Scent of Enemy From Copter in Delta," *The New York Times* (August 18, 1968).

17. "U.S. Device Sniffs for Foe From Air," *The New York Times* (May 28, 1967).

18. Quoted in Deepe.

19. U.S. House of Representatives, Committee on Appropriations, Subcommittee, *Department of Defense Appropriations for 1971, Hearings,* 91st Congress, 2d Session (Washington, D.C.: U.S. Government Printing Office, 1970), Part 6, p. 190. (Hereinafter cited as *Defense Appropriations 1971.*)

20. See Phillip H. Wiggins, "Aerial Use of Infrared Is Widening," *The New York Times* (April 14, 1968).

21. Roger Rapoport, "The Michigan Complex," *Viet-Report* (January, 1968), p. 23. This article was based on a series by Rapoport that originally appeared in the *Michigan Daily* for October 17, 18, 19, and 20, 1967.

22. *Technical Abstract Bulletin* (April 1, 1967).

23. John D. Rinaldo, Bryce D. McMichael, and John E. Walker, *Project AMPIRT—ARPA Multiband Photographic and Infrared Reconnaissance Test,* Final Technical Report (Buffalo, N.Y.: Cornell Aeronautical Laboratory, 1965), abstract. This abstract appears in Harry Cleaver, *Counter-*

insurgency Research in Thailand (East Palo Alto, Cal.: Pacific Studies Center, 1970), p. 79. The Cleaver work includes abstracts of most reports on sensor research in Thailand. In subsequent entries, reference will be made both to the document indicated in the text and to the abstract as it appears in Cleaver.

24. Dana Parker and Dale Fisher, Project AMPIRT Semi-annual Technical Report No. 1 (Ann Arbor, Mich.: University of Michigan, 1965); for abstract, see Cleaver, p. 70.

25. Dana C. Parker and William T. Pollock, *Project AMPIRT —The Second Field Trip* (Ann Arbor, Mich.: University of Michigan, 1965); for abstract, see Cleaver, p. 70.

26. *Technical Abstract Bulletin* (December 15, 1967).

27. Rapoport, "The Michigan Complex."

28. Zissis was quoted in the *Michigan Daily* (October 17, 1967).

29. *Technical Abstract Bulletin* (June 1, 1967).

30. DMS, Inc., "AN/AAS-24," *"AN" Equipment* (Greenwich, Conn., 1970).

31. DMS, Inc., "AN/AAS-14," *"AN" Equipment* (1970).

32. DMS, Inc., "AN/AAQ-5," *"AN" Equipment* (1970).

33. The best reconstruction of the CIA's hunt for Che appears in Andrew St. George, "How the U.S. Got Che," *True* (April 1969), pp. 30 *ff*.

34. See John M. Gosko, "Latins Blame the United States for Military Coups," Washington *Post* (February 5, 1968).

35. U.S. Department of State, Agency for International Development, Contract Services Division, *A.I.D. Current Technical Service Contracts As of June 30, 1966* (Washington, D.C., 1966).

36. Telephone interview with Dean Hansen, vice-president of Mark Hurd Aerial Surveys, Inc., October 2, 1968. The substance of the interview appeared in *The Guardian* (October 12, 1968).

37. The military aspects of the campaign against Che and the subsequent decision to have him executed are discussed in St. George, "How the U.S. Got Che"; Michele Ray, "In Cold Blood—The Execution of Che by the CIA," *Ramparts* (March 1968), pp. 23–37; and Richard Gott, "Gue-

vara, Debray and the CIA," *The Nation* (November 20, 1967), pp. 521–30.

38. *Technical Abstract Bulletin* (March 15, 1964).

39. Fox Butterfield, "Pentagon Papers: Vietnam Study Links '65–'66 G.I. Build-Up to Faculty Planning," *The New York Times* (July 2, 1971).

40. Quoted in Butterfield, *op. cit.*

41. McNaughton apparently gave McNamara a proposal for a barrier program on March 22, 1966. According to the Pentagon Papers, McNaughton's proposal was based on Fisher's January 3, 1966 draft memo of "A Barrier Strategy." Excerpts from the McNaughton memo were published in *The New York Times* on July 2, 1971.

42. Butterfield, *op. cit.*

43. *Electronic Battlefield*, p. 4.

44. *Ibid.*, p. 15.

45. William Beecher, "U.S. to Construct Vietnam Barrier Near Buffer Zone," *The New York Times* (September 8, 1968).

46. *Electronic Battlefield*, pp. 8–9.

47. Gene Roberts, "Work on 'McNamara Line' in Vietnam Near Standstill," *The New York Times* (March 25, 1968). See also George C. Wilson, "Pentagon Studies Effectiveness of Electronic Barrier in Vietnam," Washington *Post* (October 17, 1968).

48. *Electronic Battlefield*, pp. 9–10.

49. *Ibid.*, pp. 107–11, 118–24.

50. See George Weiss, "Battle for Control of Ho Chi Minh Trail," *Armed Forces Journal* (February 15, 1971), pp. 18–22; and John L. Frisbee, "IGLOO WHITE," *Air Force* (February 1971), pp. 48–51.

51. Quoted in William Beecher, "Sensor 'Seal' Around Vietnam Studied," *The New York Times* (February 13, 1970).

52. Beecher, "Sensor Seal."

53. "U.S. Secret Devices Conduct War by Remote Control," Miami *Herald* (August 3, 1970). See also *Electronic Battlefield*, p. 189.

54. "A New 'McNamara' Line," San Francisco *Chronicle* (October 26, 1970).

55. *Electronic Battlefield,* p. 12.
56. *Ibid.*
57. *Ibid.,* pp. 21, 33.
58. *Ibid.,* p. 17.
59. Rowland H. McLaughlin, *Acoustic and Seismic Research,* Final Report (Alexandria, Va.: Atlantic Research Corp., 1967); for abstract, see Cleaver, p. 67.
60. *Michigan Daily* (October 17, 1967).
61. William Beecher, "Way Out Weapons," *The New York Times Magazine* (March 24, 1968).
62. U.S. House of Representatives, Committee on Appropriations, Subcommittee, *Department of Defense Appropriations for 1969,* Hearings, 90th Congress, 2d Session (Washington, D.C.: U.S. Government Printing Office, 1968), Part 3, p. 107.
63. *Electronic Battlefield,* p. 97.
64. *Ibid.,* p. 111–2. See also George Weiss, "Southeast Asia Sensor Fields: More Eyes and Ears," *Armed Forces Journal* (March 1, 1971), p. 38.
65. Norman E. Goldstein, *Seismic Intruder Detection Tests* (Menlo Park, Cal.: Stanford Research Institute, 1966); for abstract, see Cleaver, pp. 44–5.
66. McLaughlin, *Acoustic and Seismic Research.*
67. *Ibid.,* Supplement. (A secret appendix to the main body of the report, which is unclassified.)
68. *Defense Appropriations 1968,* p. 295.
69. *Electronic Battlefield,* p. 73
70. *Ibid.,* pp. 6–7, 31, 73.
71. Weiss, "Southeast Asia Sensor Fields," pp. 38–9.
72. "R&D Funding Continues to Increase," *Missiles & Rockets* (March 29, 1965), p. 125.
73. J. Krebbers, *The Magnetic Field Around a Magnetized Object* (Menlo Park, Cal.: Stanford Research Institute, 1965); for abstract, see Cleaver, p. 46.
74. Russell F. Rhyne, *Preliminary Investigations of the Varian Rubidium Vapor Magnetometer in Counterinsurgency Surveillance* (Menlo Park, Cal.: Stanford Research Institute, 1967); for abstract, see Cleaver, p. 47.
75. *Electronic Battlefield,* p. 7.

76. Charles J. Schneider, Jr., "Radars for the Artilleryman," *Marine Corps Gazette* (March 1970), p. 36.
77. *Defense Appropriations 1968*, p. 295. See also "USAEPG [U.S. Army Electronic Proving Ground] Completes Tests on AN/PPS-5," *Army Research and Development Newsmagazine* (July–August 1968); Charles Mohr, "Radar Enables G.I.'s to Keep Close Eye on Enemy," *The New York Times* (May 24, 1968); and, DMS, Inc., "AN/PPS-5," *"AN" Equipment* (Greenwich, Conn., 1970).
78. DMS, Inc., "AN/PPS-6," *"AN" Equipment* (Greenwich, Conn., 1970).
79. Review of Special Laboratories, Massachusetts Institute of Technology, *Proceedings*, May 2, 1969.
80. *Electronic Battlefield*, p. 179.
81. DMS, Inc., "AN/PPS-9," and "AN/PPS-10," *"AN" Equipment* (Greenwich, Conn., 1970).
82. DMS, Inc., "Night Vision—Army," *Electronic Systems* (Greenwich, Conn., 1970).
83. *Defense Appropriations 1971*, p. 190.
84. For more on the operation of image-intensification devices, see Mort Schultz, "How the Army Learned to See in the Dark," *Popular Mechanics* (January 1969), pp. 80 *ff*.
85. DMS, Inc., "Night Vision—Army."
86. *Ibid*.
87. DMS, Inc., "PAVE," *Electronic Systems* (Greenwich, Conn., 1971).
88. DMS, Inc., "Night Vision—Air Force," *Electronic Systems* (Greenwich, Conn., 1969).
89. *Electronic Battlefield*, p. 67.
90. *Product Engineering*, February 16, 1970.
91. Westmoreland, 1969 AUSA Address.
92. *Defense Appropriations 1971*, p. 193.
93. *Electronic Battlefield*, p. 192.
94. *Defense Appropriations 1971*, p. 194.
95. *Electronic Battlefield*, p. 193.
96. For background on ADSAF and component systems, see Harry W. O. Kinnard, "Narrowing the Combat Intelligence Gap," *Army* (August 1969), pp. 22–6; William R. Reed, "Automation—Force Effectiveness Multiplier," *Defense Industry Bulletin* (March 1970), pp. 7–13; and

DMS, Inc., "ADSAF," *Electronic Systems* (Greenwich, Conn., 1970).

97. DMS, Inc., "ADSAF."

98. *Ibid.*

99. *Ibid.*

100. U.S. House of Representatives, Committee on Appropriations, Subcommittee, *Department of Defense Appropriations for 1970, Hearings,* 91st Congress, 1st Session (Washington, D.C.: U.S. Government Printing Office, 1969), Part 5, p. 707. See also DMS, Inc., "ADSAF."

101. "ADSAF."

102. Westmoreland, AUSA 1969 Address.

103. *Electronic Battlefield,* p. 202.

104. Leonard Sullivan, Jr., "Research and Development for Vietnam," *Science and Technology* (October 1968), pp. 35–6.

CHAPTER 8:
THE SCIENCE OF MERCENARIZATION

1. The most thorough documentation on U.S. mercenary payments to Korea, Thailand, and the Philippines appears in the hearings of Senator Symington's subcommittee on United States Security Agreements and Commitments Abroad. The full citation reads: U.S. Senate, Committee on Foreign Relations, *United States Security Agreements and Commitments Abroad, Hearings,* 2 vols. (Washington, D.C.: U.S. Government Printing Office, 1971).

2. Information on Project Agile is not easy to come by; the portrait of Agile presented in this chapter was pieced together from hundreds of clues obtained from a great variety of sources. The only official discussion of the project occurs during the annual Congressional hearings on Department of Defense appropriations; usually, the most detailed information is brought out in the hearings held by the Department of Defense Subcommittee of the House Appropriations Committee. McGraw-Hill's Defense Marketing Service (DMS) publications also contain basic information. The only document provided by

the Pentagon itself is a small brochure entitled *Advanced Research Projects Agency Activities* (Washington, D.C.: U.S. Department of Defense, 1966). All further information has come from articles which describe one aspect of Agile activities or which refer to Agile only tangentially.

3. *Defense Appropriations 1971*, p. 750.

4. U.S. House of Representatives, Committee on Appropriations, Subcommittee, *Department of Defense Appropriations for 1969, Hearings,* 90th Congress, 2d Session (Washington, D.C.: U.S. Government Printing Office, 1968), Part 2, p. 590. (Hereinafter cited as *Defense Appropriations 1969*).

5. Cited in *Defense Appropriations 1971*, pp. 750–1.

6. U.S. Department of the Navy, Office of Naval Research, *Directory of Department of Defense Information Analysis Centers* (Washington, D.C., 1965).

7. *Defense Appropriations 1971*, p. 751.

8. *Ibid.*

9. "Vietnam: Canned *Nucmom*," *Newsweek* (November 5, 1962), p. 63.

10. "Weapons Sought for Remote Wars," *The New York Times* (January 27, 1964). The nature of Agile's relationship to MACV is specified in *Defense Appropriations 1971*, p. 751.

11. Tompkins, *The Weapons of World War III*, p. 123.

12. "Doctor Says GI's Bullets Are Like Outlawed 'Dum-Dum,' " Washington *Post*, December 8, 1970.

13. For background on Agile's Vietnam communications project, see *Defense Appropriations 1971*, p. 736; "R&D Funding Continues to Increase," *Missiles and Rockets* (March 29, 1965), p. 128; Luther J. Carter, "Vietnam: Jungle Conflict Poses New R&D Problems," *Science,* vol. 152 (April 8, 1966), p. 189; and John R. Shirley, et al., *Communications Research and Development Data Collection Program in the Republic of Vietnam*, Semiannual Reports (Chicago: Booz-Allen Applied Research, Inc., 1966–7).

14. See Dorothy K. Clark and Charles R. Wyman, *An Exploratory Analysis of the Reporting, Measuring, and Evaluating of Revolutionary Development in South Viet-*

nam (McLean, Va.: Research Analysis Corp., 1967); and Erwin R. Brigham, "Pacification Measurement," *Military Review* (May 1970), pp. 47–55.

15. "Vietnam: Canned *Nucmom*," p. 63.

16. William A. Nighswonger, *Rural Pacification in Vietnam: 1962–1965.* Doctoral thesis, the American University, 1966, abstract. Nighswonger's thesis was published as *Rural Pacification in Vietnam* (New York: Praeger, 1966). (All subsequent references are to the Praeger edition.)

17. Nighswonger, *Rural Pacification in Vietnam,* p. 230.

18. For background on the U.S. pacification apparatus, see Komer, "Clear, Hold and Rebuild," pp. 16–24.

19. Philip Worchel et al., *A Socio-Psychological Study of Regional/Popular Forces in Vietnam,* Final Report (Cambridge, Mass.: Simulmatics Corp., 1967), abstract.

20. Komer, pp. 19–20.

21. *Defense Appropriations 1971,* p. 728.

22. Agile contracts are listed in the Commerce Department's daily publication, *Commerce Business Daily.*

23. "Remote-Area Conflict Research Sought," *Aviation Week* (November 25, 1963), p. 26.

24. "Weapons Sought for Remote Wars," *The New York Times* (January 27, 1964).

25. For background on the guerrilla situation in Thailand, see Donald Kirk, "Report from the Thailand Front," *New Leader* (September 23, 1968), pp. 6–8; Louis E. Lomax, "What Reds Plan Next in Southeast Asia," *National Observer* (January 29, 1968); and Mike Todd, "The Guerrilla Movement in Thailand," *Pacific Research and World Empire Telegram* (September 10, 1969), pp. 16–23.

26. *Defense Appropriations 1968,* pp. 175–6.

27. For background on the Agile office in Thailand, see Peter Braestrup, "Researchers Aid Thai Rebel Fight," *The New York Times* (March 20, 1967); Michael Getler, "ARPA Team Aids Thailand in Developing R&D Capability," *Technology Week* (December 19, 1966), pp. 17–8; "Fighting Guerrillas from the Lab," *Time* (October 7, 1966), pp. 69–70; and Jacques Decornoy, "Thailand: 'Laboratory' for Counterinsurgency," *Le Monde,* Weekly Selection (July 22, 1970), p. 3.

28. A fairly complete listing of all Project Agile projects in Thailand appears in Harry Cleaver, *Counterinsurgency Research in Thailand*. This study includes abstracts of Agile projects as reported in the Defense Department's *Technical Abstract Bulletin*. In subsequent entries, reference will be made both to the document indicated in the text and to the abstract as it appears in Cleaver.

29. For background on Project SEACORE, see *Defense Appropriations 1968*, p. 177.

    Specific project reports include:

    Knud Christensen and Don Neal, Environmental Research Division, *Environmental Description of Jansky and Bailey Test Site at Khao Yai, Thailand*, 2 vols. (Bangkok: Military Research and Development Center, 1966).

    Research-Engineering and Support for Tropical Communications, Semiannual Reports (Menlo Park, Cal.: Stanford Research Institute, 1963–6).

    L. G. Sturgill, *Tropical Propagation Research*, Semiannual reports (Alexandria, Virginia: Atlantic Research Corp., 1963–6).

    For abstracts of these and related studies, see Cleaver, pp. 26–9, 48–63, 100–1.

30. See D. J. Blakeslee, L. W. Huff, and R. W. Kickert, *Village Security Pilot Study, Northeast Thailand* (Bangkok: Military Research and Development Center, 1965); for abstract see Cleaver, p. 25.

31. U.S. Senate, Committee on Government Operations, Permanent Investigations Subcommittee, *Riots, Civil and Criminal Disorders, Hearings*, 91st Congress, 1st Session (Washington, D.C.: U.S. Government Printing Office, 1969), Part 21, p. 4667.

32. Angelo Gualtieri, *Communications Traffic Requirements to Support Counterinsurgency Operations Against Medium-Level Insurgency in Thailand* (Menlo Park, Cal.: Stanford Research Institute, 1966); for abstract, see Cleaver, p. 62.

    Related Studies include:

    Donald A. Price, *Survey of Existing Communications Systems in Thailand* (Menlo Park, Cal.: Stanford Research Institute, 1966).

Communications in Low-Intensity Counterinsurgency: A Study of the Border Patrol Police of Thailand (Menlo Park, Cal.: Stanford Research Institute, 1966). For abstracts of these studies, see Cleaver, pp. 62–3.

33. W. A. Hamberg and C. R. Self, *Framework and Analytical Techniques: Communist Terrorist Logistics, Southern Thailand* (Menlo Park, Cal.: Stanford Research Institute, 1967).

34. Getler, p. 17.

35. Zalin B. Grant, "What Are We Doing in Thailand?," *New Republic* (May 24, 1969), p. 19.

36. *Defense Appropriations 1968*, p. 170. The best source of information on U.S. military and paramilitary programs in Thailand is U. S. Senate, Committee on Foreign Relations, Subcommittee, *United States Security Agreements and Commitments Abroad—Kingdom of Thailand, Hearings,* 91st Congress, 1st Session (Washington, D.C.: U.S. Government Printing Office, 1970), Part 3. (These hearings will hereinafter be cited as: *Commitments/Thailand*.)

37. For background on the Public Safety Program in Thailand, see *Commitments/Thailand*, p. 817; and Tep Sarmonpal, "Thailand's Front Line," *IPA Review* (October 1968), pp. 2–3. For funding information and policy guidelines, see U.S. Department of State, Agency for International Development, *Program and Project Data Presentation to the Congress for Fiscal Year 1970* (Washington, D.C., 1969), "Narrative for Thailand," pp. 7–8. (Hereinafter cited as *Project Data Presentation—Thailand*.)

38. See *Commitments/Thailand*, pp. 617–21 and 629–31; and *Project Data Presentation—Thailand*, pp. 5, 8–9. U.S.-backed civic action projects are also discussed in Grant, "What Are We Doing in Thailand?," p. 21; Chaiyo Krasin, "Military Civic Action in Thailand," *Military Review* (January 1968), pp. 75–7; and Peter Braestrup, "U.S. Helps Thailand at Village Level in Effort to Thwart Reds," *The New York Times* (December 27, 1966).

39. "U.S. Modernizing Thai Forces for Post-Vietnam," *Washington Evening Star* (May 14, 1969). See also the discussion of U.S. Special Forces activities in *Commitments/Thailand*, pp. 772–5 and 834–5.

40. "U.S. Modernizing Thai Forces for Post-Vietnam," Washington *Evening Star* (May 14, 1969).
41. For background on the assistance program, see *Commitments/Thailand,* pp. 629–30, 632–6. See also "Laird, in Bangkok, Pledges More Arms Aid in 1970," *The New York Times* (January 8, 1971).
42. Glenn P. Elliot, "Army Support Activities in Thailand," *Army Digest* (February 1970), p. 45.
43. Terence Smith, "Grim Report to SEATO Says Communist Insurgency Grows," *The New York Times* (September 11, 1968).
44. John Stirling, "Meo Revolt Smolders in Hills of Thailand," *The New York Times* (April 14, 1969).
45. *Commitments/Thailand,* pp. 627–8.
46. Robert Trumbull, "Experts Find Outlook Gloomy in Asia," *The New York Times* (January 13, 1971).
47. *Defense Appropriations 1971,* p. 750.
48. *Ibid.*
49. *Ibid.,* p. 749.
50. *Ibid.,* p. 730.
51. *Ibid.,* p. 731.
52. U.S. House of Representatives, Committee on Appropriations, Subcommittee, *Department of Defense Appropriations for 1970, Hearings,* 91st Congress, 1st Session (Washington, D.C.: U.S. Government Printing Office, 1969), Part 5, p. 815.
53. *Ibid.,* p. 816.
54. *Congressional Record,* August 12, 1969, p. S9731.
55. *Defense Appropriations 1971,* p. 726.
56. *Ibid.,* p. 728.

CHAPTER 9:
"THE FIRST LINE OF DEFENSE"

1. This chapter is an elaboration of several earlier studies published by the author. It also draws upon the research of several other individuals, among them Marilyn McNabb, Marietta Wickes, Joe Stork, and D. Gareth Porter. The successive work of McNabb, Wickes, and Stork resulted in two publications, Wickes's "The U.S. Polices the

World," *EPICA Reports* (May 1970), pp. 6–10, published by the Ecumenical Program for Inter-American Communication and Action of Washington, D.C., and Stork's "How America Builds the Global Police State," *Hard Times* (August 10–7, 1970), pp. 1–4. Porter's work appeared in "Saigon's Secret Police," *The Nation* (April 27, 1970), pp. 498–500. The author's earlier publications include "U.S. Police Operations/Latin America," *NACLA Newsletter* (January 1970), pp. 9–11, "U.S. Police Assistance Programs in Latin America," *NACLA Newsletter* (May–June 1970), pp. 28–31; and "Policing the Empire," *Commonweal* (September 18, 1970), pp. 455–61.

2. Nelson A. Rockefeller, "Quality of Life in the Americas—Report of a Presidential Mission for the Western Hemisphere," *Department of State Bulletin* (December 8, 1969), p. 503.

3. *Ibid.*, p. 506.

4. U.S. Senate, Committee on Appropriations, *Foreign Assistance Appropriations, 1965, Hearings,* 89th Congress, 2d Session (Washington, D.C.: U.S. Government Printing Office, 1964), p. 72. (Hereinafter cited as *Foreign Assistance 1965.*)

5. *Ibid.*, pp. 72–3.

6. U.S. Senate, Committee on Foreign Relations, Subcommittee on American Republics Affairs, *Survey of the Alliance for Progress.* Compilation of Studies and Hearings, 91st Congress, 1st Session (Washington, D.C.: U.S. Government Printing Office, 1969), p. 414.

7. David G. Epstein, "The Police Role in Counterinsurgency Efforts," *Journal of Criminal Law, Criminology and Police Science,* vol. 59 (1968), p. 148.

8. Robert Thompson, *Defeating Communist Insurgency* (New York: Praeger, 1966), p. 85.

9. Address by Maxwell D. Taylor, Graduation Exercise, International Police Academy, Washington, D.C., December 17, 1965. (U.S. Agency for International Development press release, same date.)

10. Cited by Holmes Alexander in "The Inside Story of Venezuela," undated article inserted in *Foreign Assistance 1965,* p. 76.

11. Barber and Ronning, p. 98.
12. All gross statistics on Office of Public Safety spending are taken from U.S. Department of State, Agency for International Development, Statistics and Reports Division, *Operations Report*. This document is published three times annually; data for the previous fiscal year are published in the edition subtitled "Data as of June 30, [year]."
13. U.S. Agency for International Development, *Program and Project Data Presentation to the Congress for Fiscal Year 1972* (Washington, D.C., 1971). (Hereinafter cited as *Project Data Presentation 1972*.)
14. A complete breakdown of the Public Safety Program budget in the Dominican Republic appears in U.S. Department of State, Agency for International Development, *Project Budget Submission FY 1969: Dominican Republic* (Washington, D.C., 1967), p. 94.
15. *Project Data Presentation 1972*.
16. A description of the process by which a country project is initiated appears in John George, "Police Assistance," an unpublished paper prepared for the Inter-University Seminar on Armed Forces and Society [n.p, n.d], pp. 18–19. George is identified as a former Public Safety Advisor to Africa.
17. USAID, *Operations Report*, Data as of June 30, 1968.
18. George, "Police Assistance," pp. 12, 16.
19. [Byron Engle], "A.I.D. Assistance to Civil Security Forces," U.S. Department of State, Agency for International Development, Office of Public Safety, press release, February 11, 1970.
20. U.S. House of Representatives, Committee on Appropriations, *Foreign Assistance and Related Agencies Appropriations for 1969, Hearings,* 90th Congress, 2d Session, 1968, Part 2, p. 1617.
21. From an unpublished Office of Public Safety report quoted by John George in "Police Assistance," pp. 25–6. George, as former Public Safety Advisor, presumably had access to the OPS files in the State Department.
22. John Bartlow Martin, *Overtaken by Events* (Garden City, N.Y.: Doubleday, 1966), p. 122.

23. U.S. Department of State, Agency for International Development, *Project Data Summary FY 1966: Dominican Republic* (Washington, D.C., 1965), p. III–92.

24. U.S. Department of State, Agency for International Development, *Project Data Summary FY 1968: Dominican Republic* (Washington, D.C., 1966), p. II–131.

25. For a discussion of the Public Safety mission in the Dominican Republic, see the interview with David Fairchild in the *NACLA Newsletter* (November 1970), p. 8. Fairchild was the Assistant Program Officer, USAID, Santo Domingo, April 1966–September 1967.

26. U.S. Department of State, Agency for International Development, *Program and Project Data Presentation to the Congress for Fiscal Year 1971* (Washington, D.C., 1970), p. 26. (Hereinafter cited as *Project Data Presentation 1971.*)

27. Paul Katz, *Republic of Colombia Police Communications Survey Report* (Washington, D.C., 1963). Published under the auspices of the U.S. Department of State, Agency for International Development, Office of Public Safety.

28. *Project Data Presentation 1971*, p. 90.

29. From an unpublished Office of Public Safety report quoted by John George, "Police Assistance," p. 23.

30. *Foreign Assistance 1965*, p. 82.

31. *Ibid.*, p. 75.

32. *Ibid.*

33. Summary of a statement by Engle as reported by Robert Thompson, "U.S. Agency 'Waylays' Communist Subversion," Los Angeles *Times* (February 10, 1963).

34. *Ibid.*

35. "A.I.D. Assistance to Civil Security Forces."

36. U.S. Department of State, Agency for International Development, Office of Public Safety, *Program Guide— Public Safety Training* (Washington, D.C., 1968), p. 1.

37. The best description of International Police Academy activities appears in David Sanford, "Agitators in a Fertilizer Factory," *New Republic* (February 11, 1967), pp. 16–18.

38. *Program Guide—Public Safety Training*, pp. 21–33.

39. See Peter T. Chew, "America's Global Peace Officers," *Kiwanis Magazine* (April 1969), p. 23.

40. *Program Guide—Public Safety Training,* pp. 15–19.
41. "The IPA Faculty," *IPA Review* (January 1967), p. 11. *IPA Review* is published by the U.S. Department of State, Agency for International Development, Office of Public Safety.
42. Sanford, "Agitators," p. 17.
43. For background on the police program of the Michigan State University Group operation in South Vietnam, see Martin Nicolaus, "The Professor, the Policeman and the Peasant," *Viet-Report* (February 1966), pp. 16–21; and Robert Scigliano and Guy H. Fox, *Technical Assistance in Vietnam—The MSU Experience* (New York: Praeger, 1965), pp. 14–23. See also the *Final Report Covering Activities of the Michigan State University Vietnam Advisory Group* . . . (Saigon, 1962), pp. 45–51.
44. U.S. Department of State, Agency for International Development, Office of Public Safety, *The Role of Public Safety in Support of the National Police of Vietnam* (Washington, D.C., 1969), pp. 3–5. (Hereinafter cited as *The Role of Public Safety.*)
45. "Foreword" to E. H. Adkins, Jr., *The Police and Resources Control in Counter-Insurgency* (Saigon, 1964), p. v. This manual was published under the auspices of the U.S. Operations Mission to Vietnam, Public Safety Division.
46. *The Role of Public Safety,* p. 5. For more on the organization and activities of the National Police, see David E. Shepherd, Jr., "Republic of Vietnam's National Police," *Military Review* (June 1971), pp. 69–74.
47. E. H. Adkins, Jr., *The Police and Resources Control,* p. 1.
48. *Project Data Presentation 1971,* p. 76.
49. *Project Data Presentation 1972.*
50. *The Role of Public Safety,* pp. 8–9.
51. Nicolaus, "The Professor, the Policeman and the Peasant," p. 19.
52. *The Role of Public Safety,* p. 11.
53. Porter, "Saigon's Secret Police," p. 500.
54. For background on Operation Phoenix, see Peter R. Kann, "The Invisible Foe: New Intelligence Push Attempts to Wipe Out Vietcong Underground," *Wall Street Journal*

(September 5, 1968); Joseph B. Treaster, "Behind the Intelligence Curtain," *The New York Times* (October 1, 1969); and James P. Sterba, "The Controversial Operation Phoenix: How It Roots Out Vietcong Suspects," *The New York Times* (February 18, 1970).

55. See Felix Belair, Jr., "U.S. Aide Defends Pacification Program in Vietnam Despite Killings of Civilians," *The New York Times* (July 20, 1971); and Tad Szulc, "U.S. Official in Saigon Denies 'Counter-Terror' Charge," *The New York Times* (February 18, 1970).

56. *The Role of Public Safety,* p. 13.

57. *Project Data Presentations 1971,* p. 78.

58. See Gloria Emerson, "Americans Find Brutality in South Vietnamese Jail," *The New York Times* (July 7, 1970); and "Tiger Cage Camp to Get New Cells," *The New York Times* (February 21, 1971).

59. *Project Data Presentations 1971,* p. 75.

60. *Project Data Presentation 1972.*

61. *The Role of Public Safety,* pp. 9–10.

62. For background on the CIA role in Phoenix, see sources cited in notes 54 and 55.

63. Rockefeller, *op. cit.,* pp. 516–17.

CHAPTER 10:
THE LATIN AMERICAN MILITARY

1. "We're Going to Lose Latin America," *U.S. News & World Report* (July 31, 1961), p. 69.

2. John Gerassi, *The Great Fear* (New York: Macmillan, 1963).

3. Nelson A. Rockefeller, "Quality of Life in the Americas— Report of a Presidential Mission for the Western Hemisphere," Department of State Bulletin (December 8, 1969), p. 507.

4. *Ibid.,* pp. 502–3.

5. Charles A. Meyer, "U.S. Military Assistance Policy Toward Latin America," *Department of State Bulletin* (August 4, 1969), p. 101.

6. U.S. House of Representatives, Committee on Foreign

Affairs, *Foreign Assistance Act of 1967, Hearings,* 90th Congress, 1st Session (Washington, D.C.: U.S. Government Printing Office, 1967), p. 536. (Hereafter cited as *Foreign Assistance 1967.*)

7. Rockefeller, pp. 502–15.

8. Lucian W. Pye, "Armies in the Process of Political Modernization," *European Journal of Sociology,* vol. 2 (1961), p. 84.

9. Lucian W. Pye, "Military Development in the New Countries," pp. 29–30.

10. *Ibid.,* p. 31.

11. Meyer, p. 101.

12. Quoted in Dan Gottlieb, "Military Dictatorships: Why Rockefeller's Wrong" *Washington Monthly* (May 1970), p. 64.

13. Edward Lieuwen, "The Latin American Military," a report incorporated into U.S. Senate, Committee on Foreign Relations, Subcommittee on American Republics Affairs, *Survey of the Alliance for Progress,* Compilation of Studies and Hearings (Washington, D.C.: U.S. Government Printing Office, 1969), p. 113.

14. *Ibid.*

15. For text of the agreement with Ecuador (which served as a model for the subsequent agreements), see *Department of State Bulletin* (March 3, 1952), pp. 336 *ff.*

16. Sam Pope Brewer, "Americas' Defense Gains Despite Foes," *The New York Times* (April 28, 1953).

17. U.S. House of Representatives, Committee on Appropriations, *Mutual Security Appropriations for 1960, Hearings,* 86th Congress, 1st Session (Washington, D.C.: U.S. Government Printing Office, 1959), p. 736.

18. U.S. Department of Defense, Office of the Assistant Secretary of Defense for International Security Affairs, *Military Assistance Facts* (Washington, D.C., 1969), pp. 16–17, 21.

19. Lieuwen, p. 115.

20. General Robert J. Wood, Address before the Los Angeles World Affairs Council, December 3, 1964, quoted in Barber and Ronning, p. 35.

21. *Foreign Assistance 1967,* p. 117.

22. *Ibid.*

23. *Ibid.,* p. 118.

24. U.S. House of Representatives, Committee on Appropriations, Subcommittee, *Foreign Assistance and Related Agencies Appropriations for 1971, Hearings,* 91st Congress, 2d Session (Washington, D.C.: U.S. Government Printing Office, 1970), Part 1, p. 389. (Hereinafter cited as *Foreign Assistance 1971.*)

25. Lieuwen, p. 117.

26. *Foreign Assistance 1967,* p. 540.

27. Joseph Novitski, "Latin Lands Turning to Europe for Arms," *The New York Times* (May 4, 1971).

28. *Foreign Assistance 1971,* pp. 388–9.

29. Benjamin Welles, "Nixon Moving to Meet Latin Pleas for More Arms Aid," *The New York Times* (May 19, 1971).

30. U.S. Department of Defense, Office of the Assistant Secretary of Defense for International Security Affairs, *Military Assistance and Foreign Military Sales Facts* (Washington, D.C., 1970), pp. 24–5.

31. Raymond J. Barrett, "Arms Dilemma for the Developing World," *Military Review* (April 1970), p. 33.

32. "Facts Behind U.S. Policy Regarding Sale of Military Aircraft to Latin America," U.S. Department of State press release, October 30, 1967.

33. Barrett, p. 35.

34. Rockefeller, p. 516.

35. *Ibid.,* pp. 517–18.

36. Meyer, p. 102.

37. U.S. House of Representatives, Committee on Appropriations, Subcommittee, *Foreign Operations Appropriations for 1964, Hearings,* 88th Congress, 1st Session (Washington, D.C.: U.S. Government Printing Office, 1963), Part 2, p. 84.

38. U.S. Department of the Army, Office of the Deputy Chief of Staff for Military Operations, Civil Affairs Directorate, Civic Action Branch, *Military Civic Action* (Washington, D.C., 1963), p. 1.

39. Barber and Ronning, pp. 54–63.

40. *Military Civic Action,* p. 2.

41. *Ibid.*, p. 1.
42. Pye, "Armies in Modernization," p. 84; "Military Development in the New Countries," p. 31.
43. *Military Civic Action,* p. 3. See also Guy J. Pauker, *Notes on Non-Military Measures in Control of Insurgency* (Santa Monica, Cal.: RAND Corporation, 1962), pp. 1–6; and Edward B. Glick, *Peaceful Conflict: The Non-Military Use of the Military* (Harrisburg, Pa.: Stackpole Books, 1967), pp. 158–65.
44. *Military Civic Action,* p. 3; Glick, p. 68.
45. *Congressional Record,* May 25, 1961, p. H8880, as quoted in Barber and Ronning, p. 73.
46. Remarks of Dean Rusk at the dedication of the Inter-American Defense College, U.S. Department of State press release, October 9, 1962.
47. *Military Civic Action,* pp. 4–5.
48. *Ibid.,* pp. 6–10.
49. Barber and Ronning, pp. 194, 228–9.
50. U.S. Army Southern Command, *Final Report: Fourth Conference of the American Armies* (Fort Amador, Panama Canal Zone, 1963).
51. Barber and Ronning, pp. 199–200.
52. American University, Center for Research in Social Systems, *Work Program, Fiscal Year 1967* (Washington, D.C., 1966), p. 13.
53. *Foreign Assistance 1967,* pp. 540–1.
54. Barber and Ronning, pp. 131–2.
55. *Fourth Conference of the American Armies,* p. 70.
56. *Foreign Assistance 1971,* p. 389.
57. U.S. House of Representatives, Committee on Appropriations, Subcommittee, *Foreign Operations Appropriations for 1963, Hearings,* 87th Congress, 2d Session (Washington, D.C.: U.S. Government Printing Office, 1962), Part 1, p. 359.
58. *Foreign Assistance 1971,* p. 391.
59. *Foreign Assistance 1967,* p. 179.
60. Robert S. McNamara, testimony before Senate Appropriations Committee, April 20, 1966, as quoted in Lieuwen, p. 120.

61. Lieuwen, p. 121–2.
62. *Foreign Assistance 1971,* p. 391.
63. Rockefeller, p. 517.
64. For background on USARSA, see U.S. House of Representatives, Committee on Foreign Affairs, Subcommittee on National Security Policy and Scientific Developments, *Special Study Mission to Latin America on Military Assistance Training* . . . . Report, 91st Congress, 2d Session (Washington, D.C.: U.S. Government Printing Office, 1970), pp. 27–8. (Hereinafter cited as *Military Assistance Training.*) See also "U.S. Army School of the Americas," *Military Review* (April 1970), pp. 88–93; and "Bridge of the Americas," *Army Digest* (September 1968), pp. 12–14.
65. "U.S. Army School of the Americas," pp. 90–1.
66. "Bridge of the Americas," p. 14.
67. For background on IAAFA, see "U.S. Air Forces Southern Command," *Air Force* (May 1971), pp. 110–11; and *Military Assistance Training,* pp. 25–7.
68. Barber and Ronning, pp. 162–3.
69. Cited in "The Inter-American Defense College," *Military Review* (April 1970), pp. 20–1.
70. "Inter-American Defense College," pp. 20–7.
71. Institute of International Education, *Military Assistance Training Programs of the U.S. Government* (New York: 1964), pp. 26–8.
72. Barber and Ronning, p. 149.
73. Edwin Martin, "Communist Subversion in the Western Hemisphere—Continued," A Statement Before the Latin American Subcommittee of the House Foreign Affairs Committee, February 18, 1963, *Department of State Bulletin* (March 18, 1963), pp. 406–7.
74. Barber and Ronning, pp. 152–4.
75. Quoted in Philippe Nourry, "Camping Tonight, Camping Tonight," *Atlas* (May 1968), p. 19. (Translation from *Le Figaro,* Paris).
76. Geoffrey Kemp, *Some Relationships Between U.S. Military Training in Latin America and Weapons Acquisition Patterns, 1959–1969* (Cambridge, Mass.: MIT Center for International Studies, 1970), pp. 16–56.

77. St. George, "How the U.S. Got Che."

78. *Military Assistance Training Report,* pp. 3–20. See also J. Bina Machado, "The Making of Brazilian Staff Officers," *Military Review* (April 1970), pp. 75–81.

79. "U.S.A.I.D. in the Dominican Republic—An Inside View," *NACLA Newsletter,* vol. 4 (November 1970), pp. 6–7.

80. Joseph C. Goulden, "A Real Good Relationship," *The Nation* (June 1, 1970), p. 646.

81. *Military Assistance Training Report,* pp. 9–20.

82. See John M. Goshko, "Latins Blame the United States for Military Coups," Washington *Post* (February 5, 1968).

83. *Military Assistance Training Report,* pp. 7–8.

84. *Ibid.,* p. 5.

CHAPTER 11:
THE GREAT SOUTH ASIAN WAR

1. This chapter is based on a number of earlier articles by the author, particularly "The Great South Asian War," *The Nation* (March 9, 1970), pp. 265–73; "The Sun Never Sets on America's Empire," *Commonweal* (May 22, 1970), pp. 239–43; and, "The Mercenarization of the Third World," *NACLA Newsletter,* vol. 4 (November 1970), pp. 11–12.

2. For background on the growth of America's military involvement in Southeast Asia, see Committee of Concerned Asian Scholars, *The Indochina Story* (New York: Bantam Books, 1970); Marvin and Susan Gettleman and Lawrence and Carol Kaplan, *Conflict in Indochina* (New York: Random House, 1970); and George McT. Kahin and John W. Lewis, *The United States in Vietnam* (New York: Dell, 1967).

3. James D. Atkinson, "Who Will Dominate the Strategic Indian Ocean Area in the 1970's?," *Navy* (September 1968), inserted in the *Congressional Record,* October 14, 1968, p. E8998.

4. The author's understanding of the Pacific Basin as an economic unit developed through study of research materials prepared by the Pacific Studies Center (PSC) in East Palo Alto, California; *Pacific Basin Reports* in San

Francisco; and the West Coast Office of *Leviathan* magazine, also in San Francisco. For a pioneering study of this subject, see Peter Wiley, "Vietnam and the Pacific Rim Strategy," *Leviathan* (June 1969), pp. 4–7. Additional documentation has been published in the PSC newsletter, *Pacific Research and World Empire Telegram*, and in *Pacific Basin Reports*, a bimonthly survey of economic developments in the region.

5. "The Pacific Basin," *Forbes* (November 1, 1970), p. 28.

6. Rudolph A. Peterson, in *California Business Magazine* (September–October 1968), as quoted in Wiley, p. 7.

7. *Direction of Trade* (March 1970), pp. 87–8. *Direction of Trade* is published by the International Monetary Fund and the International Bank for Reconstruction and Development.

8. For more on U.S. trade with Asia, see "World Trade Outlook," *International Commerce* (July 14, 1969), especially pp. 35–54. *International Commerce* is published by the U.S. Department of Commerce.

9. David T. Devlin and George R. Kruer, "The International Investment Position of the United States," *Survey of Current Business*, vol. 50 (October 1970), pp. 21–38. *Survey of Current Business* is published by the U. S. Department of Commerce.

10. For background on the offshore oil discoveries, see Gabriel Kolko, "Oiling the Escalator," *New Republic* (March 13, 1971), pp. 18–20; Louis Kraar, "Report from Southeast Asia," *Fortune* (March 1970), pp. 45–6; "Offshore Oil Fever," *Pacific Basin Reports* (February 1971), pp. 35–45; Selig S. Harrison, "Oil Rush in the East China Sea Becomes a Three-Nation Issue," Washington *Post* (October 14, 1970); and "Four Major Oil Companies Plan South Korean Offshore Search," *The New York Times* (March 16, 1970).

11. Kraar, p. 45.

12. Kolko, "Oiling the Escalator," pp. 19–20.

13. Quoted in *Pacific Basin Reports* (February 1971), p. 35. Rockefeller made the prediction at a 1970 "Asian financial forum" sponsored by his bank in Singapore.

14. T. B. Millar, "The Indian and Pacific Oceans: Some Strate-

gic Considerations," *Adelphi Papers,* No. 57 (May 1969), p. 6.

15. Rocco M. Paone, "The Soviet Threat in the Indian Ocean," *Military Review* (December 1970), p. 49.

16. U.S. Department of Defense, *The 1970 Defense Budget and Defense Program for Fiscal Years 1970–74,* A Statement by Secretary of Defense Clark M. Clifford (Washington, D.C., 1969), p. 11. (Hereinafter cited as *Defense Budget 1970.*)

17. Quoted in "Laird Tells U.S. Role After Viet," San Francisco *Examiner,* April 13, 1971.

18. *Defense Budget 1970,* p. 76.

19. See John W. Finney, "Nixon: What Does His 'Asian Doctrine' Mean?," *The New York Times* (January 11, 1970); and Saville R. Davis, "Limited Helping Role for U.S. in Asia?," *Christian Science Monitor* (July 26, 1969).

20. Richard Nixon, *U.S. Foreign Policy in the 1970's,* Report to the Congress, February 18, 1970 (Washington, D.C.: U.S. Government Printing Office, 1970), pp. 55–6.

21. U.S. Senate, Committee on Foreign Relations, *Perspective on Asia: The New U.S. Doctrine and Southeast Asia,* Report of Senator Mike Mansfield, 91st Congress, 1st Session (Washington, D.C.: U.S. Government Printing Office, 1969), p. 3.

22. *Foreign Assistance 1971,* p. 307.

23. Laird's clarification was made at a Pentagon press conference on January 20, 1970. Quoted by Murrey Marder, "Nixon Doctrine: Wider Scope," *Washington Post* (January 21, 1971).

24. For background on the lowland/highland rivalry in Vietnam, see Hickey and Bernard B. Fall, *The Two Vietnams: A Political and Military Analysis* (New York: Praeger, 1964), revised edition.

25. Fall, *The Two Vietnams,* pp. 148–52.

26. Donald Duncan, *The New Legions* (New York: Pocket Books, 1967), p. 156.

27. *Ibid.,* p. 157.

28. Prouty, "The Secret Team and the Games They Play," p. 9.

29. Quoted in "The Case of the Green Berets," *Newsweek* (August 25, 1969), p. 31.

30. Peter Dale Scott, "Laos: The Story Nixon Won't Tell," *New York Review of Books* (April 9, 1970).

31. For background on the Green Beret mission in Vietnam, see "The Case of the Green Berets," pp. 26–33; L. Fletcher Prouty, "Green Berets and the CIA," *New Republic* (August 30, 1969), pp. 9–10; and Horace Sutton, "The Ghostly War of the Green Berets," *Saturday Review* (October 18, 1969), pp. 23 *ff*.

32. Gloria Emerson, "Isolated Outpost is Home to Montagnard Families," *The New York Times* (August 10, 1970).

33. *Ibid.*

34. Quoted in George McArthur, "Green Berets—Saying Goodby to Themselves," *Los Angeles Times* (February 25, 1971).

35. "Green Berets, in War Since '62, Being Phased Out This Year," *The New York Times* (July 12, 1970).

36. "U.S. Sends Lon Nol Mercenary Units," *The New York Times* (May 4, 1970).

37. T. Jeff Williams, "Cambodian Mercenaries Head Biggest Operation," Washington *Evening Star* (May 11, 1970).

38. Henry Kamm, "U.S. Runs a Secret Laotian Army," *The New York Times* (October 26, 1969).

39. Michael Malloy, "How the U.S. Created the Secret Army in Laos," *National Observer* (November 17, 1969).

40. Jack Anderson, "No End Seen to the Hidden War in Laos," Washington *Post* (July 31, 1970).

41. Quoted in Peter R. Kann, "The Secret War," *Wall Street Journal* (December 18, 1969).

42. Henry Kamm, "Clandestine Army Turned Tide in Vital Region," *The New York Times* (October 28, 1969).

43. U.S. Senate, Committee on Foreign Relations, Subcommittee, *United States Security Agreements and Commitments Abroad—Kingdom of Laos,* Hearings, 91st Congress, 1st Session (Washington, D.C.: U.S. Government Printing Office, 1970), Part 2, p. 553. (Hereinafter cited as *Commitments/Laos.*)

44. *Ibid.*, p. 371.

45. "The Labyrinthine War," *Far Eastern Economic Review* (April 16, 1970).

46. *Commitments/Laos,* p. 527.

47. *Ibid.,* pp. 528–36.

48. U.S. Senate, Committee on Foreign Relations, *Laos: April 1970,* Staff report, 92nd Congress, 1st Session, 1971.

49. Articles based on the unauthorized visit to Long Cheng include Jack Foisie, "Reporters See Many Flights Leave Secret Base in Laos," Washington *Post* (February 25, 1970); and T. D. Allman, " 'Secret' U.S.-Run Base Deep in Laos Seems Placid," *The New York Times* (March 6, 1970).

50. Edward M. Kennedy, "The Forgotten Casualties," *Commonweal* (October 30, 1970), p. 119.

51. "The Secret U.S. Losses in Laos," San Francisco *Chronicle.*

52. Michael Morrow, "Report on Burma Rebel Training," San Francisco *Chronicle* (October 16, 1970); "CIA's Spy Teams Inside Red China," San Francisco *Chronicle* (September 4, 1970).

53. U.S. Department of Defense, Office of the Assistant Secretary of Defense for International Security Affairs, *Military Assistance and Foreign Military Sales Facts* (Washington, D.C., 1971), p. 10. (Hereinafter cited as *Military Assistance & Sales 1970.*)

54. Data from John N. Irwin II, "New Approaches to International Security," *Department of State Bulletin* (February 22, 1971), p. 226.

55. U.S. Agency for International Development, Office of Statistics and Reports, *U.S. Overseas Loans and Grants, July 1, 1945–June 30, 1970* (Washington, D.C., 1971).

56. U.S. Department of Defense, Office of the Assistant Secretary of Defense for International Security Affairs, *Military Assistance Facts* (Washington, D.C., 1969), p. 18; data for 1969 and 1970 only from *Military Assistance & Sales 1971,* p. 12. For a discussion of such aid, see Peter Grose, "$3.4-Billion Surplus Arms Given to Allies in 19 Years," *The New York Times* (April 1, 1970).

57. For data on transfers of equipment, see James P. Sterba, "Main U.S. Aim: Training Vietnamese," *The New York*

Times (October 4, 1970); for data on 1972 Pentagon aid to Vietnam, see U.S. Senate, Committee on Foreign Relations, *Foreign Assistance Legislation, Fiscal Year 1972, Hearings,* 92d Congress, 1st Session, 1971, pp. 381–4.

58. *Military Assistance & Sales 1970,* p. 17.

59. For discussion of U.S. training programs, see: Drew Middleton, "Thousands of Foreign Military Men Studying in U.S.," *The New York Times;* and Richard Homan, "Vietnamization Training Up," Washington *Post* (February 23, 1970).

60. *Commitments/Thailand,* p. 657. For discussion, see Richard Halloran, "U.S. Costs to Get Thais to Join War Put at $1-Billion," *The New York Times* (December 1, 1969); and John W. Finney, "U.S. Pays Thailand $50-Million a Year for Vietnam Aid," *The New York Times* (June 8, 1970).

61. Richard Halloran, "Korea's Vietnam Troops Cost the U.S. $1-Billion," *The New York Times* (September 13, 1970).

62. U.S. Senate, Committee on Foreign Relations, Subcommittee, *United States Security Agreements and Commitments Abroad—Republic of Korea,* Hearings, 91st Congress, 2d Session (Washington, D.C.: U.S. Government Printing Office, 1970), Part 6, pp. 1549–50. (Hereinafter cited as *Commitments/Korea.*)

63. *Ibid.,* pp. 1545, 1570–3.

64. See Tad Szulc, "U.S. Outlays for Vietnam Aid Korea and Philippines," *The New York Times* (January 26, 1970).

65. *Commitments/Korea,* p. 1542.

66. *Ibid.,* p. 1565.

67. *Ibid.,* p. 1552.

68. Ralph Blumenthal, "U.S. Officer Says Thai Unit in War Is Worth the Cost," *The New York Times* (December 3, 1969).

69. T. D. Allman, "Declining U.S. Aid Brings First Crisis of War to Thais," Washington *Post* (July 19, 1970).

70. *Congressional Record,* June 26, 1970, p. S10010.

71. U.S. Department of Defense, *Fiscal Year 1971 Defense Program and Budget,* A Statement by Secretary of Defense Melvin R. Laird (Washington, D.C., 1970), p. 57.

72. John W. Finney, "Arms for Cambodia Voted," *The New York Times* (December 23, 1970).

73. Bernard D. Nossiter, "U.S. Arms Aid Up 25% in '71 to $6.7 Billion," Washington *Post* (February 3, 1971).

74. "Increased Foreign Military Sales Inescapable Under Nixon Doctrine," *Armed Forces Journal* (November 2, 1970), p. 22.

75. *Army Research and Development Newsmagazine* (June–July, 1969).

76. Vice President Spiro Agnew, Arrival Statement, Canberra, Australia, January 10, 1970, recorded in "Vice President Agnew Visits Asia," *Department of State Bulletin* (February 23, 1970), pp. 198–200.

77. "Agnew, in Canberra, Holds News Parley," *The New York Times* (January 15, 1970).

78. Quoted in James M. Naughton, "Agnew Gives Australia Partnership Vow," *The New York Times* (January 14, 1970).

79. John Gorton, quoted in Robert Trumbull, "Australian Build-up Expected in Asia," *The New York Times* (December 28, 1968).

80. "Australia Vital Link in U.S. Spy Satellite Net," Los Angeles *Times* (December 13, 1970). See also Bob Cooksey, "Beyond Pine Gap—U.S. Bases in Australia and New Zealand," *Dissent* (Melbourne, Winter 1970), pp. 3–6.

81. Robert Trumbull, "Back of the Outback, a Vital U.S. Radio Base," *The New York Times* (April 12, 1969).

82. See Trumbull, "Australian Build-up Expected"; David Winder, "Defense Gap Galvanizes Commonwealth in Pacific," *Christian Science Monitor* (June 18, 1969); and "Australia, New Zealand Reassure Malaysia, Singapore," *SEATO Record*, pp. 18–19. *SEATO Record* is published by SEATO Headquarters in Bangkok, Thailand.

83. *Defense Budget 1970*, pp. 11, 76.

84. T. B. Millar, "The Indian and Pacific Oceans," p. 2.

85. Congressional Quarterly Service, *Global Defense: U.S. Military Commitments Abroad* (Washington, D.C., 1969), pp. 37–8. For a list of U.S. bases in Asia, see *NACLA Newsletter*, vol. 4 (October 1970), pp. 18–22.

86. See John Mecklin, "Building by the Billion in Vietnam," *Fortune* (September 1966), pp. 113–15 *ff.*

87. For a discussion of the base at Khorat, see John Hughes, "Could Thailand Be the Next Vietnam?" *Christian Science Monitor* (July 23, 1969).

88. See James P. Sterba, "4 Berets Linked to a Secret Unit," *The New York Times* (August 15, 1969); and Joseph B. Treaster, "Behind the Intelligence Curtain," *The New York Times* (October 1, 1969).

89. Kamm, "U.S. Runs a Secret Laotian Army."

90. See Henry Kamm, "Joint U.S.-Laotian Center Coordinates Air Strikes," *The New York Times* (March 8, 1970); and Henry S. Bradsher, "Udorn Air Base in Thailand U.S. Mainstay in Laos Fight," *Washington Star* (March 15, 1970).

91. "New Defense Line in the Pacific," *U.S. News & World Report*, August 7, 1967, pp. 52–3.

92. See Neil Sheehan, "U.S. Said to Keep Nerve Gas Abroad at Major Bases," *The New York Times* (July 19, 1969); George C. Wilson, "Nerve Gas Stored on Okinawa," *Washington Post* (July 23, 1969); and, Robert Keatley, "Okinawa Mishap Bares Overseas Deployment of Chemical Weapons," *Wall Street Journal* (July 18, 1969).

93. David K. Willis, "U.S. and Japan Head for Okinawa Showdown," *Christian Science Monitor* (September 11, 1969); and Takashi Oka, "Sato Stakes Career on Return of Okinawa to Japan," *The New York Times* (November 8, 1969). For the text of the Nixon-Sato communique on the reversion of Okinawa, see *Department of State Bulletin,* December 15, 1969, pp. 555–8.

94. See Clyde H. Farnsworth, "Rogers and Aichi Report Final Agreement on Okinawa Treaty," *The New York Times* (June 10, 1971).

95. See "Micronesia Viewed for U.S. Bases," *Christian Science Monitor* (April 29, 1969); William D. Hartley, "Micronesia Stirs Concern in U.S.," *Wall Street Journal* (October 15, 1969); "Micronesia Eyed for U.S. Bases," *Honolulu Star-Bulletin* (April 30, 1969).

96. "New Defense Line in the Pacific," p. 52.

97. "U.S. Asks Thailand to Receive B52s," San Francisco *Examiner* (October 14, 1970).

98. "Taiwan Extends Air Base Runway," *The New York Times* (July 31, 1970).

99. Trumbull, "Back of the Outback."

100. See "U.S. and Britain Plan Indian Ocean Base," *The New York Times* (December 16, 1970); Robert C. Toth, "U.S., Britain to Build Base in Indian Ocean," Los Angeles *Times* (December 15, 1970); and Robert D. Heinl, Jr., "U.S. Flag over Diego Garcia: Challenging the Soviet Fleet," *Armed Forces Journal* (February 1, 1971).

101. T. B. Millar, "The Indian and Pacific Oceans," p. 15.

102. Quoted in Heinl, "Diego Garcia."

103. "U.S. Navy Shows Interest in Singapore for Repair Work," *The New York Times* (July 6, 1969).

104. James M. Naughton, "Agnew Hints at Aid to Four Nations," *The New York Times* (January 10, 1970).

105. "U.S. Asks Thailand to Receive B52s."

106. For background on the role of Japan in American defense strategy, see these two excellent articles: Herbert P. Bix, "The Security Treaty System and the Japanese Military-Industrial Complex," *Bulletin of the Concerned Asian Scholars*, vol. 2 (January 1970), pp. 30–53; and, Jim Shoch, "Pacific Partnership: How Japan and the United States are Joining Hands to Dominate Asia," *Pacific Research & World Empire Telegram* (November–December 1969), pp. 2–17.

107. Richard M. Nixon, "Asia After Vietnam," *Foreign Affairs*, October 1967, p. 120.

108. *Department of State Bulletin*, June 23, 1969, p. 531.

109. For background on Japan's military capability, see Bix, "Security Treaty System," pp. 30–3; "How Japan Is Reviving Its Military Machine," *U.S. News & World Report* (October 27, 1969), pp. 91–2; William Beecher, "Japan, 25 Years After Surrender, Builds Protective Might," *The New York Times* (August 15, 1970); and David K. Willis, "Japan Building Up Its Defenses," *Christian Science Monitor* (August 21, 1969).

110. See Beecher, "Japan Builds Protective Might"; Willis, "Japan Building Defenses"; Philip Shabecoff, "Japanese

Budget for 1970 Includes the Sharpest Increase in Defense Spending Since World War II," *The New York Times* (January 25, 1970); and Selig S. Harrison, "Japan Arms Makers Push Buildup," Washington *Post* (November 7, 1969).

111. See discussion of "The Japanese Military-Industrial Complex" in Bix, pp. 33–42.

112. Quoted by Harrison, "Japan Arms Makers."

113. See Takashi Oka, "Japan's Defense Plans Call for Naval Expansion," *The New York Times* (August 20, 1969); Alex Campbell, "Sun Up in Asia," *New Republic,* July 5, 1969, pp. 16–18; and "Japanese Warships Pay a Visit to Singapore," *The New York Times* (October 6, 1969).

RESEARCH
GUIDE

While many books have been written on the strategy and tactics of guerrilla and counterguerrilla warfare, very little has been written on the actual preparations undertaken by the United States for engaging in such conflicts. With the exception of John S. Tompkins' *The Weapons of World War III*, no book explores the development of counterinsurgency tactics and techniques in the early 1960's, and recent chronicles of the Vietnam war have been exclusively concerned with the historical chain of events that led to the American intervention. An investigation of U.S. planning for future Vietnams therefore involves the examination of a great number of unrelated documents in order to assemble those needed for such a study. While many of the relevant documents are of a highly specialized nature or otherwise difficult to locate in an ordinary library, they are not necessarily secret or closed to public inspection. Since an important objective of this book is to demonstrate that concerned civilians can acquire the data needed to conduct a serious investigation of military policies, we are including here a short guide to research on the U.S. defense establishment.*

* This guide has been adapted from the military section of the *NACLA Research Methodology Guide*, published by the North

HEARINGS

The basic source of information on U.S. military strategy and weapons development is the annual series of hearings held by Congressional committees on the Department of Defense (DoD) budget. These hearings are usually held in the spring, and the transcripts are published in the summer or fall. Copies are available from the Congressional committees themselves, from one's own Senators and Representatives, and from the Government Printing Office; they are also stored in Government Depository Libraries (usually the largest municipal and/or university library in each state—a complete list of these libraries appears in the *Monthly Catalog of United States Government Publications*).

Four sets of budget hearings are held each year: in the Senate, hearings are held on *Authorizations for Military Procurement* by the Armed Services Committee and on *Department of Defense Appropriations* by the DoD Subcommittee of the Committee on Appropriations; in the House, hearings are held on *Military Posture and Legislation to Authorize Appropriations* by the Armed Services Committee and on *Department of Defense Appropriations* by the DoD Subcommittee of the Committee on Appropriations.

Special hearings on military matters are periodically held by various Congressional committees and subcommitees, and are often a valuable source of information. For a complete list of such documents, consult the *Monthly Catalog of United States Government Publications* (available in most libraries).

MILITARY PERIODICALS

After the Congressional hearings, the most valuable sources of information on military affairs are the various military peri-

American Congress on Latin America. Readers who plan a serious study of the military are advised to obtain the *NACLA Guide* (available for $1.25 from NACLA, Box 57, Cathedral Station, New York, N.Y. 10025, and from NACLA–West, Box 226, Berkeley, California 94701).

odicals published by the Department of Defense, the military associations, and private concerns. Most of these magazines are indexed in the *Air University Library Index of Military Periodicals,* available in most large libraries. Pentagon periodicals are sold by the U.S. Government Printing Office (GPO), Washington, D.C. 20402. Among the most consistently useful military periodicals are:

Air Force: monthly journal of the Air Force Association (1750 Pennsylvania Avenue N.W., Washington, D.C. 20006). Subscription included in annual membership fee of $7.00.

Airman: official monthly publication of the U.S. Air Force. Available from the GPO for $7.50 per year.

Armed Forces Journal: published monthly by Army and Navy Journal, Inc. (1710 Connecticut Avenue N.W., Washington, D.C. 20009). Annual subscription is $10.00.

Army: monthly journal of the Association of the U.S. Army (1529 18th Street N.W., Washington, D.C. 20006). Subscription included with annual membership fee of $7.50.

Army Research and Development Newsmagazine: published bimonthly by the Army Research Office. Available from the GPO for $2.25 per year.

Aviation Week and Space Technology: published weekly by McGraw-Hill Publications (subscription address: *Aviation Week,* P.O. Box 430, Hightstown, N.J. 08520). Annual subscription is $10.00.

Defense Management Journal: published quarterly by the Office of the Assistant Secretary of Defense for Installations and Logistics. Available from the GPO for $1.50 per year.

Marine Corps Gazette: monthly journal of the Marine Corps Association (Box 1775, Marine Corps Base, Quantico, Virginia 22134). Subscription included with annual membership fee of $5.00.

Military Review: monthly journal of the U.S. Army Command and General Staff College (Fort Leavenworth, Kansas 66027). Available from the College for $5.00 per year. (Spanish and Portuguese editions are also available.)

Ordnance: bimonthly journal of the American Ordnance Association (Union Trust Building, 740 15th Street N.W., Washington, D.C. 20005). Subscription included with annual membership fee of $7.00.

Seapower: monthly journal of the Navy League of the United States (818 18th Street N.W., Washington, D.C. 20006). Annual subscription is $3.00.

Soldiers: official monthly publication of the U.S. Army. Available from the GPO for $9.50 per year.

U.S. Naval Institute Proceedings: monthly journal of the U.S. Naval Institute (Annapolis, Maryland 21402). Annual subscription is $12.50.

DEFENSE POSTURE AND ORGANIZATION

A general survey of the status of U.S. military forces and of planned weapons systems appears in the annual "posture statement" of the Secretary of Defense, presented to the House Armed Services Committee at the start of each year's hearings on the DoD budget. The posture statement is usually reproduced in the DoD budget hearings and is sold separately by the Government Printing Office. The Department of Defense also publishes an *Annual Report,* which is also available from the GPO (these reports usually appear several years late—the 1966 edition, for instance, went on sale in 1970). All major DoD agencies are identified and described in the *U.S. Government Organization Manual,* published annually and distributed by the GPO.

Among books on the U.S. military apparatus, attention should be paid to the "Praeger Library of U.S. Government Departments and Agencies," published by Frederick A. Praeger, Inc. (111 Fourth Avenue, New York, N.Y. 10003). Titles in this series include: *The Department of Defense* by C. W. Borklund; *The United States Navy* by Daniel J. Carrison; *The United States Marine Corps* by James A. Donovan, Jr.; *The United States Air Force* by Monro MacCloskey; and *The United States Army* by Vernon Pizer. Each volume in this series contains a short history of the service and a general description of its organization. Praeger also publishes *A Guide to National Defense* by Patrick W. Powers, which provides an overview of the national security establishment.

Each year (usually in the spring), *Air Force* magazine publishes an "Almanac Issue," which identifies the major U.S. Air Force commands and agencies, and describes most U.S. military aircraft. *Army* magazine publishes an annual "Green Book," usually in the fall, which identifies and describes the major Army commands. The Institute for Strategic Studies (18 Adam Street, London, England) publishes *The Military Balance,* an annual survey of the military capabilities of the major nations.

WEAPONS SYSTEMS

In general, the best sources of information on new weapons systems are the hearings and periodicals listed above (see in particular the Research and Development section of the hearings before the House Committee on Appropriations). *Armed Forces Journal* and *Aviation Week* are especially useful for studying the debates on proposed weapons systems, while *Ordnance* often features detailed descriptions of selected military hardware. Three valuable reference books published annually in England, and available in libraries here, are: *Jane's Fighting Ships, Jane's Aircraft,* and *Jane's Weapons Systems.* Chemical, biological, incendiary, and antipersonnel weapons are described in *The Weapons of Counterinsurgency,* available for $1.00 from NARMIC (160 N. 15th Street, Philadelphia, Pennsylvania 19102).

Technical information on standard U.S. military equipment is contained in Army, Navy, Air Force and Marine Corps field manuals, technical manuals, and training manuals. These documents, if not classified, are listed in the *Monthly Catalog of U.S. Government Publications,* and are available from the Government Printing Office. These manuals are also stored in the Government Depository Libraries, listed in the *Monthly Catalog.*

MILITARY AID AND ARMS SALES

Basic statistical data on U.S. military assistance and arms sales are provided in *Military Assistance and Foreign Military Sales*

Facts (published annually by the Office of the Assistant Secretary of Defense for International Security Affairs, The Pentagon, Washington, D.C. 20301), and *U.S. Overseas Loans and Grants* (published annually by the Office of Statistics and Reports, Agency for International Development, U.S. Department of State, Washington, D.C. 20523). Military assistance procedures and regulations are contained in *Information and Guidance on Military Assistance Grant Aid and Foreign Military Sales* (distributed by the Evaluation Division, Directorate of Military Assistance, U.S. Air Force, The Pentagon, Washington, D.C. 20330).

The most comprehensive description of the military aid program appears in the annual hearings on Foreign Assistance appropriations. In the House, hearings are held on the *Foreign Assistance Act* by the Committee on Foreign Affairs and on *Foreign Assistance Appropriations* by the Committee on Appropriations. In the Senate, hearings are held on *Foreign Assistance Appropriations* by the Committee on Appropriations, and on *Foreign Assistance Legislation* by the Committee on Foreign Relations. Special hearings on military assistance to particular countries or regions are also held from time to time— consult the *Monthly Catalog of U.S. Government Publications* for titles.

A compendium of military assistance data is contained in *U.S. Military and Police Operations in the Third World,* available for 60¢ from NACLA (Box 226, Berkeley, California 94701, and Box 57, Cathedral Station, New York, N. Y. 10025). Basic books on U.S. military assistance and arms sales include: Harold A. Hovey, *United States Military Assistance: A Study of Policies and Practices* (New York: Praeger, 1965); and George Thayer, *The War Business: The International Trade in Armaments* (New York: Simon and Schuster, 1969). For a more detailed analysis, see the studies published by the "Arms Control Project" of MIT's Center for International Studies (for a price list of these studies, write: Center for International Studies, Massachusetts Institute of Technology, Cambridge, Massachusetts 02139). Much data is also contained in *The Arms Trade With the Third World,* published in 1971 by the Stockholm International Peace Research Institute.

**WHERE TO GO
FOR MORE INFORMATION**

"Establishment" Organizations:

U.S. Department of Defense, Office of the Assistant Secretary of Defense for Public Affairs (The Pentagon, Washington, D.C. 20301; telephone 202–OX–7–5131). This office will answer questions pertaining to DoD affairs and supply copies of DoD press releases.

American Ordnance Association (Union Trust Building, 740 15th Street N.W., Washington, D.C. 20005). The official lobby for the military-industrial complex. Publishes *Ordnance* magazine.

Association of the United States Army (1529 18th Street N.W., Washington, D.C. 20006). Publishes *Army* magazine.

The Air Force Association (1750 Pennsylvania Avenue N.W., Washington, D.C. 20006). Publishes *Air Force* magazine.

The Navy League of the United States (818 18th Street N.W., Washington, D.C. 20006). Publishes *Seapower* magazine.

The Marine Corps Association (Box 1775 Marine Corps Base, Quantico, Virginia 22134). Publishes *Marine Corps Gazette*.

National Security Industrial Association (Suite 700, Union Trust Building, 740 15th Street N.W., Washington, D.C. 20005). Another lobbyist for the military-industrial complex. Publishes various reports available to the public (write for price list).

National Strategy Information Center (130 East 67th Street, New York, N.Y. 10021). Publishes a series of studies on strategy questions (write for price list).

Institute for Strategic Studies (18 Adam Street, London WC2, England). Publishes *The Military Balance,* an annual survey of comparative military strengths; *The Strategic Survey,* a yearbook on strategy questions; and the *Adelphi Papers,* a series of essays on military matters. (Write the Institute directly for a complete list of its publications.)

Stockholm International Peace Research Institute (SIPRI, Sveavägen 166, S-113 46 Stockholm, Sweden). Publishes the

SIPRI Yearbook of World Armamenents and Disarmament and other studies (write for price list).

"Anti-Establishment" Organizations:

Africa Research Group (P.O. Box 213, Cambridge, Massachusetts 02138). Publishes a series of studies on neocolonialism in Africa (write for price list).

National Action/Research on the Military-Industrial Complex (NARMIC) of the American Friends Service Committee (160 N. 15th Street, Philadelphia, Pennsylvania 19102; telephone: 215–LO–3–9372). Publishes studies and handbooks on the military, and assists local antimilitary projects (write or call for information).

North American Congress on Latin America (NACLA, Box 226, Berkeley, California 94701, and Box 57, Cathedral Station, New York, N. Y. 10025). Publishes the *NACLA Newsletter* and studies on U.S. military, economic, and cultural operations in Latin America and the Third World (write for price list).

Pacific Studies Center (1963 University Avenue, East Palo Alto, California 94303). Publishes *Pacific Research and World Empire Telegram* and other studies on imperialism in the Pacific Basin area (write for price list).

Committee of Concerned Asian Scholars (9 Sutter Street, San Francisco, California 94104). Publishes the *Bulletin of Concerned Asian Scholars* and other studies.

RESEARCH
BIBLIOGRAPHY

GENERAL:
STUDIES OF REVOLUTIONARY
WARFARE AND COUNTERINSURGENCY

Ahmad, Eqbal. "Revolutionary War and Counter-Insurgency." *Journal of International Affairs* 25 (1971): 1–47.

————. "The Theory and Fallacies of Counterinsurgency." *The Nation*, August 2, 1971, pp. 70–85.

Beavers, Roy. "A Doctrine for Limited War." *U.S. Naval Institute Proceedings*, October 1970, pp. 26–34.

Bloomfield, Lincoln P., and Leiss, Amelia C. *Controlling Small Wars: A Strategy for the 1970's.* New York: Knopf, 1969.

Condit, D. M., and Cooper, Bert. *Challenge and Response in Internal Conflict.* 3 vols. Center for Research in Social Systems. Washington, D.C.: American University, 1967 and 1968.

Connolly, Stephen, and Lightbourne, William. "Patrolling the Empire: The New Counterinsurgency." *Journal of Contemporary Revolutions* 3 (Spring 1971): 82–96.

Eckstein, Harry, ed. *Internal War: Problems and Approaches.* New York: Free Press, 1964.

Fall, Bernard, ed. *Ho Chi Minh on Revolution: Selected Writings, 1920–1966.* New York: Praeger, 1967.

Giap, Vo Nguyen. *People's War, People's Army.* New York: Praeger, 1962.

Greene, T. N., ed. *The Guerrilla and How to Fight Him.* New York: Praeger, 1962.

Guevara, Ernesto Che. *Guerrilla Warfare.* New York: Monthly Review Press, 1961.

Leites, Nathan, and Wolf, Charles, Jr. *Rebellion and Authority: An Analytic Essay on Insurgency Conflicts.* Chicago: Markham, 1970.

Mallin, Jay, ed. *Strategy for Conquest: Communist Documents on Guerrilla Warfare.* Coral Gables, Fla.: University of Miami Press, 1970.

Mao Tse-tung. *On Protracted War.* 3rd ed. Peking: Foreign Languages Press, 1966.

McCuen, John J. *The Art of Counter-Revolutionary Warfare.* Harrisburg, Pa.: Stackpole Books, 1966.

————. "Can We Win Revolutionary Wars?" *Army,* December 1969, pp. 16–22.

Osanka, Franklin Mark, ed. *Modern Guerrilla Warfare.* New York: Free Press, 1962.

Pustay, John S. *Counterinsurgency Warfare.* New York: Free Press, 1965.

Rejai, Mostafa, ed. *Mao Tse-tung on Revolution and War.* Garden City, N.Y.: Doubleday, 1968.

Scott, Andrew M., et al. *Insurgency.* Chapel Hill: University of North Carolina Press, 1970.

Stetler, Russell, ed. *The Military Art of People's War: Selected Writings of General Vo Nguyen Giap.* New York: Monthly Review Press, 1970.

Thompson, Robert. *Defeating Communist Insurgency.* New York: Praeger, 1966.

————. *Revolutionary War in World Strategy, 1945–1969.* New York: Taplinger, 1970.

Wolf, Charles, Jr. *Insurgency and Counterinsurgency: New Myths and Old Realities.* Santa Monica, Cal.: RAND Corp., 1965.

————. *United States Policy and the Third World*. Boston: Little, Brown, 1967.

CHAPTER 1:
FROM DETERRENCE TO COUNTERINSURGENCY

Ginsburgh, Robert N. *U.S. Military Strategy in the Sixties*. New York: W. W. Norton, 1965.
Hilsman, Roger. *To Move a Nation*. Garden City, N. Y.: Doubleday, 1967.
Osgood, Robert E. "The Reappraisal of Limited War." *Adelphi Papers* 54 (February 1969): 41–54.
Prouty, L. Fletcher. "The Secret Team and the Games They Play." *The Washington Monthly*, May 1970, pp. 11–19.
Rostow, Walt W. *The United States in the World Arena*. New York: Harper & Row, 1960.
Sorenson, Theodore. *Kennedy*. New York: Harper & Row, 1965.
Stavins, Ralph; Barnet, Richard J.; and Raskin, Marcus G. *Washington Plans an Aggressive War*. New York: Random House, 1971.
Taylor, Maxwell D. *The Uncertain Trumpet*. New York: Harper & Row, 1960.
U.S. Senate, Committee on Foreign Relations. *The Foreign Aid Program*. Compilation of Studies and Surveys Prepared Under the Direction of the Special Committee to Study the Foreign Aid Program. Washington, D.C.: Government Printing Office, 1957.

CHAPTER 2:
RESTRUCTURING THE PENTAGON

Borklund, C. W. *Men of the Pentagon*. New York: Praeger, 1966.
————. *The Department of Defense*. New York: Praeger, 1968.
Enthoven, Alain C., and Smith, K. Wayne. *How Much Is Enough?* New York: Harper & Row, 1971.
Halberstam, David. "The Programming of Robert McNamara." *Harper's*, February 1971, pp. 37–40.

Hitch, Charles J. *Decision Making for Defense.* Berkeley: University of California Press, 1965.

McNamara, Robert S. *The Essence of Security.* New York: Harper & Row, 1968.

Melman, Seymour. *Pentagon Capitalism: The Political Economy of War.* New York: McGraw-Hill, 1970.

Powers, Patrick W. *A Guide to National Defense.* New York: Praeger, 1964.

Raymond, Jack. *Power at the Pentagon.* New York: Harper & Row, 1964.

Roherty, James M. *Decisions of Robert S. McNamara.* Coral Gables, Fla.: University of Miami Press, 1970.

Trewhitt, Henry L. *McNamara: His Ordeal in the Pentagon.* New York: Harper & Row, 1971.

Yarmolinsky, Adam. *The Military Establishment.* New York: Harper & Row, 1971.

CHAPTER 3:
THE SCIENTIFIC MERCENARIES

Buchanan, William W., ed. *Industrial Research Laboratories in the United States.* 12th ed. Washington, D.C.: Bowker, 1965.

Caldwell, Lynton K., ed. *Science, Technology and Public Policy: A Selected and Annotated Bibliography.* Department of Government. Bloomington, Ind.: Indiana University, 1969.

East-West Center, in cooperation with the International Program of Michigan State University. *The International Programs of American Universities.* 2d ed. East Lansing, Mich.: University of Michigan Press, 1966.

Gardner, John W. *A.I.D. and the Universities.* New York: Education and World Affairs, 1964.

Grissom, Tom. *Bibliography on the Integration of Education, Science, the Military, and Ideology in Postwar America.* East Palo Alto, Cal.: Pacific Studies Center, 1970.

Horowitz, David. "The Sinews of Empire." *Ramparts,* October 1969, pp. 32–42.

Klare, Michael T. "The Military Research Network." *The Nation,* October 12, 1970, pp. 327–32.

Lyons, Gene M., and Morton, Louis. *Schools for Strategy.* New York: Praeger, 1965.

North American Congress on Latin America. *The University–Military–Police Complex.* New York: North American Congress on Latin America, 1970.

Palmer, A.M., and Kruzas, A. T., eds. *Research Centers Directory.* 2d ed. Detroit: Gale Research Co., 1966.

Price, William J. "Defense Research and the University." *Defense Industry Bulletin,* July 1970, pp. 16–19.

Ridgeway, James. *The Closed Corporation.* New York: Random House, 1968.

Shapero, Albert, et al. *The Role of the University in Defense R&D.* Menlo Park, Cal.: Stanford Research Institute, 1966.

U.S. Department of State. *Research Centers on the Developing Areas.* External Research Staff. Washington, D.C.: Government Printing Office, 1964.

———. *Language and Area Study Programs in American Universities.* Washington, D.C.: Government Printing Office, 1964.

———. *University Centers of Foreign Affairs Research.* Office of External Research. Washington, D.C.: Government Printing Office, 1968.

U.S. House of Representatives. *Conflicts Between the Federal Research Programs and the Nation's Goals for Higher Education.* 18th Report of the Committee on Government Operations, 89th Congress, 1st Session, 1965.

U.S. National Referral Center for Science and Technology. *A Directory of Information Resources in the United States: Social Sciences.* Washington, D.C.: Government Printing Office, 1965.

U.S. National Science Foundation. *Federal Funds for Research, Development and Other Scientific Activities, Fiscal Years 1969, 1970, and 1971.* Washington, D.C.: Government Printing Office, 1970.

———. *Federal Support to Universities and Colleges, Fiscal Year 1968.* Washington, D.C.: Government Printing Office, 1970.

U.S. Senate. *An Inventory of Government Concern With R&D.*
A bibliography prepared for the Subcommittee on Government Research of the Senate Committee on Government Operations, vol. 1, 88th and 89th Congresses, 1966;
vol. 2, 90th Congress, 1st Session, 1968.

CHAPTER 4:
SOCIAL SYSTEMS ENGINEERING

Africa Research Group. *African Studies in America: The Ex-
tended Family.* Cambridge, Mass.: Africa Research Group,
1969.
Brightman, Carol, and Klare, Michael. "Social Research and
Counterinsurgency: The Science of Neocolonialism."
NACLA Newsletter 3 (February 1970), 11–14, and 4
(March 1970), 1–7.
Conley, Michael. "Military Value of Social Sciences in Insur-
gent Environment." *Army Research and Development
Newsmagazine,* November 1966, pp. 22–3.
FAR Horizons. Published bimonthly for the Foreign Area Re-
search Coordination Group by the Office of External
Research, U.S. Department of State.
Foreign Affairs Research Papers Available. Monthly Accessions
List of the Foreign Affairs Research Documentation
Center. Office of External Research. Washington, D.C.:
U.S. Department of State.
Horowitz, Irving Louis, ed. *The Rise and Fall of Project Camelot.*
Cambridge, Mass.: MIT Press, 1967.
National Academy of Sciences. *The Behavioral Sciences and
the Federal Government.* Washington, D.C.: National
Academy of Sciences, 1968.
North American Congress on Latin America. *Subliminal War-
fare: The Role of Latin American Studies.* New York:
North American Congress on Latin America, 1970.
U.S. Agency for International Development. *AID Research Pro-
gram 1962–1971: Project Objectives and Results.* Office
of Research and University Relations. Washington, D.C.:
Agency for International Development, 1971.
U.S. Department of State. *Government-Supported Research:*

International Affairs. Office of External Research. Washington, D.C.: U.S. Department of State, 1970.

U.S. House of Representatives. *Behavioral Sciences and the National Security.* Committee on Foreign Affairs. *Hearings,* Part 9, 89th Congress, 2d Session, 1966.

U.S. Senate. *Defense Department Sponsored Foreign Affairs Research.* Committee on Foreign Relations. *Hearings,* 90th Congress, 2d Session, 1968.

Wolf, Eric, and Jorgensen, Joseph. "Anthropology on the Warpath in Thailand." *New York Review of Books,* November 19, 1970.

CHAPTER 5:
THE COUNTERINSURGENCY RESEARCH NETWORK

American Friends Service Committee. *The Weapons of Counterinsurgency: Chemical, Biological, Antipersonnel, Incendiary.* National Action/Research on the Military-Industrial Complex. Philadelphia, Pa.: American Friends Service Committee, 1970.

Ardman, Harvey. "How Vietnam Tested U.S. Army Planning." *American Legion Magazine,* February 1970, pp. 8–13.

Beecher, William. "Way Out Weapons." *New York Times Magazine,* March 24, 1968, pp. 49 *ff.*

Carter, Luther J. "Vietnam: Jungle Conflict Poses New R&D Problems." *Science* 152 (April 8, 1962), 187–90.

Curran, Lawrence J., and David, Heather M. "DoD, Services Gear to Manage War." *Missiles and Rockets,* March 28, 1966, pp. 132–41.

Data Publications, Inc. *Major R&D Facilities of the Federal Government.* 1970 ed. Washington, D.C.: Data Publications, Inc., 1970.

De Percin, F. P.; Albert, Leo; and Hilton, Donald C. "Army Advancing Combat Capability in Environmental Extremes." *Army Research and Development Newsmagazine,* January 1967, pp. 22–4.

Norman, Lloyd. "War Without Gadgets." *Army,* December 1966, pp. 53–9.

"R&D Funding Continues to Increase." *Missiles and Rockets,* March 29, 1965, pp. 125–9.

Sullivan, Leonard, Jr. "Research and Development for Vietnam." *Science and Technology,* October 1968, pp. 28–38.

Tompkins, John S. *The Weapons of World War III.* Garden City, N.Y.: Doubleday, 1966.

U.S. Department of Defense. "R&D Support of the War in Vietnam." Memorandum inserted in *Military Posture and Legislation to Authorize Appropriations.* U.S. House of Representatives, Committee on Armed Services, *Hearings,* 90th Congress, 1st Session, 1967, pp. 1426–34.

U.S. National Science Foundation. *Directory of Federal R&D Installations.* Washington, D.C.: U.S. Government Printing Office, 1970.

CHAPTER 6:
STRATEGIC MOBILITY AND INTERVENTION

Coffey, J. I. "Technology and Strategic Mobility." *Adelphi Papers* 46 (March 1968), 15–27.

Democratic Study Group of the U.S. House of Representatives. "The Fiscal Year 1970 Defense Budget." Memorandum inserted in the *Congressional Record,* September 26, 1969, pp. E7877–88.

Els, Theodore Vander. "The Challenge of Strategic Mobility." *Military Review,* February 1970, pp. 48–57.

Klein, Tom. "The Capacity to Intervene." *The Pentagon Watchers: Students Report on the National Security State.* Edited by Leonard S. Rodberg and Derek Shearer. Garden City, N.Y.: Doubleday, 1970.

Members of Congress for Peace Through Law. *Report on Military Spending.* Washington, D.C.: Members of Congress for Peace Through Law, 1970.

Rice, Berkeley. *The C-5A Scandal.* Boston: Houghton Mifflin, 1971.

CHAPTER 7:
"THE ELECTRONIC BATTLEFIELD"

American Friends Service Committee. *The Components and Manufacturers of the Electronic Battlefield.* National

Action/Research on the Military-Industrial Complex. Philadelphia, Pa.: American Friends Service Committee, 1971.

Dickson, Paul, and Rothchild, John. "The Electronic Battlefield: Wiring Down the War." *The Washington Monthly*, May 1971, pp. 6–14.

Frisbee, John L. "IGLOO WHITE." *Air Force*, February 1971, pp. 48–51.

Haseltine, William. "The Automated Air War." *The New Republic*, October 16, 1971, pp. 15–17.

Heiman, Grover. "Beep to Bang." *Armed Forces Management*, July 1970, pp. 36–9.

Kinnard, Henry W. O. "Narrowing the Combat Intelligence Gap." *Army*, August 1969, pp. 22–6.

Reed, Wilson R. "Automation: Force Effectiveness Multiplier." *Defense Industry Bulletin*, March 1970, pp. 7–13.

U.S. Senate. *Investigation into Electronic Battlefield Program.* Armed Services Committee, Electronic Battlefield Subcommittee. *Hearings*, 91st Congress, 2d Session, 1971.

Weaver, Kenneth. "Remote Sensing: New Eyes to See the World." *National Geographic*, January 1969, pp. 46–73.

Weiss, George. "Battle for Control of the Ho Chi Minh Trail." *Armed Forces Journal*, February 15, 1971, pp. 18–22.

———. "Southeast Asia Sensor Fields: More Eyes and Ears." *Armed Forces Journal*, March 1, 1971, pp. 38–9.

CHAPTER 8:
THE SCIENCE OF MERCENARIZATION

Cleaver, Harry. *Counterinsurgency Research in Thailand.* East Palo Alto, Cal.: Pacific Studies Center, 1970.

"Fighting Guerrillas from the Lab." *Time*, October 7, 1966, pp. 69–70.

Getler, Michael. "ARPA Team Aids Thailand in Developing R&D Capability." *Technology Week*, December 19, 1966, pp. 17–18.

Klare, Michael. "Thailand: Counterinsurgency's Proving Ground." *The Nation*, April 26, 1971, pp. 527–31.

CHAPTER 9:
"THE FIRST LINE OF DEFENSE"

"A.I.D. Police Programs for Latin America, 1971–72." NACLA Newsletter 5 (July–August 1971), 1–31.

Chew, Peter T. "America's Global Peace Officers." Kiwanis, April 1969, pp. 22–4.

[Engle, Byron.] "A.I.D. Assistance to Civil Security Forces." U.S. Agency for International Development press release, February 11, 1970. Reproduced in NACLA Newsletter 4 (September 1970), 21–3.

Epstein, David G. "The Police Role in Counterinsurgency Efforts." The Journal of Criminal Law, Criminology and Police Science 59 (1968), 148–51.

Johnson, U. Alexis. "The Role of Police Forces in a Changing World." Department of State Bulletin, September 13, 1971, pp. 280–3.

Klare, Michael. "U.S. Police Assistance Programs in Latin America." NACLA Newsletter 4 (May–June 1970), 28–31.

————. "Policing the Empire." Commonweal, September 18, 1970, pp. 455–61.

Porter, D. Gareth. "Saigon's Secret Police." The Nation, April 27, 1970, pp. 498–500.

Sanford, David. "Agitators in a Fertilizer Factory." New Republic, February 11, 1967, pp. 16–18.

Shepherd, David E., Jr. "Republic of Vietnam's National Police." Military Review, June 1971, pp. 69–74.

Stork, Joe. "How America Builds the Global Police State." Hard Times, August 10–17, 1970, pp. 1–4.

U.S. Department of State. Program Guide: Public Safety Training. Agency for International Development, Office of Public Safety. Washington, D.C.: Agency for International Development, 1968.

————. The Role of Public Safety in Support of the National Police of Vietnam. Washington, D.C.: Agency for International Development, 1969.

U.S. House of Representatives. U.S. Assistance Programs In Vietnam. Committee on Government Operations, Subcommittee, Hearings, 92nd Congress, 1st Session, 1971.

CHAPTER 10:
THE LATIN AMERICAN MILITARY

Barber, Willard F., and Ronning, C. Neale. *Internal Security and Military Power.* Columbus, Ohio: Ohio State University Press, 1966.

Bosch, Juan. *Pentagonism: A Substitute for Imperialism.* Translated by Helen R. Lane. New York: Grove Press, 1968.

Connolly, Stephen. "A Systematic Analysis of the United States Military in Latin America." *Journal of Contemporary Revolutions,* Summer 1970, pp. 56–70.

Flatley, Thomas W. "Latin American Armed Forces in the 1960's: A Review." *Military Review,* April 1970, pp. 10–19.

Gerassi, John. *The Great Fear.* New York: Macmillan, 1963.

Glick, Edward B. *Peaceful Conflict: The Non-Military Use of the Military.* Harrisburg, Pa.: Stackpole Books, 1967.

Haahr, James C. "Military Assistance to Latin America." *Military Review,* May 1969, pp. 12–21.

James, Daniel. "Another Vietnam in Latin America?" *Military Review,* June 1969, pp. 85–93.

Johnson, John J. " 'New Armies' Take Over in Latin America." *New York Times Magazine,* March 8, 1964, pp. 14 ff.

————. *The Military and Society in Latin America.* Stanford, Cal.: Stanford University Press, 1964.

Kemp. Geoffrey. *Some Relationships Between U.S. Military Training in Latin America and Weapons Acquisition Patterns, 1959–1969.* Center for International Studies. Cambridge, Mass.: Massachusetts Institute of Technology, 1970.

Klare, Michael. "U.S. Military Operations: Latin America." *NACLA Newsletter* 2 (October 1968), 1–8.

Lieuwen, Edwin. *Generals Vs. Presidents: Neo-Militarism in Latin America.* New York: Praeger, 1964.

————. *Arms and Politics in Latin America.* Revised ed. New York: Praeger, 1965.

————. *The United States and the Challenge to Security in Latin America.* Columbus, Ohio: Ohio State University Press, 1966.

462 Research Bibliography

Mercado Jarrin, Edgardo. "Insurgency in Latin America: Its Impact on Political and Military Strategy." *Military Review*, March 1969, pp. 10–20.

Meyer, Charles A. "U.S. Military Assistance Policy Toward Latin America." *Department of State Bulletin*, August 4, 1969, pp. 100–2.

Rockefeller, Nelson. "Quality of Life in the Americas." Report of a Presidential Mission for the Western Hemisphere, *Department of State Bulletin*, December 8, 1969, pp. 493–540.

Smith, Laun C., Jr. "Military Civic Action in Latin America." *Military Review*, January 1969, pp. 64–71.

U.S. Department of the Army. *Latin America and the Caribbean: Analytical Survey of Literature.* Department of the Army Pamphlet 550–7. Washington, D.C.: U.S. Department of the Army, 1969.

U.S. House of Representatives. *Reports of the Special Study Mission to Latin America.* Committee on Foreign Affairs, Subcommittee on National Security Policy and Scientific Developments. Committee print, 91st Congress, 2d Session, 1970.

U.S. Senate. *Survey of the Alliance for Progress.* Committee on Foreign Relations, Subcommittee on American Republics Affairs. Compilation of Studies and Hearings. Washington, D.C.: Government Printing Office, 1969.

_____. *United States Military Policies and Programs in Latin America.* Committee on Foreign Relations, Subcommittee on Western Hemisphere Affairs. *Hearings,* 91st Congress, 1st Session, 1969.

_____. *United States Policies and Programs in Brazil.* Committee on Foreign Relations, Subcommittee on Western Hemisphere Affairs. *Hearings,* 92nd Congress, 1st Session, 1971.

CHAPTER 11:
THE GREAT SOUTH ASIAN WAR

Bix, Herbert P. "The Security Treaty System and the Japanese Military-Industrial Complex." *Bulletin of the Concerned Asian Scholars* 2 (January 1970), 30–53.

Branfman, Fred. "Laos: 'No Place to Hide.'" *Bulletin of the Concerned Asian Scholars* 2 (Fall 1970), 15–46.

Burchett, Wilfred. *Vietnam Will Win.* New York: Guardian Books, 1968.

———. *The Second Indochina War.* New York: International Publishers, 1970.

Chomsky, Noam. *At War With Asia.* New York: Random House, 1970.

Committee of Concerned Asian Scholars. *The Indochina Story.* New York: Bantam Books, 1970.

Congressional Quarterly Service. *China and U.S. Far East Policy.* Washington, D.C.: Congressional Quarterly Service, 1967.

Dower, John W. "Asia and the Nixon Doctrine: 10 Points of Note." *Bulletin of the Concerned Asian Scholars* 2 (Fall 1970), 47–70.

Fall, Bernard. *The Two Viet-Nams.* 2d revised ed. New York: Praeger, 1967.

Garrett, Banning and Barkley, Katherine, with the editors of *Ramparts. Two, Three . . . Many Vietnams.* San Francisco: Canfield Press, 1971.

Gettleman, Marvin and Susan, and Kaplan, Lawrence and Carol, eds. *Conflict in Indochina.* New York: Random House, 1970.

Kahin, George McTurnan, and Lewis, John W. *The United States in Vietnam.* New York: Dell, 1967.

Kirk, Donald. *Wider War: The Struggle for Cambodia, Thailand, and Laos.* New York: Praeger, 1971.

Klare, Michael. "The Great South Asian War." *The Nation,* March 9, 1970, pp. 265–73.

———. "The Sun Never Sets on America's Empire." *Commonweal,* May 22, 1970, pp. 239–43.

———. "The Mercenarization of the Third World: U.S. Military and Police Assistance Programs." *NACLA Newsletter* 4 (November 1970), 11–31.

Millar, T. B. "The Indian and Pacific Oceans: Some Strategic Considerations." *Adelphi Papers* 57 (May 1969), 1–20.

"The Pacific Basin." *Forbes,* November 1, 1970, pp. 28–35.

Reischauer, Edwin O. *Beyond Vietnam: The United States and Asia.* New York: Knopf, 1967.

Scheer, Robert. *How the United States Got Involved in Vietnam.* Santa Barbara, Cal.: Center for the Study of Democratic Institutions, 1965.

Shoch, Jim. "Pacific Partnership: How Japan and the United States are Joining Hands to Dominate Asia." *Pacific Research and World Empire Telegram,* November–December 1969, pp. 2–17.

Thompson, Robert. *No Exit From Vietnam.* New York: David McKay, 1969.

Thomson, George G. *Problems of Strategy in the Pacific and Indian Oceans.* New York: National Strategy Information Center, 1970.

U.S. House of Representatives. *Review of the Vietnam Conflict and Its Impact on U.S. Military Commitments Abroad.* Committee on Armed Services, Special Subcommittee on National Defense Posture. Committee Report, 90th Congress, 2d Session, 1968.

U.S. Senate. *Perspective on Asia: The New U. S. Doctrine and Southeast Asia.* Committee on Foreign Relations. Report of Senator Mike Mansfield, 91st Congress, 1st Session, 1969.

_____. *Background Information Relating to Southeast Asia and Vietnam.* 6th ed., revised. Committee on Foreign Relations. Washington, D.C.: Government Printing Office, 1970.

_____. *Background Information Relating to Peace and Security in Southeast Asia and Other Areas.* Committee on Foreign Relations. Committee print, 91st Congress, 2d Session, 1970.

_____. *Vietnam Policy Proposals.* Committee on Foreign Relations. *Hearings,* 91st Congress, 2d Session, 1970.

_____. *Laos: April 1970.* Committee on Foreign Relations. Staff Report, 92d Congress, 1st Session, 1971.

Index

A Note About the Author

Michael Klare was born in 1942. He holds two degrees from Columbia University, and studied for two years at Yale University. Since 1968, he has been a staff member of the North American Congress on Latin America, an independent research group established in 1966 to study American preparations for "the next Vietnams" in Latin America. He has published articles in *The Nation, Commonweal,* and other periodicals. He currently lives in Berkeley, California.

A Note on the Type

This book was set on the Linotype in Melior, a typeface designed by Hermann Zapf and issued in 1952. Born in Nürnberg, Germany, in 1918, Zapf has been a strong influence in printing since 1939. Melior, like Times Roman, another popular twentieth-century typeface, was created specifically for use in a newspaper. With this functional end in mind, Zapf nonetheless chose to base the proportions of its letterforms on those of the Golden Section. The result is a typeface of unusual strength and surpassing subtlety.

Composed by Cherry Hill Composition, Pennsauken, New Jersey. Printed and bound by Colonial Press Inc., Clinton, Massachusetts.

Typography and binding design by Clint Anglin.